W9-CHU-208

A HISTORY OF NIGERIA

Nigeria is Africa's most populous country and the world's eighth largest oil producer, but its success has been undermined in recent decades by ethnic and religious conflict, political instability, rampant official corruption, and an ailing economy. Toyin Falola, a leading historian intimately acquainted with the region, and Matthew Heaton, who has worked extensively on African science and culture, combine their expertise to explain the context to Nigeria's recent troubles, through an exploration of its pre-colonial and colonial past and its journey from independence to statehood. By examining key themes such as colonialism, religion, slavery, nationalism, and the economy, the authors show how Nigeria's history has been swayed by the vicissitudes of the world around it, and how Nigerians have adapted to meet these challenges. This book offers a unique portrayal of a resilient people living in a country with immense, but unrealized, potential.

TOYIN FALOLA is the Frances Higginbotham Nalle Centennial Professor in History at the University of Texas at Austin. His books include *The Power of African Cultures* (2003), *Economic Reforms and Modernization in Nigeria, 1945–1965* (2004), and *A Mouth Sweeter than Salt: An African Memoir* (2004).

MATTHEW M. HEATON is a Patrice Lumumba Fellow at the University of Texas at Austin. He has co-edited multiple volumes on health and illness in Africa with Toyin Falola, including *HIV/AIDS, Illness and African Well-Being* (2007) and *Health Knowledge and Belief Systems in Africa* (2007).

A HISTORY OF NIGERIA

TOYIN FALOLA AND MATTHEW M. HEATON

University of Texas at Austin

CAMBRIDGE
UNIVERSITY PRESS

CAMBRIDGE UNIVERSITY PRESS
Cambridge, New York, Melbourne, Madrid, Cape Town, Singapore, São Paulo, Delhi

Cambridge University Press
The Edinburgh Building, Cambridge CB2 8RU, UK

Published in the United States of America by Cambridge University Press, New York

www.cambridge.org
Information on this title: www.cambridge.org/9780521681575

© Toyin Falola and Matthew M. Heaton 2008

This publication is in copyright. Subject to statutory exception
and to the provisions of relevant collective licensing agreements,
no reproduction of any part may take place without
the written permission of Cambridge University Press.

First published 2008
Reprinted 2009

Printed in the United Kingdom at the University Press, Cambridge

A catalogue record for this publication is available from the British Library

Library of Congress Cataloguing in Publication Data

Falola, Toyin.
A history of Nigeria / Toyin Falola and Matthew M. Heaton.
p.   cm.
Includes bibliographical references and index.
ISBN 978-0-521-86294-3 (hardback) – ISBN 978-0-521-68157-5 (pbk.)
1. Nigeria–History.   I. Heaton, Matthew M.   II. Title.
DT515.57.F353 2008
966.9–dc22
2007049016

ISBN 978-0-521-86294-3 hardback
ISBN 978-0-521-68157-5 paperback

Cambridge University Press has no responsibility for the persistence or
accuracy of URLs for external or third-party internet websites referred to
in this publication, and does not guarantee that any content on such
websites is, or will remain, accurate or appropriate. Information
regarding prices, travel timetables and other factual information given in
this work are correct at the time of first printing but
Cambridge University Press does not guarantee the accuracy of such
information thereafter.

For Dr. Akin Ogundiran, a dear friend and colleague

Contents

Illustrations

Maps

Acknowledgments

We owe a debt of gratitude to the many dedicated scholars of Nigeria who have helped us to fine-tune our conceptualization and presentation of this book. Funso Afolayan, Tosin Abiodun, Anene Ejikeme, Chidiebere Nwaubani, Ebenezer Obadare, Akin Ogundiran, Ann O'Hear, Mojubaolu Okome, Adebayo Oyebade, Hakeem Tijani, Emmanuel Ike Udogu, and Aribidesi Usman all read draft chapters of the manuscript and provided suggestions and critiques that have been invaluable in strengthening these chapters and improving the overall quality of the book. Special thanks also go to Sam Saverance, who created the maps, Roy Doron, Dr. Alfred Segun Fayemi, Brigitte Kowalski, Dr. Okpeh Okpeh, and Jonathan T. Reynolds, who supplied many of the pictures for this book from their personal collections, and Andrew Esiebo, who supplied the cover photo. The donation of all these individuals' time and energies is truly appreciated.

The community of Africanist scholars at the University of Texas at Austin provides much intellectual and spiritual support. We would like to thank several professors for extending their friendship and collegiality, which makes our time at the University of Texas both exciting and rewarding. The graduate students in African history at the university – Saheed Aderinto, Emily Brownell, Roy Doron, Kwame Essien, Tyler Fleming, Ann Genova, Sylvester Gundona, Adam Paddock, and Natalie Washington-Weik – also deserve mention for the vibrancy and fresh ideas they have brought to our community. We thank you all.

Chronology

9000 BCE	Late Stone Age evidence of indigenous habitation in Iwo Eleru rock shelter in southwestern Nigeria.
600 BCE	Evidence of iron technology used by Nok civilization, near present-day Abuja.
1000–1500 CE	Foundation of centralized states such as Kanem, Borno, Benin, Ife, Oyo, and the Hausa city states.
1100–1400 CE	Introduction of Islam into savanna and Sahelian states of northern Nigeria.
1300–1600	The "golden age" of the trans-Saharan trade. Gold, slaves, and other commodities are traded from the states of northern Nigeria across the Sahara desert to the states of the north African littoral, Europe, and the Middle East. The trans-Saharan trade continued through the nineteenth century, but in a diminished capacity after the rise of direct trade with Europeans on the coast in the fifteenth century AD.
1450–1850	Contacts with Europeans on the coast result in monumental changes to the political, economic, and social institutions of southern Nigerian states. The trade in slaves dominates relations between Nigerians and Europeans at this time, changing for ever the histories of four continents as goods and people engaged in a growing transatlantic trade.
1804	Beginning of Islamic revolution that results in the creation of the Sokoto Caliphate in northern Nigeria. The Sokoto Caliphate expands the frontiers of Islam and spread the religion beyond the ruling classes to common people to a greater extent than existed previously.

1807	British abolition of the slave trade. Although the trade in slaves continues from southern Nigerian ports for another forty years, trade in palm oil and other forms of "legitimate" commerce expand rapidly from this point.
1833	Final collapse of Oyo empire, which marks the beginning of sixty years of instability and war among Yoruba states in the southwest.
1841	The Niger Expedition marks the first attempt by Europeans and African Christians to spread Christianity into the interior of Nigeria. In 1846 Church Missionary Society (CMS) missionaries establish a mission at Abeokuta; from this point Christianity begins to spread rapidly in southern Nigeria for the first time. A new elite emerges in the south, educated in European mission schools and sharing many European cultural attributes. Christianity and Islam have since become the two dominant religions in Nigeria.
1861	British annexation of Lagos as a Crown Colony.
1885	Establishment of the Oil Rivers Protectorate in southeastern Nigeria, renamed the Niger Coast Protectorate in 1893.
1886	Formation of the Royal Niger Company (RNC), which monopolizes trade in the Niger basin until the revocation of its charter in 1900. In the same year a peace treaty is signed, ending the prolonged war among the Yoruba-speaking peoples of the southwest.
1887	King Ja Ja of Opobo exiled to the West Indies for abrogation of Treaty of Protection.
1893	Establishment of a British protectorate over Yoruba territories in the southwest.
1894	Revolt of Brassmen against the Royal Niger Company. In the same year, Nana, the Itsekiri governor of the river Benin, is deposed and deported for hindering British access to interior markets.
1898–1909	Ekumeku underground resistance movement fights against the RNC and British colonial rule.
1900	Creation of the Protectorate of Northern Nigeria. Extension of the northern protectorate concludes in

	1903, when British forces conquer the Sokoto Caliphate and kill the Sultan.
1902–3	The Aro Expedition, part of the British effort to "pacify" the hinterlands of eastern Nigeria.
1908	Protests in Lagos against the water rate, fueled by the reporting of Nigerian journalists such as Herbert Macaulay, often dubbed the "father of Nigerian nationalism." Macaulay and other journalists use newspapers to report on and critique the performance of the colonial government.
1912	Establishment of the Southern Nigeria Civil Service Union, later renamed the Nigerian Civil Servants' Union.
1914	Amalgamation of northern and southern protectorates.
1914–18	Nigerian troops aid the British cause in the First World War.
1920	National Congress of British West Africa (NCBWA) founded.
1923	Establishment of the Clifford Constitution, which allows for elected representation in the governance of Nigeria for the first time.
1925	West African Students' Union (WASU) founded.
1929	The "Women's War," or Aba Riots, a major protest against British indirect rule in southeastern Nigeria.
1931	Establishment of the Nigerian Union of Teachers (NUT).
1936	Nigerian Youth Movement (NYM), a political organization of young nationalists in the Lagos area, founded.
1944	Nnamdi Azikiwe founds the NCNC, the National Council of Nigeria and the Cameroons (later Nigerian Citizens), which quickly becomes an influential political party pushing for independence for Nigeria from British colonial rule. In the same year Mrs. Olufunmilayo Ransome-Kuti founds the Abeokuta Ladies' Club, later renamed the Abeokuta Women's Union (AWU), to lobby against the injustices of colonial indirect rule.
1945	Nigerian labor unions organize a General Strike, bringing work and business to a standstill. The strike

	precipitates important economic changes in the form of the first Ten Year Plan, adopted later the same year.
1946	The Richards Constitution enacted, providing a central legislature and dividing Nigeria into three regions: the North, West, and East. This is the first set of constitutional reforms that ultimately leads to independence for Nigeria.
1948	First university in Nigeria established in Ibadan.
1949	Northern People's Congress (NPC) founded under the leadership of Tafawa Balewa, Aminu Kano, and Ahmadu Bello, the *Sardauna* of Sokoto.
1951	The MacPherson Constitution amends the Richards Constitution, moving Nigeria closer to independence. In the same year the Action Group (AG), a Yoruba-dominated political party in the southwest, is founded under the leadership of Obafemi Awolowo.
1954	The Lyttleton Constitution establishes a federal system of government for Nigeria.
1956	Petroleum discovered in the Niger delta region.
1957	Regional self-government attained in the East and West.
1959	Regional self-government attained in the North.
1960	Nigeria becomes independent from the United Kingdom on October 1.
1963	Nigeria becomes a republic, replacing the queen with an indigenous president as the symbolic head of state.
1966	Military coup on January 15 brings down the First Republic and installs General John Aguiyi-Ironsi as head of state. Countercoup on July 29 brings General Yakubu Gowon to power.
1967	Emeka Ojukwu declares independence of Eastern Region as the sovereign Republic of Biafra on May 30. In the same year Gowon creates twelve states out of the existing three regions. From this point, clamor for the creation of more states becomes constant. Since 2000 Nigeria has been made up of thirty-six states and a Federal Capital Territory (FCT) at Abuja.
1967–70	Civil war between the forces of the Federal Military Government (FMG) and Biafran separatists. War

	ends with the surrender of Biafra on January 12, 1970, and the reincorporation of Biafra into Nigeria.
1971	Nigeria joins the Organization of Petroleum Exporting Countries (OPEC).
1973	Rising price of oil results in booming economy for Nigeria. Since this time Nigeria has been heavily dependent on its oil exports to supply government revenues The results have been grandiose development projects, widespread official corruption, and mismanagement of government funds.
1975	Gowon regime overthrown in coup of July 30. General Murtala Mohammed becomes the new head of state.
1976	Mohammed assassinated on February 13 in an unsuccessful coup. Mohammed's deputy, Lieutenant General Olusegun Obasanjo, takes over as head of state. The Mohammed/Obasanjo regime becomes known for its sweeping reforms in political institutions and its willingness to transfer power to civilian leadership for the first time since the 1966 coup.
1979	Political power handed to civilian administration of the Second Republic under President Alhaji Shehu Shagari. The Second Republic presides over a declining economy as the oil boom is followed by an oil bust. Nigeria becomes a debtor state, as politicians continue to spend lavishly despite the poor economic climate.
1983	Second Republic overthrown in military coup of December 31. General Muhammadu Buhari becomes head of state. The Buhari administration becomes known for its firmness on issues of integrity, corruption, and austerity, but proves unable to improve the foundering economy.
1985	General Ibrahim Badamasi Babangida overthrows the Buhari regime on August 27. Under Babangida the Nigerian economy continues its decline. The institution of a Structural Adjustment Program (SAP) brings hardship to the majority of Nigerian citizens, and the supposed long-term benefits of the SAP do not materialize.

1993	Presidential election held on June 12 to decide the civilian successor to Babangida. Chief M. K. O. Abiola, a Yoruba Muslim from the southwest, wins what has been called the freest and fairest election in Nigerian history. Shortly afterwards the election results are annulled, throwing the country into chaos. Babangida hands power to an Interim Governing Council (IGC), led by Chief Ernest Shonekan, on August 27. On November 17 the IGC is overthrown by General Sani Abacha, who becomes the new head of state.
1994–8	Under Abacha Nigeria becomes an international pariah state. Abacha refuses to recognize the election of June 12, 1993, and uses violence and manipulation to suppress dissent.
1995	Ken Saro-Wiwa and other members of the "Ogoni Nine" are executed. The executions become a symbol of the tyranny of the Abacha regime and result in international protest and condemnation.
1998	Abacha dies on June 8. Power is transferred to General Abdulsalami Abubakar, who organizes a quick transition to civilian rule.
1999	The Fourth Republic commences under the leadership of President Olusegun Obasanjo. Under Obasanjo Nigeria seeks to improve its tarnished international reputation and to stabilize the political and economic conditions in the country. Some progress is made, but most Nigerians remain impoverished, and the political process remains significantly flawed.
2006	A national census tabulates Nigeria's population at over 140 million.
2007	Inauguration of President Umaru Yar'Adua on May 29, marking the first time in Nigeria's history that power is transferred from one civilian regime to another. The transfer is controversial, however, since the elections that brought Yar'Adua to power are widely believed to have been rigged by the ruling People's Democratic Party (PDP).

Notable people in Nigerian history

Abacha, General Sani (1943–98)
Former military dictator and commander-in-chief of the armed forces, who ruled Nigeria from 1993 until his mysterious death on June 8, 1998. A career military man, Abacha was born in Kano, and began his military training at the age of nineteen. It was he who announced the overthrow of the Second Republic in 1983, when Muhammadu Buhari came to power, and he was the number two soldier during the Babangida administration. In November 1993 he overthrew the existing Interim Governing Council of Ernest Shonekan and declared himself head of state. Over the next five years Abacha battled pro-democracy groups and widespread international disapproval over his refusal to recognize the results of the 1993 election and his fierce clampdown on anti-government activism. Abacha has been most vilified for the execution of Ken Saro-Wiwa and other members of the Ogoni Nine. Under Abacha's rule, Nigeria became an international pariah state and the country's economic crisis peaked.

Abiola, Chief Moshood Kashimawo Olawale (1937–98)
Born in Abeokuta and educated at the University of Glasgow, Abiola was a Yoruba Muslim who became one of the wealthiest businessmen in Nigeria. His companies covered newspaper publishing, banking, air transportation, oil drilling, and the book trade. Through his wealth, Abiola also became one of the leading philanthropists in Nigeria. He had been an important backer of the National Party of Nigeria (NPN) government during the Second Republic, and won the nomination of the Social Democratic Party (SDP) to stand for the presidency in the election of June 12, 1993. Abiola won the election, but the results were annulled. When Abiola declared himself president anyway a year later, head of state Sani Abacha had him put in prison, where he died four years later.

Achebe, Chinua (1930–)

Author of many important books, including *Things Fall Apart, A Man of the People, No Longer at Ease, Arrow of God,* and *Anthills of the Savannah,* Achebe has become one of the most famous novelists in Africa. Born at Ogidi, in eastern Nigeria, Achebe worked as a broadcaster from 1954 to 1967, when he became a professor at the University of Nigeria, Nsukka. As an eloquent portrayer and critic of the existential crises facing Africa and Africans over the last two centuries, Achebe has spoken and worked throughout the world since the 1970s.

Aguiyi-Ironsi, Major General Johnson Thomas Umunankwe (1924–66)

One of Nigeria's most distinguished soldiers of the 1950s and 1960s, Aguiyi-Ironsi served as an equerry to Queen Elizabeth II on her royal visit to Nigeria in 1956 and as military adviser to the Nigerian High Commission in London in 1961, and was the first African commander of the United Nations peacekeeping force in the Congo crisis. In 1965 he was promoted to major general and became the general commanding officer of the Nigerian army. After the first military coup of 1966, Ironsi, as the most senior military officer, became the first military head of state of Nigeria, but only for a few months. After angering many, particularly northerners, over his perceived favoritism of Igbos and the abolition of the federal structure, he was killed in the second military coup in July, 1966.

Akintola, Chief S. L. (1910–66)

Born in Ogbomosho, Akintola's first career was as a journalist. At one point he served as editor of the *Daily Service,* the newspaper of the Nigerian Youth Movement, and he became heavily involved in nationalist politics, particularly in the Yoruba-dominated Egbe Omo Oduduwa and the Action Group, serving as deputy leader of the latter from 1955 to 1962 and as premier of the Western Region from 1959 to 1966. After a falling-out with Chief Obafemi Awolowo in 1962, Akintola abandoned the AG and founded the United People's Party (UPP), and later the Nigerian National Democratic Party (NNDP), which formed an alliance with the northern-dominated NPC government and used the power of incumbency to rig elections in 1964 and 1965. The chaos in the Western Region resulting from the 1965 elections was one of the main factors that led to the military coup of January 15, 1966. Akintola was killed in the coup.

Awolowo, Chief Obafemi (1909–87)

Founder of the Egbe Omo Oduduwa and the Action Group, both Yoruba-dominated organizations that pushed for Nigerian independence and the extension and preservation of Yoruba interests and culture in a multi-ethnic, federated Nigeria. He studied law and commerce in London in the mid-1940s and returned to Nigeria to practice law and politics. Awolowo contested the post of prime minister in the 1959 general election, but the AG lost to the NPC–NCNC coalition, and Awolowo became the leader of the opposition. After his falling out with Western Region premier S. L. Akintola in 1962, Awolowo was charged with corruption and treason and sentenced to ten years in prison. He was later pardoned by Yakubu Gowon and became a federal office-holder in the military regime. He ran for the presidency of the Second Republic in 1979 and 1983, but lost both times to Shehu Shagari. He died in May 1987.

Azikiwe, Nnamdi (1904–96)

Founder of the National Council of Nigeria and the Cameroons (later Nigerian Citizens), which became one of the largest parties vying for independence for a unified Nigeria from British colonial rule. Azikiwe was born in Zungeru, in northern Nigeria, to Igbo parents and was educated in several mission schools throughout Nigeria. He traveled to the United States for university education, where he became involved in the Pan-African movement. On his return to Nigeria he became a successful journalist and activist in the Nigerian Youth Movement, before breaking away and founding the NCNC in 1944. As its leader, Azikiwe became the first indigenous governor general of Nigeria in 1959 and its first ceremonial president in 1963. He was ousted from this position by the coup of January 15, 1966, but he never retired from politics, running unsuccessfully for president in both 1979 and 1983. The national airport in Abuja, the country's capital, is named after him.

Babangida, General Ibrahim Badamasi (1941–)

Born at Minna, in what is now Niger State, Babangida was trained at many different military institutions and held many different military posts in his career. He first rose to national prominence for his efforts in quashing the abortive coup of Lieutenant Colonel B. Suka Dimka in February 1976, in which General Murtala Mohammed was assassinated. In 1984 he became chief of army staff, a position he held until August 27, 1985, when he mounted the successful coup that removed Muhammadu

Buhari from power. Babangida became president and commander-in-chief of the armed forces, and ruled Nigeria until 1993. Babangida was responsible for the institution of the Structural Adjustment Program in the country, which brought economic hardship for many Nigerians, as well as for the complicated transition to civilian rule, which resulted in his annulment of the results of the presidential election of June 12, 1993. Babangida handed power to an Interim Governing Council on August 27, 1993, but has since remained influential in Nigerian politics.

Balewa, Alhaji Sir Abubakar Tafawa (1912–66)

Born in Tafawa Balewa Town in what is now Bauchi State, Balewa trained to become a teacher, receiving his teaching certificate in 1933. He taught at Bauchi Middle School and, after studying at the Institute of Education at the University of London, became an education officer for Bauchi province. He was one of the founding members of the Northern People's Congress, which became the largest and most powerful party in northern Nigeria and which won control of the federal legislature in the 1959 general elections. Balewa became the first prime minister of Nigeria and governed during the tumultuous First Republic. His power and promotion of the "northernization" agenda made him a prime target for the organizers of the coup of January 15, 1966, in which he was abducted and killed.

Bello, Ahmadu, the *Sardauna* of Sokoto (1910–66)

A grandson of Usman dan Fodio, Bello became the most important northern politician between the 1940s and the 1960s. Although he lost a bid to become the Sultan of Sokoto in 1938, he was named the *Sardauna* (war leader), a very important position. He went on to become a founding member and leader of the NPC, and the premier of the Northern Region in 1954. Along with Prime Minister Balewa, Bello was instrumental in promoting the "northernization" agenda of the NPC-dominated First Republic. He was killed in the coup of January 15, 1966, which ended the First Republic.

Bello, Muhammadu (1781–1837)

Son of Usman dan Fodio and one of the leaders of the Islamic revolution that resulted in the establishment of the Sokoto Caliphate. After the death of his father, Bello took over the reins of government, taking the title of Sultan of Sokoto, and continued to spread the revolution to new frontiers and to quell internal resistance. Under Bello, Islamic politics, justice, education, and culture, which had once been the reserve of the wealthy and powerful elite, began to spread throughout northern Nigeria.

Buhari, Major General Muhammadu (1942–)

Born in Daura in Katsina province of Kaduna State, Buhari trained at the Nigerian Military Training College in Kaduna and at Mons Officer Cadet School in the United Kingdom. He held many important positions under Nigeria's military regimes, including Director of Supply and Transport of the Nigerian army from 1974 to 1975, military governor of Northeastern – and, later, Borno – State from 1975 to 1976, and federal commissioner for petroleum and energy in the military administration of Olusegun Obasanjo. On December 31, 1983, he became head of state and commander-in-chief of the armed forces in the coup that overthrew the Second Republic. Buhari's military administration is probably best known for its idealistic but ultimately unsuccessful "War Against Indiscipline" (WAI), in which Nigerians were charged to be punctual to work, wait in queues, and keep their cities clean. After just twenty months, Buhari was himself overthrown in the coup that brought Ibrahim Babangida to power on August 27, 1985. Buhari has remained influential in politics, however. He ran for president in 2003 and 2007 as the candidate of the All Nigeria People's Party (ANPP), coming second both times.

Crowther, Bishop Samuel Ajayi (1809–91)

Born in Yorubaland in 1809, Crowther was captured at the age of twelve and sold to Portuguese slave traders. The ship he was being transported on was captured by a British anti-slavery patrol ship, and he was released in Freetown, Sierra Leone. In Freetown, Crowther was educated by the Church Missionary Society, and baptized in 1825. In 1841 he was chosen to accompany the Niger Expedition to establish a missionary presence in the Nigerian interior. The mission failed, and Crowther returned to the coast to work as a missionary in Badagry and Abeokuta. He was a very successful missionary, and in 1861 he was named the first African bishop of the Anglican Church, with his diocese on the river Niger. An African nationalist, Crowther believed that Africa's future should be the preserve of Africans themselves, and fought against the encroachment of British colonial rule in the late nineteenth century. He quarreled with Sir George Goldie over the activities of the Royal Niger Company and over ideas that Christianity should be used to promote British interests in the region. In 1890 he resigned his position as Bishop on the Niger. He died the next year.

Equiano, Olaudah (*c.* 1745–97)

Famous abolitionist and author of *The Interesting Narrative of Olaudah Equiano*, Equiano was born in Igboland around 1745. Kidnapped and sold into slavery around the age of eleven, Equiano lived as a slave in Virginia and England and participated in the Seven Years War of 1756–63. After the war he was sold to a slave trader in the West Indies, from whom he later bought his freedom. He returned to Great Britain in 1769 and became an active member of the abolitionist movement, giving public speeches and writing many letters to English newspapers. In 1789 he published his *Interesting Narrative*, in which he recounted his personal experiences of the horrors of slavery and the slave trade. The book was immensely successful and helped to shape people's thoughts about the slave trade, which was finally abolished in the United Kingdom in 1807, ten years after Equiano's death. In recent years questions have been raised as to the African origin of Equiano. Some scholars now claim that he was born not in Igboland but in South Carolina.

Fodio, Usman dan (1754–1817)

Fulani Islamic scholar and leader of the Islamic revolution that established the Sokoto Caliphate in northern Nigeria in the nineteenth century. Born and educated in the Hausa state of Gobir, by the late eighteenth century dan Fodio had developed a group of followers known as "the Community," who subscribed to his vociferous calls for a purification of the political and religious make-up of the region. Relations between dan Fodio and the King of Gobir deteriorated over the latter's refusal to institute sweeping Islamic reforms, and in 1804 dan Fodio fled from Gobir after an attempt had been made on his life. His followers went with him and organized a revolution against the king. Later in the year dan Fodio declared a *jihad*, or holy war, against the heretical Hausa rulers. Over the next decade dan Fodio's followers toppled the Hausa dynasties in most states in northern Nigeria and replaced them with Fulani emirs, thus bringing into existence the mighty Sokoto Caliphate, which ruled the region for the next century. In 1812 dan Fodio divided the administration of the territories under his control between his brother Abduallahi and his son Muhammadu Bello, and retired from public life. He died in 1817.

Goldie, Sir George (1846–1925)

British shipping mogul and largest shareholder in the Royal Niger Company, which became one of the tools through which British colonial rule was imposed upon Nigeria. Goldie was given a Royal Charter in 1886 to allow his company to negotiate with local rulers in the territories around the river Niger to administer the territories in the interests of free trade. The RNC quickly eroded the sovereignty of the local rulers with whom it had treaty relationships, however, and became a monopolistic company, completely controlling trade on the Niger for over fifteen years. In 1900 Goldie's charter was revoked and the territories controlled by the company came under the direct control of the British government.

Gowon, General Yakubu (1934–)

Born in what is now Plateau State, Gowon enlisted in the army in 1954 and took officer's training courses in Ghana and the United Kingdom. He served in the UN peacekeeping mission to the Congo between 1961 and 1963. After the coup of January 15, 1966, Gowon became the chief of staff of the Nigerian army under Aguiyi-Ironsi. After the second coup of July 29, 1966, in which Ironsi was killed, Gowon was chosen by the organizers of the coup to become the new head of state. Gowon ruled Nigeria for the next nine years. He was head of the Federal Military Government during the Nigerian Civil War, in which he galvanized the country under the slogan "To keep Nigeria one is a task which must be done." After the civil war he embarked on a program of "Reconciliation, rehabilitation, and reconstruction." This process was helped greatly by the oil boom that Nigeria experienced during the early 1970s. Gowon's administration after the civil war was plagued with inefficiency and corruption, however. Gowon also angered many prominent officers and politicians by prevaricating on the transfer of power back to civilian rule. On July 29, 1975, Gowon was overthrown in the military coup that brought General Murtala Mohammed to power. He went into exile in the United Kingdom until 1983, when he returned home. He completed his PhD in political science from the University of Warwick in 1984. He continues to live in Plateau State, and in 1998 was a prominent supporter of the presidential campaign of Olusegun Obasanjo.

Ja Ja, King of Opobo (1821–91)

One of the most famous resistors of the British colonial takeover of Nigeria. Born in the Amaigbo village group in southeastern Nigeria, Ja Ja was sold as a slave at the age of twelve to a chief in the coastal trading state of Bonny. Through his prowess as a trader, particularly in palm oil, Ja Ja rose to become the head of the Anna Pepple house, an extremely wealthy and powerful house in Bonny, in 1863. His success as a trader roused the ire and competition of other houses, particularly the Manilla Pepple house, headed by Oko Jumbo. In 1869 war broke out between the two houses, with the result that Ja Ja fled inland, establishing a new trading state, which he named Opobo. From the hinterland Ja Ja cut off Bonny's access to palm oil markets, and, over time, he turned Opobo into a wealthy trading state of its own. In 1884 Ja Ja signed a treaty of protection with the British guaranteeing them free trade in his realm. Not intending to live up to an agreement that would erode his competitive advantage, Ja Ja quickly abrogated the terms of the treaty, provoking the anger of the British. In 1887 the acting British consul, Harry Johnston, tricked Ja Ja on board a gunboat, ostensibly to negotiate a peaceful end to hostilities. Once on board, however, Ja Ja was arrested and taken to Accra, whence he was banished to the West Indies. He was allowed to return to Opobo in 1891, but died on the voyage home. His body was returned home and buried in Opobo.

Kano, Alhaji Aminu (1920–83)

A Fulani, educated as a school teacher at Kaduna College and the Institute of Education at the University of London, Kano worked with Tafawa Balewa at Bauchi Middle School and became one of the founding members of the Northern People's Congress. When this party became too conservative for him, however, Kano broke away and formed a new party, the Northern Elements Progressive Union (NEPU), which competed with the NPC for votes among Nigeria's northern Muslims. A champion of the poor, Kano became a populist leader, but never had enough backing from the established elite classes to win elections much beyond his base of Kano city. After the onset of military rule in 1966 Kano held many positions in the military governments, including federal commissioner of communications (1967–71) and federal commissioner for health (1971–74). Kano formed the People's Redemption Party (PRP) to contest elections during the Second Republic, and ran as the party's presidential candidate in 1979. He lost the election and died four years later, on May 18, 1983.

Lugard, Sir Frederick (1858–1945)

British colonial administrator, he worked as an army officer in Nyasaland (Malawi), Kenya, and Uganda before taking up employment in the Royal Niger Company in 1894. In 1897 he organized the West African Frontier Force (WAFF) for the British to secure the western border of the British sphere of influence in northern Nigeria against French encroachment. In

1900 Lugard became the first high commissioner of the Protectorate of Northern Nigeria after the dissolution of the RNC. He then undertook the military conquest of the Sokoto Caliphate, which was completed in 1903. As high commissioner of the northern protectorate, Lugard developed the administrative system that he called "indirect rule," by which the British ruled colonial territories through existing local rulers. Lugard left Nigeria in 1906, but returned in 1912 to oversee the amalgamation of the Nigerian protectorates into a single administrative unit, becoming the first governor general of a unified Nigeria. As governor general he extended his form of indirect rule to southern Nigeria, before retiring from public service in 1919. In 1922 he published *The Dual Mandate in British Tropical Africa*, in which he outlined in great detail his philosophy of colonial rule as a system that ought both to benefit the economy of the colonizing country and help to bring indigenous races to a higher level of "civilization." Indirect rule and the Dual Mandate became common ideologies of British colonial rule throughout Africa.

Macaulay, Herbert (1884–1946)
A grandson of Bishop Samuel Ajayi Crowther, Macaulay grew up in Lagos before undergoing training in England to become a civil engineer. He later abandoned this career path to become a journalist and esteemed critic of British colonial rule in Lagos. He founded the first daily newspaper in Nigeria, *The Lagos Daily News*, through which he informed Nigerians about the activities of their alien colonial government. He formed the first political party in Nigeria, the Nigerian National Democratic Party, which won all the seats in the Nigerian Legislative Council until the rise of the Nigerian Youth Movement in the 1930s. He later became a supporter of Nnamdi Azikiwe's National Council of Nigeria and the Cameroons. For his vociferous criticism of colonial injustices, which sometimes led to needed reforms, Macaulay has often been called the "father of Nigerian nationalism."

Mohammed, General Murtala Ramat (1938–76)
Born in Kano and educated at Government College in Zaria, Mohammed enlisted in the army in 1957 and underwent training at Sandhurst Royal Military Academy in the United Kingdom. He served in the United Nations Peacekeeping Force in the Congo, and later as an aide-de-camp to the administrator of the Western Region during the emergency there. He was made a lieutenant colonel after the military coup of January 15, 1966, that brought Aguiyi-Ironsi to power, and took

an active part in the July 29, 1966, coup that deposed Aguiyi-Ironsi. Mohammed served as a field commander in the civil war, capturing Asaba and Onitsha for the Federal Military Government, before moving to Lagos to become inspector of the Nigerian Army Signals in 1968 and, later, in August 1974, federal commissioner of communications. Mohammed became head of state and commander-in-chief of the Nigerian armed forces after the coup that toppled Yakubu Gowon on July 29, 1975. Over the next six months Mohammed undertook a series of sweeping reforms to government administration, including the compulsory retirement of thousands of military officers and civil servants, and the formation of a plan for a handover to civilian rule. On February 13, 1976, Mohammed was assassinated in an abortive coup attempt. Mohammed has been revered since as the most qualified and best-intentioned ruler in Nigerian history, although many believe his near-mythical status owes significantly to the fact that he did not live long enough to have his reputation tarnished.

Nzeogwu, Major Patrick Chukwuma (1937–67)

Born in Kaduna to Igbo parents, Nzeogwu attended St. John's College in Kaduna and later joined the Nigerian army, for which he underwent training at Sandhurst Royal Military Academy in the United Kingdom. Nzeogwu is credited as the leader of the first military coup of January 15, 1966, that ended the First Republic and resulted in the murders of prime minister Tafawa Balewa, Northern Region premier Ahmadu Bello, and Western Region premier S. L. Akintola, among many others. The coup was only partially successful, however, and, after Aguiyi-Ironsi had managed to restore stability to a shattered government, Nzeogwu was detained first in Lagos and then in the Eastern Region. Colonel Emeka Ojukwu released him from prison before the secession of the Eastern Region as the sovereign state of Biafra. Nzeogwu fought on the side of Biafra in the civil war, despite personal disagreement with the decision to secede, and was killed in battle on July 26, 1967.

Obasanjo, General Olusegun (1937–)

Born in Abeokuta, Obasanjo joined the army in 1958 and underwent officer training at Mons Officer Cadets' School in the United Kingdom. He served in the United Nations peacekeeping mission in the Congo and became commander of the Royal Engineers of the Nigerian Army in 1963. During the civil war Obasanjo served as the commander of the Ibadan Garrison from 1967 to 1969, and then as the commander of the third marine commando division on the southeastern front of Biafra. In January 1970 Obasanjo accepted the surrender of Biafra. After the coup d'etat of July 29, 1975, that brought Murtala Mohammed to power, Obasanjo became chief of staff, supreme headquarters. After Mohammed's assassination on February 13, 1976, Obasanjo became head of state and commander-in-chief of the Nigerian armed forces. As head of state, Obasanjo continued with the programs outlined by Mohammed before his death, most notably the plan to transfer power back to civilian rule. In 1979 Obasanjo became the first military ruler in Nigerian history to hand power over to a civilian administration, ushering in the Second Republic. Obasanjo retired from the military in 1979 and became a major figure in international politics, serving on numerous panels and organizations of the United Nations, World Health Organization, and Commonwealth Group. In March 1995 Obasanjo was imprisoned by Abacha for his supposed involvement in a plot to overthrow the government. After Abacha's death in 1998, Obasanjo emerged from prison to mount a presidential campaign for the newly established People's Democratic Party. Obasanjo won the election, and was re-elected in 2003 to a second term. In 2007 Obasanjo handed power to his successor, Umaru Yar'Adua, also of the PDP, marking the first time in Nigeria's history that one civilian leader transferred power to another. Obasanjo's two terms as president have been controversial: while on the one hand he has stabilized the economy and restored Nigeria's tattered international image to a degree, he has been accused of undemocratic and corrupt practices as well.

Ojukwu, Colonel Chukwuemeka Odumegwu (1933–)

Born in Zungeru, in northern Nigeria, to Igbo parents, Ojukwu was educated at King's College, Lagos, before traveling to the United Kingdom, where he studied history at Oxford. He returned from the United Kingdom in 1955 and joined the Nigerian army in 1957, serving in the United Nations Peacekeeping Force in the Congo. After the coup of January 15, 1966, that brought Aguiyi-Ironsi to power, Ojukwu was named the military governor of the Eastern Region. Ojukwu refused to recognize the second coup of July 29, 1966, that made Yakubu Gowon head of state, and, after a series of failed negotiations, Ojukwu led the Eastern Region in secession from Nigeria as the sovereign state of Biafra. In January 1970, with Biafran collapse imminent, Ojukwu fled to Ivory Coast. Pardoned in 1982, Ojukwu returned to Nigeria. Ojukwu has remained active in politics, but has not achieved any great success, losing a senate race in Anambra in 1983 and running for president as a fringe candidate during the Fourth Republic.

Ransome-Kuti, Fela (1938–97)

Son of the famous political activist Mrs. Olufunmilayo Ransome-Kuti, Fela was one of the most famous African musicians of the 1970s and 1980s. His style of music, known as Afro-beat, blended traditional African rhythms with American jazz and blues, appealing to music lovers the world over. In Nigeria, Fela was influential not only as a musician but as a political and social critic, often speaking out publicly against the venality and corruption of the Nigerian government, for which he paid a severe price. In 1978 his own mother was killed in an army raid on his compound, and he himself spent time in prison. Fela contested the 1983 presidential election, but lost to incumbent Shehu Shagari. Fela died of complications related to AIDS in 1997.

Ransome-Kuti, Chief Olufunmilayo (1900–78)

Born in Abeokuta, Mrs. Ransome-Kuti left Nigeria in 1920 to study music and domestic science at Wincham Hall College in Manchester in the United Kingdom. She returned to Nigeria and became a teacher in Abeokuta, where she began to found several women's organizations. These organizations later merged to become the Egba Women's Union and, later, the Abeokuta Women's Union. The AWU protested strongly at abuses of power on the part of the *alake* of Abeokuta during the 1940s and 1950s, achieving his temporary deportation in 1948. Ransome-Kuti also aligned the AWU with the bourgeoning nationalist movement of the NCNC, in which she held important party posts. Mrs. Ransome-Kuti's activism has pervaded her family, and four of her children have become quite famous as political activists: Fela Kuti became one of Nigeria's most politically and culturally significant musicians in the 1970s and 1980s, while Beko Ransome-Kuti, a doctor, has been detained in prison on many occasions for his protests against military regimes. Mrs. Ransome-Kuti was killed in an army raid on her son Fela's compound in 1978.

Saro-Wiwa, Kenule Beeson (1941–95)

Born at Bori in what is now Rivers State, Saro-Wiwa was educated at Government College Umuahia, the University of Ibadan, and the University of Nigeria, Nsukka. He worked as commissioner of works, land and transport for Rivers State and, later, as the state's commissioner of education. In 1987 he was appointed director of the Directorate for

Social Mobilization (DSM) in the Babangida administration, but he resigned the next year. Saro-Wiwa wrote many books, including *Sozaboy*, an account of the Nigerian Civil War, but he is most renowned for his work as the president of the Movement for the Survival of the Ogoni People (MOSOP), an organization that challenged the military regimes of Babangida and Abacha to give the Ogoni more control over Ogoni resources and revenues, as well as to reduce the environmental degradation that multinational oil companies brought to Ogoni lands. In 1994 Saro-Wiwa and eight other leaders of MOSOP were arrested for the supposed murder of four local chiefs and detained for many months before being tried, convicted, and sentenced to death by a secret military tribunal. Despite pleas from the international community for clemency and evidence that the trials were flawed, Saro-Wiwa and seven of his colleagues were executed on November 10, 1995. The execution of Saro-Wiwa cemented Nigeria's position as an international pariah state during the Abacha years, and resulted in the suspension of the country from the Commonwealth Group and half-hearted sanctions from other Western countries.

Shagari, Alhaji Shehu (1924–)

A former school teacher and early member of the Northern People's Congress, Shagari has had a very distinguished career in Nigerian politics. Elected to Nigeria's first federal House of Representatives in 1954 and appointed a parliamentary secretary in 1958, Shagari held many ministerial posts throughout the First Republic and the military regimes of the 1960s and 1970s, including minister of finance under Yakubu Gowon. In 1979 Shagari became the nominee of the National Party of Nigeria to stand for the presidency of the Second Republic. Shagari won the election, but only after a controversy that went all the way to the Nigerian Supreme Court. As president, Shagari oversaw a corrupt and ineffective government that hastened Nigeria's economic decline. After winning re-election in 1983 in polls that were widely considered to have been rigged, Shagari was overthrown in a military coup on December 31, 1983, that brought Muhammadu Buhari to power.

Soyinka, Wole (1934–)

Born near Abeokuta and educated at the University of Ibadan and Leeds University in the United Kingdom, Soyinka has become one of the giants of African theater and literature. A playwright, poet, actor, teacher, social critic, and political activist, Soyinka has written many important works, including *A Dance of the Forest*, *The Trials of Brother Jero*, *The Swamp*

Dwellers, Ake, The Years of Childhood, The Open Sore of a Continent, and many others. For his criticism of the Gowon regime Soyinka was detained between 1967 and 1969, and he lived in exile from 1971 to 1975. He went into exile again in 1994, after Abacha seized his travel documents over Soyinka's outspoken support of the June 12, 1993, elections. In 1986 Soyinka became the first African to win the Nobel Prize for literature.

Tarka, Joseph (1932–80)

Born in the Tiv division of what is now Benue State, Tarka trained as a teacher before becoming active in politics as the founder and president of the United Middle Belt Congress (UMBC), a political party that lobbied for the interests of middle belt inhabitants, who, by and large, were made up of small ethnic groups not well represented in the other major parties. In 1954 Tarka won election to the first federal House of Representatives, where he aligned his party with the Action Group of Obafemi Awolowo in united opposition to the NPC-led government. His unceasing lobbying for a separate state for the middle belt was rewarded when, in 1967, Yakubu Gowon created Benue Plateau State. Under the Gowon administration, Tarka held prominent positions, most notably as commissioner of transport and, later, commissioner of communications. He had to resign his position in 1974, however, amid allegations of corruption and abuse of power. During the Second Republic Tarka became vice-chairman of the ruling National Party of Nigeria, and he won a Senate seat just a year before he died, in London, on March 30, 1980.

Yar'Adua, Alhaji Umaru (1951–)

President of Nigeria since 2007, Yar'Adua was Olusegun Obasanjo's hand-selected successor for the presidential nomination of the People's Democratic Party. Before winning the nomination, Yar'Adua, who was currently serving as the governor of Katsina State, was not a well-known politician, although his family has exercised a good deal of political influence. His father had been a minister in the First Republic, and his brother, Musa, had been deputy head of state under Obasanjo's military administration from 1976 to 1979. Yar'Adua was imprisoned, along with his brother and Obasanjo, in 1995 for allegedly plotting to overthrow the government of Sani Abacha. Known as a quiet but stern leader who brooks little opposition, Yar'Adua has a reputation for fair play and an anti-corruption stance that is uncommon among high-level politicians in Nigeria. Nevertheless, the elections which brought him to power have been widely criticized as undemocratic and severely flawed.

Abbreviations

ABN	Association for a Better Nigeria
AC	Action Congress
AD	Alliance for Democracy
AFRC	Armed Forces Ruling Council
AG	Action Group
ANC	African National Congress (South Africa)
ANPP	All Nigeria People's Party
APP	All People's Party
AU	African Union
AWU	Abeokuta Women's Union
BCE	before the Common Era
BP	British Petroleum
bpd	barrels per day
CAN	Christian Association of Nigeria
CD	Campaign for Democracy
CDC	Constitution Drafting Committee
CE	Common Era
CFA	Communauté financière d'Afrique
CIA	Central Intelligence Agency (United States)
CMS	Church Missionary Society
DFRRI	Directorate of Food, Roads, and Rural Infrastructure
DPA	Distributable Pool Account
DSM	Directorate for Social Mobilization
ECOMOG	ECOWAS Monitoring Group
ECOWAS	Economic Community of West African States
EEC	European Economic Community
EFCC	Economic and Financial Crimes Commission
FCT	Federal Capital Territory
FDI	foreign direct investment
FEDECO	Federal Electoral Commission

FESTAC	Festival of Black Arts and Culture
FMG	Federal Military Government
FNDP	First National Development Plan
FNLA	National Front for the Liberation of Angola (Angola)
GDP	gross domestic product
GNP	gross national product
GNPP	Great Nigeria People's Party
IGC	Interim Governing Council
IMF	International Monetary Fund
INEC	Independent National Election Commission
JNI	Jama'atu Nasril Islam
K	Kobo
LSA	Late Stone Age
MAD	Movement for the Advancement of Democracy
MAMSER	Mass Mobilization for Economic Recovery, Self-reliance, and Social Justice
MASSOB	Movement for the Actualization of the Sovereign State of Biafra
MEND	Movement for the Emancipation of the Niger Delta
MOSOP	Movement for the Survival of the Ogoni People
MPLA	Popular Movement for the Liberation of Angola (Angola)
N	Naira
NADECO	National Democratic Coalition
NANS	National Association of Nigerian Students
NBA	Nigerian Bar Association
NCBWA	National Congress of British West Africa
NCNC	National Council of Nigeria and the Cameroons (later Nigerian Citizens)
NDE	National Directorate of Employment
NEC	National Electoral Commission
NEPA	Nigerian Electric Power Authority
NEPAD	New Partnership for Africa's Development
NEPU	Northern Elements Progressive Union
NITEL	Nigerian Telecommunications
NLC	Nigerian Labour Congress
NNA	Nigerian National Alliance
NNDP	Nigerian National Democratic Party
NNOC	Nigerian National Oil Company
NNPC	Nigerian National Petroleum Company
NPC	Northern People's Congress

NPFL	National Patriotic Front of Liberia (Liberia)
NPN	National Party of Nigeria
NPP	Nigerian People's Party
NRC	National Republican Convention
NSO	National Security Organization
NUT	Nigerian Union of Teachers
NYM	Nigerian Youth Movement
NYSC	National Youth Service Corps
OAU	Organization of African Unity
OIC	Organization of the Islamic Conference
OPEC	Organization of Petroleum Exporting Countries
PAC	Pan-African Congress (South Africa)
PDP	People's Democratic Party
PF	Patriotic Front (Zimbabwe)
PPA	Progressive Parties Alliance
PRP	People's Redemption Party
RNC	Royal Niger Company
SAP	Structural Adjustment Program
SCIA	Supreme Council for Islamic Affairs
SDP	Social Democratic Party
SWAPO	South West Africa People's Organization (Namibia)
UAC	United Africa Company
UMBC	United Middle Belt Congress
UN	United Nations
UNITA	Union for the Total Independence of Angola (Angola)
UPGA	United Progressive Grand Alliance
UPN	Unity Party of Nigeria
UPP	United People's Party
WAFF	West African Frontier Force
WAI	War Against Indiscipline
WASU	West African Students' Union
YBP	Years Before Present
ZANU	Zimbabwean African National Union (Zimbabwe)

Glossary

419	slang term for fraud schemes and other corrupt practices in contemporary Nigeria. Named for the criminal code number under which such cases are prosecuted.
ajele	also called *asoju oba*, which literally means "eyes of the king." These slaves, placed throughout the Oyo empire, reported directly to the *alafin* on matters affecting their assigned province.
aladura	group of indigenous Christian churches.
alafin	king of Oyo.
alake	title of the traditional ruler of Abeokuta.
Alhaji	title for a Muslim man who has completed the pilgrimage, or *hajj*. The title for a woman who has completed the pilgrimage is *alhaja*.
are ona kakanfo	commander-in-chief of the provincial army of Oyo and one of the most powerful and important officers in the *alafin*'s retinue.
basorun	leader of the Oyo Mesi.
Bayajidda	mythical founder of the Hausa city states.
cassava	a root crop that forms the basis for many staple foods in Nigeria, such as fufu, gari, and eba. Cassava is a starch and is low in protein; it is therefore usually accompanied by other foods with higher protein, vitamin, and fat levels to form a balanced diet.
Church Missionary Society	a branch of the Anglican Church, based in England, which had been active in evangelical activities in Sierra Leone but which branched out to other parts of Africa in the nineteenth century.

CMS missions were opened throughout southern Nigeria from the 1840s.

cowry small shell traditionally used as currency in southern Nigeria before and even during British colonial rule. The shells were used mainly for small local transactions. The British outlawed their importation in the early twentieth century in an effort to direct the economy towards the use of imported British coins and notes.

eghaevbo n'ogboe palace administration in Benin kingdom.

eghaevbo n'ore city administration in Benin kingdom.

Ekpe secret society in the region around Calabar and its hinterland that regulated the terms and conditions of trade in the region in the period of the transatlantic slave trade and beyond.

emir leaders of regions known as emirates in the time of the Sokoto Caliphate who reported directly to the Sultan of Sokoto.

groundnut peanut.

hajj Islamic pilgrimage to Mecca.

high-life popular music style from the 1940s and 1950s that melded traditional musical styles with American jazz and blues, as well as Caribbean samba, calypso, and salsa. Famous high-life musicians include the Ghanaian E. T. Mensah and Tunde King.

house system system of political and economic organization in the Bight of Biafra from the Niger delta to Calabar. Each house derived from a lineage and competed with other houses for political influence and control of trade with Europeans, particularly the trade in slaves.

ilari literally "scar-headed," slaves who served as administrators for the *alafin* of Oyo.

jihad holy war.

juju form of popular music in southwestern Nigeria.

kleptocracy term used to describe a political system in which one of the primary goals of the ruling politicians is the diversion of government funds into personal accounts and business ventures. Nigeria is considered by many to have functioned as a kleptocracy for most of its post-independence history.

kobo   unit of Nigerian currency, now out of circulation. One naira was equal to 100 kobo.

kofa   servants of the Sultan of Sokoto assigned to individual emirs to report on the actions of those emirs. *Kofa*s were also responsible for collecting tribute from the emirs.

kola nut   nuts of the kola tree, of which about fifteen different varieties grow in Nigeria. The nuts grow in clusters, each of which can contain ten or more nuts. The kola nut contains caffeine, which serves as a mild stimulant and appetite suppressant. Kola nuts are traditionally given to guests to welcome them, and are used in some wedding and naming ceremonies, as well as certain festivals and as sacrifices to some gods of indigenous religions.

mai   king of Kanem or Borno.

manila   a small brass rod traditionally used as currency in southern Nigeria. The British outlawed their importation in the early twentieth century in an effort to direct the economy towards the use of imported British coins and notes.

naira   main unit of Nigerian currency. The value of the naira has fallen over the years. As of 2007, its value stood at roughly 140 naira to the US dollar.

oba   king of a Yoruba or Benin state.

Oduduwa   mythical progenitor of the Yoruba people.

Okonko   secret society in the Niger delta region that regulated the terms and conditions of trade in slaves and palm oil, among other things.

ona iwefa   powerful palace slave who stood as proxy for the *alafin* of Oyo in handing down legal rulings.

ooni   king of Ife.

Oranmiyan   son of Oduduwa and mythical founder of Oyo.

osi iwefa   powerful palace slave who collected revenues and served as the *alafin* of Oyo's proxy in dealings with lineage heads such as the members of the Oyo Mesi.

otun iwefa   powerful palace slave in charge of the cult of Sango, through which the *alafin* of Oyo's office was mystified.

Oyo Mesi   chief advisory body to the *alafin* of Oyo.

palm oil   oil from the palm kernel, the fruit of the oil palm tree. Palm oil is an important ingredient in many foods, as well as being used in lubricants and illuminants.

ribat   fortress used to secure the boundaries of the Sokoto Caliphate, but which also became centers of Islamic life and culture.

Sango   god of thunder in Yoruba religion.

shari'a   Islamic legal code.

ulama   learned and powerful class of Islamic magistrates, scribes, or theologians, often trained in *madrasas*, or schools of higher Islamic learning.

uzama   group of advisers to the *oba* of Benin.

wangarawa   Islamic traders and missionaries from the western Sudan.

Westminster model   the form of parliamentary government practiced in the United Kingdom. The constitution of Nigeria's First Republic (1960–6) was heavily based on the Westminster model.

Zaghawa   early migrants into the Lake Chad region.

Zik   nickname of Nnamdi Azikiwe, Nigerian nationalist and first Nigerian governor general and president of Nigeria.

Zikists   radical, left-wing group of NCNC supporters who were willing to use any means necessary, even violence, to attain independence for Nigeria from British rule in the 1950s.

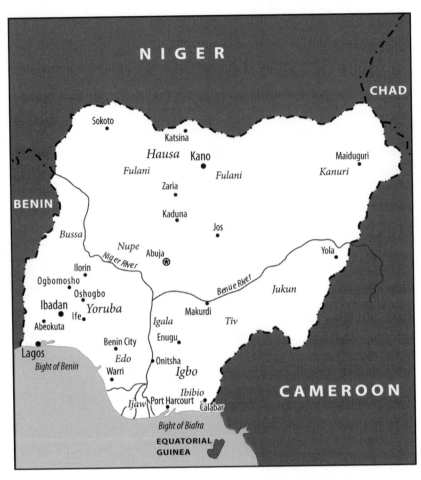

Map 1. Major cities and ethnic groups in present-day Nigeria
(courtesy Saverance Publishing Services)

Introduction

The aim of this book is to provide a general background survey of the broad themes of Nigeria's history, from the beginnings of human habitation in the region up to the early twenty-first century. The borders of modern-day Nigeria were established in 1914 by British colonizers, but the histories of the peoples that make up the Nigerian polity go back many centuries. Most general histories of Nigeria written since Nigeria gained independence from the United Kingdom in 1960 tend to focus almost exclusively on political and economic themes, and almost exclusively on the twentieth century. This book, on the other hand, aims to bring a greater chronological and thematic balance to the narrative of Nigerian history. Themes such as state formation, political institutions, commercial activities, and political economy are important, and are covered extensively in this book, but these themes featured in the history of the region well before the twentieth century, and, in many ways, events that occurred prior to the twentieth century are highly relevant to an understanding of Nigerian history in subsequent periods.

Politics and the economy are not the only barometers of history. This book also makes a special effort to illustrate social and cultural themes in Nigeria's history, such as the roles of ethnicity, religion, education, urbanization, and globalization, in the lives of Nigerian peoples and states over the centuries. The goal is not only to explain the events, policies, and circumstances that have shaped the lives of people in the Nigerian region, but also to show how Nigerians themselves have understood the world in which they have lived or currently live, and how they have influenced events in their homelands and around the world over the course of human history. Before delving into the specifics of Nigeria's long history, however, it is important to have a basic understanding of the geography and people of Nigeria, and of some of the major issues that have affected the region over the centuries.

GEOGRAPHY AND NATURAL RESOURCES

Nigeria is a large country in the west African region. Covering 356,668 square miles, Nigeria is roughly twice the size of California and three times the size of the United Kingdom. The country is bordered to the south by the Bights of Benin and Biafra, which are on the Gulf of Guinea in the Atlantic Ocean. On the west Nigeria is bordered by Benin, on the north by Niger, and on the east by Cameroon. In its extreme northeastern corner, Lake Chad separates Nigeria from the country of Chad. Nigeria stretches roughly 700 miles from west to east and 650 miles from south to north, covering an area between 3° and 15°E longitude and between 4° and 14°N latitude.

The territories that make up modern-day Nigeria exhibit diverse geographical characteristics, ranging from tropical to arid. The area around the Niger delta contains dense mangrove swamps, while the rest of the southern part of the country is heavily forested. The southern forests give way to hills and plateaus further north, in what is known as the middle belt. There are also mountains in the east. Further north still are the plains of the savanna and, in the extreme north, the semi-desert area known as the Sahel. Nigeria experiences two main seasons: the wet season, which lasts from May to October, and the dry season. Rainfall decreases from south to north, and temperatures are generally quite high throughout the country. During the dry season, a strong cool wind called the *harmattan* blows in from the Sahara, bringing relief from the heat but also carrying particles of desert sand, increasing the desertification of the northern savannas.

The main artery of commerce and communication in the region historically has been the river Niger, the third longest river in Africa, which runs for 730 miles through Nigeria. The Niger enters the country in Kebbi State in the northwest and pours into the Gulf of Guinea through its many branches in the Niger delta in southern Rivers and Delta States. The Niger joins with its main tributary, the Benue, which flows from the northeast, at Lokoja, in the central state of Kogi. Other important rivers include the Sokoto, Kaduna, and Anambra, all of which are tributaries of the Niger, as well as the Donga, Katsina Ala, and Gongola.

Nigeria's diverse geography yields a broad assortment of natural resources. Mineral wealth includes large deposits of coal, iron, tin, and columbite, as well as lead, copper, and zinc, much of which is found in the hills and plateaus of the middle belt. Small amounts of gold, silver, and diamonds have also been discovered in various places. Nigeria is most famous for its large petroleum reserves, however, located in the Niger delta. Since the 1970s petroleum has become the most important single commodity in the Nigerian economy, and sales of petroleum constitute over 90 percent of the country's export earnings, and over 75 percent of public revenues.[1] The reliance on petroleum as the main source of the country's wealth has contributed greatly to economic instability since the late 1970s, as fluctuations in world petroleum prices and high levels of corruption among government officials have made sustainable development elusive and brought extreme poverty to the majority of Nigeria's citizens.

Historically, however, petroleum has not been the lifeblood of the economies of Nigerian communities. Until recent years, agriculture formed the basis of the economic activity and lifestyle of most Nigerians. Nigeria boasts a wide variety of agricultural landscapes, yielding a broad spectrum of agricultural goods. Food crops include yams, cassava, bananas, plantains, rice, maize, millet, citrus fruits, groundnuts, cocoa, and palm produce (oil, kernels, and wine). These products are produced both for domestic consumption and for export. Cocoa production in the southwest, palm oil production in the southeast, and groundnut production in the north provided the basis of the "cash crop" economy of the colonial era, during which the production of these items was exponentially increased for the sole purpose of exportation. Non-food products are also abundant in Nigeria. Cotton, rubber, and timber, in particular, have been important products, used both in domestic manufacturing and as export commodities over the years. Animal husbandry has also been a major occupation throughout Nigeria. In the savannas of the north, in particular, cattle-rearing has been an important aspect of the economy, providing beef and milk as well as hides. Goats, guinea fowl, snails, and eggs have been major protein sources and items of trade as well. In coastal communities, fishing has been a major economic activity. Agriculture remains the main activity of the rural population; however, the contribution of agriculture as a percentage of GDP has declined since the expansion of the oil economy in the 1970s.

Another major natural resource of Nigeria is its abundant labor force. Nigeria is the most populous country in Africa. The results of a census conducted in 2006 placed the population at over 140 million people.[2] Throughout history, the labor and ingenuity of Nigerians themselves have been the primary driving force of the economy. Agricultural labor has been complemented by local craftsmanship and artisanry in such areas as blacksmithing, leather-working, construction, textile manufacturing, beer brewing, building, boatmaking, and so forth. Merchants and traders have also been important in keeping goods flowing between regions, diversifying and developing local economies. For a long time, human labor was itself a commodity that could be bought and sold. Slaves were a major item of trade for many centuries in parts of Nigeria, and played important roles in the domestic economies of many states in the Nigerian region in the centuries before the 1900s. With the onset of colonial rule in the late nineteenth and early twentieth centuries, domestic slavery was slowly eradicated; the colonial government itself used forced labor to build much of its own infrastructure, however. The instability and underdevelopment that has characterized the Nigerian economy for much of the time since independence has led to high unemployment levels, leaving Nigeria unable to utilize its labor resources effectively.

PEOPLES AND CULTURES

Nigeria's large population is very diverse, consisting of over 200 different ethno-linguistic groups. Three main ethnic groups make up the majority of the population. The Hausa, located in the northern savannas, account for roughly 21 percent of the population, while the Yoruba, located in the southwestern part of the country, make up 20 percent, and the Igbo of the southeast 17 percent.[3] Other ethnic groups with relatively large populations include the pastoral Fulani of the savannas, the Ijaw of the Niger delta region, the Kanuri of the Lake Chad region, the Ibibio in and around Calabar in the southeast, and the Nupe and Tiv of the middle belt region. Although over 250 different indigenous languages are spoken in Nigeria, English has been the official language of the country since 1960. Pidgin, a combination of indigenous languages and English that developed through hundreds of years of contact with British traders and later with colonial authorities, is also commonly used.

Nigerians belong to many different religions as well, but the vast majority identify with either Islam or Christianity. About 50 percent of the Nigerian population is Sunni Muslim.[4] Muslims are most heavily concentrated in the northern savannas, where Islam first appeared between the eleventh and fourteenth centuries CE. Until the jihad of Usman dan Fodio and the establishment of the Sokoto Caliphate in the early nineteenth century, Islam had been primarily a religion of the elite. Kings and wealthy merchants adopted elements of Islam in order to claim mystical powers and to build strong commercial and diplomatic ties with Islamic states in north Africa and the Middle East. Since the nineteenth century, however, the vast majority of the Hausa, Fulani, and Kanuri have come to identify religiously with Islam. About a third of all Yorubas are Muslim as well. Christians make up roughly 40 percent of the population, and are concentrated most heavily in the south and middle belt. Christianity first became a popular religion in the Nigerian region in the nineteenth century, as the presence of European missionaries on the coasts grew. From about the 1840s Christian missionaries began to move into the interior. The spread of Christianity was aided by the influx of "recaptive" slaves from Sierra Leone, who had converted to Christianity and returned to their communities of origin to spread the gospel, as well as to preach the virtues of anti-slavery. Approximately 10 percent of the population practices indigenous religions, which are most commonly based in conceptions of ancestor worship and reverence for both natural and supernatural phenomena.

The majority of Nigeria's population is rural, although urbanization is occurring at a rapid pace. The United Nations has estimated that, whereas in 1950 over 88 percent of Nigeria's population was rural, by 2005 only 51.7 percent lived in rural areas. Many of Nigeria's cities are becoming large and overcrowded. The two largest cities in the country are Lagos in the southwest, with a population estimated at over 9.2 million, and Kano in the north, with a population estimated at over 3.8 million.[5] Lagos is the largest cty in west Africa, and based on current growth rates it will soon be among the most populous cities in the world. Other major urban centers in Nigeria include Ibadan, Benin City, Onitsha, Ilorin, Port Harcourt, Enugu, Abuja, Jos, Kaduna, Yola, Sokoto, and Maiduguri. Agriculture remains the way of life in rural areas, where communities remain largely homogeneous, while, in urban areas, lifestyles and economic activities are more heterogeneous. Cities are places where people from many different ethnic, religious, and socio-economic backgrounds interact on a regular basis. In this way, mutual understanding and respect between people can be fostered; at the same time, however, cities tend to be places where ethnic, religious, and class tensions often erupt. One of the main factors leading to the rapid growth of Nigerian cities is the migration of young people from rural areas to urban areas for education or employment opportunities, or simply for a taste of a more cosmopolitan atmosphere.

The population of Nigeria is overwhelmingly young. As of 2005, it was estimated that 64.7 million of Nigeria's population were under the age of twenty-four, while only 2.9 percent were over the age of sixty-five. The average life expectancy in Nigeria was forty-six years, as poverty,

malnutrition, and the lack of basic health care facilities and services keep
life expectancies low. Nevertheless, the average population growth rate
stands at around 2.5 percent, which means that the ratio of young to
middle-aged and older persons continues to rise.[6]

Culturally, Nigerians are influenced both by their indigenous traditions
and by newer values and lifestyles that have been incorporated from
the West. Traditional reliance on extended family and kinship networks
remains strong throughout Nigeria, but a growing focus on smaller,
nuclear families and on individual achievement is recognizable, particularly
in urban areas. While polygamy is still a common practice in the country,
monogamous marriage is also common, particularly among Christians and
the educated elite. Traditional forms of entertainment, such as indigenous
musical styles such as juju and palm-wine music, the telling of stories or
"moonlight tales," and theatrical performances, coexist with radio, television, video cassettes, movies, computers, and other high-tech forms of
entertainment, again in urban areas in particular. Modern media forms
such as television and Nigeria's home-grown movie industry, known as
Nollywood, function in multiple cultural milieus. Some television programs and movies are based on traditional stories of long-standing local
significance, while others mimic the plots found in Western movies and
television programs, blending them with Nigerian surroundings and
situations; this illustrates the extent to which Nigerians identify both with
their traditional pasts and with the modern, global age in which they live.
The wildly popular Afrobeat music of Fela Kuti and other musicians,
which melds traditional forms of music with American jazz and funk, and
the growing popularity of hip-hop as a musical style also serve as indications of Nigerians' capacity to combine local, indigenous cultural aspects
with newer, Western influences. Incorporating Western ideas and styles
while retaining a strong foundation in indigenous traditions has been more
successful in the cultural realm than it has been in politics, however.

POLITICS AND GOVERNMENT

The borders of the modern state of Nigeria were established in 1914 when
the British colonial government amalgamated the northern and southern
protectorates of Nigeria to form a unified colonial state. The northern
and southern protectorates themselves had been the creations of British
colonial administrators, but prior to British colonial rule the diverse
societies of the Nigerian region had ruled themselves as independent
states. Many large, centralized states, such as Kanem-Borno, Benin, Oyo,

and the Sokoto Caliphate, had risen and fallen over the centuries, and many of these states had been quite strong regional powers for extended periods. Other states were smaller, and governed by decentralized political structures of local councils, chiefs, and other kinds of elites, but not by a single, central administration.

As British forces brought Nigeria under colonial rule in the late nineteenth and early twentieth centuries, they went about adapting local political institutions to meet the needs of the British themselves. Dubbed "indirect rule," the British system of governing through indigenous political institutions allowed local chiefs and elites to maintain their local authority while submitting themselves to the authority of a central apparatus of British colonial administrators. Colonial rule altered the political landscape of the region in several important ways. First, it brought together what had previously been hundreds of autonomous, independent groups of people under the single administrative umbrella of an amalgamated Nigeria. Second, the process of "indirect rule" resulted in changes in the powers of traditional political leaders. The British often misunderstood the traditional political institutions through which they governed, and often had difficulty identifying the legitimate traditional authorities. Also, the British sometimes extended powers to local rulers that they had never previously held, and in all cases they took away the sovereignty that local rulers had enjoyed previously. If an "indirect ruler" displeased the British, he would not be the local authority for long, regardless of the "traditional" basis of his authority.

Finally, the bureaucracy and economics of colonial rule dictated that a small class of English-speaking, European-educated Nigerians were needed to hold lower-level positions in the government and in European businesses. These European-educated elites enjoyed a higher standard of living than most Nigerians, but they also found that their ability to rise to the level of their capabilities was obstructed by the racist ideology of colonial rule, which viewed Africans as culturally and intellectually inferior to Europeans. It was these European-educated elites that began to organize to pressure the colonial government for greater representation for Nigerians in their own governance and for an eventual end to colonial rule in Nigeria. Leaders such as Nnamdi Azikiwe, Obafemi Awolowo, and Sir Abubakar Tafawa Balewa emerged to lead large-scale nationalist movements, which ultimately became full-fledged political parties that negotiated for independence from British rule in the years after the Second World War.

Nigeria gained independence from the United Kingdom in 1960. The nationalist leadership that won independence opted to retain Nigeria's colonial borders and to govern the country as a federated republic. Originally, the independent state of Nigeria was divided into three regions, with the Federal Capital Territory at Lagos. In 1991 the federal capital was moved from Lagos to Abuja, located in a new FCT in the center of the country. The government bureaucracy has three tiers – federal, state, and local – with each tier guaranteed certain responsibilities by the Nigerian constitution. The creation of new states has been a common theme in Nigerian politics. Nigeria was split into twelve states in 1967; this increased to nineteen in 1976, twenty-one in 1987, and thirty in 1991. Since 1996 Nigeria has been divided into thirty-six states, but clamor continues from ethnic minorities for the creation of still more.

Currently Nigeria is in its Fourth Republic, and is experiencing its longest uninterrupted period of civilian rule ever. For most of the period since independence in 1960, however, the Nigerian polity has been wracked with instability. Regional, ethnic, and religious identities have become heavily politicized. Christians from the south fear domination by the slightly more populous northern Muslims at the federal level. At the state level, ethnic minorities fear domination by larger ethnic groups: the Hausa–Fulani in the north, the Yoruba in the southwest, and the Igbo in the southeast. These ethnic and religious tensions have resulted in one civil war in Nigeria, from 1967 to 1970, as well as countless episodes of both organized attacks and spontaneous riots in which ethnic and religious minorities have been targeted. Religious and ethnic violence continues to be a regular occurrence today and shows no signs of abating.

The government has done little to mitigate the social tensions in the country; in fact, control of the government has often been at the root of ethnic and religious tensions. Control of the federal and state governments translates into access to government funds, which politicians have used corruptly to extend their own power and gain support in their own local communities. By stealing government funds for personal use and by distributing money and government contracts to cronies and allies, politicians can claim to be "taking care of their own," while at the same time growing excessively wealthy and powerful themselves. Under such a system, only those who have power or influence in the government have access to government funds, and, as such, it has become imperative for civilian politicians to maintain their positions of political power at all costs, because to lose office means being cut out of the system of patronage. As a result, elections in Nigeria have typically been characterized by high levels of violence and intimidation, as well as by manipulation of the election process and outright vote rigging, as incumbent politicians have typically preferred to guarantee their election through undemocratic means rather than allow free and fair elections, or, worse still, allow their opponents to steal elections.

The failure of civilian administrations to promote stability and rule responsibly has opened the door for the military to take a strong role in the governance of the country. In fact, Nigeria has been governed by military regimes for twenty-eight of its first forty-seven years of political independence. Military coups have been a common occurrence in Nigeria. There have been two military interventions that have brought an end to civilian regimes, and three that have replaced one military regime with another, as well as many failed coup attempts. Military regimes in Nigeria have always taken over claiming that their intent is to restore stability, end corruption, and prepare the country for a transition back to civilian rule. Military regimes themselves have proven just as irresponsible as civilian administrations, however. Military regimes are accountable only to themselves and, accordingly, are just as out of touch as, if not more so than, civilian politicians with the issues that affect the everyday lives of average Nigerians. Military regimes have been very autocratic and authoritarian, and have been more than willing to use violence to silence criticism. Military regimes have been every bit as corrupt as civilian regimes as well. Military rulers have spent lavishly on ostentatious public works projects, have stolen public funds, and have provided lax oversight of public expenditures. For much of Nigeria's post-independence history, the massive inflow of oil revenues and external loans has facilitated the corrupt and irresponsible management of public funds that has characterized both civilian and military governments.

ECONOMY AND INFRASTRUCTURE

Nigerian communities have had long-standing inter- and intranational commercial networks dating back to well before the creation of the country in 1914. The river systems served as major avenues of trade throughout the region, but beyond this there were many major roads connecting villages, towns, and regions dating back many centuries. In the northern savannas, people traded goods across the Sahara desert to north Africa, Europe, and the Middle East. The trans-Saharan trade trickled to a halt in the twentieth century with the advent of British colonial rule. The savannas were also commercially connected to the states of the forest zone, which themselves traded with the coastal states. Nigerian communities also traded east and west throughout west Africa, as well as with each other, in ways that led to historical linkages between distinct, independent states in the region that long pre-dated colonial rule. Important items of trade in the pre-colonial period included food items, salt, leather goods, weapons, horses, and textiles, all of which could be traded by barter as well as for beads, iron and copper rods, and cowry shells, which were commonly used currencies. Slaves were also an important item of trade dating back many centuries in the savanna regions of the north. After the arrival of Europeans on the coast in the fifteenth century CE, slaves became a major item of trade in the south as well. Between the sixteenth and nineteenth centuries CE, the trade in slaves with Europeans was the single most important economic activity of many states in the area in and around what is now southern Nigeria.

With the British abolition of the slave trade in 1807 came economic transformations, particularly in southern Nigeria. The slave trade continued to exist until about the 1850s; alongside the slave trade, however, there was the growth of "legitimate" commerce, or trade in non-human commodities. The most important item of "legitimate" commerce quickly became palm oil, which had long been an item of internal trade in southern Nigeria and which had been experiencing a growth in export sales since the late eighteenth century. As the British took direct political control over the territories of southern and northern Nigeria in the late nineteenth and early twentieth centuries, trade in "legitimate" commodities became the basis of the colonial economy. The colonial economy was extractive in nature, designed to mine and harvest the raw materials of Nigeria and export them in ways that profited the colonial government and European businesses. Alongside palm oil, which came mainly from the southeast, cocoa cultivation expanded in the southwest, and groundnut and cotton cultivation boomed in the north. Mineral extraction, particularly of tin, also expanded under the colonial economy, and local coal deposits were mined primarily to provide a fuel source for the railways that the colonial government built to link the sources of production with the coasts, from which raw materials were exported.

Building an infrastructure to serve the purposes of the extractive economy was an important goal of colonial rule in Nigeria. The colonial government dredged harbors, expanded riverways, and built thousands of miles of railways and roads to allow products to move more quickly and freely to the coast for export. Over time, air travel became an increasingly important method of travel as well. As of 2006 Nigeria boasted sixty-nine airports, 120,791 miles of highway, of which 37,324 miles are paved, and 2,178 miles of railways.[7] Much of the infrastructural development during the colonial period was accomplished through the exploitation of forced labor. In the years after the Second World War the colonial regime embarked upon several development planning schemes designed to enhance the industrial and manufacturing sectors of the Nigerian economy ahead of independence. These schemes, which have been extended and repackaged in the post-independence period, have for the most part failed, however, and the country's economy has remained largely dependent on the export of raw materials. Since the 1970s the vast majority of Nigerian export revenues have come from a single source: petroleum.

Since independence in 1960 the Nigerian economy has seen several peaks and troughs, largely because of its dependence on oil revenues. Petroleum production began in the late 1950s, but it was not until the "oil boom" of the 1970s that oil revenues skyrocketed. As of 2006 Nigeria was the leading oil exporter in Africa and the eighth biggest in the world by volume. The growth of the oil economy has been both a blessing and a curse for Nigeria. Oil has brought massive revenues, making Nigeria a very wealthy country in terms of increasing overall revenues and giving the country a strong potential for equitable economic growth and sustainable development over the long term. Unfortunately, this potential has gone unrealized to date. Oil revenues have been horribly mismanaged, with the result that only a very few people have benefited from Nigeria's oil wealth. The vast majority of the population continues to live in poverty, seeing few tangible results from the country's oil wealth. In the 1970s oil wealth was used to fund grand public works projects illustrating the glory and power of the military government. Corruption has also been rampant, as politicians and government officials have used Nigeria's oil wealth to line their own pockets. The fact that oil revenues accrue mainly from foreign-owned multinational corporations has led to the establishment of a "rentier state" in Nigeria – a state in which the government is dependent solely upon "rents" paid to it by non-Nigerian clients. Due to this, the Nigerian government has had little incentive to rule in the best interests of its citizens, since its power and money derive not from the population but from foreign oil companies that pay the government for the privilege of drilling on Nigerian territory.

Mismanagement of public funds and fluctuations in the price of oil have joined with political instability since the 1970s to make the Nigerian economy very unsteady. High prices have put basic goods and services out of the reach of most Nigerians, the majority of whom live below the international poverty line of $1 a day. Public utilities such as electricity and running water are erratic and unevenly distributed. Health-care and education facilities have fallen into disrepair; basic medicines, health-care equipment, and educational tools such as books, desks, chalkboards, and so on are scarce and in poor condition. Roads and vehicles are mostly run-down, making travel hazardous and expensive for most people. In many areas it is unadvisable to travel at night. Public servants regularly go unpaid, and the poverty that grips the population has resulted in high crime rates, as people smuggle, steal, and scam to make enough money to survive. Since the country returned to civilian rule in 1999, some small economic improvements have been made. Nigeria has paid off almost all its external debt, and a few new industries, such as those involving mobile phones and locally produced films, are growing rapidly. For most Nigerians, however, everyday life remains a struggle for survival; even basic needs are difficult to meet.

SUMMARY OF THE BOOK

Politics, economics, and culture are not isolated aspects of societies: they influence each other and blend in ways that are sometimes indiscernible. Nigeria is no exception. For example, the jihad of Usman dan Fodio was both politically and culturally motivated and had both political and cultural consequences. The oil boom that transformed the economy in the 1970s has had a profound impact on politics and lifestyles in Nigeria. In order to address the complex interweaving of major themes in Nigeria's history, the chapters in this book are presented chronologically. Each chapter analyzes the issues that most affected people's lives at a given time.

The first three chapters are concerned with the pre-colonial history of Nigeria. Chapter 1 discusses the formation of human societies and the creation of states in the Nigerian area in the period before 1500 CE. Chapter 2 focuses on developments in the period between 1500 and 1800, with emphasis on the consolidation of and rivalries between the Hausa states and Kanem-Borno in the northern savannas and on the effects on southern societies of the growing trade with Europeans on the coast, particularly the slave trade. Chapter 3 examines the transformations in the political and cultural landscape in the north in the first half of the nineteenth century with the creation and establishment of the Sokoto Caliphate, and looks at the effects of the economic transition from the slave trade to "legitimate" commerce on political and social institutions in the south.

The next three chapters cover the period during which Nigeria came under British colonial rule. The focus of chapter 4 is on the long, slow process by which the British took direct political control of the territories that were soon to make up the administrative unit called Nigeria. The conquest of the entire region took over fifty years, and was accomplished through various means, most commonly by treaties of protection in which local authorities ceded partial or full sovereignty to the United Kingdom. Local rulers and communities often resisted the British takeover, but were eventually "pacified" by violent means. Having established political dominance in Nigeria, the British undertook to establish a colonial administration and economy favorable to themselves. These processes are the focus of chapter 5, which discusses the development of "indirect rule" as the primary model of colonial administration and the establishment of a colonial economy based on the expansion of cash crops geared towards an export market. Many indigenous subjects resisted British efforts to change long-standing political, economic, and social institutions, but, prior to the 1930s, protests were mostly on a local level. A class of European-educated, English-speaking, middle-class Nigerians grew in number throughout the first decades of the twentieth century, however, and by the 1930s they had undertaken to establish a pan-Nigerian national consciousness and to demand the end of British colonial rule and the handing over of political control to an indigenous leadership. Chapter 6 discusses the rise of nationalist movements in Nigeria between the 1930s and 1960, when Nigeria became an independent country under the national leadership of European-educated elites.

Chapters 7 through 9 are focused on the trials and tribulations of Nigeria since independence in 1960. Chapter 7 focuses on the decade of the 1960s, a time when hopes and expectations were high. By the mid-1960s it had become clear, however, that the political class that dominated the First Republic was showing signs of corruption and undemocratic tendencies. The specter of "domination" hung in the air, as ethnic/religious groups throughout the country feared that any region that obtained control of the government would use that control to better itself at the expense of the rest of the country. These fears resulted in rigged elections in 1964 and 1965, which led to widespread communal violence and ultimately, in 1966, to the first of Nigeria's many military coups. Efforts to reduce the tensions were unsuccessful, and, in 1967, the Igbo-dominated Eastern Region seceded, declaring independence as the sovereign state of Biafra. The secession touched off a civil war, lasting from 1967 to 1970, in which the Federal Military Government ultimately succeeded in reincorporating Biafra into Nigeria.

After the civil war the military remained in power, governing throughout the 1970s. At the same time, Nigeria experienced its "oil boom." Chapter 8 discusses the failure of the military regimes of the 1970s and of the civilian regime of the Second Republic, which ruled from 1979 to 1983, to manage Nigeria's vast oil wealth. It was during this time that Nigeria became a "rentier state," dependent almost entirely on foreign companies for the funding of state initiatives. As a result, the government was not responsible to its citizens, and became increasingly corrupt and inefficient. The problems of corruption and unaccountability in government have plagued Nigeria ever since. Chapter 9 covers the period between 1983 and 2007, much of which was characterized by authoritarian military rule and stark economic decline. At the same time that military regimes became more authoritarian, however, average Nigerians became less willing to tolerate regimes that failed to govern in the best interests of their citizens. Civil society organizations proliferated during this period, both to provide an alternative source of service and support parallel to the ailing government and to pressure the government for meaningful change. Outpourings of anguish and criticism have been both peaceful and violent. Religious clashes have taken the lives of thousands in recent decades, while violence in the Niger delta, where ethnic minorities fight for greater control of their own environment and resources, has been on the rise since the 1990s. The struggles of civil society organizations were long and hard, but finally, in 1999, political power was transferred back to a democratically elected civilian adminis-tration, known as the Fourth Republic. The Fourth Republic has gone a long way towards improving Nigeria's tarnished international image, although it has yet to realize substantial improvements in the day-to-day lives of most Nigerians or to bring truly democratic institutions to the country.

Chapter 10 switches gears to discuss the effect that Nigeria and Nigerians have had on world history. The first half of the chapter focuses on Nigerians who have migrated out of the Nigerian area over time to make new homes in other parts of the world. In doing so, Nigerians have influenced the histories of virtually every part of the world: from the Americas, where large numbers of slaves from the Nigerian region mingled their traditions with those of other groups to create unique new cultures; to the Middle East and Sudan, where Nigerian pilgrims to Mecca have established permanent communities; and across Africa itself, as Nigerians have developed strong social, commercial, and cultural ties with other peoples over the generations. The second half of the chapter focuses on the impact of Nigeria's foreign policy on regional, continental, and global affairs since 1960. The goals of Nigerian foreign policy during this period have been noble, based mainly on promoting anti-colonialism and supporting liberation movements throughout Africa, as well as on improving regional economic integration and security within west Africa in particular. Although the goals have been idealistic, the overall influence and effectiveness of Nigerian foreign policy are often debatable, as the country's most visible role in international affairs came only during the oil boom years of the 1970s. Since then, the political instability and economic decline of Nigeria have left it largely marginalized in international affairs (with the exception of ECOMOG operations in Liberia and Sierra Leone) and, at times, shunned as a pariah state in the international community.

The book concludes with a short analysis of the 2007 elections, marking the first time in Nigeria's history that one civilian regime handed over power to another. Despite the superficial triumph of this accomplishment, there is no reason to see the transfer of power as a turning point in Nigeria's fortunes. The elections themselves were marred by controversy, and many of the problems that have negatively affected Nigerians in previous decades remain unresolved. Religion and ethnicity are still strong dividing lines between people; the average Nigerian is still mired in extreme poverty despite the country's immense oil wealth; and the political class is still more concerned with solidifying its own power than with governing democratically in the best interests of the majority of the population. Until issues such as these are addressed and resolved, Nigeria will remain a land of unrealized potential.

CHAPTER I

Early states and societies, 9000 BCE – 1500 CE

INTRODUCTION

This chapter discusses the early history of human habitation and the development of states in the territories of modern-day Nigeria, from the period of the earliest archeological findings in the Late Stone Age (LSA) to the coming of European traders in the late fifteenth and sixteenth centuries CE (Common Era). Archeological evidence indicates that human societies have been constantly present in all regions of Nigeria for several thousand years. Initially, their societies were decentralized in nature, focusing on small village or village-group units. Some societies, particularly in the eastern and middle belt regions of modern-day Nigeria, maintained these decentralized state structures until the advent of European colonialism. By the end of the first millennium CE, however, some societies were developing more centralized state structures, based on ideas of kingship and drawing greater resources to urban centers of political, economic, and cultural importance. In the southern, forested region, the largest of these centralized states were the kingdoms centered on Ile-Ife and Benin. In the Sahel region in the north, the empires of Kanem and Borno became increasingly powerful from the eleventh century CE, with Hausa states such as Kano, Katsina, Zaria, and Gobir beginning their ascendancy by the fifteenth century.

Both the centralized and the decentralized states had their roots in the agricultural economies of indigenous African communities, although the goods and ideas brought into these societies by immigrants often made significant marks on the politics, economies, and cultures of these states and societies. The spread of Islam in the savanna during the second millennium CE contributed greatly to the growth of centralized states. Islam provided a political cult for Kanuri, Bornoan, and Hausa leaders as well as linking their states to the wealth of the greater Islamic world through commercial and scholarly relationships. The growth of the trans-Saharan trade during this period also affected societies in the forest zone, which traded their local goods, such as salt, timber, and kola nuts, for livestock and foreign items made available through the trans-Saharan trade. Through trade and other forms of interaction, by 1500 CE societies in the areas in and around modern-day Nigeria had developed sophisticated political, economic, and/or cultural relationships with their neighbors, making the region a relatively integrated economic unit.

DEFINING PERIOD AND PLACE

General histories of Nigeria tend to refer to the period before the European colonization of west Africa in the late nineteenth and early twentieth centuries as "pre-colonial." To speak of pre-colonial Nigeria is anachronistic, however. Over the course of human history, many different groups of people have migrated into and out of the region that is now known as Nigeria. Many societies and states, and even vast empires, have risen and fallen, none of them having had any direct correlation to the Nigerian state that exists today. The boundaries of present-day Nigeria were created by the British colonial administration in the late nineteenth and early twentieth centuries. While political boundaries often coincide with physical boundaries, such as bodies of water or mountain ranges, or are established by mutual agreement between societies over generations, the boundaries adopted to create the modern state of Nigeria never had any geophysical or social significance to the indigenous peoples of the region. The only geophysical boundary of Nigeria is the Atlantic Ocean, which forms the southernmost border of the country. Nigeria's western, northern, and eastern borders are all relatively arbitrary, having been negotiated at drafting tables in Europe rather than through local processes of societal development. The country of Nigeria is thus a conglomeration of hundreds of ethnic groups, many of which straddle these arbitrary borders, which date only from the twentieth century. Therefore, to speak of the timeframe before the establishment of these boundaries as "pre-colonial Nigeria" suggests that the period is significant partly insofar as it relates to the eventual construction of modern Nigeria.

The history of social interaction in this region, however, is certainly not meaningless or non-existent before the consolidation of the modern state of Nigeria. The Nigerian people of today have many different indigenous languages, historical memories, traditional lifestyles, and social frameworks with roots reaching into the distant past. These roots must be recognized for their significant contributions to the development of human society throughout west Africa and for the historical legacies that they have left to subsequent generations. The first part of this volume is therefore devoted to the analysis of what we will call "early" societies in the territories within and straddling the boundaries of modern-day Nigeria. The geographical area under scrutiny conforms as closely as possible to the boundaries later delineated as modern Nigeria, including the surrounding areas where germane, but by no means is this meant to suggest that the present-day boundaries had any significance to the societies of the time.

ARCHEOLOGY AND EARLY SOCIETIES

The Late Stone Age, between roughly 10,000 BCE and 2000 BCE,[1] was a period of major firsts for human development in the territories in and around modern-day Nigeria. The first known human remains in this region were found in the Iwo Eleru rock shelter in what is now southwestern Nigeria, and have been dated to around 9000 BCE. While humans must have lived in the area well before this period, the LSA is unique historically for several different reasons. First, it has been widely postulated that this period was characterized by unprecedented levels of migration in the greater Nigerian area, particularly as people moved south from the savanna into the forest zones to escape the rapid desiccation of the Sahara. Second, it was during the LSA that humans in the greater Nigerian area began using stone tools, called microliths, such as arrowheads, stone axes, and so forth. The introduction of stone tools in the early LSA led to the development of pottery by about 3000 BCE in most areas and, ultimately, to the development of agriculture between 4000 and 1000 BCE, depending on the specific area in question. Finally, the development of agriculture allowed for the establishment of more permanent settlements – that is, villages and village groups – than had previously been possible. Agriculture meant a move away from hunting and gathering activities, and the centralization of food resources allowed people to congregate in larger numbers on a permanent basis.

Evidence of this process of social formation in the greater Nigerian area has been uncovered in several major archaeological sites dating from the LSA period. These sites cover the various ecological regions of modern-day Nigeria, from Apa I, Iwo Eleru, Ifetedo, and Ita-Ogbolu in the southern forested region to Itaakpa in the middle belt region, Mejiro cave, Afikpo, and Rop in the savanna zone, and Daima and other sites in the Chad Basin area of the Sahel.[2] Iwo Eleru, in the southwestern corner of the greater Nigerian area, shows distinct evidence of two phases of development: the aceramic phase, illustrated by stone tools, which lasted from roughly 10,000 to 5000 BCE; and the ceramic phase, which is characterized by stone axes and pottery, illustrating a move towards agricultural activity in the period between 5000 and 1500 BCE.

Afikpo, in the southeastern part of the greater Nigerian area, has three delineated phases of development. The first phase, dating to before 3000 BCE, has yielded a few microlithic tools, while the second phase exhibits evidence of flaked axes and some stone pottery dating from between 3000 and 500 BCE. The final phase, commencing in roughly 100 BCE, has been characterized by different types of ceramics from those of the second phase. The change to different kinds of stone tools, such as axes and adzes, between the first and second phases has been used as evidence of a switch to agricultural activity, and the discovery of pottery, used for its storage capacity, seems to confirm this theory.[3]

In the Lake Chad region of the Sahel, located in the northeastern corner of the greater Nigerian area, archeological evidence from Daima and Kursakata has shown the presence of domesticated animals, particularly sheep, goats, and cattle, from the second millennium BCE. Archeologists believe that animal husbandry probably reached this region across the Sahara from the east and north between 3000 and 2000 BCE.[4] Remains of horses, which were also brought from north Africa, have been found in archeological sites in the savanna and Sahel dating to roughly the first century BCE. Agricultural activity in the Sahel and savanna region probably began sometime in the second millennium BCE, and involved mainly cereal crops such as African rice and millet, while agriculturalists in the forest and middle belt regions relied most heavily on yam tubers and oil palm products.

The development of permanent settlements based on agricultural production allowed for the diversification of economies and the creation of more sophisticated socio-political configurations. One major example of economic diversification can be seen in the growth of iron-working in many parts of the greater Nigerian area during the first millennium BCE. Unlike those in Europe or the Near East, most west African societies transited directly from the use of stone tools to iron tools without an intervening period of using softer metals, such as copper or bronze. Evidence of iron-working and iron tools at archeological sites dates from roughly the seventh century BCE at Taruga, near Abuja, in the middle belt region. The Taruga site is also known as the center of the Nok culture, most famous in archeological circles for the large terracotta sculptures found within a 500 km radius of Taruga. At Taruga, there is evidence not only of the use of iron technology, which could have been brought from other regions through trade or migration, but also of iron smelting, which indicates a local knowledge of iron production. Other sites of archeological importance in the middle belt region include Tadun Wada, Kuchamfa, Jemaa Maitumbi, Kawu, and Kagara, all of which were smelting iron between 900 BCE and 200 CE, the recognized dates for the duration of the Nok culture.[5]

Iron-smelting activities also occurred in other regions of the greater Nigerian area. At Uffe Ijumu, in the southwest, evidence of iron smelting dates back to 160 CE,[6] while at Opi, in the southeast, the earliest dates for iron smelting may be as early as the fifth century BCE.[7] Even where there is no direct evidence of iron smelting, iron tools have been found all across the greater Nigerian area. The Afkipo site, in the southeast part of the greater Nigerian area, has yielded dates between 50 BCE and 150 CE for iron tool use,[8] while the Daima mound in the Lake Chad region of the Sahel indicates iron tool use from between 500 and 600 CE.[9]

Evidence of iron-smelting activities indicates that changes were occurring in the political economies of agricultural communities. Iron smelting is time-consuming and requires skilled labor. Professional blacksmiths were certainly responsible for the development of iron tools in the places mentioned above. This means that agricultural pursuits had become successful enough and societies had become integrated enough that full-time craftsmen could make a living at iron-working and were able to barter their skills and products for the foodstuffs that others produced. This evidence of localized economic activity based on trade is enhanced by the finding of iron tools in places where there is no direct evidence of iron smelting. The finished products of iron smelters in one region were clearly spreading to other regions, through either migration or trade, indicating the extent to which distinct communities across long distances had contact with each other during this period.

Other metals became important in the greater Nigerian area after the development of iron-working. Manipulated copper, brass, and tin became important ceremonial and luxury items during the late first millennium CE. Elaborate copper and bronze artifacts from the Igbo-Ukwu archeological site in the southeast date from the ninth century CE, while bronze and brass sculptures from Ife in the southwest date from the eleventh century CE. Items from these sites include busts of elite figures, crowns, and other regalia, as well as anklets, bracelets, necklaces, and so on.[10] Tin deposits are plentiful in the middle belt region, particularly in the Jos Plateau area; like copper, bronze, and brass, tin was used mainly for decorative purposes.

Blacksmiths and other metalworkers became very important members of early societies in the greater Nigerian area. They formed guilds to protect the quality of their products and the knowledge used to create them. Metalworkers became linked not only with the livelihoods of everyday citizens but also with the political hierarchy, making them indispensable members of communities. As David Aremu has put it,

Metal craftsmen usually enjoyed prestigious and high-status positions in their societies because of the importance of their crafts to the social and economic reproduction of the society. Skilled copper/brass/bronze workers were often associated with the monarchs and the elite that monopolized their products... [Blacksmiths] were seen as the nerve center of economic activities like hunting, farming, wood carving, palm wine tapping, medicine, fishing, cloth weaving... They were considered more important than the farmers, hunters, wood carvers, and medicine men because they manufactured some of the tools that those professions used.[11]

Thus, metalworking not only added a new dimension to the economies of agricultural societies but also made further differentiation of economies possible through the tools they produced.

ORIGIN OF STATES AND SOCIAL IDENTITIES

The move from hunting and gathering to permanent agricultural and livestock-rearing settlements during the Late Stone Age has also been seen as a starting point for the development of many of the language groups and social identities that make up present-day Nigeria. During the first millennium CE some of these societies developed loosely constructed decentralized state systems, while others developed into the first large-scale centralized states of the region by roughly 1100 CE.

The earliest states in the territories encompassing modern-day Nigeria were most certainly of a very small-scale, decentralized nature. Political structures in these societies were so fragmented that earlier generations of scholars referred to them as stateless societies. Such a characterization is misleading. True statelessness implies a lack of political authority and, therefore, the existence of anarchy, which none of these societies exhibited. A better characterization of these societies' political organization would be "decentralized," in that political hierarchy rarely reached higher than the village or village-group level, even though the overarching cultural identity could incorporate many different village groups. All

Nigerian societies must have originally functioned as decentralized states; many societies in the middle-belt region and the southeastern part of modern-day Nigeria maintained their decentralized state structures long after the development of strong, centralized states in other parts of the region, however. It is through the decentralized structures that have persisted that we can construct a broad picture of what decentralized states looked like and how they functioned in the past.

A good example of a decentralized state system is that of the Igbo in the southeastern part of modern-day Nigeria. Igbo political institutions vary rather widely across space – some groups even adopted monarchical characteristics from neighboring centralized states – but most Igbo communities remained decentralized until the arrival of the British colonialists in the early twentieth century. Although it is difficult to isolate a "typical" Igbo political system because of the decentralized nature of Igbo communities and the consequent variety across space, most contain some of the following elements. Political power in Igbo society tended to be founded on an age-based hierarchy at the village level: that is, elders, defined as the heads of patrilineal lines, were responsible for the most important decisions of a community. Multiple villages were centered on a market, which also served as a forum for village-group meetings. At the village level, all members of the community could speak their mind about village affairs, while, at the village-group level, members of secret societies tended to represent the interests of their respective villages. Decisions at the village-group level were not binding, however, as any individual village could choose whether or not to follow the guidelines of village-group councils; they could not be forced into submission. Each village-group system functioned autonomously; nevertheless, all village groups were considered Igbo, based on a common language, similar religious beliefs, and various inter-group social institutions, such as intermarriage, membership in secret societies, and common oracle worship.[12] Similar institutions existed in other decentralized societies, such as those of the Isoko, Urhobo, and Ibibio in the southeast and the Tiv of the middle belt. Such structures probably formed the basis of state formation in all societies in the region at different times throughout the first millennium CE.

Centralized states in the territories of modern-day Nigeria developed out of these decentralized states from the eleventh century CE. The most significant centralized states that had emerged by 1500 CE were the kingdoms centered on Ile-Ife and Benin in the southwestern part of the region, Kanem-Borno in the Lake Chad region of the Sahel in the northeast, and the various Hausa states in the north-central savannas.

Figure 1.1 Women selling peppers (collection of Roy Doron)

The city of Ile-Ife (or simply Ife) sits in what is today Osun State in southwestern Nigeria. Ife is credited as the birthplace and ancestral home of the Yoruba people, today one of the largest ethnic groups in Nigeria. Several variations of the Yoruba origin myth exist, but all claim that Ife was founded by a man named Oduduwa, who either came from Mecca or descended from heaven at the behest of Obatala (God) depending on the version told. While Oduduwa presumably encountered indigenous peoples in the region around Ife, he is nevertheless seen as the progenitor of the modern-day Yoruba people, largely because of the credit he is given for the establishment of a centralized state at Ife. Oduduwa's descendants are said to have spread out from Ife to found lesser kingdoms in the surrounding areas, each kingdom recognizing Ife as its predecessor and main political and cultural influence. Although archeological evidence indicates that Ife has been a site of human settlement since at least the ninth century CE, it was not until around the twelfth century that Ife was clearly a regional power.

The political system of Ife was monarchical, headed by the *ooni*. Although lines of succession for the ooniship did exist, occasionally wealthy people within the community were able to succeed to the throne, indicating that the monarchy was not strictly hereditary. The centraliz- ation of power allowed for the growth of the city of Ife and allowed it to attain regional dominance between the twelfth and the fifteenth centuries. Ife became a major trading center and a site of great wealth. During this time, most of the roads in Ife were paved with potsherds in a fishbone pattern, a very tedious and labor-intensive task. Artisans and craftsmen flocked to Ile-Ife from the surrounding regions to ply their trades. Of particular archeological renown are the elaborate bronze sculptures that were excavated in the twentieth century.[13] These facets of the social and physical make-up of Ife point to the extreme wealth and power of the *ooni* as well as to the specialization of skills and breadth of economic activity in the community.

While Ife's centralized political structure and wealth accumulation are significant in that they represent the first known centralized state in the region, the city's most important function was as a political and cultural model for other Yoruba communities. Ile-Ife became the center of Yoruba identity, the political and cultural base from which Yoruba communities derived their religious sensibilities, political institutions, and cultural reference points. Most of Ife's mystique lay in its position as the land of Oduduwa, making it not simply a site of political importance but also one of spiritual importance, because of Oduduwa's close relationship to the spiritual realm. Indeed, while the *ooni* held direct political control over the events of Ile-Ife, his physical power at no point extended throughout the entire Yoruba region. Rather, the *ooni* served as a spiritual leader for other communities, a reference point for religious and ritual matters. Other Yoruba communities had their own *oba*s (kings) who ruled over local affairs, but all of them maintained their legitimacy through their divine connection to the *ooni* of Ife. Yoruba kings from the surrounding areas saw Ife as their spiritual motherland and were buried in a sacred grove there upon their deaths. Because of this spiritual connection, Ife did not have to cement its influence through military force. Ife never maintained a standing army. Even when the political and economic might of Ife was eclipsed by the Oyo empire from the sixteenth century,[14] Ife remained the spiritual center of the Yoruba, with the rulers of Oyo even continuing to offer tribute to Ife in recognition of the divine authority that the city and its leaders possessed.[15]

The kingdom of Benin, which grew up to the east of the Yoruba areas and west of the river Niger, was the primary power in the region known today as Edoland, which encompasses much of the Edo and Delta States of contemporary Nigeria. While the Edo are a group distinct from the Yoruba, the two ethnicities are closely related historically. In fact, the political system of the Benin kingdom had much in common with the divine monarchy of Ife, as the dynastic line that ruled Benin from the fourteenth century came from Ife. The Benin kingdom probably first emerged in the tenth century CE, and was ruled by a monarchical dynasty known as the *ogiso* until around 1300, when years of misrule culminated in the overthrow of the dynasty and its replacement with a republican government. The republican government was short-lived, and the people soon looked to Ife to send them a king. The *ooni* of Ife sent his son, Oranmiyan, who upon arriving at Benin decided that only a native of the area should rule there. He thus had a son by an indigenous woman. The son, Eweka by name, became the first *oba* in the second Benin dynasty – the dynasty that continues to exist to the present day, although much reduced in stature.

Like the *ooni* of Ife, the *oba* of Benin derived his authority from a divine link to God. The *oba* of Benin also had a set of advisers, however, known as the *uzama*, made up of the hereditary heads of local clans. From about 1440, with the rise of Oba Ewuare, several important changes to the political system were established. Ewuare mystified the office of the *oba* by developing an annual festival, called the Igue, which celebrated the *oba*'s relationship with the supernatural. He also reorganized the kingdom to draw a greater distinction between the town and the *oba*'s palace. This was done physically, by building a wall around the palace, as well as administratively, through the creation of separate institutions to govern the affairs of the town and the palace. The town administration, known as the *eghaevbo n'ore*, was made up of local chiefs, while the palace administration, the *eghaevbo n'ogboe*, was a meritocracy, positions within which were open to any persons in the community provided they had superlative skills. This political reorganization greatly strengthened the authority of the *oba*.[16]

Also contributing to the authority of the *oba* was the territorial expansion that Benin undertook during and after the reign of Ewuare. Ewuare was the first of the warrior kings of Benin, and under his rule Benin grew from a small kingdom with a 15 km radius to an expanding empire that had overrun several Yoruba communities in the west and some of the western Igbo communities to the east. Several *oba*s continued the process of expansion after Ewuare, building Benin into a major imperial center.

Economically, imperial expansion was beneficial to Benin. Dependent communities paid tribute to the *oba*, who used the funds to improve the city and trade with other societies. The *oba* also charged tolls to enter the city for trading purposes and to pass along Benin waterways. Benin City, like Ife, became a major center for economic activity, including that of artisans and craftsmen (Benin is particularly famous for its bronze sculptures), cloth makers, and carpenters, to name but a few. These urban professionals were organized into guilds, like the ancient blacksmiths before them. In the outlying areas, people remained largely agricultural, but their relationship with Benin provided access to markets, while at the same time providing Benin with access to the resources that made the city wealthy. Imperial wars of expansion also allowed Benin to capture large numbers of slaves, who became the main resource fueling trade with Europeans after the sixteenth century, further expanding the wealth and power of Benin.

While Ife and Benin represented the largest centralized states in the forest zone in the period before 1500, in the Sahel zone of the Lake Chad region the empires of Kanem and, later, Borno (also called Kanem-Borno) were the dominant centralized state structures. The Kanem origin myth claims that the original Kanuri inhabitants were descended from the intermarriage of migrants from the Sahara with the indigenous agricultural communities of the Lake Chad region. The migrants, known as the Zaghawa, supposedly united the peoples of the Lake Chad region under the emerging Kanem state sometime in the eighth century CE. Surrounding groups, particularly some of the Jukun states to the south of Lake Chad, claimed their original descent from the same set of migrants.[7]

The city of Kanem, which was located to the northeast of Lake Chad, developed great wealth as a result of its agricultural pursuits and its location on one of the main routes of the trans-Saharan trade that linked the forest and savanna zones to markets in north Africa. Kanem's political system was based around the office of the *mai*, a hereditary monarchical ruler from the Saifawa dynasty, with a centralized bureaucracy of titled officers charged with carrying out the *mai*'s orders. Kanem also developed a large standing army, which it used to enforce its rule over surrounding areas. By the thirteenth century CE Kanem had become a full-scale empire, having incorporated the lands to the south and southeast of Lake Chad, as well as areas to the north, particularly in the Fezzan. Kanem maintained its imperial holdings through military force, demanding taxes and tributes from subject populations.

From the thirteenth century onwards the empire of Kanem began to crumble, however. Internal wrangling within the ruling dynastic family destabilized the political situation in the city, while growing dissent in the subject territories threatened the monarchy from without. One dissident group, the Bulala, organized against Kanem so successfully that the Saifawa rulers abandoned the city, moving to the western side of Lake

Chad. Political intrigues and battles with indigenous populations continued to plague the Saifawa; with the rise of Mai Ali Gaja around 1470, however, the new state of Borno became stabilized and began to expand. Ali Gaja established a new capital at Gazargamu, strategically located on the river Yobe, between the mineral-rich areas to the west and the agricultural lands to the east. Gazargamu, like the city of Kanem, was located on a trans-Saharan trade route, allowing for the accumulation of wealth through trade. This period marks the transition from the First Kanuri Empire to the Second Kanuri Empire, or, as it is more commonly known, the state of Borno. The successors of Ali Gaja strengthened Borno by developing relationships with other major states in the western Sudan region, as well as the central Sahara and north Africa. By the late sixteenth century Mai Idris Aloma had managed to reconquer the areas taken by the Bulala, thereby reincorporating the old Kanem empire into the new empire of Kanem-Borno.

To the south of Borno were the Jukun states. The Jukun developed several strong, centralized states and many weaker states in the region bounded to the north by Borno and to the south by the Cross River, and stretching as far west as the Jos Plateau. Jukun origin myths state that the Jukun were closely related to the Kanuri, claiming that both groups were descended from migrants from near Mecca who split up somewhere in the Sahara, with one group founding Kanem and the other moving south to create the Jukun states.

The largest of the Jukun states was Kororofa, founded sometime before the fourteenth century. Kororofa's capital was at Beipi, and it was from here that the king ruled his territories, maintaining tight central control. All administrators of Kororofa's various regions were required to reside in the capital so that the king could monitor their activities. Through its military might, Kororofa managed to bring many of the other Jukun states under its thumb in the fifteenth and sixteenth centuries, and took advantage of local resources such as fertile agricultural land, livestock, wild animals, and salt and iron ore deposits to become wealthy as a result of trade with surrounding societies and tribute from subject communities.

The Jukun states are most commonly noted in historical documents from the Hausa states for their frequent conflicts with the expanding Hausa states of Kano, Katsina, and Zaria (Zazzaa). By the end of the seventeenth century Kororofa had fallen prey to internal political pressures and droughts, which undermined the economic system, causing further political instability and eventual collapse. Other Jukun states rose to take over the position of Kororofa, but none became quite as powerful as Kororofa had been.

The Hausa states emerged later than most of the other centralized states. The Hausa states owed their rise in the fifteenth and sixteenth centuries partially to the instability created by the collapse of the First Kanuri Empire to the east and the fall of the western Sudanic kingdoms of Mali (in the fifteenth century) and Songhay (in the sixteenth century). Although the Hausa states took advantage of the shift of important trans-Saharan trade routes from Mali and Songhay towards the central savanna, it must be noted that, for this shift to have been possible, the Hausa states must have had a relatively stable state system before this time. It is believed that the foundations for most of the Hausa states were laid down in the ninth or tenth century CE. The rulers of the Hausa states also adopted Islam as a tool for consolidating their control over their regions and for improving trading relations between societies that were already Islamic in the Sahara and north Africa.

Like the Kanuri and Jukun origin myths described above, Hausa tradition claims origin from migrants from the east. The most widespread story of Hausa origin indicates that the Hausa states were created by Bayajidda, who was the son of a king of Baghdad. After a falling-out with his father, Bayajidda fled to Borno, where he married the daughter of the *mai*. Due to unhappiness and fear of the *mai*, Bayajidda later fled westward, meeting some blacksmiths, who crafted him a knife. Bayajidda took the knife and, upon reaching a place called Daura, used the knife to kill a sacred snake that had been preventing the people from using the local well. He was proclaimed a hero, and the Queen of Daura offered to marry him. She bore him a son named Bawo, who in turn had seven sons, each of whom went out from Daura to establish one of seven Hausa states: Daura, Biram, Katsina, Zaria, Kano, Rano, and Gobir. These seven states are known as the "Hausa Bakwai." Seven illegitimate sons of Bawo are claimed to have founded seven other states, known as the "Hausa Banza." These states were Zamfara, Kororofa (Kwararafa), Kebbi, Nupe, Ilorin, Gwari, and Yauri.

The Hausa states were linked by a common Hausa language and, over time, by a common religion in Islam. Administratively, however, each Hausa state was entirely autonomous, and the inhabitants of the Hausa states at this time would have identified themselves by their state affiliation — that is, to Kano, Katsina, Zaria, Gobir, and so on — and not primarily as Hausas. The political structures in each state were somewhat similar, however: each was headed by a *sarkin* (king), who developed an expansive bureaucracy to administer the various economic endeavors of the states. The savannas were characterized by fertile agricultural lands, and livestock production was also a major source of wealth for Hausa communities. As states grew around the trans-Saharan trade routes, cities expanded and immigrants began to arrive from many different regions. As in other centralized states, many of these immigrants were skilled craftsmen seeking to ply their trade, in addition to itinerant traders just passing through.

Also extremely important to the development of Hausa states, however, were the migrants from the western Sudan and the nomadic Fulani pastoralists, who brought Islam and increased trade into the region beginning in the fourteenth century. The Hausa states of Kano, Katsina, Zaria, and Gobir became the dominant states in the northern savannas at different times from the fifteenth century until the British colonial occupation in the first decade of the twentieth century, and so they will be discussed in much greater detail in succeeding chapters.[18] For now, let us turn to two of the main factors that contributed to the power of the Hausa states and Borno by 1500: the coming of Islam and the growth of Hausaland and Borno as nexus for the trans-Saharan trade.

THE COMING OF ISLAM

Islam's first appearance in the societies encompassing modern-day Nigeria came in the late eleventh century, when the King of Kanem, Humai, is said to have converted. When the Saifawa dynasty relocated to Gazargamu and established the state of Borno, Islamic influence began to spread west to the emerging Hausa states. The Hausa states also received Islamic influences beginning in the fourteenth century from *wangarawa*, traders/missionaries who migrated to the region from the kingdoms of Mali and Songhay in the western Sudan, as well as from the pastoralist Fulani, who moved into the region in the fifteenth century. The first Hausa ruler to convert to Islam was Yaji of Kano, who adopted Islam in 1370.[19] The other Hausa states followed suit between this time and the mid-seventeenth century. Islam did not spread beyond the savanna into the forest at this time. Islam was an intriguing religion to Hausa and Kanuri rulers for the local political advantages it brought, and for the ways it connected Hausaland and Borno to the larger Islamic world (and Europe) through political and trade relationships. Islam thus strengthened the power and influence of the Hausa states and Borno both at home and abroad.

Islam spread through the Hausa and Kanuri lands primarily through the travels of Islamic traders and scholars from other regions. These traders and scholars established relationships with the rulers of the states through which they traveled and in which they sometimes settled, often becoming trusted advisers to the ruling class. The adoption of Islam offered several advantages to the ruling elite in these states. First, the rituals and literacy of Islam granted rulers special spiritual knowledge that could be used to strengthen their image as spiritually powerful among their people. Second, Islam offered a new deity upon which polytheistic rulers could call for aid in battle or personal affairs. Third, the relationships garnered by Hausa and Kanuri rulers with other Islamic powers in the Sudan, Sahara, and north Africa reinforced their own power: they could call on powerful allies in times of need, and they developed strong trading relationships with other Islamic powers.

The Islamic rulers of the Hausa states and Borno developed relationships with the wider Islamic world in several ways. One way was through the propagation of Islamic learning. Itinerant Muslim scholars would often travel through the savanna and Sahelian regions of the greater Nigeria area, sometimes teaching classes on Islamic theology along the way, sometimes settling for long periods of time to establish basic Quranic schools of Islamic learning (*kutab* in Arabic, *makarantan allo* in Hausa) from which to instruct pupils, often the sons of kings and other nobility, on the basic tenets of Muslim theology. Over time, more permanent and more advanced schools (*madrasas* in Arabic, *makarantan ilimi* in Hausa) were created. Through these schools, students trained to become part of the learned and powerful class of Islamic magistrates, scribes, or theologians known as the *ulama*. By the fifteenth century Borno had at least two *madrasas*, and by 1650 the Hausa state of Katsina had a well-established *madrasa* as well.[20] Islamic scholarship also fostered relations between the states of the Nigerian region and the wider Islamic world through the sending of Hausa or Kanuri students abroad to study Islamic theology. Evidence for such activities dates to at least 1250 CE, when Kanuri students established a hostel in Cairo.[21] Islamic religious ideas also spread through the Hausa states and Borno through literacy and the books that accompanied it. In these ways, Hausa and Kanuri rulers remained connected to the wider Islamic world through the diffusion of ideas.

Another major way that Hausa and Kanuri rulers became integrated with the Islamic world was through the annual pilgrimage to Mecca. The pilgrimage, or *hajj*, is one of the five pillars of the Islamic faith: the Quran

Figure 1.2 A Zarian woman (collection of Dr. Alfred Segun Fayemi)

states that any Muslim with the means to do so must make the pilgrimage at least once in his life. Hausa and Kanuri rulers undertook the pilgrimage not only to illustrate their religious devotion but also to make other Islamic nations aware of their wealth and power. The pilgrimage also represented a major opportunity for commercial activity, and *hajjis* (those who have performed the *hajj*) often returned with luxury items from exotic places. It is stated that Mai Dunama bin Humai, of Kanem, made the pilgrimage twice during his reign in the first half of the twelfth century.[22]

Despite these important connections between the states of the Nigerian region and the wider Islamic world, it is important to note that the Islam practiced in the Hausa states and Borno was not orthodox or ubiquitous by any means. The average agricultural Hausa or Kanuri would have had little to no contact with Islamic ideas or personages at this time, as Muslim migrants and their ideas congregated mainly in the urban centers of trade and political authority. Furthermore, even the Islam practiced by Hausa and Kanuri rulers remained superficial and was infused to a large extent with pre-existing indigenous religious beliefs and practices. Just as rulers gained power from their association with Islam, they also needed to maintain a religious connection with their subjects, a vast majority of whom were not Muslim at this time. Thus, as Nehemia Levtzion has put it, rulers often were taught "only those religious obligations and practices that no one may be excused from knowing. Hence, the king was instructed only with the rudiments of Islam and was not heavily burdened from the beginning with the obligations of prescriptive Islam."[23] In Hausaland, the Bori cult of local spirits remained a central aspect of religious activity in the region, indicating the extent to which indigenous beliefs persisted despite the spread of Islam.

Although Hausa and Kanuri rulers are often accused of being only "nominal" Muslims at this time, accepting some tenets of Islam for the power, prestige, and trading relationships that came with them, it is also worth pointing out that the goals of these rulers were not always entirely instrumentalist in nature. One King of Kano, named Umaru, abdicated his throne to pursue Islamic theology in the fifteenth century, and by the sixteenth century the King of Katsina, Ibrahim Maje, had instituted elements of the Islamic *shari'a* law code in his state.[24] Thus, Islam's growth in the savanna and Sahelian areas was not immediate but incremental.

THE TRANS-SAHARAN TRADE

The spread of Islam and the growth of the trans-Saharan trade were inextricably linked in west Africa. Islam became the preferred religion of long-distance traders in these regions beginning in the tenth and eleventh centuries, and from these traders the religion spread to the rulers of the various states described above. The connection between trade and Islam is perhaps best exemplified by the *wangarawa* merchants and Islamic scholars, who spread Islam and commercial activity from the western

Sudanic states of Mali and Songhay to the Hausa states of the central savanna from the fourteenth century onwards. As trade spread to the savannas and Sahel, Islam spread with it. And, as Islam developed roots in the Hausa states and Borno, more trade ensued. Islam provided a way for traders to identify with each other and also established common values and rules upon which trade was conducted. The trans-Saharan trade existed well before the establishment of the Hausa states and Borno and continued to be an important factor in the economies of savanna and Sahelian states until the twentieth century.

The "golden age" of the trans-Saharan trade is commonly noted as having taken place between the fourteenth and sixteenth centuries. During this time, gold and slaves were the primary goods traded. Gold became increasingly valuable from the eleventh century, when many Islamic states turned to gold as their primary form of currency. By the thirteenth century European countries were also converting their currency to gold, causing the metal to be in even greater demand. Large gold deposits existed in the kingdom of Ghana, in the forest zone of west Africa, to the west of modern-day Nigeria. By the thirteenth century the kingdom of Mali had emerged as the largest miner of gold in west Africa. In order to transport the gold from these southern regions to the countries of north Africa and Europe that desired it, an elaborate trading network emerged.

Crossing the Sahara desert took between seventy and ninety days, depending on the route taken. As a result, the process was laborious and capital-intensive. Large amounts of goods had to be taken on each trip in order to make the journey economically feasible. This required supplies, most important of which were the beasts of burden that carried the goods. Originally donkeys were used, but camels were introduced over time and proved to be superior for the purpose because of their ability to traverse sand effectively and to travel long distances without water.

The routes across the Sahara changed in importance over time. The main routes passed through the western Sudanic kingdoms of Mali and Songhay before they collapsed in the fifteenth and sixteenth centuries respectively. When these kingdoms fell, the routes shifted east through the Hausa states. The importance of different goods also fluctuated over the period. Gold remained important at all times, but, from the sixteenth century, slaves became an increasingly important article of trade, especially in the central savanna. Slaves had always been a primary commodity in the trans-Saharan trade from Borno. Aside from these two goods, salt, leather goods, weapons, horses, and textiles were also traded widely, as far as north Africa, the Middle East, and Europe.[25]

The states of the savanna and Sahel served as the southern termini for the trans-Saharan trade. The Hausa in particular became traders in large numbers and spread across the savanna region and into the forest zone to conduct trade; the actual trade across the Sahara was conducted not by the Hausa, however, but by the Tuareg of the central Sahara and by north Africans who traveled to the Hausa states to purchase goods. Hausa rulers exacted tolls from traders passing through their realms and collected taxes on marketed goods. The wealth could then be invested in luxury goods from all over the world, or used for public works or for strengthening their military forces. Thus, the trans-Saharan trade made the Hausa states rich and powerful as the routes shifted eastward from the sixteenth century.

The trans-Saharan trade was important not only to the states of the savanna and the Sahel. Goods from the forest zone were also traded heavily in the savanna, if not across the Sahara. Hausa traders traded livestock and leather and iron goods to forest zone societies for grains, slaves, pepper, and, above all, kola, the caffeinated fruit of the kola tree used in medicinal and ritual practices.

The trans-Saharan trade declined in intensity somewhat with the activities of Europeans along the coast from the sixteenth century, around the same time as the Hausa states rose to dominance. European ships became increasingly important vessels for the transfer of goods, particularly slaves, out of west Africa, diminishing the importance of the overland routes over time. Nevertheless, the trans-Saharan trade remained intact, and continued to supply north Africa and lands to the east until the twentieth century.

AFRICAN ORIGINS AND INTER-STATE CONNECTIONS

Although migration played an important role in the growth of centralized states in the forest zone, savanna, and Sahel, particularly through the growth of trade and the spread of Islam in the north, immigrants should not be seen as the sole providers of state formation in the region. The decentralized and centralized states that developed during this time were all essentially indigenous in origin. Their roots lay in the development of agricultural subsistence economies from the third millennium BCE. While these states encouraged the wealth that migrants could bring, and adopted political, economic, and cultural attributes from immigrants where expedient, they nevertheless retained their African origin. It is also important to note that, although each state that emerged in the region was more or less autonomous, both centralized and decentralized states had contact with each other throughout this time period, and, as a result, developed sophisticated political, economic, and cultural relationships across societies.

Many scholars initially believed that state formation was an inherently non-African idea, and that any ideas of state centralization must have been brought into the region by foreigners. Dubbed the "Hamitic thesis," this idea that any sophisticated political, economic, or social institutions in Africa had to come only from outsiders has been seriously questioned in recent decades. Scholars now widely recognize that the structures upon which centralized states were formed in the region pre-dated outside influence, and it is increasingly clear that many of the centralized states that developed in much of the area under discussion emerged from the decentralized formations that preceded them, not solely from the outside influence of immigrants.

Hamitic scholars based their assertions of the external origins of states on several types of evidence. Commonly cited were the origin myths that proclaimed that the founders of centralized states all migrated from elsewhere. This explanation is flawed for two reasons. First, although many origin myths in the societies of the Nigerian region indicate state creation through migration, not all do. Many traditions of autochthonous origin are also present in the region. Second, it must be noted, for example, that both the immigrant Zaghawa from the Kanuri myth and the Baghdadi prince Bayajidda from the Hausa myth encountered indigenous populations that already seemed to have social structures in place at the time of their arrival. Daura had a queen when Bayajidda arrived, and the indigenous peoples of the Kanuri legend are described as agricultural at the very least. Thus, even in cases where migrants are known to have influenced social structures and where they appear in origin myths as performing this function, the original African socio-political structures must be seen as the foundations upon which these states were built.

The kingship institutions that dominated the centralized states in west Africa also convinced scholars of the non-African origin of state formation processes. Scholars argued that the "divine kingship" institutions that cropped up in African states were identical to those that had emerged in Egypt and the Near East, thus indicating that those responsible for state formation in west Africa must have come from these places. Subsequent research has shown that a variety of different kingship types exist in the societies that developed in the territories of modern-day Nigeria, however, and that none of them mirror identically the divine kingship institutions of

Egypt or the Near East, in that they do not recognize their monarch as the permanent, human embodiment of a deity. Rather, most kingship institutions in the area were characterized by a close relationship between the office of the king and the spiritual world without the monarch himself being supernatural. It is quite likely, in fact, that these kingship institutions grew out of the spiritual-cum-political institutions of decentralized states, which also derived their political authority, albeit circumscribed, from spiritual sources. One such example is the institution of the secret society, prevalent in many decentralized societies, which claimed authority over certain aspects of traditional life through a secret group of community leaders. The authority of such institutions usually derived from spiritual sources. A second possible outlet for the emergence of spiritually based kingship may have been the oracle system, in which a human being would become the medium through which the wishes of the gods were articulated. This kind of human custodianship over the gods' orders could easily have evolved into a "divine" kingship over time.[26]

Having illustrated the African origin of both centralized and decentralized states in the Nigerian region, it is important to note the ways in which these African states maintained relations with each other. Trade was the most important factor linking different societies. No region was economically independent: the regions relied on each other for goods they could not produce, making good inter-group relations of paramount importance. In addition, maintaining trade routes was an inter-state task that required members of all communities to contribute to clearing brush, providing security, and performing other duties that made trading as convenient as possible.

Trade was not the only activity that inspired inter-group relations. Social and cultural organizations such as age grades, secret societies, and oracles also facilitated good inter-group relations by providing levels of identity that stretched beyond individual community lines. Also crossing community lines was the common practice of intermarriage, which brought people from different backgrounds into new communities and forged cultural and biological ties between them. Closely related to intermarriage and trade was migration. People relocated across the region as a result of trading activity, intermarriage, displacement through war, and the slave trade. As a result, cultural barriers remained porous. Cultural activities such as festivals, food preparation techniques, and even words from different languages circulated across state and community lines. These activities, dishes, or words often became fully incorporated aspects of societies in which they did not originate.

Indeed, many origin myths in the societies of the Nigerian region speak to the antiquity of the inter-group relationships that existed in these areas. The Nupe, in the middle belt region, trace their ancestry to an Igala prince, also in the middle belt but further east. The Igala have traditions that link their origin to the Yoruba in the southwest. The Idoma claim descent from the Jukun, and the Efik, from the southeast, claim their origin in intermarriage between an Igbo man and an Ibibio woman. The Urhobo, from the Niger delta, claim their society was founded by the son of an *oba* (king) of the Benin dynasty to the west. Such traditions clearly indicate the African origin of these societies. More importantly, they illustrate the political and social connections that existed between groups that considered themselves distinct but related.

CONCLUSION

Human habitation in the areas in and around modern-day Nigeria goes back many thousands of years. Societies in this region developed agricultural techniques, craftsmanship in areas such as pottery, leather-working, and iron-working, among others, and engaged in trade between groups. Over time these societies developed into both decentralized and highly centralized states. Decentralized states organized politically around chiefs and councils at the village and village-group level, while centralized states, such as those of Ife, Benin, the Hausa states, and Kanem-Borno, developed kingship institutions that placed political and, to some extent, spiritual authority in the person of the king, who ruled from a capital city. Cities became the focal points of centralized states, as the bases of political authority and as the centers of trade.

In the savanna and Sahelian states of the north, the advent of Islam and the trans-Saharan trade aided in the growth of centralized states and contributed to the accumulation of wealth in these areas. Nevertheless, it must be remembered that all social state formations in the Nigerian region had essentially indigenous African origins, although they were certainly willing to incorporate outside influences over time. The states that formed in the territories in and around modern-day Nigeria in the second millennium CE were politically autonomous, but in many ways they were economically and socially interdependent, trading on a large scale with each other and developing social and cultural linkages through intermarriage, commercial and spiritual organizations, and diplomatic contacts.

Thus, by 1500 the territories in and around modern-day Nigeria constituted a dynamic area characterized by the existence of several powerful centralized states and the proliferation of hundreds of smaller decentralized states. These states were involved in political, economic, and cultural activities that both linked them together and accentuated their distinct contributions to the region as a whole. Trade remained the most important factor linking groups and buttressing the power of the centralized states. After 1500, with the establishment of Europeans on the Atlantic coast as permanent trading partners, this trade increasingly shifted towards one item: slaves. The transatlantic slave trade would have a transformative impact on the individuals and the states of this region between the sixteenth and nineteenth centuries.

CHAPTER 2

Slavery, state, and society, c. 1500 – c. 1800

INTRODUCTION

This chapter focuses on the formation and consolidation of states in the Nigerian area from the sixteenth through eighteenth centuries AD. During this period, large, centralized states built upon strong agrarian bases, generating surpluses that allowed for economic diversification and engagement in regional and international trade. One such diversification was the growth of an international trade in slaves, particularly out of the south. This chapter emphasizes the role that slavery and the slave trade played in social relations and in the establishment and consolidation of political power in states throughout the Nigerian region. It is important to note that slavery and the slave trade were not the main factors in the formation of these states, most of which existed in one form or another before the arrival of European traders on the coasts in the late fifteenth century. From the 1500s through the 1800s, however, the trade in slaves did provide important sources of revenue and access to items such as guns and European luxury goods that contributed greatly to the consolidation of wealth and power in many states. In the states of the northern savannas and the Sahel, the institution of slavery had deep roots, and connections with the trans-Saharan trade routes meant that markets for slave exports had existed for several centuries. As the main trans-Saharan trade routes moved east in the fifteenth and sixteenth centuries, coinciding with the expansion and consolidation of the Hausa states and the Borno empire, tensions between these states mounted. The result was widespread warfare and raiding between states, in which the taking of slaves for eventual sale in the trans-Saharan markets became both a tactic and a goal.

In the states of the southern forest zone, it is much more difficult to determine the antiquity of slavery as a social institution. By the sixteenth century, however, forms of slavery were definitely being adopted in these states, and sometimes they became extremely important aspects of social and political structure. In the case of the Oyo empire, which grew to become one of the largest states in the Nigerian region between the seventeenth and nineteenth centuries, slaves provided the bureaucratic and military backbone of society, while in many coastal states, particularly in the southeast, slaves became an increasingly important force in the political economy, often working as domestic or agricultural labor but also as slave raiders and traders in their own right. Some slaves even became exceedingly wealthy and powerful leaders of their communities in these areas.

The entrenchment of slavery as a social institution and as the backbone of politics and economies in southern Nigeria was fueled primarily by the arrival of Europeans on the coasts from the late fifteenth century. Early trade with Europeans focused on much the same items that regional trade had focused on for centuries: gold, textiles, foodstuffs, and slaves. By the seventeenth century, however, slaves had become by far the dominant commodity traded on the coasts. During the seventeenth and eighteenth centuries, the trade in human beings was a major source of wealth for states in the south, becoming the primary export of most states in this region. Over time, the transatlantic trade even began to direct slaves away from the time-tested markets of the Sahara towards the coast.

The transatlantic trade reshaped societies in the south in the period before 1800 around the commercial activities of the slave trade. This reorientation of commercial activity set the stage for even more rapid and transformative changes in the nineteenth century. In these ways the growth of the slave trade with Europeans in the period from 1500 to 1800 represented both a continuation of long-standing ways of life and a point of embarkation for changes to come.

SLAVERY AND SOCIETY IN THE NIGERIAN REGION

Slavery is a dynamic institution. The uses and treatment of slaves have varied significantly in different places and have been transformed over time. The form of chattel slavery that became popular in the Americas as a result of the transatlantic slave trade does not represent the way in which unfree labor functioned in African societies. In the Nigerian region, the forms of social bondage were diverse and complicated, but were generally more benign and integrative than in the Americas. The Hausa states in the savanna and Borno in the Sahel had long-standing institutions of slavery; the slavery in these areas was by and large integrative and domestic in nature, however. Islam had many rules governing the taking, treatment, and manumission of slaves. In the southern regions, institutions of social bondage had certainly existed for a long time, yet it is difficult to say with any certainty that these institutions constituted slavery prior to the sixteenth century. Other forms of social bondage existed and continued to exist alongside slavery as the importance of slavery as a social institution became more prevalent from the sixteenth century onwards.

One example of an alternative form of social bondage was pawnship, whereby the head of a family would offer one of his children as a pawn to a creditor until the debt had been repaid. In the meantime, the labor of the pawn essentially served as the interest on the debt.[1] Young females were the most prized pawns, and if the female pawn married into the creditor's family the debt was canceled and the families joined together as kin. If a pawn died before the debt had been paid, then the debtor family would send another pawn to replace him or her. The pawn was therefore socially bound to the family of the creditor, but the arrangement was not permanent. Thus, pawnship served as an institution of social bondage separate from and alongside slavery until well into the twentieth century.

Kinship ties were the most important element of social relations in most societies in and around modern-day Nigeria. Kinship networks contained connected lineages. Each lineage was based on the idea of a common ancestry, in which each person in the lineage could trace his or her roots back to the founder of the lineage. Relationships between lineages could be strengthened through intermarriage, thereby linking the lineages and expanding the kinship group. Individuals' identities were primarily centered on kinship links. Pawnship was a form of social bondage that allowed unfree laborers to retain ties to their families, while also offering the opportunity to expand kinship ties by marrying into their creditor's family.

Slaves, on the other hand, lacked such kinship ties. Having been taken into slavery primarily as a result of having been captured in war or kidnapped, or as a punishment for a criminal offense, slaves were stripped of their kinship ties and sold to masters in different kinship networks, usually in places distant from their point of origin. Slaves were thus totally dependent upon their owners, no longer having their own kinship network to protect them. The further a slave traveled before sale the more valuable the slave was, as there was less prospect for escape, making slaves more inclined to adapt to their new circumstances and become integrated into their new surroundings. Young people were also more prized as slaves than adults because of their adaptability, as well as for their energy and, among females, for their reproductive capacity and potential as wives.

The lack of kinship ties made slavery much more versatile than other forms of social bondage, such as pawnship, that allowed for unfree labor to retain kinship connections. Slaves could be sold for money or traded for goods, with value added over distance. Slaves could also be given as gifts to family members and political supporters or as tribute to imperial overlords. Slaves were also used as sacrificial offerings in religious ceremonies in traditional settings. Non-slave labor could not be used for these purposes. Female slaves served both as domestic labor and, very often, as sexual providers, particularly as concubines or in the harems of wealthy or noble Muslims in the northern savanna states. Because of this, young female slaves were always the most expensive and abundant slaves traded across the Sahara to the Muslim countries of north Africa and the Middle East.[2]

Despite the disadvantages that outright slavery placed on the enslaved, however, the institution of slavery in most African societies functioned differently from and more compassionately than the chattel slavery that emerged in the Americas. Slaves in African societies usually had the opportunity to integrate themselves into their new communities through assimilation, and, over time, marriage and childbirth, much as pawns did. Slaves did not constitute a class in the African setting. They tended to live with the family that owned them as dependents within the household and tended to do the same type of work as other family members. Slaves of agricultural owners performed agricultural duties; slaves of artisans apprenticed as artisans. Slaves were acculturated by the families in which they lived and, over time, might even marry into the family, thereby becoming ostensibly emancipated through their relationship to free persons. The children of such slaves would be free as well.[3]

In the savanna regions, slavery was often governed by Islamic law. The Quran permits the enslavement of non-believers, making areas of recent conversion and areas on the frontiers of Islam prime arenas for the enslavement of non-Muslims. Borno and the Hausa states of the savanna existed on the fringes of the Muslim world and so had large pools of non-Muslim neighbors from which to draw potential slaves. Islam also provides for the humane treatment of slaves and their ultimate incorporation into Muslim society, however. Ideally, individuals could remain slaves only until they became Muslim, since it was a sin to enslave a fellow Muslim. While this ideal was not always practiced (indeed, Muslim rulers in the savannas often complained that fellow Muslims were being taken into slavery in raids by their enemies),[4] other checks on the institution also existed in Islam. Concubines could not be sold once they gave birth to their first child by a free man, and the child itself would be free at birth. Manumission of a slave was also a common penance for sins committed under Islam. Furthermore, the giving of alms is one of the five pillars of Islam. Therefore, manumitting slaves could also serve as a religious expression, an act of recognition for the generosity of God.[5]

The ability of slaves to be integrated into new kinship networks and to be emancipated in the slave systems of societies in the Nigerian region meant that slaves were, by and large, not a self-reproducing pool. New slaves were constantly infused into communities as old slaves died, became integrated into their communities, or became fully emancipated. As a result, markets always existed for the buying and selling of slaves. The market for slaves was also buoyed by the versatility of slaves. Because slaves were not defined by the kind of labor they performed but by their lack of kinship ties, slaves could be used for virtually any kind of labor in these societies. As such, a slave's social status was not necessarily linked to his or her condition of servitude. Slaves' tasks could, and often did, consist of menial or physical labor, but not necessarily to a greater extent than free persons experienced. Slaves performed agricultural labor, apprenticed as artisans, and served as domestic labor within households. The social status of slaves could also be very high, however, depending on the status of their owner. Slaves of nobles and royals often played important roles in the military or the administration of the state. Some slaves even became so powerful as to become the heads of lineages and the governors of territories, sometimes even owning their own slaves, as we will see later in this chapter and the next. As the slave trade became an increasingly important sector of the economies of states in the seventeenth and eighteenth centuries, particularly in the societies of southern Nigeria, slave traders employed captive slaves to help in the process of acquiring more slaves.[6]

The versatility of slaves as commodities, accompanied by the tendency to incorporate slaves into existing social networks, allowed for the institution of slavery to exist in African societies without becoming a defining feature of those societies. Slaves served primarily as a supplement to free labor, not as a replacement for it. Slaves also became important items of trade, serving as major commodities in the trans-Saharan trade for many centuries, and, from the sixteenth century, in the transatlantic trade with Europeans on the coast. The way in which each of these trades functioned was closely linked to political developments in the trading states of the Nigerian region.

SLAVERY, STATE, AND SOCIETY IN THE SAVANNA

The value and versatility of slaves had made them an important aspect of the trans-Saharan trade for centuries before the coming of Europeans and the establishment of the transatlantic trade on the coast. Indeed, slaves had been a particularly important commodity of the trans-Saharan trade at least since the establishment of kingdoms in the savanna and their association with the Muslim states of north Africa from about the eleventh century, if not earlier. Slaves were an excellent commodity for trade over the harsh Sahara desert for several reasons. First, as mentioned above, slaves increased in value with distance from their point of origin. Second, large pools of potential slaves existed in the savannas, as the Hausa states and Borno fought with their neighbors and each other, taking war captives who could then be turned into profit through sale on the trans-Saharan market. Third, transportation conditions were poor across the sandy, dry Sahara. Donkeys and camels could carry only a certain amount of weight, and overheads were always high because of the danger of the trip and the possibility that animals would get lost or die on the journey, making their cargo impossible to transport. As such, the trans-Saharan trade had always focused most heavily on luxury items that had a high value-to-weight ratio, such as gold, salt, and textiles. Slaves, like gold, were very valuable, but, unlike other commodities, they were self-transporting, and could even be used as porters themselves if necessary, making them particularly efficient items in the trans-Saharan trade.

Numbers for the trade in slaves across the Sahara are speculative at best, but Paul Lovejoy has suggested that in the period from 650 to 1600 AD the total number of slaves exported across the Sahara was in the region of 4,820,000; he admits, however, that the number could be as little as a half of this or, equally, significantly higher. These uncertainties are borne out by the relative lack of statistical evidence available. The total number suggested by Lovejoy supposes an average number of 3,000–8,000 slaves per year traversing each of the main trans-Saharan routes.[7] The figure for the seventeenth century is likely to have been in the realm of 800,000 slaves for the trans-Saharan trade as a whole. In the eighteenth century, however, the number of slaves transported across the Sahara declined drastically, due to the growth of the transatlantic trade with Europeans along the coast.

It must be noted that the numbers provided above are estimates for the trans-Saharan trade as a whole, and are not confined solely to slaves exported from the Hausa states and Borno. Indeed, prior to the sixteenth century a significant percentage of the total slave trade was conducted through the kingdoms of the western Sudan, most notably Mali and Songhay. Nevertheless, the Hausa states and Kanem (and its successor state of Borno) had both traded in slaves from early days, and the slave trade across the Sahara had been an important aspect of the political economy of these states throughout their periods of expansion and consolidation, although the overall scale of their involvement relative to the whole is impossible to gauge.[8]

Borno's contribution to the trans-Saharan trade in slaves probably reached its peak in the sixteenth century. During this period, Borno expanded rapidly through many wars with neighboring states. The period is best exemplified in the reign of Mai Idris Aloma (1569/70–1619), considered to be the greatest of Borno's leaders. At the time that Idris rose to power, Borno was beset from all sides and from within by threats to its security. Famines had ravaged the area during the reigns of Aloma's two predecessors, weakening the state and making it susceptible to invasion. The boundaries with the Hausa states to the west and the Teda and Tuareg to the north and northwest were not secure. Meanwhile, the Bulala, who had ousted the Borno regime from Kanem in the fifteenth century, were still a threat in the east. The Jukun states to the south, most notably Kororofa (Kwararafa), had risen in power and begun to raid territory claimed by Borno. Meanwhile, within the Borno kingdom, non-Muslim groups such as the So and the Ngizim remained unintegrated into Borno society.[9]

Idris initiated many military campaigns against these groups during his reign, and by the time of his death he had managed to pacify the borders on the north and northwest. He had also defeated the Bulala and brought them under the control of Borno, although without incorporating the lands of the old Kanem state into the Borno empire to any degree. Campaigns against the Hausa states to the west were less successful. Owing to the relative power of the Hausa states, Borno was never able to bring these states into its empire. Idris Aloma was able to expand westwards against Kano, however, thereby securing the western border to some extent. The Jukun remained a menacing threat throughout the seventeenth century, but Idris was able to bring under control many of the non-Muslim groups within the borders of Borno, thereby strengthening the internal security situation.

Idris Aloma's wars and raids did more than secure the political authority of the *mai* over an expanding Borno empire. His military activities also had profound implications for the economic growth of Borno. His campaigns against internal enemies led to a surge in war captives, who were then sold as slaves across the Sahara, particularly to markets in Tripoli and Cairo. Idris's predecessor, Mai Dunama, had established contact with the Ottoman Turks in Tripoli as early as 1555, and had established a trade there. Contacts with Cairo had pre-dated this

Figure 2.1 European-styled building in Badagry (collection of Brigitte Kowalski)

occurrence, and during Idris Aloma's reign contacts were also made with Morocco. Slaves captured in Borno's many wars were traded across the Sahara for horses and, most importantly in the sixteenth and seventeenth centuries, guns and musketeers. The trade with Tripoli became increasingly important and by the mid-seventeenth century was very lucrative, hinging to a great degree on the trade in slaves. For instance, a caravan reaching Tripoli from Borno in 1638 traded "thirty eunuchs, a hundred young negroes, fifty maidens and a golden tortoise, among many other items," for "200 choice horses, fifteen young European renegades, several muskets and swords."[10] Trading slaves for military equipment, Idris and other *mais* of Borno used Turkish horses, guns, and musketeers to gain a military advantage over their foes, routing them in battle thanks to their superior technology and military organization, thereby gaining more war captives who could be sold for yet more goods across the Sahara. In this way, Borno reached its highest level of power and influence during the sixteenth and seventeenth centuries.

The eighteenth century was not as kind to the *mais* of Borno. Having effectively secured their borders relative to previous centuries, with the exception of occasional Jukun raids, it appears that Borno reduced its military campaigns and, subsequently, its importation of firearms, basking in the relative peace that had been established, in contrast to the previous centuries of warfare. The droughts that had undermined the power of Idris Aloma's predecessors returned, however, causing three major famines lasting several years each in the period from 1700 to 1750.[11] Under such circumstances, the empire of Borno shrank considerably from its peak size in the seventeenth century, and lost much of its western territories to the Sokoto jihadists in the early nineteenth century, as discussed in the next chapter.

In Hausaland, the period from 1500 to 1800 was characterized by frequent wars between the various states. Regional power shifts occurred as states fought to gain access to markets and trade routes, to exact tribute from each other, or to capture new slaves for domestic use or export. At no point did any single Hausa state enjoy total dominance over all other Hausa states, but at different times during this period several different Hausa states enjoyed greater power relative to their neighbors, before ceding their elevated position to other rising states through losses on the battlefield or economic decline.

At the beginning of this period, around 1500, Kano was the most powerful Hausa state, having subjected both Katsina and Zaria to tributary positions in the first decade of the sixteenth century. Kano's position was by no means secure, however. Embattled from the east by Borno forces, from the southeast by regular Kororofa raids, and to the north by constant military rivalry with the rising power of Katsina, Kano also suffered from occasional famines that threatened its internal stability. Nevertheless, through its position on a major trans-Saharan trade route and the economic activity of the commercial and artisan class that resided within the city, Kano managed to maintain regional power. After over a century of prolonged antagonism, Kano and Katsina proclaimed peace by the mid-seventeenth century, partly out of the need to present a united front against the Kororofa attacks that beset both their eastern borders.[12] Katsina managed to reach its own peak of power and stability in the eighteenth century despite regular attacks from Kano, Zamfara, and Gobir, its three nearest neighbors and regional rivals in the seventeenth and eighteenth centuries.

Further to the west, Kebbi had surfaced as the most important state by the seventeenth century, although Gobir (to its east) and Zamfara (to its southeast) were expanding rapidly through wars with not only Kebbi but also with Kano and Katsina. Kebbi finally fell to a combined attack by Gobir, Zamfara, and the forces of the Sultan of Ahir, a loosely organized conglomeration of nomadic groups to the north of Hausaland. Gobir emerged as the new power in the region after the fall of Kebbi. Taking over parts of Kebbi, Gobir also expanded to the south and southeast, effectively stifling the expansion of Zamfara, which also wished to expand into these regions. By the mid-eighteenth century Gobir had become powerful enough to launch several attacks on Kano, although none strong enough to cause serious damage to the city.[13]

Thus, hundreds of years of warfare between Hausa states had resulted in the establishment of three particularly powerful states by 1800, Kano, Katsina, and Gobir, with Kebbi and Zamfara also of relative importance. Beyond the military might necessary to maintain power during this time period, the strength of these states was also based on their economic prowess. While much of the production and trade of the Hausa states was based on free labor and commodities such as gold, grain, livestock, and leather goods, slaves were also an important aspect of the Hausa states' economies. It is clear that during the sixteenth century Kano's infrastructure developed enormously, largely because of an increase in the number of slaves used for the production of agricultural goods, as porters and guards on trade routes, as soldiers in the many military campaigns against neighbors, and, as was seen in Borno, as export items used to purchase goods from north Africa, particularly horses.[14] The acquisition of slaves was probably a motivating factor behind some of the wars and raids that Hausa states conducted against each other, as slaves were equated with other kinds of wealth during this period, both for the labor that they could perform and for the price that they could get at market.

Until the eighteenth century the primary direction of the slave trade was towards north Africa via the trans-Saharan routes. In the eighteenth century, however, the Hausa trade in slaves turned southwards, towards the transatlantic trade conducted by Europeans on the coast. For instance, Hausa traders from Kano traded slaves south for such important European items as "textiles and beads, cowry shells, as well as brass, iron, and, to a lesser degree, firearms and ammunition."[15] Although Hausa traders had reached the coast by the early eighteenth century, most Hausa trade with Europeans was conducted through middlemen who controlled the trade routes between Hausaland and the Atlantic Ocean, most notably the Yoruba state of Oyo, which rose to prominence from the sixteenth century.

SLAVERY AND STATE FORMATION IN THE OYO EMPIRE

The empire of Oyo was based around the city of Oyo Ile, situated south of the river Niger in the savanna zone near its convergence with the forest zone in what is today the northeastern corner of Oyo State. It is unclear when exactly the town of Oyo Ile was founded, but archaeological testing indicates that the town was inhabited as early as the eighth century AD.[16] Oyo Ile was a well-established urban center by the fifteenth century, when the neighboring Nupe sacked the city. The Oyo monarchy sought refuge among the Borgu, another neighboring people, to the west, where it reconstituted itself. By the early sixteenth century Oyo had moved its capital to Igboho, roughly forty miles west of Oyo Ile, and sometime in the late sixteenth century, under the reign of Ajiboyede, the Oyo defeated the Nupe and reclaimed Oyo Ile.[17]

From about 1600 Oyo underwent rapid expansion into the forest zone to the south and southeast, becoming one of the largest empires in the Nigerian region. At its largest size in the eighteenth century, the Oyo empire stretched from the river Moshi in the north down the river Niger in the east to Ogudu, which was a Nupe settlement. In the east, Oyo may have stretched as far as the river Osin in Igbomina territory, while, in the southeast, Oyo bordered on the lands of the Ekiti and the state of Ife. Oyo reached as far south as the present town of Oyo, while the river Opara marked the western boundary of the empire. In all, the area of the empire was somewhere in the range of 18,000 square miles.[18]

Although Oyo Ile stood in the savanna and cohabited with middle belt neighbors such as the Nupe and Borgu, Oyo was essentially a Yoruba state, although some political and cultural exchanges did occur between Oyo and its neighbors. As was the case with most Yoruba states, the leader of Oyo, known as the *alafin*, traced his authority back to descendants of Oduduwa, the founder of the Yoruba people, who spread out from Ife. Oyo's tradition claims that the city was founded by Oranmiyan, a son of Oduduwa. This link to Oduduwa and Ife was not the only foundation upon which the *alafin*'s authority rested, however. The *alafin* also claimed descent from Sango, an early King of Oyo later deified as the god of thunder, further mystifying the office of *alafin* and connecting it to the realm of the gods.

The office of *alafin* apparently had supreme authority, and only the *alafin* or one of his proxies could make policy decisions, order executions, and create and confer titles. Over time, the royal lineage also took more and more direct control over the functioning of the slave trade, one of Oyo's most prosperous enterprises. Despite this supreme authority, however, the *alafin* did have several checks on his authority. The main political unit of Oyo was the lineage, and the *alafin*'s lineage was just one of many, although undoubtedly the most powerful. Each lineage had a head, and the head of each important lineage had a duty to perform for the state. Lineage heads held political, religious, or military offices in the city or in the provinces of the empire and were responsible for the day-to-day administration of their purview. Local lineage heads often served as patrons for communities in the provinces of the empire. In return for tribute, these chiefs would lobby on behalf of their constituent communities for favors from the *alafin*.

The most important lineage heads, aside from the *alafin* himself, held positions in the Oyo Mesi, a non-royal organization that served as the chief advisory body to the alafin. The Oyo Mesi led the army of Oyo Ile, and its members served as the custodians of many religious centers for the city, among other duties. The Oyo Mesi also had the prerogative to approve of the royal lineage's choice of a new *alafin* and could enact regime change by ordering disgraced or ineffective *alafin*s to commit suicide.

Such powers made it possible for the Oyo Mesi to exert significant, sometimes even disruptive, control over the office of *alafin*. The most famous example is the case of Gaha, who, as the *basorun*, or leader, of the Oyo Mesi from 1754 to 1774, secured the suicides of two *alafin*s, Labisi and Awonbioju. Gaha then forced Awonbioju's successor, Agboluaje, to accede to Gaha's authority, over which issue Agboluaje eventually committed suicide. It is speculated that Gaha may also have been responsible for the death of Agboluaje's successor, Majeogbe, supposedly through magic or poisoning. Gaha was eventually overthrown by Alafin Abiodun, who called upon aid from the provinces of Oyo to end Gaha's tyrannical rule.[19]

That the office of *alafin* did not crumble under the instability created by Basorun Gaha and the Oyo Mesi is a testament to the organization of the *alafin*'s palace administration, which rested heavily on slaves with positions of high authority and responsibility. It is clear that, from the reconquest of Oyo Ile in the late sixteenth century, slaves had performed integral duties within the palace administration, not only in the everyday affairs of running the palace but also in ruling the city of Oyo Ile and the provinces of the Oyo empire. Three eunuchs, known as the *ona iwefa* (eunuch of the middle), *otun iwefa* (eunuch of the right), and *osi iwefa* (eunuch of the left), were the most senior titled slaves and were the highest authority next to the *alafin* himself in judicial, religious, and administrative matters respectively. The *ona iwefa* stood as proxy for the *alafin* in handing down legal rulings, while the *otun iwefa* was in charge of the cult of Sango, through which the *alafin*'s office was mystified. The *osi iwefa* collected revenues and served as the *alafin*'s proxy in dealings with lineage heads such as the members of the Oyo Mesi.[20]

Beneath these three titled eunuchs was a larger class of palace slaves known as the *ilari*, meaning "scar-heads," a reference to the incisions made in their heads into which magical substances were rubbed, initiating them into their new rank. These slaves numbered several hundred if not thousands, and were under the purview of the *osi iwefa*. Ilari served the *alafin* as tax collectors, messengers, and bodyguards. To enable the *alafin* to keep an eye on events in the provinces of the empire, a group of slaves known as the *ajele* or *asoju oba* (eyes of the king) were placed throughout the Oyo empire and reported directly to the *alafin* on matters affecting their assigned province.

The reliance on slaves for the overseeing of the *alafin*'s affairs stabilized royal authority in two ways. First, since the duties of slaves were so diffused and carried such importance, royal authority could be maintained even if the *alafin* himself was ineffective or was suffering through periods of instability, as in the period of Basorun Gaha. Second, since slaves had no lineage of their own and therefore no power to gain, other than that which could be conferred upon them by the *alafin*, their dependent status made them particularly stable and trustworthy underlings. In this way, the Oyo empire managed to thrive on a series of checks and balances between royal and non-royal lineages, propped up by a fairly dense bureaucracy based on slave labor.

Slaves also served much the same functions in Oyo as they did in other regions of the greater Nigerian area during the 1500–1800 period. Slaves performed agricultural work, performed domestic duties, trained as artisans, and served in the military. With slaves such an important aspect of the politics and economy of Oyo, it is no surprise that the trade in slaves was also a central element in the rise of Oyo.[21] Oyo traded slaves captured in war, and to a smaller extent convicted criminals, as well as European goods attained through southern trade, to Hausa states in exchange for Hausa slaves and, perhaps most importantly, the horses upon which Oyo built the cavalry it used to dominate the region militarily. Oyo also traded slaves south to the coast after 1650 in exchange for European luxury goods, cowry shells, which were the standard currency of Oyo, and, during the eighteenth century, a limited supply of firearms.

Oyo's involvement in the slave trade was not restricted to the slaves acquired in Oyo's own military campaigns. Oyo's strategic position between the southern forest zone and the Hausa states put Oyo in a prime position to capitalize on the flow of goods between the two regions. Oyo thus served as a middleman, imposing heavy financial burdens on traders wishing to pass through Oyo territory to sell their wares on the other side. Hausa merchants wishing to move south and forest zone traders wishing to trade north found that they were forced to pay heavy dues when passing through Oyo territory. Ultimately, most merchants found it in their own

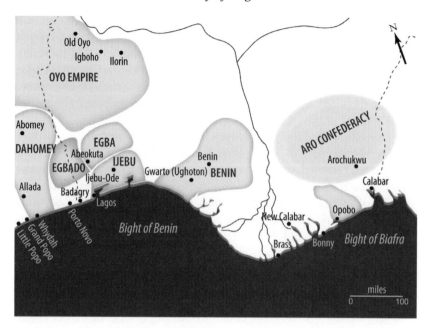

Map 2.1 Bights of Benin and Biafra (courtesy Saverance Publishing Services)

economic interest simply to sell their wares in Oyo, rather than pay the dues necessary to pass through Oyo. Oyo merchants could then re-export these goods in whatever direction they chose, at inflated prices. Government traders within Oyo did not pay the fees to pass through Oyo and as such they were at a competitive advantage over other traders in the region. This was particularly true of the trade in slaves, which the royal lineage of Oyo itself dominated in the eighteenth century.[22] With slaves and the slave trade playing such an important role in the politics and economy of Oyo, it is no wonder that Oyo was particularly invested in the unfolding of events in the coastal area to its south, known as the Bight of Benin, or the Slave Coast, where the slave trade with Europeans dominated commercial activity in the seventeenth and eighteenth centuries.

SLAVE TRADING AND THE POLITICAL ECONOMY
OF COASTAL STATES

The first Europeans to arrive on the west African coast were the Portuguese, who had established a trading post with the Benin kingdom at Gwarto (Ughoton) by 1480. Initially, trade between Europeans and

African peoples centered on luxury goods such as textiles, pepper, and gold, with slaves making up only a small percentage of the overall trade. Slaves did not become an important aspect of the Atlantic trade until the discovery of the Americas and the establishment of plantation labor there from the sixteenth century, and slaves did not become the dominant item of Atlantic trade until later, in the seventeenth and eighteenth centuries.

The Bini initially were eager to trade with the Portuguese in non-human goods, but, with the rising demand for slaves in the first half of the sixteenth century, the *oba* of Benin severely restricted the sale of male slaves in 1550,[23] forcing the Portuguese and other European traders, notably the English and the Dutch, to search for other ports along the coast from which to purchase human cargo. The growth of slaving ports occurred both to the west of Benin, along what is known as the Bight of Benin, and to the east, in the Bight of Biafra, which stretched from the Niger delta to Calabar, in the extreme southeast of modern-day Nigeria. Major slaving ports along the Bight of Benin at different times included, from west to east, Grand and Little Popo, Whydah (Ouidah), Offra, Jakin, Epe, Apa, Porto Novo, Badagry, and Lagos. In the Bight of Biafra, three main slaving ports emerged. These were, from west to east, Elem Kalabari (also called New Calabar), Bonny, and Calabar (also known as Old Calabar).

The total numbers of slaves exported are difficult to calculate, but Lovejoy estimates that between 1600 and 1800 the ports of the Bight of Benin shipped out 1,473,100 slaves, with over 1.2 million of these slaves being dispatched in the eighteenth century alone.[24] In fact, between 1676 and 1730 the Bight of Benin shipped 730,000 slaves, a remarkable 42 percent of all the slaves taken from Africa during this period.[25] For the eighteenth century as a whole, the Bight of Benin was responsible for 20 percent of total slave exports from Africa. A similar expansion of the slave trade occurred in the Bight of Biafra in the eighteenth century. Prior to that century the Bight of Biafra had supplied some slaves to the European market, but probably fewer than 1,000 per year, mainly through Calabar.[26] Over the course of the eighteenth century, however, somewhere in the realm of 900,000 slaves were sold in the ports of the Bight of Biafra – roughly 15 percent of all the slaves taken from Africa during this period. Slave exports from the Bight of Biafra reached a peak of 175,400 in the 1780s, an average of 17,500 per year,[27] before exports were reduced again in the nineteenth century as a result of the British abolition of the transatlantic slave trade in 1807.

In both the Bight of Benin and the Bight of Biafra, slaves were sold at the coast by communities increasingly organized towards the specific end of selling slaves. Slave supplies came mostly from the hinterlands in both places, however. Slaves were procured through wars and raids by hinterland states in the Bight of Benin, particularly the large, centralized states of Dahomey and Oyo, which raided their weaker neighbors and each other for slaves. These slaves were then sold to coastal merchants, who in turn sold them to European traders. In the hinterlands of the Bight of Biafra, wars and raids were also common, but kidnappings, enslavements of criminals, and enslavements through the religious decree of a major hinterland oracle called Arochukwu also contributed in a major way to slave supplies. This rapid and exponential growth of the slave trade along the Bights of Benin and Biafra during the seventeenth and eighteenth centuries had significant impacts on the political, economic, and social structures of communities both along the coast of these regions and in their hinterlands.

Slaves in the Bight of Benin were sold to Europeans only on the coast. Europeans did not venture inland to capture or purchase slaves themselves. Most slaves were captured in wars and raids conducted by Africans in the interior and were then transported to the coast to be sold to European traders. In this way, trade with Europeans, although conducted only on the coast, also had a significant impact on the hinterlands. As the sale of slaves to Europeans became increasingly lucrative, particularly after the Dutch and English began to replace the Portuguese as dominant trading partners in the seventeenth century, the rulers of the coastal states of the Bight of Benin sought ways to control the trade in slaves in order to maximize their own profit and minimize that of the slave-procuring societies to the north. The coastal kingdoms of Hueda and Allada attempted to enforce their role as middlemen between the Europeans and hinterland states such as Oyo and Dahomey, just as the Oyo government enforced its role as middleman between Hausa traders and communities in the forest zone. Around 1717–18, both the King of Hueda, who controlled the important port of Whydah at the western edge of the Bight of Benin, and the King of Allada, who controlled the ports of Offra and Jakin further east, attempted to tighten their control of the slave trade in their respective regions. The King of Hueda forbade hinterland traders to sell slaves on the coast at all, forcing them to sell their slaves to a royal agent and thereby establishing a royal monopoly over the trade with Europeans. In Allada, the king did not outlaw all trade in slaves by hinterland merchants, but did reserve as his sole right the purchase of

Figure 2.2 A mother and child in Ibadan (collection of Roy Doron)

firearms and cowry shells, two of the most common items for which slaves were traded.[28]

This move by the coastal states to restrict access to European traders threatened the economies of the hinterland states, which accumulated many of the slaves who were later sold on the coast. By monopolizing the trade on the coast, the Kings of Hueda and Allada could effectively set the prices at which they bought slaves from the hinterland merchants and at which they would turn around and sell the same slaves to the Europeans. The royal monopoly of the coastal trade threatened to funnel the lion's share of the profit gained by the slave trade directly into the coffers of the ruling lineages of Hueda and Allada. The possibility of being cut off from the profits of the slave trade infuriated Dahomey, the nearest inland state and one of the chief providers of slaves to the coast. Dahomey's power had been on the rise for some time, and in 1724 King Agaja of Dahomey sent troops to conquer Allada, taking control of the port of Jakin. In 1727 Agaja attacked Hueda, bringing Whydah into Dahomey's fold and effectively ending the coastal monopoly of the slave trade.

Having gained control of the most important ports for European trade, Dahomey then attempted to restrict access to the ports by other hinterland states, most notably Oyo. The threat this posed to Oyo's commerce, which increasingly relied on the sale of slaves at the coast, caused Oyo to intervene against Dahomey. Between 1726 and 1730 Oyo embarked upon numerous expeditions against Dahomey, which resulted in Dahomey becoming tributary to Oyo. While this situation presumably made Oyo the most powerful state in the economic sphere of the Bight of Benin, it is clear that even Dahomey's tributary status did not result in free and unfettered access to Whydah for Oyo slave traders. Conflict between Dahomey and Oyo continued until the 1740s, and even as late as the 1780s it is reported that King Kplenga of Dahomey had attempted to reinstate a royal monopoly of the slave trade in the region.[29]

Although Oyo continued to use Whydah as its main center for slave trading until the 1770s, the instability brought about by the poor relations with Dahomey caused Oyo merchants and administrators to develop new routes to the coast further east, in an effort to circumvent Dahomey. Oyo merchants traded with Europeans at the ports of Allada until Dahomey destroyed Jakin in 1732, at which point the Oyo trade moved further east to Badagry and Porto Novo. Wishing to avoid the high prices for slaves imposed by Dahomian agents at Whydah, Europeans were more than willing to travel the extra distance to trade in the new markets further east. Both Badagry and Porto Novo immediately became embroiled in conflict with Dahomey, Oyo, and each other over matters of trade and tribute, and from the 1760s an increasing amount of trade moved yet further east, to the emerging port of Lagos, which became the major center of trade on the Bight of Benin in the nineteenth century.[30]

In the Bight of Biafra, the trade in slaves intensified only in the eighteenth century, with the three main ports of Bonny, Elem Kalabari, and Calabar accounting for roughly 90 percent of all trade with Europeans during this time. Despite the great profits available, the slave trade in the Bight of Biafra was not dominated by the activities of centralized states as it was in the Bight of Benin. The societies of southeastern Nigeria, where the Bight of Biafra is located, maintained their decentralized political structures, and, as a result, the slave trade tended to be dominated not by the states but by strong, relatively localized commercial interests. The lack of centralized states in the Bight of Biafra meant that slaves tended not to be procured through wars to the extent that they were in the Bight of Benin. Enslavement in the Bight of Biafra was much more commonly the result of judicial rulings, orders by oracles, and, above all, kidnapping. As in the Bight of Benin, most slave procurement in the Bight of Biafra took place in the hinterland, from where slaves were sold down the river Niger to slave traders in Bonny or Elem Kalabari, or down the Cross River to Calabar. Slave traders in the ports then sold the slaves to Europeans on the coast, as in the Bight of Benin.

The growth in the power, prestige, and wealth of slave traders in the Bight of Biafra occurred in different ways on the coast and in the hinterland, but the result in all places was a reorientation of power away from traditional political and religious authorities in favor of new forms of social organization centered on protecting the commercial interests of the slave trade, in which royal lineages were certainly involved but not necessarily in control. The two most important new social organizations were the house system and the secret society, the largest of which was known as Ekpe.

In the Ijo-speaking communities of the eastern Niger delta, the *canoe house* became the organizational unit responsible for conducting the slave trade with Europeans. A canoe house was a branch of a lineage that had developed enough wealth, most likely through the trade in slaves, to equip a war canoe of fifty soldiers that could be put at the disposal of the state in times of peril. The ability to equip a war canoe served two functions. First, it illustrated the power of the house – and, by extension, the house head – in the community, thereby establishing the house as an important actor in local affairs. Second, the war canoe could itself be used for the procurement of more slaves. Slaves could then be sold for more wealth or incorporated into the house. Those slaves incorporated into the house would help in the procurement of more slaves. Over time, slaves became assimilated into their new houses, and through marriage, or bravery in battle or slave raiding, could become fully integrated into the house, even to the point of becoming the house head.[31] House systems such as these had emerged in both Bonny and Elem Kalabari by the end of the seventeenth century.

In Calabar, the center of the Efik people, the house system functioned in much the same way, but with the added element of the secret society of Ekpe. Made up of elite members of the community, which mostly meant those who had attained wealth through the slave trade, the Ekpe society established laws and resolved legal disputes between members of the society in the interest of keeping credit and commerce flowing smoothly. The laws of Ekpe were religiously sanctioned by a forest spirit of the same name, and those who did not abide by the rules of the Ekpe society suffered crippling economic and physical consequences. Economic sanctions included boycotting an offender so that he could not trade, marking an offender's property so that it could not be used until the mark was removed (thereby freezing the offender's assets), destroying property, and imposing fines. On a physical level, Ekpe could arrest and detain

offenders and order executions.[32] Since slaves were an important part of
the commercial activities of the slave trade, they were also allowed to join
Ekpe, and could even achieve ranks of distinction within it. Ekpe became
the legal backbone of Calabar in the seventeenth century and had spread
into the hinterland by the early eighteenth century, becoming the legal
basis for the conduct of the slave trade in the interior as well.

As was the case in the Bight of Benin, the vast majority of slave procurement activities in the Bight of Biafra occurred in the interior. No group
has been more associated with the process of slave acquisition in the
hinterland of the Bight of Biafra during the eighteenth century than the Aro.
The Aro were a subgroup of the Igbo who became the leading commercial
actors in the interior of the Bight of Biafra through their association with
Arochukwu, an oracle of astounding power not only among Igbo groups but
also among the Ijaw and Ibibio. Also known as Ibiniukpabi, the oracle
inhabited a cave near a stream located at the bottom of a steep hillside in Aro
territory, and the Aro were its custodians. As a result of this exalted religious
duty the Aro termed themselves the "children of Chukwu [God]" and
thereby elevated their status relative to other groups in the region.

The oracle of Arochukwu was important to the Aro dominance of the
slave trade in the interior in two ways. First, the Aro proclamations of
religious title allowed them to perform commercial activities, most
profitable among which was the slave trade, without fear of molestation
from competing groups. Aro merchants were able to travel in any places
where people believed in the Arochukwu oracle and were able to control
commerce in these places through alliances with other elite political and
commercial actors, or through the establishment of new Aro communities, often called colonies, in the area. The Aro also adopted the Ekpe
secret society, which linked them with merchants throughout the interior,
thereby further cementing commercial connections. Moreover, the Aro
were missionaries for the Arochukwu oracle when they traveled, serving as
proxies for the oracle in judicial decisions, as well as helping individuals
to pray to the oracle for happiness and prosperity. In this way, the Aro
served as goodwill ambassadors for the oracle, establishing strong religious connections with outlying communities that then translated into
beneficial trading relationships. Through these methods the Aro became
the dominant purchasers of slaves in the area between the lower Niger
and the Cross River, and therefore the dominant suppliers of slaves to the
canoe houses of the coastal states.

The Arochukwu oracle also served to support Aro ascendancy in the
slave trade as a supplier of slaves in its own right. Individuals from

surrounding areas undertook to visit the oracle in search of justice or aid. Sometimes the oracle demanded a price for such assistance, usually in the form of slaves, whom it would "eat." Sometimes the oracle would demand slaves as the judicial penalty, and sometimes the oracle would enslave persons as part of its judgment. The slaves demanded by the oracle were then engulfed by the mouth of the cave, from where they were escorted to the Cross River, which led them to Calabar for ultimate sale to the Europeans.[33]

While surrounding groups stood in awe of the oracle at Arochukwu, the Aro themselves did not hold the oracle in such high regard. Rather, they manipulated the oracle to achieve commercial dominance in the region. According to Opoko and Obi-Ani, "[I]n the town of Arochukwu itself . . . the indigenes did not disguise the fact that the oracle was a fraud manipulated by some selfish, though entrepreneurial, individuals in their midst in order to exploit outsiders and hold them in perpetual awe."[34] Nevertheless, the Aro managed to keep the secret of the oracle to themselves, while simultaneously invoking the oracle to enhance their own authority and bring a sense of overarching law and order throughout a region known for its decentralized political institutions and high level of internal strife. The Aro also conducted investigations to make sure that the "decisions" of the oracle were reasonable and just, and therefore likely to perpetuate respect for the power of the oracle among the surrounding communities. The ploy worked, and the Aro applied the religious authority of the oracle to maintain a stranglehold on the slave market in the interior of the Bight of Biafra throughout the eighteenth and nineteenth centuries.

CONCLUSION

By the turn of the nineteenth century slavery and the slave trade with Europeans had become integral aspects of the economies of states and societies throughout the greater Nigerian area. The institution of slavery had existed in the states of the greater Nigerian area for a long time before 1500, although these slaves tended to be assimilated into their new societies and tended to perform tasks similar to the ones performed by free men and women. In the north, Borno and the Hausa states had sustained a trade in slaves with north Africa through the trans-Saharan trade routes for several centuries before 1500, and wars and slave raiding became an important aspect of the political wrangling between Borno and its neighbors and between the Hausa states and their neighbors in the savanna in the period between 1500 and 1800. Oyo became an important power in the period after 1650, serving as a middleman between the Hausa states and the markets of the coast. Slavery was an institution that was central to Oyo political power, and the slave trade fueled Oyo's military and economic might.

On the coast, two main centers for trade with Europeans emerged – in the Bight of Benin in the west and the Bight of Biafra in the east – and slaves had become the commodity of choice by the mid-seventeenth century. In the Bight of Benin, states attempted to control the slave trade throughout the eighteenth century, the result being frequent wars, political instability, and a movement of trade from west to east, as both Oyo and European traders attempted to circumvent the controls over the slave trade attempted by Dahomey. In the Bight of Biafra, no such states dominated the slave trade, but strong commercial interests did emerge. On the coast these interests took the form of canoe houses, while in the interior the Aro dominated the slave trade through their relationship to the powerful oracle, Arochukwu. The Ekpe secret society provided the regulation needed to maintain a smooth flow of trade.

Over the 1500–1800 period slavery became an increasingly ingrained institution in many states of the Nigerian region. The demand for slaves created by the growth of the Atlantic trade with Europeans resulted in the creation of ever larger supplies of slaves. These slaves were not only sold to the Europeans but were also integrated into the economic systems of the societies in the region in terms of agricultural production, domestic service, and further slave production through their employment in canoe houses or in the armies of various slaving states. By 1800 many states in the Nigerian region, with the notable exception of Benin, were heavily dependent on slavery and the slave trade for their political stability and economic wealth. This dependence on slavery and the slave trade would contribute greatly to the revolutionary changes of the nineteenth century, both in the south and in the north.

CHAPTER 3

Political and economic transformations in the nineteenth century

INTRODUCTION

The nineteenth century brought great changes to the states in the Nigerian region. Although social formations within the various geographical regions remained diverse, several relatively large, centralized states came to dominate geopolitical and economic dynamics during this time period. In the northern savanna zones, the Islamic jihad of Usman dan Fodio led to the establishment of the Sokoto Caliphate, an expansive state that brought under one government all the Hausa states, as well as some former provinces of Borno and lands that had once been under the control of Oyo and the Jukun states, in the south and southeast respectively. Although dan Fodio and his successors were never able to implement the ideal Islamic state that they sought to build, they had nevertheless reconfigured the political and cultural landscape of the northern savanna towards a primary identification with Islam by the time British colonial forces sacked Sokoto in 1903.

In the southern region of the greater Nigerian area, political and economic transformations occurred as well. In the southwest, the empire of Oyo fell in the early nineteenth century, ushering in an age of intra-regional warfare as new Yoruba states fought for dominance over the areas that had previously been stabilized by the rule of the *alafin*. Simultaneously, the British abolition of the slave trade in 1807 led to an overt attempt to redirect trade away from human cargo and towards items of "legitimate" commerce. In the south, palm oil became the primary article of "legitimate" commerce. The transition from a focus on slave trading to a focus on palm oil production was a slow process that brought about social and economic transitions over the course of the nineteenth century, on the coasts and in the interiors of the Bights of Benin and Biafra and in the Niger delta region. The slave trade itself persisted into the 1850s, however, and the institution of slavery expanded in many parts of these regions due to the labor-intensive nature of palm oil production. The social foundations and infrastructure that had existed at the height of the slave trade in the seventeenth and eighteenth centuries therefore persisted to a considerable degree in the era of "legitimate" commerce, although with increased access to international markets for small-scale producers, of whom many were women and slaves.

THE SOKOTO CALIPHATE

The Islamic jihad, led mostly by Fulani reformers, that resulted in the establishment of the Sokoto Caliphate in the savanna area of what is now northern Nigeria and southern Niger began officially in 1804 with Shehu Usman dan Fodio's *hijra* (flight) from Gobir to Gudu. During the first half of the nineteenth century the government of Sokoto consolidated the savanna states, which had warred almost continuously over the previous several centuries, under one administrative system. The Sokoto Caliphate was dedicated to purging the region of what it considered "mixed Islam" in an effort to recreate the perfect, pious society established in Arabia under the leadership of the Prophet Muhammad, the founder of the Islamic faith, in the seventh century AD. Although the Sokoto administration failed to bring about this perfect society, the political consolidation and cultural transformation that took place in the savanna region during the nineteenth century were nothing less than remarkable. By 1810 the caliphate had vanquished all the Hausa states and had also brought provinces that had previously been under the influence of Borno under a new Islamic government. Over the next two decades, emirates were added to the south and southeast of Hausaland.

Although the jihad that resulted in the creation of the Sokoto Caliphate began officially in 1804, it must be recognized that the revolution in the savanna at this time did not materialize out of thin air. The jihad had roots that stretched back well into the eighteenth century, in the efforts of Islamic scholars – most, but not all, of whom were ethnic Fulani – to urge reforms upon the states of the western and central Sudan, which they considered to be both pagan and corrupt. It will be remembered that, although Islam had been introduced into the savanna region of the greater Nigerian area no later than the fifteenth century, the religion had been adopted by the rulers of the various states mostly superficially. While some Hausa kings had adopted Islam, their successors often repudiated the religion, returning to indigenous religions for their spiritual guidance. Furthermore, even though some Hausa kings had no doubt been devout Muslims, they had not been able to entrench Islam throughout their kingdoms and had been more than willing to allow Islam to exist alongside indigenous religions and to be mixed with these religions for political reasons. Since one of the principal beliefs of fundamental Islam is that society and government should be ordered solely upon the teaching of the Prophet Muhammad, Fulani clerics of the eighteenth century accused the ruling elite of the western and central Sudan of illegitimacy because of their inability or unwillingness to adopt wholesale Islamic governing principles and social mores. Islamic reformist movements led two successful jihads in the western Sudan in the eighteenth century: the first was that of Alfa Ba in the Futa Jallon region of the Senegambia in 1727–8; the second was that of Abd al-Qadir in the Futa Toro region in the 1770s, a jihad that came to an end with Qadir's murder in 1796.[1]

At the same time that these jihads were occurring in the western Sudan, a similar Islamic reformist movement was growing in the central Sudan in the area of the Hausa states. By the 1780s a Fulani cleric named Usman dan Fodio had become the leader of this reform movement.[2] An immensely charismatic and influential orator, dan Fodio preached and taught throughout the region encompassed by the Hausa states of Gobir, Kebbi, Katsina, and Zamfara. In his travels, he developed a large following among Hausa, Fulani, and Tuareg residents, both peasant and learned. Although dan Fodio was a devout Muslim scholar who believed in the establishment of a state guided by the principles of classical Islam by any means necessary, his preferred method for most of his career was to achieve change through internal reform, not through war. He preached to the masses, who, he believed, practiced mixed Islam, on the proper methods of performing religious rites and duties. He also sought to raise awareness about the un-Islamic activities that he believed the Hausa ruling elite perpetrated. These sins included failure to adhere to the Islamic juridical code, the *shari'a*; levying types of taxes that were not listed as acceptable in the Quran; the enslavement of Muslims; and the corruption of leaders who demanded bribes for political favors, lived ostentatiously in lavish palaces, ignored the Islamic injunction against immodest dress, and did not adhere to Islamic dietary restrictions.[3] Despite the depth and breadth of these charges, dan Fodio believed that the system could be reformed peacefully from within, through pressure that he and his followers could exert on the ruling authorities of the Hausa states. Throughout the period from the 1770s until the outbreak of hostilities in 1804, dan Fodio lobbied tirelessly to transform the system from within, and in this he was relatively successful for a long while. From 1774 to 1785 dan Fodio urged Bawa, the Sultan of Gobir, to overturn excessive taxes, among other demands, which Bawa finally agreed to do in 1785 when it was clear that dan Fodio's popularity was on the rise.[4]

Despite these concessions, the governing elite of Gobir certainly saw dan Fodio's increasingly popular movement more as a threat to their own power base than as a partnership in bringing about much-needed Islamic reforms. Indeed, after such a long period of refusal, Bawa, although he was himself a proclaimed Muslim and Gobir was a nominally Muslim state, probably acquiesced to dan Fodio's demands less out of any sincere spiritual repentance than out of a desire to avoid further confrontation. In the decades after Bawa's reforms, subsequent sultans in Gobir began to combat dan Fodio's movement more and more openly. In 1801 Sultan Bunu claimed that only those subjects of Gobir whose fathers had been Muslim could themselves claim to be Muslim, thereby attempting to reduce the size of dan Fodio's movement, which was now large enough to be known simply as "the Community." Bunu also sought to curb fundamentalist Islamic cultural influence in Gobir by prohibiting men from wearing turbans and women from wearing veils.[5] Two years later, upon Bunu's death, Yunfa, a former pupil of dan Fodio's, succeeded to the office of sultan in Gobir. Dan Fodio had been instrumental in securing Yunfa's succession and expected Yunfa's administration to adopt many of his reforms. This was not to be, however, as Yunfa soon came to see dan Fodio as a threat to his power, even going so far as to make an attempt on dan Fodio's life.

The Community did not take kindly to Yunfa's belligerent attitude and many of its members tried to emigrate from Gobir and Gobir-controlled regions. One particular group, under Abd al-Salam, moved to Kebbi, arousing the ire of Yunfa, who sent an expeditionary force to bring them back forcibly, in the process killing many and destroying the town in which they had settled. Yunfa then threatened dan Fodio with similar treatment if he did not leave Gobir immediately. Dan Fodio obliged, moving west to Gudu on February 21, 1804. Calling this move his *hijra*, after the Prophet Muhammad's famed flight from Mecca to Medina, dan Fodio now prepared his followers for the coming jihad against recalcitrant unbelievers such as Yunfa.[6]

Those who believed in dan Fodio's message of Islamic reform, as well as subjects of Hausa states who were simply fed up with what they considered oppressive misgovernance, flocked to dan Fodio's aid. War with Gobir began almost immediately, and ended in 1808 with the defeat of Yunfa and the retreat of the Gobir ruling class to the north. The jihad also encompassed other parts of Hausaland, and, by 1810, most of the Hausa states, which had existed independently for hundreds of years, had come under the control of the newly established Islamic caliphate, the metropolitan center of which encompassed the former states of Gobir, Zamfara, and Kebbi, where dan Fodio's Community had been based. Also coming under the purview of the newly established caliphate were the former Hausa states of Kano, Katsina, and Zazzau, as well as several territories which had previously been administered by Borno. The jihad continued to the southeast and south of Hausaland, where, by the 1830s, the Sokoto Caliphate had taken control of much of the territory formerly ruled by the Jukun and Nupe, and toppled the Oyo empire, bringing the territory around Oyo Ile into the new emirate of Ilorin. Thus, in the space of just over five years, the religious movement of Usman dan Fodio had united all of previously fragmented Hausaland under one Islamic state, and within thirty years this became one of the largest states ever established in west Africa.

Immediately after the new Islamic state had been consolidated, dan Fodio retired from the running of the caliphate to focus on spiritual and scholarly concerns. Although he retained the title of caliph, or shehu (sheikh), as he was more commonly called, dan Fodio delegated the day-to-day administration to his son, Muhammadu Bello, and his brother, Abdullahi. The caliphate was divided into two parts, the larger, eastern portion ruled by Bello from the town of Sokoto, and the western portion overseen by Abdullahi at Gwandu. Upon dan Fodio's death in 1817 Bello was named the new caliph. It was Bello who undertook the onerous task of developing the administrative mechanism by which the unwieldy caliphate would be governed.

The strategic method that dan Fodio had utilized to extend the jihad rapidly had been to name any leader who took up the fight in his name as his "flag-bearer," his sanctioned proxy in whatever region he happened to be operating. When these "flag-bearers" won, they were instantly named the new rulers of the region they had conquered. In many cases, this meant little more than replacing the previous ruler with themselves, leaving the extant political structures more or less intact. As such, the Sokoto Caliphate became a conglomeration of decentralized provinces, called emirates, run by almost entirely independent emirs. These emirs all claimed allegiance to the caliph and sent annual tribute to Sokoto or Gwandu, depending on their location. New emirs had to be approved by the caliph; the caliph almost always approved of whoever had been locally

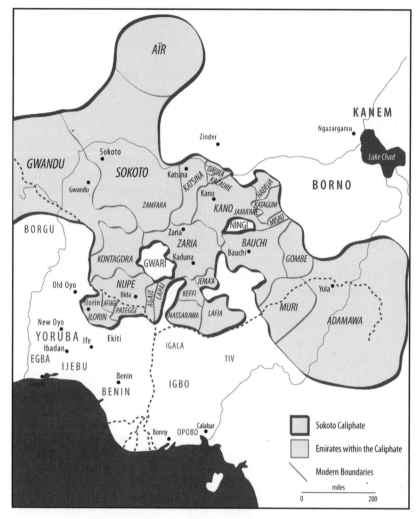

Map 3.1 The Sokoto Caliphate at its greatest territorial limits
(courtesy Saverance Publishing Services)

nominated, however, and rarely interfered in the administration of the
emirates in any significant fashion.[7]

While this process served dan Fodio's purposes well, there were
obvious drawbacks that Bello had to address in the early years of his
administration. First, while dan Fodio assumed that all the "flag-bearers"
who took up the jihad on his behalf did so out of religious zeal for a pure,

Islamic society, this was not necessarily the case; and it turned out that many had taken up the jihad for worldly gain. Second, even among those who had undertaken the jihad for spiritual reasons, there was no guarantee that subsequent generations of emirs would share the same religious sentiment and would not rule the emirate for their own personal gain. Indeed, cracks in the edifice of the Sokoto structure began to emerge soon after dan Fodio's death, when Abd al-Salam, the follower who had instigated the jihad with his emigration from Gobir, rebelled against the caliphate in 1817 because he was unhappy with the small amount of territory he had been given to govern.[8] Although Abd al-Salam was killed and the rebellion defeated, the revolt by one of the earliest political figures of the jihad illustrated the tenuous nature of a large, decentralized state presumably based on the principles of purified Islam and not on the accumulation of power, prestige, or wealth.

In order to establish some kind of central authority over the emirates of the caliphate, Bello developed several new governing strategies. First, he instituted the *kofa* system to improve communication between the center and the emirates. *Kofas* served much the same purpose that the *asoju* did for the *alafin* of Oyo.[9] *Kofas* were assigned to individual emirs and were responsible for keeping abreast of the affairs of that emirate and for relaying pertinent information back to the caliph in Sokoto. They advised the caliph on matters within their emirate and served as intermediaries between emirs and the caliph, insofar as requests made by the emirs to the caliph were funneled through the *kofa*. *Kofas* were also responsible for collecting the required tribute from the emirs, for which they were rewarded with a share.[10] Through the *kofa* system, Bello imposed the presence of the central governing authority even if he rarely used the *kofas* to exert coercive control over the emirs. Since Bello chose *kofas* from his own entourage, he could be sure that they shared his religious convictions and served for the purpose of establishing a purified Islamic state, as opposed to the emirs, whom he did not choose directly and whose motives were often suspect.

Another way in which Bello curbed the power of the emirates and amplified his central authority was through the establishment of *ribats* throughout the provinces. The *ribat* was a fortress, originally utilized by the Prophet Muhammad to secure the boundaries between Dar al-Islam (the land of Islam) and Dar al-Harb (the land of war) or Dar al-Kufr (the land of non-believers). Bello augmented the system of the Prophet slightly, however, in that he placed *ribats* not only on the frontiers of the caliphate but also well within its borders. Thus, through their physical presence alone, *ribats* served the purpose of illustrating the power of the caliph to the emirs and to local populations alike, as well as indicating to all the people in the region that they were protected by that caliph as inhabitants of Dar al-Islam. The *ribats* also became centers of Islamic culture in the regions where they were established. While they housed a garrison for military purposes, they also housed local *ulama*, or learned Muslims, who preached, prayed, and conducted Islamic ceremonies such as weddings and funerals. Through the founding of *ribats*, Bello brought the preachings and practices of Islam closer to his subjects, making the religion more familiar and more palatable to communities that had previously been inclined to practice Islam in conjunction with indigenous religions, if they had been inclined to practice Islam at all. The military and scholarly postings to *ribats* were also made by Bello, ensuring yet again that he had loyal and like-minded allies in place to counteract the possible machinations of restless emirs.[11]

These administrative tools helped Bello to stabilize the caliphate under his own strong, individual rule; they were not enough to guarantee long-term security or stability over all the territories of the caliphate, however. The defeated Hausa kings, of Gobir and Kebbi in particular, continued to fight against the caliphate from their reconstituted positions to the north. Territorial disputes with Borno to the east were ongoing, and the southern emirates were still attempting to take the jihad further into non-Muslim territories. In addition to the external threats and conflicts that continually beset the caliphate, internal strife grew as well. Although Bello had established enough caliphal authority over the emirates to keep the caliphate mostly stable, the power of the caliph did not spread evenly or thoroughly throughout the caliphate. Tensions between Sokoto and some emirates became heightened, particularly after Bello's death in 1837. While in certain emirates the caliph utilized his authority strongly, as in Zaria, where in the 1840s alone the caliph deposed several emirs for unwillingness to accept policies dictated from Sokoto,[12] in other areas the caliph was unable to quash open revolts against his authority. Two such revolts were the uprising of Emir Buhari of Hadeija from 1851 to 1863, and the rebellion of Yusuf bin Abdullah, which touched off the Kano civil war, which lasted from 1893 to 1895.

The story of Buhari's uprising is one of a quest for personal power and wealth at the expense of the caliphate. Buhari had become Emir of Hadeija, one of the emirates carved out of what had been Borno territory, around 1848. Buhari's main goal as emir was to maintain power at any cost. He thus developed a reputation for ruthlessness in his own cause, even going so far as to have his primary political opponent, a cousin

Figure 3.1 The Kano Mosque horsemen (collection of Jonathan T. Reynolds)

named Auyo Nalara, assassinated. When the caliph, Aliyu Baba, learned of Buhari's misdeeds, he summoned Buhari to defend himself. When Buhari refused to present himself before the caliph, Aliyu Baba deposed him. Buhari then renounced the authority of the caliph and withdrew to the northeast, where he gained succor and support from Borno. In 1851 he attacked and reclaimed Hadeija. He then initiated a twelve-year assault on neighboring emirates loyal to the caliph. Buhari frequently raided communities in the region, taking booty and slaves through which he enriched himself. At no point between 1851 and 1863, when Buhari died, was Sokoto able to oust him and reclaim Hadeija. After Buhari's death, however, Hadeija was reincorporated into the Sokoto Caliphate.[13]

The rebellion of Yusuf bin Abdullahi in Kano, unlike that of Buhari, was centered less in a desire for personal aggrandizement than in a legitimate succession dispute. After the death of the Emir of Kano, whose name was Muhammad Bello (not to be confused with the former caliph), in 1893, Kano residents expected the widely popular Yusuf b. Abdullahi to be named the next emir. Caliph Abdurrahman, however, chose the emir's elder son, Tukur, instead. This decision was accepted neither by Yusuf nor by a large percentage of Kano's residents, who followed Yusuf out of Kano to Takai, where Yusuf attempted to set up his own government.

Abdurrahman ordered military action against Yusuf. Since Sokoto had no standing army, however, the caliph's personal ability to conduct military expeditions was limited without help from surrounding emirates. Emirs were reluctant to send aid to the caliph in this situation, as many believed that the appointment of Tukur had been a poor decision. In 1894 Yusuf defeated Tukur's army but died himself shortly thereafter. Yusuf's brother, Aliyu, succeeded him and carried on the fight against Tukur, capturing Kano later the same year. Tukur fled, but was captured and killed in 1895. At this point, with both Tukur and Yusuf dead, Abdurrahman appointed Aliyu the next Emir of Kano, thus ending the dispute and satisfying both the Kano residents and the emirs who believed that injustice had been done.[14]

These two examples are given to illustrate that, despite the fact that the Sokoto Caliphate was a large state with a central authority, the central authority was often tenuous and expressed unevenly over time and space. The caliph could not necessarily impose his will upon the emirates; often he needed their support to implement his own policy decisions. The relative weakness of the caliph, as illustrated by events such as Buhari's uprising and the Kano civil war, has been used by some authors to portray the Sokoto Caliphate as essentially a failed revolution that was unable to live up to the Islamic ideals set forth by Usman dan Fodio.[15] According to this argument, men such as Buhari demonstrated the underlying hypocrisies of the Sokoto revolution, proving that the thrust for power on the part of the Fulani was less about inculcating religious piety in government and society than it was about simply replacing Hausa leaders with themselves. From this perspective, the jihad was more of an ethnic conflict than a religiously inspired revolution. Adding fuel to the interpretation that the Fulani simply used Islam as a tool to usurp the Hausa monarchies was the fact that many of the reforms that the jihadists endorsed during the jihad were not carried out afterwards. Taxation and tribute continued; even the cattle tax that dan Fodio had argued was not sanctioned by the Quran was not outlawed after the jihad.[16] Concerns that Muslims had been enslaving Muslims under Hausa regimes were not addressed: in fact, evidence indicates that the number of slaves in the savanna actually increased under the Sokoto Caliphate as the jihad spread to new regions. Sokoto was even willing to accept slaves as part of the requisite annual tribute it received from its emirates.[17]

This issue of who could legitimately be raided and enslaved as part of the jihad actually provoked something of a theological debate between the triumvirate of dan Fodio, Bello, and Abdullahi, and al-Kanemi, the

Muslim warlord who effectively mobilized Borno's forces to repel the Fulani jihadists in the Lake Chad region. Borno itself had been highly Islamized since as early as the eleventh century, yet al-Kanemi argued that Fulani raids continually intruded upon his territory in the name of jihad. Since he and his people were Muslim, al-Kanemi argued, the raiders were the ones in breach of the Islamic code for their actions. Bello, who was responsible for most of the Sokoto correspondence on this issue, argued that al-Kanemi's forces were helping the Hausa against the jihad, were threatening jihadists' lives and property, and were engaging in heathen practices such as worshipping gods and fetishes other than Allah,[18] all of which made al-Kanemi's people no better than the non-believers and corrupted Muslims against whom the jihad was directed. The war with Borno reached a stalemate by 1812, but the ideological debate that it evoked illustrated further the philosophical complexities upon which the Sokoto Caliphate was based. The question over what defined acceptable Islamic practice was one that was never fully resolved during the existence of the Sokoto regime.

These gray areas in the ideology of the revolution, coupled with the indication that many of the emirs did not seem as dedicated to the fundamentalist beliefs of the jihad as were the clerical leaders such as dan Fodio and Bello, fueled the argument by later scholars that the Sokoto revolution was more of a Fulani uprising than an Islamic one.[19] Indeed, all but one of the original "flag-bearers" who became the first emirs of the Sokoto Caliphate were Fulani, and not Hausa, in ethnic origin. This apparently compelling evidence for the ethnic basis of the revolution is easily complicated, however.[20] In fact, although most of the leadership of the jihad was Fulani, the progenitors of the revolution, such as dan Fodio and Bello, rarely mentioned ethnicity in their writings, focusing much more heavily on the Islamic nature of their movement. This indicates that, among those who instigated the revolution, the religious transformation of government and society was the primary goal.[21]

The fact that most of the leadership was Fulani can be explained in less conspiratorial terms. As a Fulani himself, dan Fodio could tap into a community of itinerant Fulani pastoralists who had spread themselves across the savannas over the course of several centuries. Thus, when the call for jihad went out, the Fulani were the first to hear it and the first to mount an attack.[22] Added to this, any non-Fulani with the means to launch jihad very probably already had vested interests in the status quo represented by the Hausa rulers and, as such, were unlikely to take up arms against the established regime.[23] Although the Fulani had lived in the savanna region in and around the Hausa states for several centuries, they had remained mostly pastoralist and had not become integrated into the government apparatus of the local states to any significant degree. This made them more likely candidates to lead a revolution than Hausas, who were to one extent or another bound up with the existing power structure. As a final point, it must be noted that, even though the leadership of the jihad was primarily Fulani, the make-up of "the Community" was ethnically mixed, containing Fulani, Hausa, and Tuareg followers of dan Fodio.[24]

Although it cannot be denied that the Islamic ideals for which dan Fodio initiated the revolution were not shared by all his Fulani emirs, this alone cannot be used as evidence that the Sokoto Caliphate ultimately failed in its endeavor to entrench Islam in its subject population. On the political level, it is clear that the revolution remained incomplete, as Fulani emirs in many cases simply picked up where Hausa kings left off. On the economic and cultural levels, however, it is evident that the leadership of Sokoto had a profound impact. Economically, the Hausa states, which had fought each other for centuries over control of trade routes, now developed their agriculture and markets without fear of raids or wars in most places. Hausa states were able to trade freely with each other as well since they were now regulated by the same overarching political system. The boundaries of Hausa commercial activities also expanded along with the jihad, as trade followed the flag. The growth of the economy of the savannas under the Sokoto Caliphate had negative consequences, however, for much of the peasantry. Slave raiding continued and even increased in some places during the nineteenth century. Large-scale plantations, often worked by slave labor, proliferated along the savannas of the Sokoto Caliphate in the nineteenth century. The jihad also resulted in massive population movements, as long-standing urban areas were destroyed and new ones were built, including Sokoto itself.

Culturally, local populations across the Sokoto Caliphate increasingly came to identify themselves primarily as Muslims and only secondarily as citizens of their local emirates. The presence of an overarching Sokoto government that defined itself in classical Islamic terms, even though it retained to a great extent the non-Islamic political structures of the Hausa kings, left the impression on many that they lived in an Islamic state and therefore they were all unified by a common religion. Contributing to the growth of an Islamic identity among the masses in the savanna were the spread of Islamic culture through Bello's *ribats*, the expansion of Islamic primary education throughout the caliphate – which resulted in an increase in Arabic literacy – and an expansion in Islamic architecture and dress. Music and lyrical verse increasingly took the form of panegyrics to the Prophet Muhammad and to the architects of the Sokoto Caliphate, dan Fodio in particular, often in the vernacular Hausa language.[25] The *shari'a* became the basis for jurisprudence across the caliphate.[26] Although traditional Hausa legal customs, such as those regulating conflict resolution, courtship, and marriage, among others, continued to exist, they became infused with Islamic justifications. As Mary Wren Bivins has put it:

> The assimilation of normative Islam and, ultimately, Shari'a into the habits and thoughts of Hausa people enjoyed popularity as a topic of discussion in the tatsuniyoyi, where stereotypes of the teacher and the judge only thinly disguised the questions posed about these living symbols of Islamic authenticity and authority. The broader question is how Hausa Muslims were educated in their obligations as Believers and motivated to use the formal instruments of Shari'a to solve personal problems. For Hausa Muslims Shari'a did not exercise complete and monolithic control over litigation, but was one of several possibilities for finding legal relief. The choice was real, personal, and most likely weighed on the balance of personal experience and social identity as often as that of faith.[27]

Indications such as Bivins' that Islam did not become the monolithic source of social organization and identity formation in the nineteenth century have led many scholars to argue that the Islamic revolution in the Sokoto Caliphate remained unrealized. Sultans and emirs, particularly after Bello's time, did abandon the religious motivations of the jihad for more materialistic goals, therefore limiting the extent to which the local populations attained a "true" experience of an Islamic state and a true conversion of identity.[28] Indeed, differing interpretations of the ideal Islamic state developed within the caliphate, with Sufi sects such as the Qadiriyya and Tijaniyya competing for adherents to their particular brands of mysticism. Over time, emirs throughout the caliphate enforced elements of *shari'a* law differently, if at all, and sultans eventually reintroduced some of the taxes deemed un-Islamic by dan Fodio. The Islamic revolution was by no means completed or perfected under the Sokoto Caliphate. Nevertheless, Islam permeated the lifestyles and values of the savannas to a greater extent than at any time previously. By the time Sokoto fell to British colonial forces in 1903 most of the savanna region of what is now northern Nigeria was more culturally united than at any other time in its history, and this unity was based heavily on a shared experience of life in an Islamic state.

POLITICAL AND ECONOMIC TRANSFORMATIONS
IN THE SOUTH

The southern regions of the greater Nigerian area also saw a considerable amount of change in the nineteenth century. The century began with Oyo as the major power in the southwest and a major supplier of slaves to the coastal ports of Porto Novo and Lagos. Internal conflicts in the early nineteenth century resulted in Oyo's collapse by the 1830s, however. The nineteenth century became a century of wars in the region, as Yoruba states previously held in check by the might of Oyo fought to fill the power vacuum created by Oyo's decline.

The period between 1790 and 1830 saw a gradual whittling away of Oyo's power, both at the center in Oyo Ile and in the many provinces that Oyo had previously dominated. The beginning of the decline of Oyo can be dated as early as the 1750s, when the crisis between the *alafin* and the Oyo Mesi reached its crescendo in the usurpation of the *alafin*'s authority by Basorun Gaha. Although Gaha was eventually laid low and the office and powers of the *alafin* were restored to Abiodun in 1774, the political tensions between the *alafin* and the Oyo Mesi were not resolved, and the *alafin*'s control was never again as strong as it had been in the seventeenth and early eighteenth centuries. Although tensions between the *alafin* and the Oyo Mesi continued to exist, perhaps the most damaging blow to the *alafin*'s power base came from the revolt of Afonja, who held the title of *are ona kakanfo*. The *are ona kakanfo* was the commander-in-chief of the provincial army and one of the most powerful and important officers in the *alafin*'s retinue. Afonja, who was also the ruler of Ilorin, a provincial town to the southeast of Oyo Ile, conspired with other Oyo chiefs to remove Abiodun's successor, Alafin Awole, from power by military means. Afonja's motives were partly a lack of belief in the administrative capabilities of Awole and partly a personal desire for the position of *alafin*. Afonja's forces took Oyo Ile in 1796 and forced Awole to commit suicide. Afonja no doubt believed that he would be named the next *alafin* for his role in Awole's deposition; the Oyo Mesi chose instead a prince named Adebo, however. Perceiving this as a slap in the face, Afonja declared his independence from Oyo and retired to Ilorin, from where he mounted an all-out offensive against Oyo Ile and nearby provinces.

Afonja's rebellion remained stagnant for twenty years. While Oyo was not able to defeat him and bring Ilorin back under its control, neither was Afonja able to inflict any serious defeats on Oyo. In 1817, however, Afonja sought and received aid from Muslims keen on extending the jihad of Usman dan Fodio into Oyo territory. Islam had made gains in Oyo territory from at least the sixteenth century, both among the free population and as the professed religion of many of the Hausa slaves who had been sold to Oyo over time. Although Afonja was not a Muslim himself he saw the benefits to be gained by association with the jihad, and, as a result, he called on Muslims in Oyo to revolt. The revolt turned the tables in Afonja's favor initially, but he soon became wary of his Fulani allies and ordered them out of Ilorin. The Fulani, under the leadership of Abd al-Salam, in turn revolted against Afonja, killing him in 1823 and incorporating Ilorin into the Sokoto Caliphate, with Abd al-Salam as the first Emir of Ilorin.

At the same time that these political crises near the center were occurring, Oyo was also losing control of its outlying provinces. By the 1790s this process was already well under way, and, largely because of instability at and around the capital, Oyo could do little to prevent the losses. In fact, Oyo had begun to lose military dominance as early as the 1780s, when it suffered defeats at the hands of both Borgu and Nupe, its closest neighbors in the savanna region. Nupe in particular was a rising power by the early nineteenth century, and had extended its raids to its north and east. The Nupe lands were eventually incorporated into the Sokoto Caliphate, becoming the emirates of Bida, Agaie, Lapai, Lafiagi, and Tsonga.[29] So dire was the situation that some traditions say Oyo was paying tribute to Nupe by 1790.[30] As the relative weakness of Oyo became recognized, other challenges to Oyo control were soon mounted. The Egba, located in the area west of Ife and north of Lagos, had revolted and gained independence from Oyo by around 1796. Although some of this territory later came back under Oyo's rule, most of it did not. Around 1817 Oyo's main ally, Owu, was besieged by Ife and Ijebu forces, and was ultimately razed around 1822. Dahomey continued to put up resistance to Oyo's control of routes to the coast, and had cut off Oyo's access to Porto Novo by 1807, forcing Oyo to move its slaves further east, to Lagos, for sale. A full-scale revolt by Dahomey occurred later, in 1823, resulting in the termination of the tributary relationship with Oyo. By 1830 Egbado, Oyo's most southwesterly province, located to the west of Egbaland, had fallen to the Dahomians, putting a final end to Oyo's influence in the forest zone south of its capital of Oyo Ile.[31]

By the 1820s Oyo had lost control of its routes to the sea, by which it partook of trade in slaves and other items with European merchants. Meanwhile, the city of Oyo Ile itself was under constant attack from

Sokoto forces based in Ilorin. Under such conditions Oyo could no longer afford to buy the horses that made up its cavalry, and, in any case, the slaves upon whose talents the cavalry was built had been largely Hausa imports who were now in direct opposition to Oyo. By 1833 Ilorin had sacked Oyo Ile and taken over most of the other important towns in its vicinity.

The collapse of Oyo led to a surge of refugees heading south into the forest, where the cavalry of Ilorin could not reach them. Here the royal regime of Oyo reconstituted itself, although in a much diminished capacity, at New Oyo. Other refugees from Oyo founded new states in the forest and began to battle to fill the political vacuum created by the fall of Oyo. Of these, the city states of Ibadan and Ijaye became the most powerful. Both cities had been founded in the 1820s by early refugees from Oyo. While these cities had become the new power centers in the Yoruba region by the 1830s, they each still maintained technical allegiance to the *alafin* of Oyo, even though they functioned as completely autonomous entities with their own individualized political systems. Ijaye developed a monarchical institution of its own with hereditary inheritance; Ibadan developed into something of a military meritocracy, where any capable commander could assume some stake in the governance of the city and its growing dependencies. Egba refugees from the Owu war also moved south and west to found the city of Abeokuta, which quickly grew into a bustling urban center.

The movement of refugees and the reorientation of political and military power after the fall of Oyo led to a series of protracted wars between Yoruba states.[32] In these wars, Ibadan emerged as the dominant power. In 1840 Ibadan successfully confronted the forces of Ilorin at Ogbomosho, putting an end to the southward push of the Sokoto jihadists. Having fought off Ilorin, Ibadan then turned its attention to Ijaye, its rival to the west, defeating it in 1862. Having gained control of its northern and western fronts, Ibadan then turned its gaze south in an effort to regain access to the sea through Egba and Ijebu lands. Moves against the Egba and Ijebu resulted in all-out war in Yorubaland beginning in 1877, when forces from Egba, Ijebu, Ekiti, Ijesa, and Ife all joined to fight against Ibadan domination in what has been dubbed the Ekitiparapo War. The state of warfare lasted for sixteen years, and was ended only with the negotiation of peace in 1886 by the British, who used the opportunity to gain a foothold in Yorubaland. British intervention ultimately resulted in the consolidation of a protectorate, which initiated colonial rule in the region in 1893.

The Yoruba wars of the nineteenth century were more than a political phenomenon. They also had significant social and cultural implications. The large numbers of refugees created by these wars migrated to all parts of Yorubaland, significantly altering the demographic make-up of the region. As a result, cultural practices diffused throughout the region with them. For instance, as Ade Ajayi has noted, Oyo refugees brought with them wherever they went practices such as "the Oyo narrow male-operated loom as opposed to the women's broad loom, clothed *egungun* as opposed to those covered with grass or palm fronds, drums slung from the shoulder as opposed to standing drums, and the royal cult of Sango."[33] Although fleeing the Islamic jihad of Ilorin, many of the Oyo refugees were themselves Muslim, and their movement south meant more Islamic activity in the forest zone as a result.

Another major sociocultural transformation in nineteenth-century Yorubaland was rapid urbanization. Although the Yoruba had long been an urban people in comparison to most west African groups, the exigencies of almost constant warfare intensified this trend significantly in the nineteenth century. It became important for people to move to cities for several reasons. First, they moved to cities to avoid raids by rival armies. Second, they moved to cities in order to take advantage of strength in numbers. Third, cities developed walls and maintained a military presence, making them more defensible positions and therefore more attractive to refugees wishing to avoid capture and possible enslavement by enemy armies.

From a military standpoint, the Yoruba wars of the nineteenth century are also significant because they represent the first time that firearms were used in large numbers in the region. As noted previously, Oyo's power had been based primarily on the use of cavalry; in the forest zone, however, the tsetse fly and dense foliage made the maintenance and employment of cavalry impossible. To balance this tactical disadvantage, the new Yoruba powers in the forest zone began to use European firearms in warfare in significant numbers for the first time.

At the same time that the wars between the Yoruba states in the southwest were occurring, transformations in the economic structure of both the southwest and the southeast were also under way. In 1800 the slave trade was still the most important aspect of relations with the Europeans on the coast, both in the Bight of Benin and in the Bight of Biafra. The British abolished the slave trade in 1807, however.[34] While this did not initially affect the volume of the slave traffic out of the bights to any great extent, British naval security on the coasts and a decrease in demand for slaves in the Americas reduced the transatlantic slave trade to negligible levels by 1850. In its place, the British promoted what they called "legitimate commerce," by which they meant trade in non-human commodities, such as gold or agricultural products. Palm oil and, later, palm kernels became by far the most important commodities traded in the southern Nigerian area by the 1840s.

Palm oil is made from the fruit of the oil palm tree, which comes in two varieties, *Elaeis oleifera* and *Elaeis guineensis*, the latter being indigenous to western and central Africa. The southern, forested region of southern Nigeria is home to the largest and densest accumulation of oil palms in the world, making the region a natural source for an expansion in the external trade in palm oil. Palm oil had been a staple food product in the region for many centuries because of its palatable taste and high nutritional value, and thus there had existed an internal trade within the Nigerian region long before the nineteenth century. An external trade in palm oil also existed alongside the transatlantic slave trade, as merchants sold large quantities of palm oil to Europeans to feed their chattel cargo on the long voyage to the Americas.

Palm oil exports had been on the increase well before the abolition of the transatlantic slave trade. In fact, palm oil exports from west Africa were on the rise from the late eighteenth century, well before the abolition of the slave trade. British merchants bought increasing amounts of palm oil not only to sustain slaves on the middle passage but also for direct export to the United Kingdom, where palm oil was becoming valuable as a fatty substance from which candles, soap, and industrial lubricants could be made. By the 1780s Liverpool, in England, was importing an average of 40 tons of palm oil each year, most of which came from the west coast of Africa. In 1815, only eight years after the abolition of the slave trade, the United Kingdom imported over 2,000 tons of palm oil from west Africa. Of this, 1,200 tons came from Old Calabar on the Bight of Benin.[35] For the remainder of the century, most of the palm products exported to the United Kingdom came from the Bight of Biafra and, to a lesser extent, from the Bight of Benin. The Bight of Biafra was by far the most productive region for palm oil exports, in no small part because its hinterland held the densest population of oil palms in all of west Africa. By the 1840s Bonny had outstripped Old Calabar as the largest exporter of palm oil. Combined, these two ports shipped out over 12,000 tons of palm oil per year in the 1840s, and by the 1850s this number had risen to over 20,000 tons, which accounted for two-thirds of all the palm oil exported to the United Kingdom from west Africa at this time.[36]

Figure 3.2 A cloth-dyer in Kano (collection of Jonathan T. Reynolds)

The exponential increase in the growth of the palm oil trade, particularly after 1815, has led to the conclusion that its growth was somehow related to a decline in the slave trade after its abolition. This interpretation is in no small part influenced by the fact that British officials themselves promoted palm oil as a "legitimate" article of trade capable of replacing slaves. The conclusion that increased palm oil exports were linked to the reduction of slave exports is based on the assumption that the transatlantic slave trade declined rapidly after its official abolition by the United Kingdom, however. This is simply not true. At the same time that the palm oil trade was increasing so rapidly, the slave trade continued to exist and even thrive in some places. For instance, in the 1820s, more than a decade after the official abolition of the slave trade by the United Kingdom, the Bight of Benin exported roughly 115,000 slaves, while the Bight of Biafra exported over 127,000 – numbers slightly lower than, but comparable to, the volume of trade in the second half of the eighteenth century. In fact, between 1800 and 1867 as many as a million slaves may have gone through the ports on the Bights of Benin and Biafra, even though the slave trade was technically illegal for the vast majority of these years.[37] The slave trade declined to marginal levels only after 1850, as a result of a combination of factors, the most significant of which were the increased vigilance of British antislavery naval activities off the coast and the abolition of the slave trade by several of the largest markets in the Americas, most notably Brazil, which outlawed further importation of slaves in 1850, thereby reducing the demand for fresh slaves from Africa.[38] Thus, it must be concluded that, in the first half of the nineteenth century, the palm oil trade expanded in spite of the continuation of the slave trade and not because of its decline.[39]

Production of palm oil was a labor-intensive process. First, a harvester had to climb the oil palm tree and pluck the palm fruit clusters. These were then taken home, where the palm nuts had to be individually separated from the core. The nuts then had to be cooked until they were soft enough for the oil to be squeezed from them. This was done in much the same way that wine is extracted from grapes: the nuts were placed in elevated vats and stomped, letting the oil run downhill into waiting containers. Using this method, 300 pounds of palm fruit were required in order to produce 36 pounds of palm oil. It has been estimated that it would take three to five days of labor for one person to produce one 36-pound tin of palm oil.[40]

The high labor load necessary for palm oil production resulted in significant changes to the socio-economic make-up of the southern zone of the Nigerian region.[41] Two different systems of labor organization emerged to produce palm oil. One of these systems was the plantation, which utilized slave labor in the production process. The other system was individual production in smallholdings, based primarily around a family unit. Slaves could be incorporated into this system as well, but in smaller numbers and in a manner similar to the assimilation-based slavery discussed in the previous chapter. In both systems, women, whether slave or free, were responsible for most of the labor associated with palm oil production.

Large-scale plantations for the production of palm oil were more common in the interior of the Bight of Benin than in that of the Bight of Biafra. As the transatlantic slave trade subsided, more and more slaves were diverted towards domestic use, for agricultural labor, as porters for "legitimate trade" articles, or for military purposes. Thus, not only did the promotion of "legitimate trade" fail to bring an end to the slave trade, but it actually increased the desirability of slaves within the domestic economy, which allowed the institution of slavery and the internal slave trade to persist quite openly until well into the twentieth century. In the southwest, the wars of the nineteenth century brought about a reappropriation of people, property, and land throughout the Yoruba region. Successful warlords were able to establish ownership of large tracts of land and large numbers of slaves as a result of their military conquests. Land and slaves were then often organized towards palm oil production.[42] One famous example of such a warlord was Kurumi, who took over Ijaye in 1829. By 1859 he is reported to have had over 300 wives and over 1,000 slaves, most of whom would have been in his service either as soldiers or as agricultural laborers on his expansive farmlands. Kurumi is just one example of many Yoruba warlords with similar wealth and power during the nineteenth century.[43]

Plantations also existed in the Bight of Biafra outside Old Calabar and in the hinterland regions. Plantation slaves in this region cultivated mostly food items for the local population, not palm oil for export.[44] The majority of the palm produce in the Niger delta region and in the Cross River area inland of the Bight of Biafra was supplied by smallholders. These were small-scale, family-based enterprises that produced palm oil from the fruits of trees located on their own plots of land. Unlike the slave trade, which required a relatively large outlay of capital and military capability, the palm oil trade exhibited relatively low barriers to entry. Anyone with enough labor to run a family farm could divert some of that labor to palm oil production, and, given the abundance of oil palm trees in the Bight of Biafra, many farmers were able to do just that. Although slaves could supplement family labor in these enterprises, they were used only in small numbers and only if the smallholder was successful enough to be able to afford to expand his or her operation. More commonly, smallholders would take multiple wives, who then engaged in much of the labor associated with palm oil production.

While men were generally responsible for the harvest of palm fruit, women did most of the remaining labor, including removing the palm nuts, cooking them, and extracting the oil. Women were also heavily engaged in the process of transporting palm oil to market and selling it to middlemen, who then transported the oil to the coast for sale to Europeans.[45] The ability of women to participate in the palm oil business marked another significant diversion from the slave trade, which, because of its militaristic nature, had been dominated by men. In fact, palm oil production became so dominated by women in the Biafran hinterland that coastal middlemen began extending credit to the wives of important men in the Ngwa-Igbo region of the interior.[46]

If the growth of the palm oil trade in the nineteenth century led to the greater involvement of women in commercial activities, it also offered opportunities for slaves to improve their lot. In parts of the Yoruba region, slaves were often allowed to engage in palm oil dealings on their own behalf, particularly after the British occupation of Lagos in 1851.[47] In the delta states and in the Bight of Biafra, slaves were able to gain power and prestige through trading in palm oil, just as they had through involvement in the slave trade. Perhaps the best example of this in the second half of the nineteenth century is Ja Ja, who spent his early life as a slave in one of the most important houses in Bonny. Born in 1821, Ja Ja developed a reputation as an excellent trader as a young man, so much so that he was able to buy his freedom, and, in 1863, he was named the head of his house, called Anna Pepple House, making him one of the most powerful men in Bonny. Ja Ja's rise to prominence had been based in the trade in palm oil, among other items, and, as head of his house, Ja Ja actively sought to extend his control over the palm oil markets. He did so partly by helping his own slaves to trade on their own account, and also by developing relationships of dependency with other houses in Bonny. Ja Ja's increasing wealth, power, and popularity were seen as a threat by other powerful house heads in Bonny, particularly Oko Jumbo, head of the House of Manilla Pepple. In 1869 Anna Pepple and Manilla Pepple went to war, with the result that Ja Ja evacuated Bonny and started his own state upriver at a site called Opobo. From Opobo, Ja Ja warred with Bonny. By 1872 Ja Ja had won the war. By depriving Bonny middlemen of access to the palm oil belts of the hinterland, Ja Ja quickly built Opobo into one of the leading ports for palm-oil exports.[48]

While this is an extreme example, Ja Ja's rise to power through trade in palm oil and other items is an indication of the doors that were open, however slightly, for slaves to achieve upward mobility through "legitimate" commerce. The commercial opportunities available to marginalized groups such as women, slaves, and smallholder farmers should not be seen as evidence of a widespread upheaval in the social order that had been developed during the heyday of the transatlantic slave trade. In fact, the simultaneous existence of the slave and palm oil trades from the 1780s through the 1850s allowed plenty of time for the groups empowered by centuries of slave trading to develop new strategies to maintain control over shifting economic markets.[49] It must be remembered that even Ja Ja rose to power through established power structures, gaining his authority and influence as the leader of a house that had attained its might through slave trading in the seventeenth and eighteenth centuries.

In fact, it was not uncommon for the same lineages, firms, or houses that had enriched themselves through the sale of human cargo to switch gears and continue to enrich themselves through trade in "legitimate" articles such as palm oil or other agricultural goods. Wealthy members of the Okonko societies in the southeast were able to do this, for instance, by dominating the labor supply. Since the production of palm oil was carried out mostly by dependants, wives, and slaves, wealthy men, who could afford more of all these, were able to build large-scale operations and thereby retain a significant percentage of the total market despite the rise of smallholders. Title-holders, many of whom had gained their titles as productive slave traders, were able to claim land rights over much of the territory on which oil palms grew, thereby limiting smallholders' access and organizing the production of palm oil towards their own ends.

Slave traders had also come to dominate the interior trading routes. These same routes were also used to transport palm oil, thereby giving the already privileged classes an advantage in the distribution of palm oil as well.[50] In Calabar, the Ekpe society was able to incorporate successful palm oil traders, including slaves, in a way that allowed Ekpe to remain the most powerful social and economic institution in Calabar even after the slave trade had declined to negligible levels.[51] Thus, the transition from the slave trade to "legitimate" commerce allowed for some changes in the social and economic framework of the southern parts of the Nigerian region, but did not represent an abrupt or revolutionary break with previous modes of social organization.

CONCLUSION

By the second half of the nineteenth century the Sokoto Caliphate had consolidated the previously fragmented political landscape of the savanna under a single government based on Islamic law. At the same time, the Caliphate was well under way in its process of transforming the social and cultural make-up of savanna communities in the direction of a primary identification with Islam, thereby uniting the people of the savanna to a greater extent than they had ever experienced previously.

In the south, the Yoruba wars of the nineteenth century that led to the fall of Oyo and the establishment of new powers in the region – notably Ibadan, Ijaye, and Abeokuta – had brought about great instability, as large numbers of refugees migrated to all parts of the region and political authority increasingly took the form of warlords brandishing European-made firearms. At the same time, an economic transition was occurring throughout the southern region as the slave trade, abolished by the United Kingdom in 1807, was slowly being replaced by "legitimate" commerce, which in the Nigerian area took the form of trade in palm oil and, later, palm kernels. The slave trade continued to exist until the 1850s, and the new trade in palm products developed upon the social institutions and infrastructures developed during the slave trade era, although with greater opportunities for smallholding farmers, women, and, to a certain degree, slaves to improve their social and economic positions.

The arrival of British colonialism in the Nigerian region had its origins in the events that took place in the forest zone in the south during the second half of the nineteenth century. The promotion of "legitimate" commerce had meant that British commercial interests were increasingly concerned with the political stability of the region. The Yoruba wars in the southwest alarmed many British observers, as did the continuation of slavery and the slave trade within the region. By the second half of the nineteenth century the wheels were in motion for an eventual colonial takeover of the territories that would become southern Nigeria. By the first decade of the twentieth century British forces had also overrun Sokoto and its emirates, bringing into existence the British protectorates that were later consolidated into the single colonial administrative unit of Nigeria. The forces that led to the colonization of Nigeria, as well as the political and social make-up of the protectorates, are examined in the next chapter.

CHAPTER 4

Transition to British colonial rule, 1850 – 1903

INTRODUCTION

By about 1850 political and economic transformations had begun to alter the make-up of states in the Nigerian region, to a greater or lesser degree. As the savanna was reconfigured into an Islamic empire centered on Sokoto, the states of Yorubaland grappled with the collapse of the Oyo empire. In the Niger delta and Calabar, established slave traders began to transform their business practices and power bases towards palm oil exports and were dealing with new forms of competition. Also affecting political, economic, and social processes was the growing influence of British agents, in the form of Christian missionaries, trading interests, and political officials, all of whom were primarily concerned with increasing British influence against what they saw as the nefarious activities of indigenous rulers and other European powers, notably France and Germany. The power and influence of the British became tangible from around the middle of the nineteenth century, and by the end of the century circumstances had led to a dovetailing of British interests that resulted in the colonial occupation of the territories that would become Nigeria.

This chapter explains, first, the British motives for their colonial takeover in the second half of the nineteenth century and, second, the process of colonial takeover in the different parts of the Nigerian region: Lagos and Yorubaland in the southwest; the Niger delta, Calabar, and their hinterlands in the southeast; the territories surrounding the rivers Niger and Benue; and, finally, the emirates of the Sokoto Caliphate. The circumstances under which colonial rule took hold were different in each of these regions, with the result that the process of colonization was drawn out: over forty years elapsed between the annexation of Lagos in 1861 and the occupation of Sokoto in 1903. Differing regional circumstances also meant that different tactics were attempted in order to gain control of these regions. In the end, however, the most common and

most effective tool of colonial expansion was the British willingness
to use superior military might to subdue any opposition violently.
By 1903 British predominance had been extended at the barrel of a gun
to create the Colony and Protectorate of Lagos, the Protectorate of
Southern Nigeria, and the Protectorate of Northern Nigeria where
previously had existed autonomous, independent states under indigenous leadership.

MOTIVES FOR COLONIZATION

British interests in the greater Nigerian area took different forms in the
second half of the nineteenth century, but there was general agreement
that these interests would be best met through increased British influence
in the local affairs of indigenous communities. Some felt that their goals
could be achieved through British intermediary action with sovereign
indigenous leaders; others felt that circumstances could best be altered in
their favor through more direct British political control. Both methods
were attempted, as will be seen in the next section, but in the end the
latter approach held sway. The primary actors pushing for greater British
involvement were Christian missionaries, who wanted the areas converted
to anti-slavery, to "legitimate" commerce, and, ultimately, to ideas of
Christian "civilization." These missionaries were more than willing to
undertake this task themselves, but most felt that their job could be made
much easier with protection and assistance from British political and
military resources. British trading interests also lobbied hard for British
intervention, to regulate what they saw as the chaotic situation arising
from increased competition among British firms and the monopolistic
practices of indigenous middlemen, particularly in the coastal states of the
Bight of Biafra. Finally, British politicians themselves began to see the
need for a stronger political presence in the Nigerian region as French and
German traders and military expeditions moved dangerously close to the
British sphere of influence, especially around the navigable rivers of the
interior: the Niger and the Benue. The British found themselves caught
up in the "Scramble for Africa" that gathered steam after the Berlin
Conference of 1884–5, more or less forced to take direct control of the
entire area lest they lose their dominant influence in matters of trade and
politics to other European powers. Into the mix were thrown indigenous
rulers who courted British missionaries and political agents in the hope
that they would be valuable allies who could help the rulers to achieve
greater power vis-à-vis local rivals, either not realizing the consequences of

giving the British a foothold in their country or not being equipped to prevent these consequences.

Christian missionaries became influential in local politics in the territories of southern Nigeria from the 1840s. Although Christianity had been introduced to the region by Portuguese traders as early as the fifteenth century, few Africans converted and the religion did not spread at all beyond the coast. Christian missionaries did not begin to see Africa as a viable environment for the spread of their religion until the first half of the nineteenth century. From the 1840s onwards, however, missionary activity expanded rapidly. In Yorubaland, where Christian missionaries had previously been confined to Lagos, a group from the Church Missionary Society landed at Badagry in 1842, and its members found their way to Abeokuta in 1846, where they were joined later that year by the Wesleyan Missionary Society. In 1850 the American Southern Baptist Mission set up a mission in Abeokuta as well. While missionaries were still denied access to Ijebu territory to the east of the Egba, they continued to work their way north through Egba territory, establishing themselves as far north as Ilorin by the 1890s. In the southeast, the Presbyterian Church founded its first mission at Calabar in the 1840s, while, in the Niger delta, mission work began slightly later with the establishment of a CMS mission in 1857 at Onitsha under the leadership of Samuel Ajayi Crowther. Roman Catholic organizations, the largest of which was the Holy Ghost Fathers, also became quite successful in the latter part of the nineteenth century in Lagos, Abeokuta, Oyo, and Ibadan, as well as throughout the southeast. Christian missionary groups even attempted to compete with Islam in the north. The CMS made some headway among peoples in the savanna, particularly the Nupe and non-Muslim middle belt groups around the river Niger, and established missions in the emirates of Yola, Bida, and Zaria. Ultimately, however, Christianity did not spread significantly in the Islamic territories of the Sokoto Caliphate, even after British rule was established in the first years of the twentieth century.[1]

Two factors helped Christian missionaries to spread throughout the coastal and forest zones in the nineteenth century to a greater degree than had been possible before. First, the rulers of many indigenous communities saw it as being in their best interests to admit and encourage Christian missionaries at this time. From a spiritual standpoint, they thought that inviting the Christian god into their realm might give them a supernatural advantage over local rivals. From a commercial standpoint, the schools that the missionaries established focused heavily on speaking, reading, and writing in English, all of which helped Africans to trade more effectively with the British at a time of increased competition resulting from the shift from the slave trade to "legitimate" commerce. At the same time, African leaders recognized the link between Christian missionaries and British military power, which was becoming an increasingly important force in the region, particularly after the ousting of Kosoko from Lagos in 1851 (discussed below). Leaders of African communities therefore saw Christian missionaries as ambassadors through whom they could enlist British support against their enemies.

The second factor aiding the spread of Christianity at this time was a new focus on the part of missionaries on improving communication with local communities by learning their languages and developing an understanding of their cultures and histories. Christian missionaries in the nineteenth century put indigenous languages such as Yoruba and Igbo into writing for the first time, developed the first written dictionaries of these languages, and undertook the first written histories of culture groups in the Nigerian region.[2] Missionaries also translated the Bible into vernacular languages and printed it, to spread the Gospel more quickly and thoroughly, something that would have previously been unthinkable.

As part of the effort to strengthen ties and improve communications and relations, Christian missionaries began to promote Christianized Africans as valuable proselytizers. The strategy was for Africans who knew local languages and customs to go into communities and explain Christianity in terms to which their countrymen could relate. African missionaries in the nineteenth century were often former slaves who had been seized en route to the Americas by the British navy's anti-slavery squadron in the Atlantic and sent to Sierra Leone, a British west African colony founded in 1822 specifically for the purpose of depositing recaptured slaves back on African soil. While in Sierra Leone, freed slaves often learned English and converted to Christianity. From the 1830s some of these freed slaves began returning to their original homes, often explicitly to spread their new faith.[3] Perhaps the most famous example of a recaptive slave turned Christian missionary in the Nigerian region was Samuel Ajayi Crowther. Born in Yorubaland, Crowther was captured as a slave during the Yoruba wars accompanying the fall of Oyo. The slave ship carrying him across the Atlantic was captured by the Royal Navy, and Crowther was sent to Freetown, Sierra Leone, where he was baptized into the Anglican Church in 1825. Crowther returned to Yorubaland as one of the leaders of the Niger Expedition of 1841, the first major attempt to spread Christianity into the interior of the Nigerian region, and then as one of the founding members of the CMS mission in Abeokuta five years later. In 1857 he moved to Onitsha to run the highly successful CMS mission on the Niger, and for his untiring evangelical efforts he was named the Bishop of the Niger in 1862, becoming the first indigenous African bishop of the Anglican Church. Crowther was only one of many recaptured slaves who returned home to spread Christianity and fight against the slave trade that had so nearly destroyed their lives. European missionaries were also important figures in the spread of Christianity; for much of the nineteenth century, however, Africans themselves dominated missionary activity in the Nigerian region, communicating with local chiefs and leaders about the benefits Christianity could bring to their societies, only to be forced from positions of leadership in the Church after the 1880s.

Many indigenous leaders welcomed Christian missionaries in the belief that these missionaries would help them gain influence with their god and with British political agents against their rivals in times of political instability and economic transformation. The missionaries, however, were more concerned with spreading their religion and ending slavery and the slave trade than with helping indigenous rulers meet their political goals. Although missionaries did deal directly with African leaders, urging them to join in the fight against the evils of slavery and the slave trade and to engage in "legitimate" commerce, most believed that indigenous cultures were far inferior to European, Christian culture and therefore needed complete undermining and overhauling to bring about a more "civilized" society. As such, most missionaries believed that the British would be a more powerful and effective partner in achieving these ends than traditional rulers, who had a vested interest in the status quo. Not only did they believe that British rule would result in the final removal of slavery and the slave trade, they also believed that it would provide the means for the furtherance of the evangelical mission into areas that had previously been impenetrable, such as Ijebuland and the Sokoto Caliphate. Christian missionaries, particularly the Europeans among them, therefore lobbied hard for the British government to protect them and their efforts in southern Nigeria, and urged the British government repeatedly to intervene to end the practice of slavery and the ongoing slave trade. Internal political pressure from Christian groups therefore played a role in British decisions to intervene more heavily in local political disputes in the second half of the nineteenth century.[4]

The activities of British traders in the second half of the nineteenth century also led to deeper British involvement in the politics of indigenous states. While British trading interests were concerned that the ongoing instability in Yorubaland was causing roads to be blocked to trade, the primary trading concerns by this time were operating out of the Niger delta and Calabar. With the decline of the slave trade from the 1850s, the trade in palm products had become the most important commercial activity in the region. The palm oil trade offered fewer barriers to entry than the slave trade, and the oil palm tree grew abundantly in the hinterland of the Bight of Biafra.[5] As a result, competition in the Niger delta and further east in Calabar increased among African producers and middlemen in the second half of the nineteenth century, particularly as slaves themselves began to trade on their own behalf. Added to this increased competition among middlemen was the increase in the number of European trading firms on the coast. This included older companies that had been involved in the coastal trade for a long time as well as newcomers hoping to get rich from the lucrative palm oil trade. This increased competition among both European firms and Delta and Calabari traders resulted in high tensions in the region throughout the second half of the nineteenth century.

Tensions were so high because of the business model of the palm oil trade, known as the "trust" system.[6] Under the trust system, British firms on the coast would pay credit to coastal middlemen to procure a specified amount of palm oil. The middlemen would use part of this credit to purchase palm oil from hinterland dealers. They would then bring the palm oil back to the British firms in completion of the bargain. The trust system caused increased tensions for many reasons. First, increased competition among Delta and Calabari traders meant that they were in a weakened position vis-à-vis the British firms, which could lower prices by playing them off against each other. Sometimes Delta traders would refuse to trade at low rates, or would look for better rates from different British firms. This angered British traders, particularly from the larger companies, who held the largest amount of middleman debt. Second, the more established British firms could extend so much credit to Delta traders that they could never repay it and, therefore, could not embark on deals with newer British firms, even if these firms were offering better terms. Third, disputes between British creditors and Delta debtors often broke out, with the result that British firms commandeered property from the traders, often in a fashion incommensurate to the outstanding debt.

Given the growing problems with the trust system, it is not surprising that British firms were eager to bypass the African middleman altogether. Before the second half of the nineteenth century European traders had been forced to rely on middlemen for two reasons. First, malaria threatened to cut short the life of any European who ventured beyond the coast. Second, Europeans were unfamiliar with the complicated series of rivers, streams, and inlets that made up the Niger delta. Only middlemen knew how to get from the coast to their hinterland suppliers, therefore effectively controlling the trade in hinterland goods. Beginning in the early nineteenth century, however, middleman dominance of the trade routes to the interior began to be jeopardized as British explorers began trying to unlock the mysteries of the interior, particularly the pathways of the Niger.[7] Originally coming at the Niger from the west, British explorers such as Mungo Park, Hugh Clapperton, and the Lander brothers had no idea that the Niger of the western Sudan was the same river that poured out into the many rivulets of the delta so many hundreds of miles away. Mungo Park, who journeyed from Timbuktu to the Niger in 1805, was the first European to discover that the river flowed to the east.[8] Killed at the rapids at Bussa, however, Park was unable to follow the river to its termination. In the 1820s Clapperton revealed that the Niger flowed through Hausaland, and, after his death, his servant Richard Lander followed the Niger to its confluence with the Benue. In 1830 Lander and his brother were able to travel all the way from Bussa to Brass, in the Niger delta, proving the Niger to be one of the longest and most promising trading rivers in the world.

The discovery by Europeans of the extent of the river Niger led to attempts to spread British missionary and trading influence into the interior. The first such attempt was the failed Niger Expedition of 1841, which was charged to establish a mission and a model farm. Most of the European members of this mission died, and no long-term effects followed from it. In 1854, however, Dr. William Balfour Baikie led a much more successful expedition in conjunction with the establishment of the Niger Mission in the Niger delta under Samuel Ajayi Crowther. Baikie's expedition made use of quinine as a prophylactic against malaria and proved that Europeans could survive in the interior. The expedition was a success and led to the establishment of missions at Onitsha and Lokoja.

Baikie's success led directly to attempts to spread British trade into the interior. In 1857 Macgregor Laird established the first steamer business on the Niger. Although his business ultimately failed due to competition and the violent opposition of both British coastal firms and their middlemen contractors, Laird proved that interior trade on the Niger could be profitable, if competition could be limited. The possibility that British firms could bypass the coastal middlemen who had dominated trade for centuries threatened to ruin the local economies of places such as Bonny,

Brass, Opobo, and Calabar, the last-mentioned of which sat on the Cross River, as well as the profit margins of established British firms that relied on the trust system. The instability brought about by such tensions led directly to calls on the part of both British traders and coastal middlemen for the British to aid them in restoring equilibrium to the system, which, in turn, laid the foundation for British colonization of the region.

While the local circumstances encountered by Christian missionaries and traders resulted in a growing demand for more direct British interference in the politics of the greater Nigerian area, also influencing British decisions to act were the interests of other European countries in west Africa, particularly France and Germany, in the last quarter of the nineteenth century. In the late 1870s the French began an aggressive push to expand their political and economic influence in west Africa, and began pushing east from Senegal into the western Sudan and the upper reaches of the river Niger. By 1881 the French government had begun to build a railway from Senegal to the upper Niger, and had begun to compete with British firms on the lower Niger, having established stations at Abo, Onitsha, and Egga. German efforts to move into the Nigerian region began almost simultaneously. As early as 1880 Germany had conducted exploratory missions to the Benue, and by 1884 had annexed the Cameroons, the western border of which was dangerously near Calabar in the south and the northern border of which threatened to give Germany unfettered access to the Benue and, by extension, the Niger.

The new moves towards imperial expansion into previously uncolonized areas of Africa, both in west Africa and in other regions of the continent, resulted in the famous Berlin Conference of 1884–5. This conference laid out the rules for European territorial acquisition in Africa. The most important rules for declaring control over African lands were the upholding of the long-established practice of signing treaties of "protection" with indigenous rulers for the creation of "protectorates," and the "effective occupation" with military forces of any full-fledged colonies. The Berlin Conference therefore marks the official beginning of the "Scramble for Africa," in which the European countries agreed among themselves how to slice up the continent for their own strategic and material gain.[9] The British now feared that, if French or German interests gained access to the Niger, they might "effectively occupy" the area, thereby staking a claim for political control over the entire river. With political control would come high protective tariffs that would threaten to oust British traders from the Niger altogether. Therefore, in order to prevent such a catastrophe, the British government became increasingly willing to take the necessary steps to assert its own political power over the region, through treaty wherever possible, through force wherever necessary.

ESTABLISHMENT OF BRITISH PROTECTORATES
IN THE SOUTH

The spread of Christian missionaries and British trading interests and, after the 1880s, the need to keep out French and German interests dovetailed, influencing the decisions of the consuls appointed to oversee British affairs in the coastal states of the Bights of Benin and Biafra to interfere more and more heavily in the local politics of the coastal states from the 1850s. Interference in local politics eventually led to direct British control of the coastal states between 1861 and 1885. Having annexed the coasts, British political interests moved inland, adding to their existing protectorates the Yoruba states and the states on the rivers Niger and Benue. The activities of Sir George Goldie's chartered Royal Niger Company were instrumental in gaining ultimate control of the Niger and Benue for the British. With the Niger secured by 1900, British military might turned its attention towards the emirates of the Sokoto Caliphate. In a series of offensives led by Frederick Lugard, British forces finally brought down the caliphate, killing the caliph in battle in July 1903 and thereby bringing under British imperial control the lands that were soon to make up a fully amalgamated Nigerian protectorate.

The colonization of Nigeria took over forty years to complete and was accomplished in a series of British maneuvers emanating from Lagos in the west, which became the base for all colonial operations in Yorubaland, and from the trading states of the Niger delta and Calabar in the east. Direct British interference in Lagos politics began in 1851, when missionaries at Abeokuta convinced John Beecroft, the British consul for the Bights of Benin and Biafra, to use his military power to unseat Kosoko, the reigning King of Lagos, in favor of a rival claimant, an Egba royal named Akitoye. Kosoko had been belligerent towards both missionaries and British trading activity in Lagos, and had made no serious effort to end the ongoing slave trade in the region. Furthermore, missionaries felt that he, along with his allies in Dahomey, posed a significant threat to Egba security. The Egba, surrounded by enemies and recognizing their perilous position, had been the first group in the region to welcome Christian missionaries in the hope of attracting exactly this kind of support for British protection. Beecroft hoped that replacing Kosoko

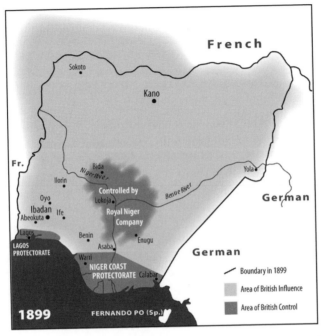

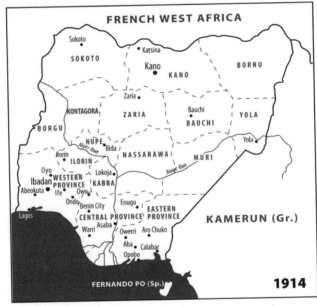

Map 4.1 British Colonial Nigeria (courtesy Saverance Publishing Services)

with Akitoye would bring an end to the slave trade, stabilize the region for the spread of "legitimate" commerce, and open Lagos as a port to Abeokuta for the expansion of British missionary and trading enterprise. Therefore, in December 1851 he ordered the bombardment of Lagos, forcing Kosoko to flee. Akitoye was put on the throne under the pre-condition that he sign an anti-slave-trade treaty. Unfortunately, over the next ten years Akitoye and his successors were unable to bring the stability to the region that the British had hoped for, and, in 1861, Lagos was annexed as a British colony under the direct political control of a British governor. The colonization of Nigeria had officially begun.

From Lagos the British made their way inland, slowly bringing Yorubaland under British rule. The first major coup in the hinterland occurred in 1886, when the British intervened to end the arduous Ekitiparapo War between Ibadan and the alliance of Ekiti, Ijesa, Egba, Ijebu, and Ife forces. All sides were weary of fighting this war, which had been going on for fifteen years, and welcomed the British as peacemakers. The British terms, while bringing an end to the main fighting of the war, opened the door to full-scale colonization, however. The treaty ending the war declared that all signatory combatants would direct future dis-putes with each other to the British governor in Lagos for resolution. Furthermore, all parties agreed to the promotion of free trade, which, of course, translated into greater access for British commercial interests to interior markets.

The British used this treaty as justification for the occupation of Ijebuland in 1892. The Ijebu had always been suspicious of the motives of white people in their country – whether missionary, commercial, or political agents – and had outlawed them entirely for most of the nine-teenth century. When the Ijebu king refused to discuss trade terms with the acting governor of Lagos on a trip to Ijebuland in 1891, the British used this as an excuse to occupy the territory forcibly. British troops subdued the Ijebu in four days of fighting, sending a message to the rest of Yorubaland that the British were the new supreme power in the region and were willing to use their superior military machinery to get their way. When British officials circulated a new treaty of protection to the Yoruba states in 1893, most Yoruba leaders saw the writing on the wall and signed away their sovereignty, becoming part of the expanded Colony and Protectorate of Lagos. Only the reconstituted New Oyo offered signifi-cant physical resistance to the British at this time. Oyo soon met the fate of Ijebu, however. The town of New Oyo was bombarded on November 12, 1894, and brought forcibly under British colonial rule.

In the port cities of the Bight of Biafra, as in Yorubaland, the promotion of anti-slavery and British trading interests was a key aspect of the British rhetoric that led to colonization. Regulation was greatly needed in the fiercely competitive commercial atmosphere of the Bight of Biafra, and both local traders and British firms looked to the British consul to negotiate balances to the trust system and to settle disputes. Indigenous political leaders sought the friendship of the consul as an ally against rivals, preferring to cede authority to the British rather than to local competitors. The consul achieved a position of great power through his position as intermediary. When disputes over kingships or chieftaincies arose, the favorites of the consul usually ended up winning out. Over time, then, the consul became something of a puppet-master, able to place in a position of authority whoever was willing to carry out his policies. In the early days of consular authority, this mostly meant abiding by treaties agreeing to a platform of anti-slavery, free trade, and the allowing of missionary activity in the relevant territories. By the 1880s, however, it meant signing over sovereignty to the British government in the form of treaties of protection.

The growing power of the consul from the middle of the nineteenth century can be seen in the case of Calabar.[10] The kings of Calabar's two most powerful towns, Eyo II of Creek Town (often referred to by British agents as King Honesty II, due to his pro-British attitude) and Eyamba V of Duke Town, both welcomed Christian missionaries in 1846, believing that this would lead to stronger relationships with the British consul and therefore increased trade and political support. The missionaries, however, were concerned over the lingering ritual practice of human sacrifice of slaves in Calabar and pressured the consul, Beecroft, to intervene to end the practice. Beecroft negotiated a treaty in 1850 with Eyo and Archibong I, who had succeeded Eyamba in 1849, banning human sacrifice and the killing of twins, which was also a common practice among the Efik. When Old Town, a weaker neighbor of Creek Town and Duke Town, sacrificed a number of slaves in 1855, Beecroft demolished the town by bombardment and forced its king to sign a similar treaty as a precondition for rebuilding.[11] Under such circumstances, the king had little option but to agree. Beecroft had also become the kingmaker of Duke Town by this time and had been directly responsible for the ascent of Archibong I to the throne in 1849, as well as that of his successor, Duke Ephraim, in 1852. Beecroft's support for these rulers was, of course, conditional on their promise to maintain good relations with the British, which ultimately meant doing as the consul wished.

The kings of Calabar, as in other coastal states of the Bight of Biafra, agreed to such political dependence because they believed it would bring more trade and more friendly relationships with the British, which would ultimately make them more powerful and wealthy vis-à-vis other local rulers as well as vis-à-vis British trading enterprises. Unfortunately, neither of these goals was ultimately achieved. The consul, whose primary function was to protect British interests, usually favored British firms in disputes and intervened in local politics in a way that benefited increased British trade at the expense of the local dealers. For instance, a court of equity was established in Calabar in 1856 to settle disputes between British firms and local traders. The court was made up of a group of voting members, a majority of whom came from the major British firms, with the consul himself as chairman. Because of the make-up of the court, decisions rarely favored local dealers. The Calabar court had been based on a similar court established by Beecroft in Bonny in 1850. The granting of judicial authority to such an alien institution simultaneously empowered British trading interests at the expense of local middlemen and undermined the sovereign authority of indigenous rulers in the Bight of Biafra.

In the delta states, political interference proceeded along a similar tack. In a meeting of the Bonny Court of Equity in 1853, Beecroft deposed King Pepple of Bonny, who had recently instigated a war with the town of Elem Kalabari. King Pepple had been a thorn in the side of British trade interests for over twenty years, consistently refusing to give up his control of interior markets and openly engaging in hostilities with anyone who challenged his pre-eminence in these areas. Pepple's successor, Dappo, was forced to sign a treaty that made the court of equity the supreme judicial authority in Bonny, prevented the king from engaging in trade himself, and prevented the king from waging war without the approval of the British supercargoes. Bonny declined quickly thereafter, and, with the civil war that led to Ja Ja's creation of Opobo in 1869, ceased to be the most prominent state in the delta. Ja Ja's ability to control the hinterland markets from Opobo meant that the European traders, while initially angered by this move, ultimately accepted Ja Ja as the predominant ruler of the region and officially recognized Opobo in 1873. Ja Ja was by far the most powerful ruler in the Bight of Biafra by this point, because he had been able to maintain control of his markets more effectively than other local rulers, who had increasingly been brought under the thumb of the British consul through such treaties as that signed by Dappo of Bonny.

By the time of the Berlin Conference in 1884–5, British concerns had ceased to be primarily over how to bypass the coastal middlemen in the Bight of Biafra and had turned towards how to prevent the French and Germans from undercutting British interests, especially on the Niger and Benue. French trading vessels had appeared in the delta in 1880, and the French had developed trading posts at several points on the upper Niger. Meanwhile, Germany was encroaching upon Calabar and the Benue from the east, annexing the Cameroons in 1884. Thus, in 1884–5, the British consul, Hewett, traversed the entire coastal region from Calabar into the western delta, and, through the power of his office, had little difficulty convincing local rulers to sign his treaties of protection. These treaties essentially gave the United Kingdom political sovereignty over the signer's territory, allowing the British to conduct foreign relations on the part of the ruler and to interfere in local politics in the interest of peace and free trade. Even Ja Ja signed a treaty, although warily and with reservations. In 1885 Hewett declared the setting up of the Oil Rivers Protectorate in the name of the United Kingdom. When Ja Ja later violated the terms of the treaty of protection by continuing to deny British traders access to his hinterland markets, he was deposed and exiled to the West Indies as a warning to other local rulers of the consequences of insubordination.[12] A similar fate met Nana, the Itsekiri governor of the river Benin, who was deposed and deported in 1894 after refusing British traders access to the Urhobo markets of his hinterland.[13]

In 1891 Sir Claude Macdonald developed an official governing structure for the protectorate and became its first consul general. The territory was renamed the Niger Coast Protectorate in 1893, and continued under this name for the remainder of the nineteenth century. In 1897 the kingdom of Benin was forcibly brought into the protectorate, expanding its western boundary to reach the eastern limits of the Lagos protectorate.[14]

THE ROYAL NIGER COMPANY

With the Niger delta and Calabar effectively under British political control after 1885, the British had only to shore up their interests on the navigable reaches of the Niger and Benue against encroachment by France and Germany. Rather than proclaim protectorate status over the Niger and Benue, however, the British took a different approach, granting a royal charter to George Goldie's National African Company in 1886.[15] The royal charter gave the National African Company, soon renamed the

Royal Niger Company, the power to control the political administration and trade policies of any local territories with which it could gain legal treaties, provided that the company did not interfere in local religions, laws, or customs, except insofar as was necessary to discourage the practice of slavery. Under the terms of the charter, the RNC came to control the trade on the Niger between the delta and Nupe and on the Benue as far as Yola. Political power varied from treaty zone to treaty zone, but administration was only the secondary objective of the company: the primary objective was to monopolize the trade of the navigable rivers of the Nigerian interior.

From the perspective of the British parliament, the granting of the charter was initially a smart move. The administration of the "Niger Territories," as they were called in the charter, was to be conducted by the Royal Niger Company itself, and paid for by company revenues, and not by the British government. Nevertheless, the charter established a British sphere of influence over the Niger and Benue and apparently kept France and Germany from gaining a foothold on these strategically and commercially important rivers. Thus, the British government got to have its cake and eat it too. From Goldie's perspective, the charter represented a potential goldmine. Goldie's outlook had long been that commercial profitability for European firms on the Niger was hindered primarily by too much competition between firms. Therefore, he had made his reputation on the Niger by amalgamating the different trading interests on the Niger in a way that Macgregor Laird, for instance, had been unable to do. In 1879 Goldie had successfully drawn together the three largest British firms operating on the Niger – Holland Jacques and Company, in which Goldie himself owned a controlling interest, Miller Brothers, and James Pinnock – to create the United African Company. The company was reorganized into the National African Company in 1882, amending its constitution to allow it greater leeway in attaining political rights of administration both from the British government and from the local rulers with whom the company negotiated treaties. As head of the National African Company, Goldie bought out three French competitors in 1884, making the company by far the largest firm on the Niger. Goldie's ambitions had always been overtly monopolistic, and, although the royal charter he received technically obliged him to promote free trade, it also gave him the power to organize that trade in a way that would exclude all possible rivals. Under Goldie, the Royal Niger Company became a commercial empire of its own, crowding out both foreign and local trade in a bid to end competition on the Niger.

Figure 4.1 Street scene in present-day Ibadan (collection of Roy Doron)

Despite the emphasis placed on promoting free trade, Goldie never-theless achieved his chartered monopoly legally. Although treaties varied in structure and terms from signatory to signatory, at the very least they usually gave the company jurisdiction over all trade in the signatory's dominions and forced the signatory to refer rival companies to the RNC for access to the Niger. Some treaties achieved more, essentially giving the company political sovereignty over the signatory's territories, although it is unclear whether these treaties were legitimate or whether the signatories fully understood their implications. In any case, the treaties with local rulers ensured that the RNC was the only authority legally permitted to negotiate terms of trade on the Niger, with the result that the company could then set those terms heavily in its favor. Goldie then used the power given him by the royal charter and his hodgepodge accumulation of treaties to exclude all competition. The RNC established high tariffs on imports and exports, which had to be paid upon entering or exiting the Niger at the company's base in the delta town of Akassa. Furthermore, in order to trade at all, foreign traders had to pay £100 for a license and an additional £100 if they intended to trade in alcohol. Such restrictions effectively excluded all small-scale traders, who would find it difficult to raise the capital necessary to get started. To prevent larger firms from trading, the company set import duties on war materials and alcohol at near 100 percent, making it unprofitable for firms other than the RNC to import these goods. Guns and alcohol had become the accepted goods through which trade negotiations were initiated with local rulers on the Niger, and without them foreign firms stood little chance of establishing trading relationships on the Niger or Benue.

Such policies made the Royal Niger Company extremely unpopular both among the other British supercargoes, who now recognized that Goldie had succeeded in simply replacing the monopoly of the coastal middlemen with that of his own company, and among the indigenous populations, whose rights to trade on the Niger had been reduced or eliminated. The decidedly monopolistic activities of the RNC provoked widespread criticism of the company in west Africa and in the United Kingdom alike. Investigations into the company's business and administrative practices were even undertaken by parliament between 1889 and 1891, but the resulting report by Claude Macdonald was mostly favorable to the company, and, while Macdonald proposed several reforms to curb the company's monopoly, such as allowing delta traders from Brass and Elem Kalabari to use the Niger without paying taxes, these reforms were never implemented and the company was able to continue to operate as before. As of 1891 the British government was willing to sacrifice its stance on free trade in order to have the Niger administered on behalf of the United Kingdom, keeping the French and Germans out, without the financial burden of direct colonial occupation.

By the end of the nineteenth century, however, the worm had turned and the Royal Niger Company had lost its political capital even with Whitehall, which, to the delight of Goldie's detractors, revoked the company's charter in 1899. Three events led to the downfall of the RNC and convinced the British that direct colonial administration would be the only effective means of governing the "Niger Territories". First, by 1895 the Conservative Party had taken control of parliament from William Gladstone's Liberals. Joseph Chamberlain, an ardent imperialist, became colonial secretary under Lord Salisbury's new administration. Chamberlain looked askance at government by chartered companies, preferring the accountability and progressive possibilities of full-scale colonial rule through the Colonial Office.

Second, at the same time that Chamberlain took over at the Colonial Office, the Royal Niger Company was proving how ineffective it actually was at promoting peace, stability, and free trade. The catastrophe that illustrated the evils of company rule occurred among the Brass, a people located in the mangrove swamps of the Niger delta.[16] The Brass were historically a trading people. The dense mangrove swamps in which they lived were an inhospitable environment for agricultural activity, and so the Brass had always exported such items as salt, fish, and European luxury items in exchange for imports of foodstuffs from the interior. The primary channel for their trading activities had always been the Niger. With the onset of company rule, however, it was no longer legal for the Brass to conduct trade on the Niger. Technically, the Brass were part of the Oil Rivers Protectorate, and, as such, constituted a foreign interest on the Niger, required to pay all the licensing fees and import and export duties that the company imposed. The Brass obviously could not afford these charges, since they were specifically designed to prevent competition on the Niger. Efforts at smuggling and attempts to find alternative trade routes were made, but none were particularly successful. The Brass imported less and less food, and eventually they began to starve.

Resentful that the company apparently wanted them to "eat dirt" rather than trade on the Niger, the Brass planned a revolt against the RNC. Knowing they were probably consigning themselves to a violent end at the hands of the British rather than the slow demise of starvation, Brass forces under the leadership of King Koko attacked the Royal Niger Company's headquarters at Akassa on December 29, 1894, carrying off as much company property as they could and destroying warehouses and machinery. They even kidnapped several company employees, whom they later ritualistically ate as part of a spiritual ceremony to combat the smallpox epidemic that was also terrorizing their community.

Despite the outright barbarity of the attack against the RNC, the general consensus in the United Kingdom was that the company had provoked this response by its cut-throat business practices. Goldie demanded revenge, however, and so Macdonald was forced to bring his subjects under the gun. He ordered the town of Nembe to be bombarded, but the job was done half-heartedly and the Brass were never fully brought into submission. Most political and trading interests believed that the Royal Niger Company was ultimately responsible for the desperate situation in which the Brass had found themselves, and were unwilling to devote their own resources to a battle that Goldie had instigated and now wanted others to fight for him.

Third, and the final nail in the RNC's coffin, was the falling-out between Chamberlain and Goldie over the protection of the northwestern frontier of the company.[17] Despite the company's presence on the Niger and its preponderance of treaties claiming exclusive rights to trade, the French had not given up their quest to expand their political influence and develop trading networks on the river. The French made regular efforts to establish a base on the northern part of the river, and, after acquiring Dahomey in 1889, they were able to send expeditions from Nikki eastward, occupying Fort D'Arenberg in Borgu in 1894. In December of the same year a French gunboat brazenly forced its way up the Niger from the delta before running aground 100 miles upstream. The real threat came in 1897, however, when the French occupied Bussa on the Niger, very near the Royal Niger Company's treaty zone but not technically within it. From this position, France could conceivably build up the military strength necessary to challenge company jurisdiction over the Niger. Chamberlain wanted Goldie to use company forces to secure company territories and force the French out; Goldie was reluctant to do this. Goldie had recently undertaken wars against Nupe and Ilorin, bringing them under company rule, partly to keep out the French and partly to prevent British colonial expeditions moving north from Yoruba territory from undermining his position as the administrative power over the Niger.

Goldie now felt his company's position threatened. He demanded that his charter be renewed and that Chamberlain do something to bring the Brass situation under control before he would undertake yet another expensive military operation to protect the Niger for the United Kingdom. Chamberlain had little intention of meeting either of Goldie's demands. Instead, Chamberlain created the West African Frontier Force under Frederick Lugard. Lugard, an accomplished colonial officer who had been instrumental in bringing the east African territory of Uganda under British rule in 1892, was working by this time as an employee of the Royal Niger Company. He was charged with mounting a campaign for the Colonial Office, independent of the company, to push the French back from the Niger. Chamberlain then negotiated with Goldie over the terms of revocation of the company's charter. Once Goldie was satisfied with the financial arrangements, he agreed to divert company resources towards the WAFF campaign. Lugard's forces advanced and the French retreated from Borgu, leaving the Niger as firmly as ever in British hands. On January 1, 1900, the Royal Niger Company ceased to be the governing authority of the Niger and Benue. Its southern territories in the palm oil zone near the Niger delta were amalgamated into the Niger Coast Protectorate, forming the new Protectorate of Southern Nigeria. The company's northern territories, including Ilorin, became the Protectorate of Northern Nigeria. The Colonial Office bypassed Goldie and named Lugard the first high commissioner of the northern protectorate. Few wept for the passing of

Figure 4.2 The Water House, Lagos (collection of Brigitte Kowalski)

the Royal Niger Company, the monopolistic activities of which had finally come to an end.[18]

COLLAPSE OF THE SOKOTO CALIPHATE

Lugard now faced the task of expanding his newly founded protectorate over the territories of the Sokoto Caliphate.[19] The reorganization of the "Niger Territories" into the northern and southern protectorates illustrated the importance that the British now placed on establishing full-fledged imperial control over the rivers Niger and Benue. Even the colonization of riverine states did not guarantee their safety and stability as far as the British were concerned, however, as long as the Sokoto Caliphate continued to exist to their north. Sokoto posed a problem to British rule for two reasons. First, Lugard feared that, since the caliph had been the suzerain over territories such as Bida, Ilorin, and Yola, which were now under British protection, the influence of the caliph would undermine Lugard's own authority, and could conceivably lead to internal revolts within British-controlled territories. Second, the Sokoto Caliphate offered yet another avenue through which the French might make a play for the Niger. By 1900 the French had expanded their rule over most of the western Sudan, including the territories directly to the north and west of Sokoto. Thus, if the French conquered the caliphate before the British moved to do so, the French would be able to move their forces all the way down to the banks of the Niger from the north. To prevent French encroachment, the Royal Niger Company had attempted to establish a military post and a British Resident in Sokoto in 1899, but had been rebuffed by the caliph. The resistance of the caliph to British influence convinced Lugard that the only effective way of securing the protectorate and, by extension, the rivers Niger and Benue, was the military conquest of Sokoto and its incorporation into the Protectorate of Northern Nigeria.

The decentralized nature of the caliphate worked against it in the ensuing campaign against the British takeover. The caliphate's lack of a standing army meant that large numbers of troops could not be dispatched at any given time, and the emirates were left mostly to fend for themselves against the British onslaught. Lugard's first move was to shore up British control of the emirates of Bida and Kontagora on the Niger and Yola on the Benue. The emirs of these states had recently been hostile to company rule, so Lugard took troops into their territories, deposed the emirs, and replaced them with new emirs whose primary qualification to rule was willingness to submit to Lugard's authority. From these places, Lugard's forces moved north into Bauchi and Gombe, and by 1902 Lugard had conquered Zaria. British forces now faced their greatest challenges, in Kano and in Sokoto itself. Kano was occupied after only minor resistance on February 3, 1903, but fighting outside the city continued for several weeks afterwards. In the end, the emir fled and the Kanawa troops surrendered by early March. Caliph Attahiru put up a stiff fight for Sokoto on March 15, but eventually he, too, was forced to flee, and Sokoto fell to British troops. Not content to allow the head of such a vast empire possibly to reconstitute himself elsewhere, Lugard's forces pursued Attahiru, killing him finally on July 27 at the Second Battle of Burmi, some 200 miles southeast of Kano on the river Gongola.

The mighty caliphate founded by Usman dan Fodio was no more. Many of its most prominent citizens, rather than submit to alien, non-Islamic rule, fled east to escape their persecutors. Some went on pilgrimage to Mecca, others to aid the millenarian campaign of the Mahdi against the British in Sudan. The caliphate's territories were incorporated into the Protectorate of Northern Nigeria under emirs willing to accept British colonial rule. Borno, which had always retained its independence from Sokoto, was occupied by British forces and brought into the protectorate as well, in 1904.[20]

INDIGENOUS RESISTANCE AND BRITISH VIOLENCE

The conquest of Sokoto was the final act in setting the boundaries of the British Protectorates of Northern and Southern Nigeria. But this does not mean that from 1903 all the peoples within those boundaries were subjected to British colonial rule. What the conquest of Sokoto did represent was the end of British efforts at control through diplomacy. Many parts of the protectorates continued to put up fierce resistance to British rule, and slowly, over the first decade of the twentieth century, these pockets of resistance were brought to submission by British guns. In 1901–2, British forces from the southern protectorate moved north into the heart of Igboland to rout the Aro, whom the British believed to be the political overlords of the entire region.[21] The Aro succumbed quickly, but the British soon realized that the conquest of the Aro did not lead automatically to the subjugation of all the Igbo and Ibibio. As discussed in previous chapters, the Aro were a ritual/spiritual power in Igboland, but political power was decentralized to a great extent, meaning that British forces found themselves conquering the interior essentially village by village over the next decade.

A similar situation predominated just to the west of Igboland in the interior of the Niger delta, where Urhobo, Isoko, and Ukwuani communities put up resistance to British control until 1914. In the western Igbo area around Asaba and Onitsha, on the Niger, the Ekumeku movement caused trouble for British forces periodically from the 1880s until its final defeat in 1909. Ekumeku was an organization established by western Igbo communities as a communal defense system. Whenever one community faced a military threat, surrounding communities sent soldiers to combat the threat. Afterwards, these soldiers returned home. The decentralized nature of Ekumeku made it difficult for British forces to combat, as the units dispersed over a large space and the leaders and soldiers could be easily replaced if captured or killed. Ekumeku had risen against the Royal Niger Company in 1898 and had achieved concessions from the company after a prolonged period of inconclusive fighting. The movement then dispersed, but rose again in 1900 to defend Asaba and its hinterland against the new government of the protectorate. Defeated in 1902, Ekumeku rose again in 1904 and again in 1909, when the movement was finally annihilated by overwhelming British force.[22]

A point must be made here on the role of violence in the British colonial takeover of Nigeria. The use or threat of violence on the part of the British must be seen as the single most important factor allowing them to assume

Figure 4.3 The Niger–Benue confluence at Lokoja (collection of Dr. Okpeh Okpeh)

political control over the territories that made up the various protectorates of Nigeria. To refuse to play by British rules was to sign one's own death or deportation warrant. British military might, in the form of the Royal Navy, cannons, and machine guns, and the willingness of the British to use military means to protect the interests of the United Kingdom and her allies made the British a desirable ally for many indigenous rulers against local rivals. These rulers therefore welcomed missionaries and traders, and signed British treaties, hoping that this would persuade the British to intervene in their favor in local disputes. We have seen this in the case of the Egba in Yorubaland. Other rulers, such as Ja Ja of Opobo, were wary of British motives, but signed treaties anyway to avoid provoking immediate conflict with a superior military power. Still others, such as Caliph Attahiru, resisted British encroachment outright, and saw their power, and often their lives, come to a swift and merciless end.

Even under such circumstances, the various states and societies of the Nigerian region did not succumb to British colonial rule without a fight. Indeed, heavy resistance met British incursions at almost every turn. Much has been made of the question whether or not indigenous rulers understood the full implications of the treaties they signed with the British that so undermined their sovereign ability to administer their territories, politically and commercially.[23] Indeed, many may not have understood the implications. Whether they did or not, however, it is clear that few rulers ceded their sovereignty willingly. Some, such as the warlords of Ibadan who aided in the British capture of Oyo, perpetuated their power by aiding British attacks against neighboring groups, staying in the good graces of the British as long as possible. Others, such as Ja Ja of Opobo and the Emir of Yola, extended their rule by signing the treaties that effectively opened their trade routes and erased their ability to conduct foreign policy, only later to be ousted forcibly for continuing to restrict access to their hinterlands and to court relationships with other foreign powers. Others, such as many of the ruling elites of the Sokoto Caliphate, resisted by emigrating from the territory they had once ruled, refusing to come under the thumb of an alien power.

Indigenous rulers were not the only actors that resisted British incursion. Some resistance movements organized themselves from a more grassroots level. The unfortunate people of Brass, for instance, were uniformly opposed to the disastrous policies of RNC rule. Although their resistance was led by their king, the sentiments against the company were widespread, even among the growing Christian community, the members of which favored "legitimate" commerce, anti-slavery, and the suppression of the liquor trade. The community as a whole took part in the raid on Akassa. At the same time, the Ekumeku movement represented a resistance effort with deep-rooted origins in the social fabric of the decentralized western Igbo communities. The Ekumeku movement was able to fight against British colonial rule for more than two decades, even in circumstances where their leaders had been neutralized. Socially based resistance movements proved problematic for the extension of British control over parts of the protectorates until well into the twentieth century, particularly in the interior of the Niger delta and the Bight of Biafra.

The widespread resistance, both passive and active, that the British faced in their bid to establish colonial rule was crushed only by violence. Sometimes this violence removed an obstinate ruler in favor of a more malleable one. Sometimes this violence took the form of bombarding a state or region to the point at which resistance could no longer be maintained. The use of violence also served as a warning to other rulers or populations who might be considering an intransigent approach. Therefore, at the end of the nineteenth century and into the twentieth, the British extended their colonial grasp over Nigeria more as a result of superior military might and the willingness to use violence to achieve their ends than as a result of any other set of factors.

CONCLUSION

The colonization of Nigeria was a prolonged process, taking more than forty years to accomplish. Local circumstances and the influence of missionaries, traders, or French and German incursions tended to dictate the process of colonization; in the end however, territories were brought into submission only by the use of force. Colonization brought under the sole rule of the United Kingdom previously independent states that had been interconnected commercially and to some extent culturally over the previous centuries, but had not experienced political unification of any kind. The process of governing the conglomeration of states that was soon to become amalgamated into a single Nigeria was thus, by necessity, inorganic, alien, and transformative. The peoples and institutions of the Nigerian region were changed deeply and permanently in the latter half of the nineteenth century. The next chapter discusses the political, economic, and social changes that British colonial administration brought about in the first part of the twentieth century.

CHAPTER 5

Colonial society to 1929

INTRODUCTION

Colonial rule by the United Kingdom brought many changes to the societies of Nigeria. Charged with the tasks of governing the territories of Nigeria, expanding the commerce of the country, and promoting "progress" and "civilization" for peoples they considered inferior and backward, British colonial officers went about restructuring Nigerian societies in the years after their colonial conquest. The purpose of colonial rule was, theoretically, to alter only those customs, traditions, and institutions that the British deemed harmful to Nigerian progress, leaving existing political and social institutions intact to the greatest degree possible. In practice, however, colonial policies made transformative changes to Nigerian societies in many ways, particularly in southern Nigeria, which saw the most significant alterations to political institutions and economic orientation. The purpose of this chapter is to examine the structure of colonial society and the response of Nigerians to the British regime from the beginning of colonial rule up to 1929.

During this period the British colonial administration utilized the concept of "indirect rule" – rule through traditional kings and chiefs – to govern local areas in each of the British protectorates. Originally, indirect rule operated differently in different regions, as determined in large part by the administrative outlook of the British authorities in each protectorate and by the diversity of indigenous political institutions throughout the protectorates. After the amalgamation of the Nigerian territories in 1914, however, the specific framework of indirect rule developed by Frederick Lugard in the Protectorate of Northern Nigeria was extended to all of newly unified Nigeria. Indirect rule claimed to respect traditional political institutions and promote continuity between indigenous and colonial regimes, but in practice indirect rule alienated traditional authorities from their subject populations through their association with the colonial regime. Furthermore, traditional rulers found that they maintained their power at the behest of

British colonial officers, who made sure that colonial directives were enforced at all times. Insubordinate indigenous rulers soon found themselves ousted and their places taken by more malleable replacements.

British colonial rule also affected the Nigerian economy. The colonial economic model focused on expanding Nigeria's import-export markets through increased cash crop and mineral production, thereby creating an extractive economy based on the export of raw materials and the import of finished goods and luxury items. The British also instituted a cash economy based on the UK currency and forced Nigerians into wage labor, transforming in a few short years the processes of agricultural production and capital accumulation that had developed among Nigerian communities over centuries. This was done primarily as a means to redirect economic activity towards external markets and thereby make the colonial endeavor self-sustaining for the colonial government and profitable for British and European business.

The changes in the political and economic structures of Nigerian communities also led to significant social changes. Cities grew rapidly as people moved to urban areas looking for jobs in the colonial service or in commercial firms. Traditional age and gender roles shifted as people reacted to the new labor requirements of the colonial economy. A new class of European-educated, literate, English-speaking Nigerian Christians emerged in southern Nigeria, keen on holding the colonial regime responsible for its actions and demanding a greater role for Nigerians in their own governance.

The upheaval of the early colonial period resulted in high tensions between ruler and subject, particularly in southern Nigeria, where the impact of colonial rule was most intense. In the course of such monumental change, many mobilized to protect their own interests in a colonial system that often seemed to disregard their well-being. Some people organized, demonstrated, and even rioted in the effort to make their voices heard. Others tried to enter into dialogue with the colonial government to have their needs addressed. At the core of all responses to colonial rule was a sense that Nigerians themselves knew how best to structure their societies and did not need to be told how to do things by an alien regime. By the late 1920s anti-colonial resistance, which until then had been mostly a local phenomenon, was poised to become a full-fledged nationalist movement.

COLONIAL ADMINISTRATION

The development of British colonial administration in the Nigerian protectorates was not a process of unified or consistent planning and implementation. On the contrary, colonial administrations emerged over time in each region of Nigeria primarily as a response to the specific circumstances of that region. Although distinct colonial administrations had emerged independently in each protectorate by the early twentieth century, they did have two overarching commonalities. First, all relied philosophically on the concept that British colonial rule should be maximally beneficial both to the British and to the peoples of Nigeria. This was dubbed the "Dual Mandate" by Frederick Lugard in the 1920s,[1] and the British argued that it was their duty to run the colonies efficiently and effectively so that the United Kingdom itself might benefit from extracting Nigeria's raw materials and from the opening up of Nigerian societies to European markets. At the same time, the British claimed to be bringing "progress" and "civilization" to otherwise backward African societies by developing the economy, eradicating slavery in all its forms, weeding out the corruption they believed existed in traditional political institutions, promoting a work ethic they believed traditional societies lacked, and educating populations on European conceptions of health, hygiene, and cleanliness, among other things.

The second similarity between the colonial administrations that emerged in the Nigerian protectorates was the belief in indirect rule as the most effective way to fulfill the Dual Mandate. The point of indirect rule was to govern through existing indigenous rulers. Under indirect rule, traditional kings and chiefs were allowed to continue governing their territories through traditional political and social institutions in a way to which the populations were accustomed. Traditional rulers were also subordinated to British colonial officers, however, whose job it was to make sure they conformed broadly to the values of "civilized" governance – that is, the abolition of slavery, the promotion of legitimate commerce, and the acceptance of free trade in their territories. In principle, British colonial officers in every region of Nigeria embraced the idea of governing as far as possible through the traditional ruling class. They felt that indirect rule optimally balanced alien with indigenous governance so as to promote the stability and continuity necessary for the gradual development of broader political, economic, and social transformations in Nigerian societies over the long term. From the British perspective, indirect rule allowed Nigerian cultures to maintain those traditions and customs that were valuable and effective, while weeding out the few practices that hindered the development of Nigerian societies.

In theory, indirect rule made sense to the colonial mind. In practice, it often did not work as planned. In southeastern Nigeria, British colonial officers had an extremely difficult time even identifying who the "traditional" rulers of the region were. The process began in the 1890s with the establishment of the Niger Coast Protectorate under the administration of Claude Macdonald. Building on the court of equity established by British consuls on the Oil Rivers in the 1850s, Macdonald had developed a native court in the coastal communities of Calabar by 1892. This native court consisted of representatives from the main ruling houses of Calabar, with the British governor general as the president, and served as a court of appeal for the many minor courts that adjudicated disputes over the larger Cross Rivers area. Soon afterwards, similar native courts were established in Bonny, Degema, and Buguma.[2]

The native court system established on the coast spread into the interior with the British pacification campaigns of the early twentieth century that brought southeastern Nigeria under colonial rule. The British found the setting up of native courts difficult to accomplish in the interior, however, because the political landscape differed greatly from that of the coast. Rather than being centered on autocratic heads of households as in the coastal city states, government among the Igbo, Ibibio, Urhobo, and other hinterland societies was based on village or village-group councils along the lines of a representative democracy. To the extent that chiefs existed in these areas, they were little more than figureheads whose most important duty was ritual oversight; they did not have significant political authority over villages or village groups.[3] Confounded by the lack of local paramount chiefs, British colonial officers did not know who should be approached to sit on the native courts. In order to find worthy elites for positions on the courts, the British resorted either to "consultation" with local people to determine whom they most revered or to the arbitrary selection of a local community member based on his perceived leadership capabilities.

The authority of the native courts derived entirely from the British "certificate of recognition," or warrant, that a court member received on taking office and not necessarily from any organic relationship to traditional political institutions. The members of the native courts in the southeast therefore came to be known by the derogatory term "warrant chiefs": indigenous rulers created entirely by the process of establishing indirect rule. The warrant chiefs became poor representations of the traditional governing apparatus in the protectorate, alien replacements who engendered little respect from the subjects under their jurisdiction. The institution of the native court system gave executive and judicial powers to individuals who had no traditional claim to them. The British often chose people with little or no standing in their communities to sit on the court, even after consultation with local communities. Afigbo has noted that sometimes, when the British asked communities to produce their "chiefs," the local populations assumed that, once handed over, the chiefs were to be killed. Other communities thought that the British were asking for tribute. In both cases, the communities pointed the British to unimportant people, social outcasts or slaves, thereby protecting their true leaders from the machinations of a hostile occupying force. Second, the jurisdiction that the British granted to native courts often straddled village groups or crossed ethnic boundaries, placing the warrant chiefs in a position of political power over communities that did not even recognize them as members of the community, let alone as members of a legitimate governing body.[4]

Systems of colonial administration began to develop in southwestern Nigeria from the 1860s. In the Colony of Lagos, British colonial officers ruled more directly than in any other part of Nigeria. Because it had been a Crown Colony since 1861, Lagos was officially British territory, as opposed to the rest of Nigeria, which was British-protected territory. Lagos came under the direct suzerainty of the British monarch, and the inhabitants of Lagos had all the rights of British citizens. As a result, colonial officials took control of the day-to-day administration of Lagos in a manner unlike any other part of Nigeria. Traditional elites were involved in the colonial administration, but not to the extent they were elsewhere. Administration in Lagos was very much directed by the colonial governor, although local elites did play a substantial role as advisers to him. Under the administration of Governor William MacGregor (1899–1904), a Legislative Council and a Central Native Council made up of members of the traditional ruling elite were established, with MacGregor himself as president. The function of these bodies was to advise the governor on traditional Yoruba law regarding such issues as land ownership, marriage customs, and ceremonial procedures. While the governor retained the sole right to make decisions on these matters, the councils incorporated the traditional elite to some extent and in principle prevented the governor from angering or alienating his Lagosian subjects through rash or uninformed decisions. In this way, the traditional elite maintained some power, although significantly reduced, and the colonial government was able to present itself as concerned with the preservation of local culture.[5]

Colonial administration took a different form in the Protectorate of Lagos, which encompassed the Yoruba-dominated states of the mainland.

Although the governor of the Lagos colony was also the supreme administrator of the Lagos protectorate, the power of the British colonial government was somewhat mitigated by the terms of the various treaties of protection signed with individual Yoruba leaders in the 1890s. These treaties differed throughout Yorubaland; they all guaranteed some kind of "independence" for the existing ruling authorities, however, particularly over internal affairs. For the most part, the colonial government in Lagos was content to allow traditional rulers to maintain their authority, preferring not to define too closely what "independence" actually meant, so as not to upset the political stability that had emerged in the region. Some administrative reorganization was required, however, to bring the protectorate under British control. MacGregor extended his Native Council Ordinance into Yorubaland, recognizing native councils where they already existed and creating them where they did not. Throughout the protectorate, however, the most prominent chief served as the president of the Native Council, unlike the situation in Lagos, where the British governor himself held this position. The local British officer served only in an "advisory" capacity; he did not make decisions, but he did indicate to the council what decisions should be made in order to please the British colonial government. Failure to please the colonial government often led to reprisals, as in 1901, when MacGregor had several chiefs fined and one imprisoned for the execution of a purported thief. The ruling on the execution was completely within the jurisdiction of the Native Council, but MacGregor's view that it was unjust led to direct colonial intervention.[6]

Establishing systems of indirect rule in southern Nigeria required a significant amount of British reformulation of traditional political institutions. This differed from the Protectorate of Northern Nigeria, where Lugard's administration (1900–6) was able simply to replace the administrative superstructure that had governed the Sokoto Caliphate with a British duplicate. Although the Sultan of Sokoto had been deposed and killed, the Fulani emirs and non-Muslim chiefs retained control over their respective emirates and regions, which were renamed native authorities. Whereas their power had previously derived from their relationship with the Sultan of Sokoto, they now maintained their power at the pleasure of the British high commissioner – that is, Lugard and his successors. The *kofa* who had once overseen the activities of the emirs on behalf of the Sultan of Sokoto was replaced with a British Resident, who reported directly to the high commissioner and whose duty it was to transmit orders from the high commissioner to the emirs and chiefs and to serve as "a watchful adviser not ... an interfering ruler," just as district officers were charged to do in the southern protectorates.[7] The power of traditional rulers to adjudicate in their territories was retained in the Native Courts Proclamation of 1902, which allowed existing legal systems to remain intact. Emirs also maintained their power and responsibility to tax their subject populations and to pay tribute to the British colonial government.[8]

The indirect rule regimes in the southern and northern protectorates developed separately and, as a result, differed significantly. Whereas indirect rule in the south was mostly conducted through councils of traditional rulers, in the north power in any given region was centralized in the hands of a single emir, or, in the non-Muslim areas, of a paramount chief. In the southern protectorates colonial officials tended to favor the extension of European education and modern social services. In Lagos, for example, the colonial government had established a Medical Department, which employed eleven European and three African doctors by 1898, a police service, and a Public Works Department charged with the maintenance of public buildings and roads and the extension of electric lighting, telegraphs, piers, and public transport, among other things.[9] In the southeast, Ralph Moor became a champion of the use of the colonial government to extend European education in the early part of the twentieth century.[10]

In direct contrast, colonial officials in the north explicitly forbade colonial government expenditure on such social services, in the interests of both parsimony and cultural preservation. The development of modern social services under Lugard's indirect rule was to be undertaken by native administrations themselves at their own expense and on their own terms. Lugard believed that for the colonial government itself to embark on such activities was a direct violation of the Dual Mandate, in that it constituted unnecessary colonial expenditure and purposelessly brought about the erosion of traditional social structures. Also in the name of preserving traditional cultures, Lugard and his successors severely restricted the access of Christian missionaries to the Muslim areas of northern Nigeria. As a result, the inhabitants of northern Nigeria did not have the access to European education that southerners had. By the time the Colonial Office decided to amalgamate the northern and southern provinces of Nigeria into a single administrative unit in 1912, the two regions were already on very different paths.

THE AMALGAMATION OF NIGERIA

The ostensible reason for amalgamating the Nigerian protectorates was economic. Despite the efforts of Lugard and his successors to reorganize the finances of northern Nigeria, the economy of the northern protectorate had floundered under indirect rule and had not become fully self-financing as of 1914. Taxation had not produced enough revenue to cover the administrative needs of the protectorate, and commerce had not grown sufficiently to make the region profitable. To finance itself, the northern protectorate relied on annual subsidies from southern Nigeria and an imperial grant-in-aid from the British government to the tune of approximately £300,000 per year.[11] Both the Colonial Office and Lugard believed that centralizing the protectorates under a single administration would be economically beneficial. Amalgamation would allow for a streamlining of existing expenses and would allow the central administration to divert resources as it saw fit – allocating southern revenue to the north as necessary. It would also allow for the centralization of infrastructural and development schemes, reducing waste and eventually bringing about the integration of the southern and northern economies on a much greater scale. The amalgamation of the Colony and Protectorate of Lagos with the Niger Coast Protectorate to form a single Protectorate of Southern Nigeria occurred in 1906.[12] Lugard, who had left northern Nigeria in 1906, was brought back in 1912 to oversee the amalgamation of the southern and northern protectorates. This process was completed in 1914, with Lugard becoming the first governor general of a unified Nigeria, a position he held until 1919.

Lugard's main goal as governor general of a unified Nigeria was to centralize the administrative apparatus. Lugard believed that the models that had been developed in southern Nigeria amounted to little more than administrative chaos. He found the variations in structure and procedure that existed across space unacceptable. He also believed that the "indirect" rule established in southern Nigeria was, in fact, far too direct, in that the British colonial officers had far too much power and influence over the affairs of the native courts and councils. Failing to recognize that the systems that had been established in southern Nigeria had emerged as responses to the variation in social make-up of communities in southern Nigeria, Lugard instead tried to impose on southern Nigeria the system of administration established in the north: ostensibly making emirs out of southern kings and chiefs. Always searching for paramount chiefs in whom to invest sole authority, Lugard extended to traditional rulers in southern Nigeria powers and duties that they had never traditionally held, disregarding his self-professed duty to preserve traditional institutions and widening the rift created by colonialism between indigenous rulers and their subjects.

Nowhere were the effects of Lugard's systematization of indirect rule more apparent than in the realm of revenue collection. Indirect rule in the north derived colonial and native authority revenue primarily from the direct taxation of the population. This tax was collected by the emir and placed in the native treasury. The emir and his servants all received salaries paid from the native treasury, and all other public expenditures came from the native treasury funds as well. This system worked in the north, where the population had a long history of paying taxes to emirs and where emirs had a long history of paying tribute to an imperial authority. In southern Nigeria, colonial revenues had been collected and allocated very differently. In the southwest, the primary source of revenue came in the form of customs duties. In the southeast, the native courts had a native treasury system, but revenues were primarily obtained through fees and fines imposed by the court. In neither of these regions was there a history of direct taxation; nor did the indigenous rulers traditionally have the unilateral power to collect taxes. In neither region were colonial revenues used to pay salaries to indigenous rulers.

Despite both indigenous tradition and established colonial practice in southern Nigeria, Lugard insisted that the establishment of native treasuries funded by direct taxation throughout Nigeria was the cornerstone of effective colonial administration and "civilized" governance. He argued that direct taxation served as an indication to indigenous populations of the power that traditional chiefs and kings still held, despite the British presence. He also argued that it was imperative that indigenous rulers be allocated salaries paid by the native treasury in order to reduce corruption and make them indebted to the central colonial government.[13] Although Lugard received reports from various colonial officers in southern Nigeria indicating that direct taxation was not practicable in most areas of southern Nigeria, he went ahead with his administrative overhaul, imposing direct taxation on Benin in 1914, Oyo in 1916, Abeokuta in 1918, and parts of southeastern Nigeria by 1926. Lugard's indirect rule therefore did no more to preserve traditional societies in southern Nigeria than had the systems devised by his predecessors; in fact, it led to significant political and social changes.

THE COLONIAL ECONOMY

Just as colonial rule altered traditional political institutions in the name of "civilization," so too did it transform the economy of Nigeria. Ideally, the British believed that they could bring Nigerian societies into "civilization" through the development of a "modern" economy. By expanding the commercial infrastructure and promoting increased trade throughout Nigeria, British colonial administrators believed that they were fulfilling the dictates of the Dual Mandate, making the colonial endeavor profitable for both European merchants and Nigerian producers. In fact, the colonial economy did far more to enrich existing British commercial interests than to develop Nigerian industry and commerce into a viable, modern economy.[14]

The British approach to economic development had three main objectives. The first goal was the expansion of Nigerian commerce through the exportation of raw materials – cash crops and minerals – and the importation of European finished goods. To facilitate this increased commerce, the British made large-scale improvements to the transportation and communication infrastructure of Nigeria, building roads, railways, telegraphs, and ports, and expanding the navigable waterways. The second goal was to bring Nigeria into a cash economy based on the UK currency. The third goal was to force Nigerians to work for that currency. Over time, colonial economic policy resulted in the growing dependence of Nigerians on an export economy dominated by European firms with which indigenous Nigerian enterprise could not compete and which conducted business primarily with a view towards European profitability at the expense of Nigerian producers.

The most important export crops produced in colonial Nigeria were groundnuts and cotton in the north, cocoa in the southwest, and palm produce in the southeast. Subsistence crops such as cassava, yam, and millet remained important throughout the period; the British economic scheme was to divert as much agricultural production as possible towards the exportation of cash crops, however, with the result that subsistence farming suffered under the colonial regime. The exportation of cash crops grew exponentially in the period before 1930. For instance, between 1900 and 1904 Nigeria exported an average of 475 tons of groundnuts per year. Between 1925 and 1929 this annual figure had grown to nearly 109,068 tons. Cotton exports rose from an average of 132 tons a year in 1900–4 to 6,038 tons by 1925–9. Cocoa exports expanded from an average of 305 tons a year over the period 1900–4 to an average of 45,483 tons between 1925 and 1929. Annual exports of palm oil averaged 53,729 tons between 1900 and 1904, compared to 124,716 tons between 1925 and 1929. Palm kernel exports grew from an average of 120,778 tons per year in the period 1900–4 to an average of 255,469 tons per year between 1925 and 1929.[15]

The main mineral exports of Nigeria were tin and, to a lesser degree, gold, silver, lead, and diamonds.[16] The mining of coal, discovered in the southeast near the city of Enugu, also became a major endeavor of the colonial government, which extracted it mainly for the internal use of the railway.[17] Tin, found primarily in the middle belt in the area around Bauchi and on the Jos Plateau, was exported to the tune of only 212 tons in 1907. By 1930, however, annual exports exceeded 12,000 tons.[18] The extraction of gold, diamonds, and other precious metals was erratic, and did not see the sustainable growth of other export industries, because of the relative paucity of these minerals.

To facilitate the export of the commodities mentioned above, the colonial government undertook large-scale projects to improve the transportation infrastructure of Nigeria. Railways were built to connect the major cities of Nigeria. By 1900 a railway line was in operation between Lagos and Ibadan. This line reached Oshogbo in 1907 and the river Niger at Jebba in 1909. In the north the original plan was to create lines connecting major trade centers with the river Niger. Once goods reached the Niger they could be shipped to the coast. A short line connecting Zungeru to the river Kaduna, a feeder of the Niger, had been built by 1902. By 1907 a line designed to connect Zungeru, Zaria, and Kano with the Niger at Baro had begun construction. On January 1, 1912, the Lagos line joined with the Kano line, making it possible for goods to be shipped from the north straight to Lagos. By 1916 a line had been completed between the coastal city of Port Harcourt in the southeast and Enugu, which was the main source of coal for the railway. This eastern line connected with the western line at Kaduna in 1926.[19] Railways allowed for larger amounts of goods to be transported over longer distances more quickly. This had huge implications for the export economy. For instance, in 1910 exports of groundnuts from northern Nigeria amounted to only 1,179 tons; when the railway reached Kano in 1911 exports jumped immediately, to 19,288 tons.[20] By 1915 groundnut exports had risen to approximately 41,000 tons a year, and the railway played a significant role in this growth.[21]

The colonial government also undertook to expand the capacity of Nigeria's navigable waterways. Swamps were dredged to allow larger ships to dock at Nigeria's ports. Inland rivers and tributaries were deepened and widened to allow larger watercraft to engage in the transport of goods. The colonial government also built paved roads, particularly in southern Nigeria, to connect rural zones of agricultural production to the railways, as well as to make it easier for government officials, the military, and the police to move around the countryside. Telegraph cables were constructed, particularly along the railway lines, to improve communication and keep the trains running smoothly.

Cash crop production, whether of cocoa, groundnuts, or palm produce, was dominated by small-scale producers who continued to use traditional methods of growing, harvesting, and preparing products for market. The existence of many small-scale producers meant that they competed with each other when the time came to sell their goods, which kept prices low. Further adding to the difficulties of small-scale farmers, cash crops were produced in the Nigerian interior but had to be exported from the coast. Farmers therefore either had to pay to get their goods to the coast themselves, or sell to middlemen, who transported the goods to the coast and sold them to the European shipping firms at a slightly higher price.

All this competition between Nigerians benefited the European firms, which did not face such competition among themselves. Prior to the First World War German firms competed seriously with British firms for Nigerian exports. With the outbreak of war, however, German businesses were expelled from Nigeria, only to return after the war in a much-diminished capacity.[22] By 1939 a mere seven European firms controlled over two-thirds of all Nigeria's export trade. The largest was the United Africa Company (UAC), which was a branch of the larger Anglo-Dutch consortium Unilever. The UAC controlled 40 percent of Nigeria's export economy by 1939, while the parent company, Unilever, controlled 80 percent of the total external trade of Nigeria.[23] This dominance by a few large firms, many of which operated under the umbrella of a huge parent corporation, allowed these firms to keep prices for goods bought very low, while prices for goods sold were inflated. Large European-owned mining operations also dominated mineral extraction. Several mining firms, such as Ropp Tin and the Naraguta Company, were extracting tin from the Jos Plateau by the first decade of the twentieth century, each making over 100 percent profits by 1914.[24]

The exploitative nature of the colonial economy ensured that very little sustainable development occurred during the colonial period. Neither the profit-mongering European firms nor the stingy colonial government were willing to invest in the long-term development of Nigeria in the period before the Second World War. European firms took their profits back to Europe, enriching shareholders at the expense of exploited Nigerian labor. Because so much of the wealth of Nigeria was being extracted for European profits, very few Nigerians earned enough to invest in local development projects of their own. A few local industries continued to flourish, such as traditional textile weaving, brewing, and blacksmithing, but most other Nigerian craftwork could not compete with the huge quantities of cheaper European imports that flooded the markets.[25] Nigerians became producers for and workers in an extractive economy that did little for the long-term development of their country.

The question that must be asked, then, is why Nigerians participated in a colonial economy that benefited European firms so much more than themselves. Nigerians had many different motivations for involving themselves in the colonial economy. For many, the export economy was initially quite profitable. In some regions, the British colonial economy simply encouraged the expansion of production in commodities that were already under cultivation. For instance, groundnuts, cotton, and palm oil had been grown for domestic use in Nigeria for centuries. The British simply encouraged Nigerian farmers to produce more of these commodities than was needed for domestic consumption and to sell the surplus for export. Thus, many farmers viewed the export economy as a source of supplemental income and were more than willing to take advantage of it. Prior to the late 1920s many farmers were able to make a decent living growing new crops that had no domestic use. Cocoa, which was not consumed locally and had not been cultivated in Nigeria before the expansion of the export economy, made many small farmers relatively wealthy in the first three decades of the twentieth century. Sara S. Berry has noted that prosperity from cocoa exports allowed many farmers to increase the consumption of both locally produced goods and imports. By 1929 so many cocoa farmers in Yorubaland had re-roofed their houses with imported sheets of corrugated iron that these iron sheets had become symbols of the prosperity of the region.[26]

Other work in the colonial economy was less attractive. Foreign firms and the colonial government needed Nigerian labor as well. Mining companies needed miners; shipping companies needed dock workers; railway companies needed freight haulers; and the colonial government needed workers to build the roads, railway lines, ports, and public buildings on which the colonial economy depended. Both foreign firms and the colonial government relied heavily on Nigerian wage laborers to do this work. These jobs paid poorly. They involved hard, sometimes dangerous, manual labor. They often required workers to travel long distances to work, and there was little to no opportunity for promotion or pay raises to make the work palatable. Added to this, there was a general labor shortage through much of Nigeria in the early colonial period. Foreign firms and the colonial government therefore found it extremely difficult to attract the wage laborers they needed to develop the economy and maximize their profits.

The colonial government used several approaches to push Nigerians into wage labor. Forced labor was common. Throughout Nigeria, native administrations were coerced to supply laborers, sometimes as a substitute for taxes, and workers were usually paid a pittance for their efforts.[27] The colonial government employed forced labor to build railways, ports, and roads. Mining companies received conscripted labor from native administrations in the north. Even the use of forced labor did not solve the labor shortage problems, however. Clearly, these were not jobs that many indigenous workers chose to do, and many resisted the methods of obtaining forced labor. Even with wage contracts, conditions for mine employees were poor. Many mine workers were not paid enough to feed and clothe themselves; they often fled or joined the military to get out of their forced or contracted labor terms.[28] In southwestern Nigeria, colonial officials lamented the fact that many forced laborers absconded from their duties to return to the cocoa fields, where they received better compensation and worked more freely.[29]

The colonial government therefore had to come up with other ways to coerce Nigerians to work in the colonial economy. One way was to make Nigerians dependent on cash money in the form of imported British currency, which could be obtained only by engaging in the colonial economy, either as a producer or as paid labor. Many different forms of currency existed in Nigeria in the early twentieth century. The cowry shell and the manila (a curved rod of copper or brass) were the most widely used, particularly in southern Nigeria, but gold dust, liquor, guns, and all sorts of foreign coins were also in circulation. Barter trade in commodity items also continued to be common. The British decided to streamline the Nigerian monetary system in order to solidify the prices of goods and to force Nigerians to work for cash that only the British could provide. In 1902 the colonial government outlawed the importation of manilas and fixed the price in sterling of existing manilas.[30] Cowry importation was prohibited in 1904.[31] UK coins and paper money were imported and circulated as the only legitimate legal tender.

The introduction and systematization of a cash economy based on British-imported currency forced Nigerians into the colonial economy in insidious ways. Any transaction concerning the colonial government or the European trading firms was conducted in the new cash currency. This meant that any producer wishing to sell to the British was paid in cash, thereby quickly increasing the circulation, availability, and legitimacy of the new currency. Likewise, anyone wishing to purchase British imports had to pay in cash. Imports of such items as cheap textiles, liquor,

Figure 5.1 A typical street-side market in Ibadan (collection of Roy Doron)

matches, kerosene, tobacco, books, electronic goods, and medicines were becoming increasingly popular in Nigeria, particularly among the growing class of European-educated Nigerians in the south. The desire for British luxury goods meant that more and more Nigerians were willing to take wage labor jobs with the colonial government or European firms in order to earn the cash necessary to purchase imported wares. Furthermore, and most importantly from the perspective of the majority of rural Nigerians, all colonial taxes had to be paid in cash. The imposition of direct taxes made it virtually impossible for Nigerians to avoid participating in the colonial economy to some degree. In order to pay taxes and keep individuals and their families on the good side of the law, many Nigerians found themselves engaged in the wage labor force at least part-time.

From the late 1920s the Nigerian economy was affected by the global depression that gripped the world. After the Second World War, however, the colonial administration began to make significant changes to the colonial economic model, undertaking large development and modernization schemes to appease the calls of a growing body of Nigerian nationalists for greater economic, and political, independence. These developments are discussed in detail in the next chapter.

SOCIAL AND CULTURAL DEVELOPMENTS

The changes in Nigeria's political and economic structures brought about by colonialism also led to social and cultural changes. The labor needs of the colonial economy led to widespread urbanization.[32] The urban population increased rapidly as people migrated to cities in droves looking for work as manual laborers. Others migrated to cities to trade, taking advantage of the proximity of the railways. The majority of migrant laborers were young men who had come to the cities to make money to support their families back in the rural villages of Nigeria. For instance, on the Jos Plateau the ever-increasing labor needs of tin-mining companies led to large influxes of migrant male labor. As Bill Freund has noted, in 1914 the mining companies employed an average of 17,833 daily paid laborers; by 1920 this number had risen to 22,976, and by 1928 to 39,959.[33] Many people also migrated to cities to serve the needs of these young, kinless men. Many moved to the cities to become self-employed, working as craftspeople, barbers, and tailors, or selling food or other items in the large urban markets. The population of Nigeria's urban areas skyrocketed during the colonial period. For instance, the population of Lagos was estimated at 42,000 in 1901. By 1931 the population had grown to approximately 126,000.[34] Other cities saw similar growth rates, if not in such large numbers.

The extraction of male labor to serve the needs of the colonial export economy through cash cropping and manual wage labor increased the labor responsibilities and economic activity of women, particularly in southern Nigeria. The increased production of cash crops and the labor shortages brought about by the increased wage labor needs of the colonial economy combined to affect negatively the production of foodstuffs in southern Nigeria. As labor was diverted to meet the needs of the colonial economy, the internal economy suffered. In southeastern Nigeria, women became increasingly responsible for food production. This led to the adoption of cassava as a food source in this region, because cassava grows more abundantly in poor soil and is less labor-intensive in its cultivation than yam. The manpower shortages caused by Nigerian troop conscription during the First World War and the high death rates from the influenza pandemic that followed the war also contributed to the increased cultivation of cassava by women.[35] Cassava production therefore became largely a woman's business.[36]

While this detracted from women's previous economic position in the palm produce economy, it also brought commercial opportunities, as women began selling surplus cassava to the expanding urban areas of southeastern Nigeria that increasingly needed food imports to support their growing non-agricultural workforce.[37] In southwestern Nigeria, urbanization and the growth of the cocoa market also led to decreases in food production. Unlike the situation in southeastern Nigeria, however, in Yoruba society women traditionally did not farm extensively; their relationship to food production was limited to processing and cooking. Therefore, in southwestern Nigeria, the decrease in food production did not lead to the diversification of crops or the adoption of subsistence farming by women but, rather, to the more generalized importation of foodstuffs. Women increasingly became responsible for importing, because they had traditionally been responsible for food preparation. In importing foodstuffs, women became increasingly involved in the colonial economy, and many began to make money as traders in their own right.[38]

Another major cultural development brought about by colonial rule was the growth of the class of Western-educated Nigerians. Until roughly the last decade of the nineteenth century the majority of European-educated Africans in Nigeria were "recaptive" slaves or their descendants, known as Saro, who had returned to Nigeria from Sierra Leone. The list of Saro included such men as Samuel Ajayi Crowther, the famed Bishop of the Niger, who returned to Nigeria in the nineteenth century and became instrumental in the establishment of Christian missions in southern Nigeria.[39]

Many Nigerian communities were ambivalent towards the expansion of Christian missionaries and their schools at first. Some Nigerian societies saw Christianity as a threat to traditional ways of life as well as to traditional political and economic institutions. For example, the Ijebu of Yorubaland completely forbade white men and Christians to enter their territory before the 1880s, because they feared that missionaries were agents of British imperialism. Likewise, Ja Ja, the King of Opobo, had seen Christianity as a threat to his commercial activity and, by extension, his power base in the Niger delta region. Since Christianity promoted a belief in only one God, this meant that under Christian doctrine the spiritual basis of the Okonko and Ekpe societies became unacceptable. Therefore, Ja Ja feared that the spread of Christianity in the Niger delta would ultimately lead to the deterioration of commercial relations between coastal traders and their inland suppliers – relations that had been based on a common religious tradition – and therefore fought against the spread of missionaries until his exile to the West Indies at British hands in 1887.

By the late nineteenth century, however, increasing numbers of Nigerians were taking advantage of the opportunities that a European education in a mission school could offer, of which the most notable was the ability to read and write in English. With the onset of colonial administration and the expansion of the colonial economy based on increased import-export commerce from the 1890s, the ability to read and write in English became the stepping stone to a middle-class career. European-educated Nigerians could find reasonably paid jobs as clerks in the native courts or councils, or in other civil service positions in the colonial regime. They could also work as clerks or intermediaries for the European trading firms that dominated the export trade. Still others went into the service of the Church, often becoming teachers in the very schools in which they had been educated. The 1921 census indicated that there were approximately 32,000 European-educated southern Nigerians, roughly 0.5 percent of the population. Another 4 percent of the population reportedly had attained what the colonial government called "imperfect" education, meaning they had begun but not completed primary schooling.[40]

For the most part, European education in Nigeria was limited to primary education or industrial training. It was not initially thought that secondary schools or universities would be necessary or practical in Nigeria. European education was limited mostly to rudimentary reading and writing skills, as well as instruction in Christian theology. The vast majority of European-educated Nigerians therefore received at best full primary education; many received only a partial primary education. By 1926, however, there were eighteen secondary schools in Nigeria, although high admission fees limited attendance. A very small percentage of students found opportunities for post-secondary education abroad, either in Sierra Leone or in the United Kingdom, and became the few Nigerian doctors, lawyers, and engineers of the colonial era. By 1921 southern Nigeria boasted only seventy-three professionals with such training.[41]

Education opportunities remained limited; even those who received the most limited training improved their chances of finding employment with the colonial government or the European trading firms, however. In 1881 the colonial government in Lagos employed forty-five civil servants. By 1901 over 1,100 civil servants and commercial clerks worked in Lagos. This number rose to over 5,300 by 1921.[42] The expansion of the colonial export economy therefore had a significant impact on the demand for European education in southern Nigeria, where the bulk of European commerce took place.

European education remained primarily limited to southern Nigeria, partly because European education was most useful in southern Nigeria but also because European education remained the domain of the Christian missions, the activities of which were overwhelmingly limited to southern Nigeria. The colonial government did not compete with mission schools in the south, allowing the Christian missions to educate at their own expense the literate Nigerians who filled the lower levels of the colonial bureaucracy. As of 1921 there were over 2,200 schools in southern Nigeria and over 90 percent of these schools received no financial assistance from the colonial government.[43] Only a handful of mission schools were in operation in northern Nigeria, where Lugard and his successors had restricted missionary enterprise on the grounds of Islamic cultural preservation. Enrollment in non-Quranic primary schools in northern Nigeria stood at 2 percent of the level in southern Nigeria in 1913.[44]

European education did have an effect on the behaviors and beliefs of the Nigerians who received it, molding them over the decades into what has been called an African middle class – African in heritage, but with many European tastes and values. The European-educated population inhabited a cultural milieu influenced both by their indigenous roots and by the lifestyle provided by their foreign education. Because European education was so firmly linked to the Christian missions, most of the Nigerians who were educated in the European fashion also became practicing Christians and assimilated many of the values of nineteenth- and twentieth-century Christianity into their own lifestyles. While many Nigerian communities continued to allow the institution of domestic slavery, most European-educated Nigerians believed in the anti-slavery cause. While most Nigerian societies practiced polygamy as a means of enhancing a family's productive capacity, European-educated Nigerians tended to choose monogamous, Christian marriages.[45]

Because their skills earned them coveted and relatively high-paying jobs with the colonial administration or European trading firms in the cities, the European-educated elite was also exposed to and receptive of British culture in a way that poorer, rural Nigerians were not. A taste transfer therefore occurred among the members of the European-educated middle class, as they began to identify, at least in part, with the culture in which they were educated and in which they worked. The European-educated middle class earned better wages and therefore had greater purchasing power than other Nigerians. As a result, they bought more imports than other Nigerians, particularly luxury items such as European clothing, hats and shoes, books, radio sets, and automobiles, as well as building European-style homes.[46] Possessing such items became a status marker, visibly setting European-educated Nigerians apart from their "uneducated" compatriots.

Even though European-educated Nigerians understood that they had gained much under colonial rule, they also had good reasons to reproach the colonial regime. British colonial rule was founded on the ideology that Africans, as a race, were inferior to Europeans and needed gradual amelioration under British supervision; this was the basis of the Dual Mandate. As a result of this ideology, the same European employers that gave jobs to European-educated Nigerians based on their individual merits also kept them subjugated based on their racial background. Lugard, for example, disdained the European-educated Nigerians, claiming that mission schools inculcated in their pupils "discontent, impatience of any control, and an unjustifiable assumption of self-importance in the individual," all of which made the European-educated Nigerian a threat to both British rule and traditional social norms.[47] The ideal Nigerian was one who had attained enough education to be useful to the colonial system but not enough to think himself the intellectual equal of the white man. Within the colonial government and European firms, only low-level bureaucratic positions were filled by Nigerians, and there was little opportunity for promotion or advancement within the colonial government or European firm once hired.

Nevertheless, the European-educated middle-class Nigerians relished their position as cultural intermediaries to a great extent. Many European-educated Nigerians believed in the "civilizing mission" of the British colonial adventure. They owed their own heightened material and social position to the "civilizing" influence of Christianity and mission education. They saw themselves as links between the old, traditional ways and the new, modern lifestyles, and advocated to their countrymen the values of anti-slavery, commerce, and Christianity. At the same time, however, European-educated Nigerians were constantly reminded of their Africanness, which was treated by Europeans as evidence of weakness, savagery, and corruption. European-educated Nigerians, by and large, refused to see their indigenous heritage this way; rather, they wore it as a badge of pride. Just as European-educated Nigerians promoted the benefits of the "civilizing mission" to other Nigerians, they also promoted the values of indigenous Nigerian societies among themselves and to the British colonial administration, in an effort to illustrate both pride in their heritage and the capacity of Nigerians to advance on their own terms. They sought to prove both to the British and to other Nigerians that "civilization" did not have to mean the abandonment of one's heritage and the imitation of a foreign lifestyle.

European-educated middle-class Nigerians consciously promulgated an identity that blended the "traditional" and the "modern," showing that these two classifications were not mutually exclusive. While continuing to believe in the benefits of European education and Christian values, middle-class Nigerians also embraced their local African cultures. They took pride in wearing traditional dress as well as European clothing. Many middle-class Nigerians changed their Christian names to traditional names and gave their children traditional names. They promoted the use of indigenous languages alongside English in school and in everyday use, and developed African histories to be taught alongside European history in schools.[48] New African-led churches were built and swelled their congregations in the early twentieth century. These African churches broke with the European churches over both cultural and doctrinal issues. They preached Christian values but adapted their teachings to fit better the cultural peculiarities of Nigerian communities, incorporating indigenous cultural elements such as traditional singing, drumming, and dancing, group baptisms, and tolerance of polygamy. African churches with indigenous leaders were also better equipped than European-led churches to understand the problems that their congregations experienced and to offer them solace and advice.[49]

Efforts on the part of European-educated elites to distinguish themselves from a British culture that did not view them as equals were accompanied by direct protests and criticisms directed at the colonial regime, which continued to exclude European-educated Nigerians from the processes of government and to subordinate traditional authorities to alien domination. An independent Nigerian press emerged in the late nineteenth century and quickly became the tool through which literate Nigerians criticized the colonial government and made their demands known. Over fifty different newspapers were printed in Nigeria between 1880 and 1937. Most newspapers in the early colonial period were based in Lagos, as was a large percentage of the literate Nigerian community. From the 1920s, however, newspapers were established in urban areas throughout southern Nigeria, from Ibadan, Abeokuta, Ijebu-Ode, and Oshogbo in the southwest to Calabar, Aba, Onitsha, Enugu, and Port Harcourt in the southeast.[50] Newspapers were printed both in English and in indigenous languages, and some, such as *Eko Akete* of Lagos, were bilingual.

Figure 5.2 Girl reading a newspaper (collection of Roy Doron)

Literate elites used newspapers to reach all elements of Nigerian society. Perhaps the most famous newspaperman in the first decades of the colonial period in Nigeria was Herbert Macaulay, the European-educated grandson of Bishop Samuel Ajayi Crowther. After taking a degree in civil engineering and becoming disillusioned with the civilizing mission of British colonial rule, Macaulay changed career paths and became a respected journalist in Lagos. Macaulay's newspapers, such as the *Lagos Daily News*, leveled passionate criticism at the colonial regime and earned him the title "father of Nigerian nationalism." Newspapers spoke to the colonial government, urging reform, criticizing policies that negatively affected Nigerians, and pushing for a greater involvement of Nigerians in their own government. They spoke to other literate Nigerians, building a community of people aware of the issues of the day and offering a forum through which to voice their concerns. They also spoke to the illiterate masses, who got the news by word of mouth or through public readings, informing them of how government actions were affecting their lives. Elites also used newspapers to spread their message of African pride, ingenuity, and intelligence, actively opposing the racist ideologies put forward by the colonial regime. In this way, newspapers became an early avenue of peaceful protest and a catalyst for the nationalist sentiments that developed over time.

Beyond the European-educated elite, working-class Nigerians and peasant farmers also had good reasons to feel frustrated with the colonial regime and the changes that colonial rule had brought to traditional political, economic, and social structures. Particularly in southern Nigeria, indirect rule had alienated indigenous authorities from their subjects. Whereas chiefs and kings had traditionally maintained power by ruling in a fashion that pleased their subjects, under colonial rule traditional elites maintained power by pleasing the British colonial authorities first and foremost. The colonial economy forced people to work for cash, commandeered labor on a regular basis, and affected gender and generational relations as traditional economic roles became blurred and were refashioned to meet the needs of increased cash cropping, decreased food production, and expansion in the import-export market. Nothing aroused more ire among the common people of southern Nigeria, however, than the new forms of taxation that accompanied colonial rule.

Anti-tax protests became one of the most common forms of anti-colonial resistance that emerged in southern Nigeria in the first three decades of the twentieth century. As early as 1908 massive protests against the colonial government took place in Lagos in opposition to the water rate, which charged Lagosians against their will for the development of a new water scheme that would reduce Lagosians' reliance on well and rain water. The move was opposed by both the local chiefs and Herbert Macaulay, who had become the leading voice of the European-educated elements in Lagos through his newspapers.[51] The protests were carried out mostly by average Nigerians, however, indicating both the disaffection produced by colonial taxation policies in Nigeria and the ability of poor Nigerian workers to make their voices heard.

Other mass protests against taxation occurred in other parts of southern Nigeria, particularly after the amalgamation of the northern and southern protectorates and the extension of direct taxation to the south after 1914. Riots took place in Oyo the first time taxes were collected in 1916,[52] and in Abeokuta the Egba rebelled against direct taxation in 1918. In both places, people were expressing frustration with a system that gave traditional elites powers that they had never possessed previously. Neither the *alafin* of Oyo nor the *alake* of Abeokuta traditionally had the power unilaterally to impose or collect taxes. In Abeokuta, it had become so difficult for the *alake* to exercise this new authority that tax collectors often resorted to force, going so far as to strip uncooperative women naked in public spaces to see if they were old enough to pay taxes.[53] Such actions further alienated the Egba masses from their traditional leaders, leading to widespread rioting in which the telegraph and railways were destroyed in protest against the colonial regime.

Direct taxation did not reach southeastern Nigeria until 1926, but it faced similar opposition. Whereas in Abeokuta the poll tax applied to men and women alike, in southeastern Nigeria originally only men were taxed. A census had been conducted in 1926 to determine who was eligible for taxation in the region, and taxation was subsequently introduced. In 1928, however, an assistant district officer in Owerri Province ordered local warrant chiefs to conduct another census. Women in the region feared that a new census meant they were soon to be taxed as well. Already burdened with supporting families and helping men to pay their taxes, the women of southeastern Nigeria held mass demonstrations and spread the protest throughout the region. The protests came to be called the "Women's War" among the Igbo; they were less ceremoniously dubbed the "Aba Riots" by the British. Over the course of November and December 1929 women from Owerri to Calabar looted factories and destroyed Native Court buildings and property, as well as the homes of those associated with the Native Courts. By the time colonial troops restored order late in December fifty-five women had been killed. The fact that the Women's War was organized and carried out almost entirely by women, who overwhelmingly did not have access to European education at this time, is another indication of how frustrated average Nigerians were with the colonial regime and its puppet indirect rulers. The Women's War also illustrated the capacity of average Nigerians to organize and voice their opposition to colonial policy despite the obstacles.

These forms of anti-colonial resistance saw mixed results. Most managed to achieve some tangible improvements, but none were able to achieve their full goals. Protests against taxation did not result in the repeal of taxation policies; in the case of the Women's War, however, the widespread resistance to the poll tax prompted an inquiry into the legitimacy of indirect rule in the region. The result was a government report condemning the warrant chief system as illegitimate. Over the course of 1931 and 1932 the colonial government sponsored in-depth anthropological research, which resulted in a reorganization of the administrative system in the region. By 1935 many different forms of native administration existed in southeastern Nigeria, most based to some extent on clan or village councils, and these forms of administration were much more in tune with traditional political models than the warrant chief system had been.[54] In Lagos, the criticisms of the European-educated middle class and the mass mobilization of the common people resulted in minor changes in the political structure of southern Nigeria. In 1922 the colonial government set up a new constitution creating a Legislative Council of forty-six members, twenty-seven officials, and nineteen non-officials. Of the non-officials, three were to be elected by adult males in Lagos and one in Calabar.[55] This was the first instance of elected African representation on a Legislative Council in British Africa.

To the extent that anti-colonial activity resulted in reforms or redress on the part of the colonial government, it must be noted, it occurred only at the local level in the period before 1930. Demonstrations, protests, riots, and criticisms at this time mainly engaged with the colonial regime within a local context – in Lagos where people protested against a local water rate, for example, or in select cities of northern Nigeria, where government clerks struck for better working conditions in 1912.[56] Protests and criticisms occasionally spilled out from local areas to become regional affairs, as the Women's War of 1929 clearly illustrates, but there was no coherent Nigeria-wide nationalist movement at this time. Indeed, prior to the 1930s nothing like a Nigerian national identity had yet emerged. This would change as a result of developments in the 1930s and 1940s.

CONCLUSION

In the period before 1930 the British colonial regime developed and implemented its program for imperial dominance in Nigeria. Indirect rule became the cheapest, easiest, and most ideologically attractive way to justify the colonial presence. Indirect rule theoretically preserved indigenous political institutions, but the nature of these institutions was significantly altered by the colonial presence. The colonial economy likewise transformed the agricultural activities and work patterns of Nigerians, expanding the export economy, promoting wage labor, and forcing people to work for cash. Political and economic changes led to social changes as cities grew, gender roles shifted, and a new class of middle-class elites emerged that was both indebted to and frustrated by the colonial system. As people struggled to negotiate these rapid changes, they found ways to vent their frustrations with the overbearing, racist colonial regime, through dialogue where possible and through demonstrations, protests, and violent outbursts where necessary.

The year 1929 marks a turning point in Nigerian history in several ways. First, the economy of Nigeria faltered in the late 1920s, as Nigeria began to feel the effects of the global depression that characterized the inter-war years for so many countries. As prices for exports fell, so too did willingness to tolerate the colonial regime that justified its presence on the idea that it provided progress, security, and modern civilization. The depression significantly affected Nigerians' attitudes towards the colonial government, creating widespread disaffection and providing an impetus for the burgeoning nationalist movement that also emerged in the 1930s. While resistance to British colonial rule existed and thrived from the very beginning of the colonial regime, this resistance was primarily at the local level and pushed for reform within the colonial system rather than independence from the colonial system. The Women's War of 1929 might be seen as a viable turning point in the trajectory of anti-colonial resistance. The war started in a local setting as a response to conditions in Owerri Province, but, because the issues addressed by the protesters were salient in surrounding regions, the resistance spread to a regional level. Beginning in the 1930s, a new generation of anti-colonial activists was emerging to fight not only for local improvements within the colonial system but also for complete independence for the whole of Nigeria from British rule.

CHAPTER 6

Nationalist movements and independence, 1929 – 1960

INTRODUCTION

The first three decades of the twentieth century saw the establishment and entrenchment of British colonial administration in Nigeria. Along with colonial rule came transformations to Nigerian economies and societies. While the colonial system brought some material benefits to a few European-educated intellectuals, by and large it alienated and frustrated most Nigerians, who believed that colonial rule eroded traditional cultures and institutions. Colonial rule also exploited Nigerian labor, both manual and intellectual, in a way that profited European firms far more than Nigerians themselves. Colonial rule had inspired anti-colonial resistance from the very beginning, although it had not organized around a pan-Nigerian consciousness, instead making appeals to race consciousness on the one hand and local circumstances on the other.

This early resistance to colonial rule soon, however, mushroomed into full-scale nationalist movements. Beginning in the 1930s a new generation of anti-colonial activists emerged in Nigeria, calling for greater involvement of Nigerians in the governance of Nigeria. Led by charismatic visionaries and dominated by the ever-growing class of European-educated Nigerians, the new nationalist movements placed increasing pressure on the colonial government to embark on progressive development planning measures, particularly after the Second World War. Increased spending on infrastructure, education, and health facilities made the colonial government more responsive to the needs of average Nigerians. Meanwhile, pressure from nationalist groups led to constitutional reforms in the years after the Second World War – reforms that increased Nigerian self-governance at the regional level and ultimately resulted in complete independence for Nigeria from British rule, achieved on October 1, 1960.

The nationalist movements that emerged in Nigeria from the 1930s onwards all had the same basic goal: replacing the alien British government with an indigenous Nigerian government. Beyond this commonality, however, the goals of nationalists often diverged significantly. Radical elements called for an immediate end to British rule by any means necessary, while more moderate organizations chose to work with the British authorities for a gradual loosening of the colonial yoke. Organized labor movements often had different short-term interests from the explicitly political organizations. The most intractable divisions between nationalist movements were regional, however. The nationalist movements that had emerged as pan-Nigerian efforts to promote the indigenization of the government in the 1930s devolved into regionally based political parties with memberships that were divided largely along ethnic lines by the early 1950s. The independence thus achieved in 1960 was a fragile one, unified under a federal constitution in which politically conscious ethnic groups vied for control of the central government through ethnically based political parties.

DEVELOPING A PAN-NIGERIAN IDENTITY

Prior to the 1930s Nigerians by and large did not see themselves as "Nigerians" at all. European-educated nationalists at this time believed the boundaries created by British colonial rule to be as arbitrary and illegitimate as the racist government policies that relegated otherwise qualified Africans to menial, dead-end jobs in the colonial bureaucracy or in European firms. The nationalism espoused by the literate class of Nigerians at this time tended to promote a race consciousness focusing on a dichotomy between indigenous black African subjects and alien white European rulers. Most European-educated Africans prior to the 1930s were old enough to remember a time when Africans ruled themselves, and remembered political and social structures that pre-dated those established by the colonial regime. Those who studied in the United Kingdom found an affinity with African subjects from other British African colonies, notably the Gold Coast (now Ghana) and Sierra Leone. They banded together across colonial boundaries, arguing for a "west African" identity. In 1920 west African nationalists founded the National Congress of British West Africa in the Gold Coast. Then, in 1925, Ladipo Solanke, a Nigerian, established the West African Students' Union in the United Kingdom. By the early 1930s Solanke had established branches of WASU throughout Nigeria and British west Africa. The main goals of both organizations were to foster unity among British west Africans to fight against the color bar that prevented Africans from attaining benefits commensurate with their abilities, both in the colonial system and in British society.[1]

This is not to say that nationalist sentiments did not exist prior to the 1930s. The literate class of European-educated Nigerians had been pushing for greater control over their governance long before then. Herbert Macaulay's journalism and the organization of protests in Lagos and other parts of Nigeria in the 1920s certainly indicated a strong antagonism to alien rule and a belief that Nigerians should govern themselves. These events had resulted in the implementation of the Clifford Constitution in 1923, which allowed for elected representation of Nigerians in a newly formed Legislative Council.[2]

By the early 1930s, however, a new generation of students was completing its Western education. This generation of students differed in many ways from previous generations. In Nigeria, this new generation was made up primarily of students who had been born after the advent of British colonial rule. They had never known anything but the colonial boundaries of Nigeria. Whereas previous generations of Western-educated Nigerians had come predominantly from the coastal regions, where European influence had been apparent for several decades, the new generation of students was more likely to come from the interior, where European influence was recent. They were, therefore, also more likely than previous generations of students to be the first in their families to gain a Western education, speak and write English, and travel outside Africa.[3] Unlike foreign travelers of previous generations, who went almost exclusively to the United Kingdom, an increasing number of Nigerian students in the 1930s earned degrees from African-American colleges in the United States. In sheer numbers, the new generation of Western-educated Nigerians dwarfed its predecessors. Whereas in 1912 there had been 184 primary schools in Nigeria catering to 36,670 students, by 1937 this had increased to 4,072 primary schools with an enrollment of 238,879. Secondary education grew as well. Ten secondary schools in Nigeria in 1912 had become twenty-seven by 1937, with enrollments rising from sixty-seven to 4,890.[4]

The new generation of Western-educated Nigerians continued in the footsteps of previous generations in many ways. They continued to find employment as clerical staff in the colonial government or European firms, as well as becoming teachers, clergymen, or low-level civil servants. They continued the organizational efforts of previous generations as well. Focusing not only on voicing discontent with the colonial regime, the new generation of students embarked on campaigns of "self-help," organizing kinship unions in urban centers. Membership in these unions was based on one's ethnicity or place of origin, and therefore they cannot be called "nationalist" as such. These unions served two important functions that contributed to the greater nationalist cause, however. First, they offered assistance to new urban immigrants, helping them to get situated and settled in a new environment, and involving them in local and regional politics in a way in which they would not otherwise have been. Second, these unions established linkages between the urban and rural areas. Unions organized resources to aid community development in the rural communities from which their membership originated.

Their impact in this regard was felt no more strongly, perhaps, than in the field of education. Kinship and ethnic unions financed the building of primary and secondary schools in rural areas, and sponsored scholarships to send students abroad for advanced degrees. These activities had direct implications for the growth of nationalism, because, as James S. Coleman reminds us, "a substantial number of the educated members of Nigeria's postwar elite were supported through all or part of their university training by their local unions."[5] While the leadership of such unions was mostly made up of Western-educated Nigerians, the membership included elements from all sections of Nigerian society, from agricultural workers to traditional title-holders. Ethnic unions were therefore able to bring people from different backgrounds together for the common goal of community improvement and ethnic solidarity.

"Self-help" organizations also proliferated in other forms from the late 1920s. Labor unions had begun to develop as early as 1912, with the establishment of the Southern Nigeria Civil Service Union, which later changed its name to the Nigerian Civil Servants' Union after the amalgamation of Nigeria in 1914. In 1931 the Nigerian Union of Teachers was organized, and it quickly became the largest trade union in the country. By 1946 there were 121 registered trade unions in Nigeria, representing a total membership of over 52,000. Through solidarity and cooperative action, trade unions were able to pressure the colonial government to arbitrate disputes between labor and management. The most common form of pressure was work stoppage. For example, in 1921 a strike by the Mechanics' Union of railway workers prevented a threatened wage reduction, and at Udi in 1929 coal workers were able to force the removal of illegal wage deductions through a successful strike.[6]

Cooperative societies also emerged in the cocoa-producing areas of the southwest. Cocoa producers had long been using indigenous, informal forms of cooperatives, such as labor pooling, but by the mid-1930s cooperatives had taken on a more formal, institutional shape, and were even supported by the colonial government. Unlike labor unions, which were a thorn in the side of the colonial government, cooperative societies were actually supported and encouraged by the authorities, because their main purpose was to maximize the output of the agricultural sector and make it financially self-sufficient, both of which were in the best interests of the colonial regime. Cooperative societies organized collective sales of produce, and held all surplus earnings for future development projects. Members of the cooperatives had the right to vote on the activities and procedures of the cooperative, as well as to take loans from the cooperative bank for capital investments. While cooperative societies developed first in the southwest, they quickly spread across Nigeria. By 1947 there were 692 cooperative societies operating in the country.[7]

As in previous eras, women were important activists in the "self-help" movement. The Lagos Women's League was organized in 1936 to push for greater access for women to careers in the colonial civil service. Women in the southeast continued to organize themselves and protest against unfair tax burdens and market controls, as they had done in previous decades. Perhaps the most famous champion of women's activism in this period was Olufunmilayo Ransome-Kuti, who organized the Abeokuta Ladies' Club in 1944. The club, originally founded as a charity group, soon grew into a full-fledged political organization, fighting directly with the colonial government and its representative of indirect rule, the *alake* of Abeokuta, for the alleviation of hardships placed on women under the colonial regime. Renamed the Abeokuta Women's Union in 1946, the organization gained many concessions from the colonial government and the *alake* under Ransome-Kuti's leadership, including the abolition of the flat rate tax and representation for women in the administration of Abeokuta. Having achieved these gains, Ransome-Kuti expanded her scope and developed the Nigerian Women's Union in 1949, which became a major force in the greater nationalist movement during the 1950s.[8]

By the late 1930s members of the new generation of Western-educated Nigerians had become the leaders of the anti-colonial struggle and were beginning to develop full-scale, pan-Nigerian nationalist movements. The nucleus of nationalist activity in Nigeria was Lagos, the center of the colonial government and, not coincidentally, the location of the highest concentration of Western-educated Nigerians. Lagos had been the center of the movement by Herbert Macaulay and his followers that had resulted in the establishment of the first constitution for Nigeria and the first elected members of the Legislative Council, in 1923. Since that time, Macaulay and his Nigerian National Democratic Party had dominated the political spectrum in Lagos. In 1934, however, the Lagos Youth Movement emerged to challenge Macaulay's control. Organized by Ernest Ikoli, Samuel Akinsanya, Dr. J. C. Vaughan, and H. O. Davies, the Lagos Youth Movement's main goal originally was to demand improvements in higher education. Within the space of four years, however, the movement had become the most powerful nationalist organization in Nigeria. In 1936 the name was changed to the Nigerian Youth Movement to illustrate its pan-Nigerian goals. NYM candidates soon won election to the Lagos Town Council and, in 1938, the NYM defeated Macaulay's party in the elections for the Legislative Council, ushering in a new era in Nigerian politics.

Between 1938 and 1941 the NYM became the first pan-Nigerian nationalist movement in the country's history. The movement was pan-Nigerian in the sense that its explicit aim was to unite across ethnic boundaries in order to create a common voice with which to confront the colonial government. The movement was nationalist in the sense that members pushed for greater indigenization of the civil service, better wages and working conditions for Nigerians, and more elected representation in government; in short, a Nigeria for Nigerians. The NYM saw rapid and widespread growth as its message and activities were embraced throughout Nigeria. By 1938 the movement had spread beyond Lagos, establishing branches in Ibadan, Ijebu-Ode, Warri, and Benin City in the southwest, Aba, Enugu, Port Harcourt, and Calabar in the southeast, and Jos, Kaduna, Zaria, and Kano in the north, with a combined membership of over 10,000. The NYM also established its own newspaper, *The Daily Service*, which was read by countless more Nigerians.[9]

DEPRESSION, WAR, AND POLITICAL ACTIVISM

All these organizing activities among Nigerians in the 1930s occurred in the context of a long, devastating economic depression that began in the late 1920s and lasted until the Second World War. During this period, the export market that had dominated the colonial economy collapsed. The value of total exports, which stood at over £17,000,000 in 1929, had dropped to £9,702,000 by 1938.[10] Such a stark decline in the main sector of the economy put a heavy strain on the pocketbooks of most Nigerians, even those not directly engaged in the export market. The poor economy in itself fed the desire for a large-scale nationalist movement among the people of Nigeria; the response of the colonial government and the European trading firms to the depression only exacerbated the anti-colonial sentiments further, however. Despite the suffering of the Nigerian population at large, European firms continued to make profits. Between 1932 and 1938 the profits for the United Africa Company never dipped below 9 percent of total turnover, even in the throes of widespread economic depression.[11]

One way in which European firms were able to maintain their profit margins was through unfair business practices, most notably collusion. The most outrageous example of collusion was the infamous "Cocoa Pool" incident of 1938, in which the ten European firms responsible for roughly 90 percent of cocoa exports signed a buying agreement designed to reduce the prices they paid for Nigerian cocoa. When cocoa producers caught a whiff of this agreement, they quickly organized to boycott the firms in question. The NYM itself got involved in the Cocoa Pool dilemma, sending a mission to compile a report on the business practices of the European firms to submit to the colonial government. The colonial government soon arbitrated on the dispute, agreeing to set up a commission to oversee cocoa-buying practices, and cocoa exports had resumed by April 1938. The Cocoa Pool incident illustrated to Nigerians the extent to which the colonial system deliberately sought to exploit them, and convinced many of the importance of a pan-Nigerian nationalist movement such as the NYM that could combat the colonial regime and gain redress for injustices done to Nigerians.

The activities of Nigerian nationalists and organized labor were beginning to have some impact on colonial policies by the late 1930s. The beginning of the Second World War in 1939 resulted in changes to the Nigerian political economy on a much more rapid scale, in ways that benefited the long-term goals of the nationalists. The war caused the British colonial government to institute many measures both to control the Nigerian economy and to develop the infrastructure and social services in Nigeria in an effort to marshal Nigerian resources for the war effort. Some of these measures did harm to Nigerians. The colonial government restricted imports to only those goods bought within the British Empire, thereby reducing overall trade even further. At the same time, the government established control boards to fix the prices of Nigerian exports below the international market prices. This allowed European firms to continue to operate and continue to purchase Nigerian produce that could then be diverted to the war effort, but such actions served to exploit Nigerian labor further and forced many Nigerian agricultural workers into severe poverty. Another negative effect on Nigerian communities resulted from the recruitment of thousands of young Nigerian men as soldiers sent to fight overseas. This meant that many families lost loved ones in a war in which they had little stake. It also meant that labor supplies within Nigeria became even scarcer in many places, causing crop yields in even basic foodstuffs to drop. The result was a huge increase in the prices of such staple items as yams and gari.

While the wartime economic policies of the colonial government tended to impoverish Nigerians further, in other ways wartime colonial policies brought about a surge in development initiatives that had been lacking since the amalgamation of Nigeria in 1914. To facilitate the war economy and the movement of troops and goods for the war effort, the colonial government invested more in infrastructure, building more harbors, railways, and airfields. Military hospitals were built to treat soldiers from around the empire, as troopships often docked in Nigeria en route to or from battle zones. Soldiers were not the only type of Nigerian labor that the British needed to aid their war plans; technicians, electricians, nurses, carpenters, and clerks were also needed in larger numbers than before the war. As a result, the colonial government established training centers for Nigerians to learn these skills, which were then employed in the war effort. Afterwards, many of these people continued to develop these skills and build new careers for themselves that they might otherwise not have had the opportunity to pursue.

The wartime activities of the colonial government fed the nationalist impulse among Nigerians in two ways. First, the economic policies that harmed Nigerian producers across the country illustrated further the need for self-government and an end to colonial exploitation, just as the Cocoa Pool incident had done prior to the war. Not only did Nigerian workers find it difficult to make a living, but soldiers returning to Nigeria after fighting for the United Kingdom also had a hard time finding gainful employment. Those who did manage to get work tended to earn wages far lower than those they had earned in the military. Such conditions turned many former soldiers to the nationalist cause, and provided yet another illustration to many others of the extent to which colonial rule used Nigerians more than it helped them. Second, the development initiatives conveyed to many Nigerians what the role of government should be in the post-war era. Having received a taste of government-sponsored social services, Nigerians clamored for more, and joined the nationalist fight to spread development programs throughout the country. Furthermore, the activities of the colonial government during the war proved to many that government could be a vehicle for growth, that it could single-handedly control the economy and promote development. The goal now was simply to make sure that government always did these things in a way that represented the best interests of Nigerians, not Europeans.[12]

After the war Nigerians faced many of the same problems they had faced beforehand – poverty and suppression at the hands of a seemingly uncaring alien regime – and were increasingly able to organize in ways that got the attention of the colonial government. In 1945 the colonial government was faced with a General Strike that effectively hamstrung the colonial government and economy. The economic hardships brought about by the wartime economy had resulted in huge increases in the cost of living for Nigerian workers; cost of living allowances for Nigerian government employees had not risen commensurately, however. By 1945 workers were arguing that the cost of living had skyrocketed over 200 percent, but no wage increases had been instituted since 1942. As a result, the African Civil Service Technical Workers' Union demanded a 50 percent increase in wages in 1945. When their demands were not met, seventeen unions with a combined membership of over 30,000 struck for thirty-seven days, shutting down railway, postal, and telegraph services, as well as involving technical workers in government employ.[13] The strike ended only when the colonial government assured labor leaders that their demands would be addressed. The General Strike thus demonstrated to both the colonial government and Nigerians themselves their ability to force reforms from the colonial government if they could unite and organize on a large scale.

The General Strike also marked the rise of a new force in the nationalist struggle for Nigerian unity and self-governance. The strike was actively supported through demonstrations and in the press by a young journalist named Nnamdi Azikiwe and his new organization, the National Council of Nigeria and the Cameroons (NCNC).[14] Born in 1904, Azikiwe became perhaps the most influential of the new generation of Nigerian nationalists that emerged beginning in the 1930s. The son of a Nigerian civil servant, Azikiwe was an Igbo by ethnicity, but he grew up in many different cities throughout Nigeria, experiencing first-hand the cosmopolitan nature of Nigeria's urban areas, which instilled in him a sense of nationalist solidarity that transcended ethnic boundaries. Educated in mission schools, Azikiwe traveled to the United States in 1925, where he earned degrees from Lincoln University and the University of Pennsylvania. In 1934 he moved to the

Gold Coast to become a journalist. Convicted in 1937 of sedition against the colonial government in Accra, he returned later that year to Nigeria, where he founded his own newspaper, *The West African Pilot*, and quickly rose to the leadership ranks of the NYM. By the outbreak of the Second World War Azikiwe's publications and leadership skills had made him the most revered nationalist in Nigeria.[15]

In 1941 Azikiwe split from the NYM over a dispute with Ernest Ikoli as to who should fill a vacancy on the Legislative Council. Azikiwe's candidate, Samuel Akinsanya, an Ijebu Yoruba, lost the bid. Azikiwe saw the election as having been marred by ethnic rivalry, and he left the NYM along with a large percentage of the Igbo and Ijebu membership. This split marked the beginning of the end for the NYM; in 1944, however, Azikiwe founded the NCNC, which quickly became the most prominent nationalist organization in Nigeria. Like the NYM, the NCNC was overtly concerned with fostering a pan-Nigerian identity and securing self-government for all of Nigeria. The NCNC was not a political party as such; rather, it was a conglomeration of many ethnic and social unions, with constituencies throughout Nigeria, that aligned under its banner, although its greatest support was in the south and its center of activity was Lagos. Nevertheless, the NCNC became the mouthpiece for the concerns of a broad swath of the Nigerian population.

Azikiwe and the NCNC's staunch support for the General Strike brought recognition and legitimacy to the new organization and made Azikiwe, dubbed "the Great Zik," the face of Nigerian nationalism. Further popularizing his movement, Azikiwe claimed in 1945 that the colonial government had conspired to have him assassinated, fueling sympathy for himself and the nationalist cause and contempt for the colonial authorities. After the alleged "assassination" attempt, a militant wing of the NCNC was formed in 1946. Known as the Zikists, members of this movement called for the elimination of the colonial regime by any means necessary. In pursuance of this goal, the Zikists flirted with leftist ideology and openly argued for Nigeria to become a socialist state under self-rule. Communism and socialism in their various forms increasingly appealed to Nigerian nationalists, who embraced the ideas of proletariat empowerment and anti-imperialism that leftist ideologies promoted. The Zikist movement stood at the vanguard of the radical left until its dissolution in 1950, after being outlawed for the attempted assassination of the colonial secretary. Even after the demise of the Zikist movement, however, the idea of a socialist Nigeria remained compelling to some Nigerians.[16]

DEVELOPMENT PLANNING, CONSTITUTIONAL REFORM,
AND REGIONALISM

Bowing to pressure from an increasingly organized and demanding Nigerian nationalism coming out of the Second World War, the colonial government embarked on a program of development planning and gradual internal self-government for Nigeria. By agreeing to some of the more moderate demands of the nationalists, the colonial authorities hoped to forestall militant, leftist nationalism among Nigerians. The new Labour-controlled parliament of Clement Attlee in the United Kingdom, in power from 1945 to 1951, was far more sympathetic to the agenda of the nationalists than previous administrations had been. This, coupled with the impending independence of India, the United Kingdom's largest and most treasured colony, also contributed to the willingness of British officials to move towards greater development and eventual self-government for Nigeria.

Development planning involved an influx of British money and the redirection of Nigerian revenues to develop and expand social services, infrastructure, and local industries. In 1945 the colonial government instituted a ten-year plan for Nigerian development. The plan contributed £11.3 million for the improvement of Nigeria's communication infrastructure, and £4.2 million for research and development in connection with improved agricultural methods to aid the ailing economy. The most significant aspect of the ten-year plan, however, marking a divergence from previous colonial policy, was the expansive public spending on social services. The plan earmarked £7.7 million for the expansion of education facilities. Included in education expenditure was a heavy emphasis on teacher training and secondary education, which had not previously been stressed. Increased investment and attention to education led to the rapid growth of primary and secondary schools in Nigeria in the post-war era. In 1937 there had been about 3,500 primary schools in Nigeria, catering for roughly 288,000 students, and the vast majority of these schools were in the south. By 1960 there were over 6,500 primary schools just in the southwest, and over 2,600 primary schools in the north, with a combined student population of over 1.4 million in these two regions. In 1947 there were only about 100 secondary schools in all of Nigeria. By 1960 over 700 secondary schools were in operation in the southwest alone, and over forty in the north.[17] In 1957 the southwest adopted universal primary education, granting access to free European primary education to all Nigerians in the Western Region.

Also contributing to the development of education institutions, the University College at Ibadan opened in 1948 as an extension of the University of London. For the first time, Nigerian students could receive formal preparation for university degrees in Nigeria. Students at the University College, Ibadan, actually trained for University of London examinations and earned University of London degrees. The University of Ibadan did not become a fully independent university until 1962.[18]

The ten-year plan also allocated £10.4 million for medical and health services, increasing the number of hospitals as well as mobile and stationary dispensaries in Nigeria, and expanding their capacity to treat patients with improved facilities, equipment, and training of staff. Treatment facilities for leprosy and malaria were created, vaccination campaigns against smallpox were undertaken, and treatment for such epidemic and endemic diseases as yaws, scabies, and trypanosomiasis was expanded. The plan also allocated £8 million to improve water supplies for Nigerian communities.

The ten-year plan's attention to developing the social service sector marked a new direction in colonial policy; progress was slow, however. While the plan allocated large sums for development initiatives, it did not indicate how these funds should be spent and did not offer strict oversight of the development projects. As a result, much of the funding went unused. Also, despite the efforts specified in the ten-year plan, the scope was inadequate to meet the needs of the Nigerian population as a whole. Further inhibiting the overall development of Nigeria was the fact that the ten-year plan did little to promote indigenous industry. While the plan nominally promoted research and investment in local crafts, in effect the bulk of attention was paid to expanding the agricultural economy in line with long-standing colonial economic policy. To control the agricultural markets, the colonial government also created permanent marketing boards for individual export crops, such as cocoa, groundnuts, and palm kernels. The marketing boards had complete power to set the price of commodities. The prices were set at the beginning of each harvesting season, and were geared towards the international prices prevailing at the time. Prices were always set lower than the international market price, which continued to benefit European firms, but they also provided some stability for producers by setting a floor price that all buyers were compelled to offer. While the marketing boards prevented the kind of collusion that had previously led to conflicts such as the Cocoa Pool incident, they did little to improve the living conditions of Nigerian producers. In fact, the marketing boards themselves generated huge revenue surpluses, some of which were invested in agricultural research, but most of which remained uninvested in the Nigerian economy.[19]

The Nigerian economy did begin to recover from its long depression in the years after the Second World War, however. The value of exports, which continued to fuel the Nigerian economy, stood at £23.7 million in 1946. By 1955 the total value of exports had risen to £129.8 million.[20] Economic growth was due less to the development policies of the colonial government than to general improvements in the global economy, but economic improvement, whatever its source, dampened desires for radical left-wing or violent nationalism.

While development planning made Nigeria only marginally more economically self-sufficient and independent in the 1940s and 1950s, reforms in governance and administration moved Nigerians ever closer to political independence. From 1946, when the first constitutional reforms were enacted, until the independence of Nigeria in 1960, the colonial government collaborated with moderate Western-educated elite nation-alists to develop a system of gradual self-government. Beginning in 1945 the colonial government began the Nigerianization of the senior levels of the civil service. In 1939 there had been only twenty-three Nigerians in senior levels of service; by 1947 the number had risen to 182; by 1953 it was 786, and by 1960 it was over 2,600.[21] Many of these positions were filled by nationalists. By appeasing them, the colonial government hoped to slow down the growth of the nationalist movement, but, in the process, Nigerians themselves gained greater control over the day-to-day oper-ations of the colonial administration.

Just as the Nigerianization of the civil service gave greater adminis-trative powers to Nigerians, constitutional reforms gave Nigerians greater legislative powers. Three new constitutions were introduced for Nigeria between 1945 and 1954, and each one brought Nigeria closer to full self-governance. The first constitution, known as the Richards Constitution after the colonial governor, Sir Arthur Richards, came into effect in 1947. The Richards Constitution revamped the Legislative Council created by the 1922 Clifford Constitution to allow a majority of unofficial, Nigerian members for the first time. The Northern Region was included in the central legislature for the first time, increasing the unity of Nigeria. At the same time as the Richards Constitution promoted Nigerian unity, however, it also exacerbated regional identities, creating regional houses of assembly in each of the three existing regions – that is, one for the West, one for the East, and one for the North. The Richards Constitution therefore became the first step towards a federated Nigerian state, with a unitary central legislative apparatus coupled with separate and individual legislative bodies at a regional level.

Although the Richards Constitution was designed to grant Nigerians a greater voice in their own governance, it was lambasted from all sides, particularly by Azikiwe and the NCNC, but also by other nationalist groups. The first issue was the arrogance with which the constitution was bestowed upon the Nigerian people. Rather than consulting with the leading nationalist voices of Nigeria over how to go about framing a new constitution, Richards and his staff had simply constructed it themselves and foisted it upon the country. Nationalists argued that, had Richards asked advice from them before drafting the constitution, perhaps the problems with the constitution could have been avoided. These included the fact that, despite the Legislative Council now being about to be made up of a majority of Nigerian officials, no new arrangements had been made for the direct election of those officials. Lagos and Calabar remained the only jurisdictions that voted for their Legislative Council representatives; all others were appointed by the colonial government or through the native administrations. Nationalists argued that this was not progress towards self-government, as the traditional authorities that governed the native administrations were inseparably linked to the colonial system and would appoint councilors who represented their own interests and not necessarily those of the people as a whole.

On the issue of regional houses of assembly, feelings among nationalists were mixed. On the one hand, regional legislatures marked a step backward from the pan-Nigerian goals of the new educated elite. On the other hand, nearly everyone recognized that, geographically, politically, economically, and culturally, Nigeria was an extremely diverse place, and a single unitary government was unlikely to please very many people for very long. Zik himself vacillated on the value of regional distinctions to Nigeria. Originally, he opposed the houses of assembly because he claimed they gave the regions too little real authority; later he attacked the idea of regionalism entirely, claiming it to be detrimental to the unity of Nigeria and the development of a true national consciousness. By the early 1950s Zik was again embracing the idea of regional legislatures, but now he argued that three assemblies were not enough. He pushed for the creation of eight different regions rather than the existing three, so as to make sure that ethnic minorities in each of the three existing regions would not be dominated by the larger ethnic groups in each region – that is, the Yoruba, Hausa/Fulani, and Igbo. Zik and the NCNC, however, always argued that the central government should be more powerful than the regional houses, strong enough to hold Nigeria together as a single entity.

Other parties were supportive of the idea of the regional assemblies. Nationalists in the north were particularly interested in solidifying regional distinctions. Since the Richards Constitution guaranteed the incorporation of the Northern Region into the central legislature, nationalists in the north recognized that their political fates were now linked with those of their southern neighbors. The north had developed very differently from the south, however. The north still lagged far behind the south in terms of a European-educated population. The north was also culturally distinct, claiming a population that was predominantly Muslim, whereas the south was increasingly Christian. Northerners feared that incorporation into a unitary Nigerian state would mean that they would ultimately become politically and culturally dominated by the south. Since the north lacked a large European-educated population, there were not at that time enough qualified northerners to take up positions in a European-style legislature, nor were there enough northerners to staff the civil service even of the Northern Region. In fact, the colonial civil service in the north had been dominated by transplanted southerners for most of the colonial era. More conservative elements in the north feared that a southern-dominated central legislature would force a secular state on the north, preventing northerners from governing via Islamic law, or *shari'a*.[22] For these reasons, northern political activists almost uniformly supported the predominance of regional power over central authority.

Throughout Nigeria, ethnic identities had begun to solidify and become politically meaningful by the 1940s. Although the NCNC had become the leading nationalist organization based on its pan-Nigerian motivations, ethnic affiliations were simultaneously emerging. As already discussed, ethnically based social unions had been developing in the urban areas of Nigeria for some time, and the NYM, which had been the premier nationalist organization of the late 1930s, had collapsed by 1941 after Zik and his followers withdrew over a controversy they saw as ethnically motivated. For several years afterwards the NYM continued to function, although in a diminished capacity, under the leadership of a wealthy Yoruba cocoa farmer named Obafemi Awolowo.[23] Under Awolowo the NYM became a Yoruba-dominated organization, until he left to study law in London in 1944. Beginning with his tenure in the NYM, Awolowo became the leading proponent of Yoruba nationalism, and focused his energies primarily on gaining Yoruba support behind his leadership to control the political scene in the Western Region. While in London in 1945 Awolowo founded a cultural organization called the Egbe Omo Oduduwa (literally, Society of the Descendants of Oduduwa, Oduduwa being the mythical founder of the Yoruba people). The explicit goals of the Egbe were to foster unity among Yoruba people, promote the spread of Yoruba language and culture, and work with other nationalist groups in Nigeria with the goal of facilitating the realization of Yoruba progress. When Awolowo returned to Nigeria in 1948 he established branches of the Egbe throughout the southwest.

Similar cultural organizations developed in the other regions of Nigeria. In the southeast, the Ibo Federal Union was formed in 1944 to engender solidarity among the Igbo and promote Igbo progress through supporting European education for Igbos, among other things. An amalgamation of existing local social unions, the Ibo Federal Union changed its name to the Igbo State Union in 1948 and became one of the largest groups in the NCNC. Azikiwe, an Igbo himself, served as both the president of the NCNC and the president of the Igbo State Union from 1948 to 1952. In the north, the first major cultural organization was the Bauchi General Improvement Union, founded in 1943 by Mallam Sa'ad Zungur, Mallam Aminu Kano, and Alhaji Tafawa Balewa, three of the few northerners who had attained high standards of European education at the time. Changing its name to the Northern People's Congress in 1949, its founders sought primarily to promote northern unity in the fight to maintain regional autonomy for the north in the face of what seemed like impending southern domination. The NPC was conservative in nature, and did not wish to challenge the authority of the existing political structure as other nationalist groups did. As a result, some of the more radical elements of the NPC, notably Mallam Aminu Kano, broke away to form the Northern Elements Progressive Union. NEPU members also thought that it was counterproductive to galvanize southern–northern differences, and, as a result, the union allied with the NCNC. Nevertheless, NEPU remained a fringe group in the north, which came to be politically dominated by the NPC under the leadership of Alhaji Sir Ahmadu Bello, also known as the *Sardauna* of Sokoto, by the early 1950s.[24]

From the perspective of these regionally based and/or ethnically motivated organizations the regionalization of Nigeria was a good, and even a necessary, thing. The regional houses of assembly created by the Richards Constitution therefore reinforced the attitudes and methods of these organizations by giving them something specific to fight for on a regional level. Cultural organizations also developed among smaller

Figure 6.1 The Emir of Kano celebrating Eid (collection of Jonathan T. Reynolds)

ethnic groups as well, but by the early 1950s it was becoming clear that Nigeria was congealing into three zones based on the regional divisions of the country: a Yoruba-dominated Western Region, an Igbo-dominated Eastern Region, and a Hausa/Fulani-dominated Northern Region. The constitutional reforms of 1951 changed these previously cultural distinctions into full-fledged political battle lines.

In response to the grievances of the nationalist leadership concerning the Richards Constitution, Sir John Macpherson, the new colonial governor of Nigeria who had replaced Richards in 1948, embarked on revisions to the Richards Constitution in 1950. Whereas Richards had unilaterally imposed his constitution, Macpherson made much greater efforts to include Nigerian nationalist leaders in the constitution-making process, holding a Constitutional Conference in Ibadan in 1950. The result was what has been dubbed the Macpherson Constitution of 1951, which improved upon its predecessor in several ways. The Macpherson Constitution created a Council of Ministers, made up of twelve Nigerian ministers, four from each region, and six official members. The central legislature became a House of Representatives with half the representatives allocated to the north and half divided between the southwest and southeast. Regional assemblies were expanded: in the Western and Northern Regions the regional assemblies were made bicameral, with a

House of Assembly and a House of Chiefs; in the Eastern Region the assembly remained unicameral. Greater legislative and financial powers were granted to the regional assemblies as well. The most important contribution of the Macpherson Constitution, however, was that it provided for the first general election in Nigerian history.

The advent of the general election process galvanized regional and ethnic identifications, as cultural associations organized as proper political parties to campaign for control of the various regional assemblies. In the Eastern Region, the NCNC remained the dominant party. In the southwest, Awolowo's Egbe Omo Oduduwa became the nucleus for the newly founded Action Group party, which contested for control of the Western Region. In the Northern Region, the NPC transformed itself from a cultural organization into a political party as well.[25] When the votes had been counted, Nigeria had clearly broken into regional blocs. The NCNC dominated in the Eastern Region; in the North, the NPC took all the seats; and, in the West, the AG won 49 out of 80 seats, a solid majority.

From 1951 the political parties in the Western and Eastern Regions in southern Nigeria began to push the colonial government to extend full internal self-governance to the regional assemblies. The Northern Region continued to oppose this move, however, stating that it was not ready for self-government. At the center of the controversy over self-government was the issue of the centralization of government. If one region wanted self-government, did that mean that all the regions had to have self-government? Two constitutional conferences on this issue were held in London and Lagos between July 1953 and February 1954. After grueling deliberations between the representatives of the three regions, agreements were reached on several important issues, which were incorporated into the Lyttleton Constitution of 1954, named for the British statesman Sir Oliver Lyttleton who arbitrated the conferences. The Lyttleton Constitution established Nigeria as a federation of three regions, Northern, Western, and Eastern, much as had already existed. Lagos became a Federal Territory administered by the central government.

Each region had the option of acquiring full internal self-government in 1956, but no region was compelled to become fully self-governing, and the Federation of Nigeria as a whole was to remain under British colonial authority for the time being. The central government was made up of a unicameral legislature of 184 members, of whom ninety-two came from the north, forty-two each from the west and the east, six from the British Cameroons, and two from the Federal Territory of Lagos. Federal ministers were appointed by the leader of the majority party in each region's legislature, with three ministers to be appointed from each region and one from the Cameroons. The ministers joined with the governor general, who remained a British official, and three other official ministers to form a central executive council. The Federal House of Representatives had the jurisdiction to pass legislation relating to issues on exclusive legislative lists; jurisdiction over legislation on all issues not on those lists devolved to the regional legislatures. Federal laws always overrode regional laws in cases of legislative overlap. This constitution set up the federal system of government under which Nigeria gained independence in 1960.

The Lyttleton Constitution managed to forge a middle path between the desire of some nationalists, mainly the NCNC, for a strong central government and the desires of other nationalists, most stridently the NPC, for decentralized, regional autonomy. Under the Lyttleton Constitution, both the Western and the Eastern Regions opted for self-government in 1957; the Northern Region claimed self-governance in 1959. General elections in 1954, 1956, and 1959 cemented the regionalization of political consciousness in Nigeria, as the AG, NCNC, and NPC continued to dominate their respective regions in both the regional and central legislatures.[26] In many ways, however, the various regional political parties tried to work together to form a strong national government in the second half of the 1950s.

In 1957 Alhaji Tafawa Balewa was named the first prime minister of Nigeria. The choice of Balewa illustrates the efforts of nationalists to forge a truly national government at this time. Balewa was the vice-president of the NPC, therefore representing the north. In many ways he was not the prototypical northern politician, however. He was a London-University-educated former secondary school principal, and this appealed to all elements of the nationalist community. Furthermore, he was not a member of the Fulani aristocracy, as so many of the NPC leaders were, having come from a humble background. Nor was he a member of the Hausa ethnic group that formed the majority of the northern population. Balewa was therefore able to rally the three main political parties into a national government, persuading even the opposition AG to join the NPC–NCNC coalition, which had governed since the elections that followed the adoption of the Lyttleton Constitution in 1954.

CULTURE AND SOCIETY IN POST-WAR NIGERIA

The political changes after the Second World War were accompanied by sociocultural changes. The urbanization that had accompanied colonial rule exploded in the 1950s to unprecedented levels. Lagos, which had an estimated population of 126,000 in 1931, ballooned to over 274,000 by 1951, and by 1963 was home to over 675,000 people. Lagos is the most dramatic example, but rapid urbanization occurred throughout the country. In the eastern part of the country, where no city had a population higher than 26,000 in 1931, four cities boasted populations of over 50,000 by 1952. As in previous decades, people flocked to cities for employment and other economic opportunities, but cities offered more than hope for jobs. Urban areas developed completely different cultures and lifestyles from rural areas. Cities became attractive symbols of a new, modern Nigeria to many young people who wanted a change from the traditional rural lifestyle. Cities offered urban amenities such as running water, electricity, and European schools, all of which drew people from the rural areas. Cities became cosmopolitan centers where people and cultures from throughout Nigeria, west Africa, and the world came together, learned from each other, and drew on each other, while rural areas remained more ethnically and culturally homogeneous. In some cases, the multicultural attributes of city life led to ethnic tensions, as in 1953 in Kano, where communal riots broke out during a visit by the Yoruba nationalist leader Obafemi Awolowo. The multiculturalism of cities also brought people together in more peaceful and productive ways, however, illustrating to many the commonalities of Nigerians regardless of their backgrounds. The cosmopolitan nature of Nigerian cities influenced a vibrant entertainment scene as well.

New musical styles, such as high-life and juju, emerged in Nigerian cities and became very popular from the 1930s. High-life and juju are syncretic musical styles that meld African folk music with Western jazz and blues influences, and Caribbean musical styles such as samba, salsa, and calypso, to bring new meaning to traditional musical forms. Unlike performers in previous musical cultures in west Africa, high-life musicians incorporated Western instruments such as the electric guitar and brass horns into their compositions, while juju musicians, who were most prevalent in Yoruba areas, based their music primarily on traditional instruments such as drums and shakers, but by the 1950s were incorporating Western instruments such as flutes, kazoos, and mandolins. From the end of the Second World War musicians such as E. T. Mensah,[27] known as the father of high-life music, and Tunde King, on the juju scene, became urban celebrities and left an indelible imprint on the cultural history of Nigeria.[28]

The differences in culture and lifestyle that developed between urban areas and rural areas created yet another division in Nigerian society, between modernizing urbanites and traditional, conservative rural elements. Each had different ideas about what the future of an independent Nigeria should look like, where resources should be allocated, and towards what ends. The European-educated elites that came to dominate the political scene in the post-war era tended to be acquainted with urban spaces, tended to favor modernization, and tended to see the cities as the future beacons of respectability for an independent Nigeria. Cities received the bulk of the developmental aid, and rural areas began to fall into neglect and disrepair. This, of course, led to greater urbanization, which further proved to the governing element the importance of cities to Nigeria's future growth.

DECOLONIZATION AND INDEPENDENCE

A final election was held in 1959 to determine the make-up of Nigeria's first independent government. The results gave the NPC the largest number of seats, and a majority government was formed through an NPC–NCNC coalition. The AG became the opposition party. Alhaji Tafawa Balewa maintained his position as prime minister, and Nnamdi Azikiwe took a largely ceremonial title as Nigeria's first indigenous governor general. On October 1, 1960, Nigeria became a fully sovereign state in the British Commonwealth. Tafawa Balewa stood in the square in central Lagos which was soon to bear his name and spoke to all those with a stake in the independence process. He thanked the British for their cooperation and the nationalists for their relentless work over the course of many decades. He noted that the process had been long and arduous, but declared that "history will show that the building of our nation proceeded at the wisest pace: it has been thorough, and Nigeria now stands well built upon firm foundations." It was a glorious moment for Nigeria, the culmination of nearly 100 years of striving for the ideals of freedom and democracy.

The foundations upon which Nigeria gained independence were not as firm as Balewa had declared, however. In fact, the federal machinery was very fragile. The new country, united in the euphoria of its independence, was still divided on many levels. Regionalism and ethnicity remained major problems barring the development of a national identity. Furthermore, although the three largest ethnic groups each dominated a region of Nigeria, hundreds of smaller ethnic groups feared impending domination by a larger group at the regional level. Urban and rural areas were developing along very different paths, and the working class and peasants had reason to fear that they had simply traded wealthy, elite

Figure 6.2 Sellers of locally produced textiles in Lagos (collection of Roy Doron)

British leadership for a Nigerian bourgeoisie that did not share their values or views on future prosperity.[29]

In addition, while Nigeria had gained political independence in 1960, the country was still far from being economically independent. The development planning initiatives of the post-war era had not progressed to the level of achieving sustainable development for Nigeria. The country continued to be reliant on export agriculture for the majority of its revenues, and European firms continued to control the export economy. Very little industrial development had been undertaken, and the industry that did exist was still largely owned by European companies. Nigeria's political independence was therefore coupled with a continuing economic dependence, as the country was reliant on European knowledge, connections, and technologies and on international market conditions.

Further fueling these political and economic problems facing the newly independent Nigerian nation was the discovery of petroleum in commercial quantities in the Niger delta in 1958. Petroleum would become both a blessing and a curse for Nigeria in the decades to come: the resource with the most potential to make Nigeria a strong, wealthy state, but one that has also fueled the flames of ethnic division, economic underdevelopment, and institutional corruption since the 1960s.

CHAPTER 7

Instability and civil war, 1960 – 1970

INTRODUCTION

When Nigeria achieved independence from British colonial rule on October 1, 1960, the prospects appeared promising and expectations for the future of the country were high. Nigeria was the most populous country in Africa, and the potential for economic growth was great, buoyed largely by the discovery of commercial quantities of petroleum in the Niger delta region in 1958. Nigeria was dubbed the "Giant of Africa," and many people both inside and outside the country believed that Nigeria would soon rise to claim a leading position in African and world affairs. Nigeria also saw itself as a beacon of hope and progress for other colonized peoples emerging from the yoke of alien rule. By 1970, however, Nigeria's stability and prestige had been greatly damaged by a decade of political corruption, economic underdevelopment, and military coups. Most damaging, however, was the culmination of these problems in a two-and-a-half-year civil war from 1967 to 1970 that rent the country along regional and ethnic lines, killed between 1 and 3 million people, and nearly destroyed the fragile federal bonds that held together the Nigerian state.

The underlying cause of all the problems that Nigeria experienced in the 1960s and has experienced since then is what is often called the "national question."[1] What is Nigeria? Who are Nigerians? How does a country go about developing a meaningful national identity? The geographical area now known as Nigeria was created by the British colonial administration in 1914, not by indigenous peoples themselves. Thereafter, the people within the borders of Nigeria were known to the world as "Nigerians," but in reality this designation meant little to most people, whose lives continued to be primarily centered on local communities that had existed for hundreds and thousands of years. The regional and federal emphases of the constitutions of the 1950s further undermined the development of a unified national consciousness by determining that access to power at the national level was to be derived from holding power at the regional level. The largest ethnic groups in each region – the Hausa/Fulani, Yoruba, and Igbo in the Northern, Western, and Eastern Regions respectively – therefore came to dominate their respective regions and to contest for power at the federal level. Within each region, ethnic minorities often opposed the political domination of the large ethnic groups and, as a result, they felt increasingly alienated from the political process, creating even further subdivisions of identity that detracted from the development of a single, encompassing Nigerian national identity. Since power derived most immediately from association on a sub-national level, there seemed to be very little to gain in domestic politics from identifying on a national level. As a result, when Nigeria became an independent sovereign state in 1960, in many ways it was a state without a nation.

The problem of national unity was apparent in the early 1960s, and Nigerians addressed it in many ways. Artists, scholars, and some politicians went about trying to construct a unique Nigerian culture through their art, writings, speeches, and legislation. Efforts were made to promote a strong central state and a state-run economy that focused on development initiatives across Nigeria. All these efforts were meant to bring Nigerians closer together politically, economically, and culturally, to promote commonalities and downplay differences. Ultimately, however, these efforts failed, largely because of the overwhelming trend in the political sphere towards consolidating power at the regional level at any cost. Official corruption, rigged elections, ethnic baiting, bullying, and thuggery dominated the conduct of politics in the First Republic, which existed from 1960 to 1966.[2]

The preponderance of such realpolitik tactics struck fear in the hearts of many Nigerians. Since regional identities were strong and national identity was weak, the greatest fear of most Nigerians in the 1960s was that their region would become "dominated" by another. Southerners from the Eastern and Western Regions feared northern domination, and northerners feared southern domination. These fears led to severely flawed elections in 1964 and 1965, in which all kinds of dirty tricks were used by every side. Under these circumstances, many Nigerians came to believe that the federal system was dysfunctional and that Nigeria should cease to exist in its present form. These attitudes led directly to the overthrow of the civilian democratic regime by several military officers in January 1966, and, second, to a bloody civil war between 1967 and 1970, in which the Eastern Region attempted to secede from Nigeria and establish the sovereign state of Biafra. Eventually the federal government, made up of the Northern and Western Regions and the Federal Capital Territory of Lagos, was able to reincorporate the Eastern Region, but overall the Nigerian Civil War did more to exemplify the problems associated with the national question than to solve them.

BUILDING A NATION

The need to build pride around a unified national identity for Nigeria was not a new development in the 1960s; indeed, the creation of a pan-Nigerian consciousness had been a preoccupation of nationalist activists since at least the 1930s. By the 1960s, however, the desire for a sense of national unity had spread beyond the political realm to encompass cultural activities as well. Many people began searching for ways to develop a distinct and recognizable national culture in order to bring Nigerians together as a single people and to grow national pride by contributing something distinctly Nigerian to world culture in general. Artists, writers, scholars, and politicians developed many different conceptions of what aesthetics and values best characterized Nigeria, but all were clearly concerned with promoting and analyzing Nigeria's unique traditions and history, and in this way illustrated their desire to forge a stronger national identity.

In theater and literature, Nigerians made great contributions to national culture. Chinua Achebe, perhaps Nigeria's most famous author, published his masterpiece, *Things Fall Apart*, in 1958.[3] By the early 1960s he had become one of the leading voices in the Nigerian arts. Written in English prose, *Things Fall Apart* makes use of a European language and a European medium, the novel, to tell a tale of life in Nigeria prior to and leading up to British colonial rule. Other writers told similar tales of Nigeria's traditional ways, but in a different type of language. Amos Tutuola's *The Palm-wine Drinkard*,[4] first published in 1952 and produced in the theater in the 1960s, tells the story of a man's journey with a palm-wine tapper (a worker in a traditional Nigerian industry) through the land of the dead. Rich in indigenous cosmology, the tale is also written in broken, or pidgin, English, common among Nigerians who did not have extensive European education. Other writers wrote solely in indigenous languages, but this severely restricted their markets and, therefore, their capacity to truly promote a pan-Nigerian vision. The most famous dramatist to emerge in the early 1960s was Wole Soyinka, whose *A Dance of the Forests*[5] was written to commemorate Nigerian independence in 1960. His plays became famous not only in Nigeria but throughout Africa and Europe. Soyinka's contribution to drama later earned him the distinction of becoming the first sub-Saharan African to win the Nobel Prize in literature.

Soyinka and other dramatists promoted national unity through their work in several ways. First, many of the plays written and performed at this time contained characters from many different ethnic groups in Nigeria. Soyinka's play *The Swamp Dwellers*,[6] which contains characters whose names clearly come from many different ethnicities, is a case in point. Second, productions of plays were often undertaken by theater groups in Nigerian colleges and universities. Because the universities were few in number, their make-up was very multi-ethnic, as students came from across Nigeria to earn degrees. As a result, the casts of university-produced plays were multi-ethnic in nature, often with actors playing characters of a different ethnic background from their own.[7] Finally, much of the literature of the period, including drama, was written in English, which made the works accessible to a wider audience than if they had been written in a locally specific indigenous language.

The issue of language was a tricky one in the development of national identity. On the one hand, English was clearly the language of the colonial past, an alien language that had no roots in Nigeria's cultures or traditions. For this reason, many felt its use should be limited in an independent Nigeria. At the same time, however, Nigeria itself was a creation of the colonial past, and the shared colonial experience was one of the major factors through which all Nigerians could relate to each other regardless of their other differences. Indeed, the federal government had declared English the national language of Nigeria in 1960 as one way of downplaying regionalism and ethnic tensions in the legislative process. Just as some people found English distasteful, others found it appropriate and even indispensable. Tutuola, whose *Palm-wine Drinkard* was written in pidgin English, received heavy criticism for this choice from other Nigerian literati, who felt that the use of pidgin, despite its undeniable authenticity, denigrated Nigerian intelligence and perpetuated the image of the Nigerian as barbaric and uneducated.[8]

One thing that all cultural activists could agree on, however, was that Nigeria's rich history and traditions were the foundation upon which national consciousness could and should be built. Therefore, much of the fictional writing of novelists and dramatists focused on Nigeria's pre-colonial past and incorporated distinctly indigenous symbolism. At the same time, the academics who earned degrees either in Nigeria's universities or abroad themselves turned their focus on Nigeria's pre-colonial past in such fields as history, archaeology, and anthropology. No longer content with Eurocentric interpretations of their history and traditions, Nigerian scholars contributed their first-hand understanding of their own cultures to the analysis of Nigeria's past. They also sought out the indigenous voice by incorporating oral histories into the documentary record, bringing balance to knowledge bases that had previously been constructed solely from European accounts of African affairs.[9] Through such efforts, Nigerian scholars began to rewrite Nigerian history in a way that fostered pride and promoted the overarching similarities of experience shared by peoples in all corners of Nigeria.

In the visual arts, sculptors such as Uche Okeke, Susanne Wenger, and Felix Idubor drew inspiration from the ancient sculptures found at Nok, Osogbo, and other places, but were also influenced in form and style by European production methods and aesthetics. Painters also sought to express a distinctly Nigerian style using the inspiration of traditional design motifs. Two main schools of artistic expression developed in the 1950s and 1960s: the Zaria School, based in the old Nigerian College of Art and Sciences in Zaria; and the Osogbo School, an offshoot of the Zaria School that emerged in Osogbo under the tutelage of Uli Beier and Susanne Wenger.[10]

Much of the brainstorming and labor associated with the flourishing arts scene in Nigeria in the 1960s took place in colleges and universities. Indeed, the school system became a key sector of Nigerian society in which attempts were made to foster national culture and identity, although the curricula and structure of schools continued to follow very closely the British models developed during the colonial era. Overall, access to formal education increased in the 1960s, and four new universities were opened between 1960 and 1962. These new universities contributed to the national unity of Nigeria in two ways. First, in 1960 the government established the Nigerian National University at Nsukka, in the Eastern Region. Second, Ahmadu Bello University opened in Zaria, in the Northern Region, in 1962, and the University of Lagos opened the same year. As a result, each region now contained at least one university (the Western Region claimed two universities from 1962, when the University of Ife commenced classes), equalizing access and proximity to higher education to a certain degree.[11]

Despite these efforts to develop a distinct Nigerian culture and to promote national unity through education and the arts, the national question could not be solved so easily. Ethnic and regional tensions heightened during the 1960s, culminating in civil war in 1967.

ECONOMIC DEVELOPMENT

The expansion of formal education facilities was part of a wider economic plan on the part of the First Republic to make Nigeria wealthier and more self-sufficient. In 1962 the government introduced the First National Development Plan (FNDP), designed to run until 1968, focusing on investment in agriculture, industry, and education. The FNDP anticipated an annual growth rate of 4 percent, with savings and investment both rising to 15 percent of GNP annually. In many ways, the FNDP provisions were in keeping with the previous development plans that had been in place since the end of the Second World War. In some ways, however, the development planning initiatives of the First Republic were more ambitious than previous plans. First, whereas colonial development plans were overwhelmingly interested in increasing agricultural output to boost the export economy, the independent government of the 1960s was far more concerned with attaining economic independence. Therefore, greater emphasis was placed on the development of manufacturing and industry in the 1960s. In manufacturing, tobacco, food processing, and beverages became the leading growth sectors. Import substitution was also a main goal of manufacturing development. Industrial development grew most in the mining sector, with petroleum making up the bulk of the increase. Production of crude oil grew from 46,000 barrels per day (bpd) in 1961 to 600,000 bpd in 1967.[12]

Through the FNDP and other development initiatives, the economy grew at a steady rate between 1960 and 1966. The economy also diversified considerably during this period. Agriculture, which had at its peak constituted 63.4 percent of gross national product (GNP), fell to 55.6 percent of GNP by 1966. Manufacturing grew from 3.6 percent of GNP in 1960 to 6.2 percent in 1966; mining rose from 0.9 percent of GNP in 1960 to 4.8 percent by 1966; and the distribution of goods increased from 9.1 percent to 14 percent in the same period. The economy as a whole was improving slowly, with national incomes growing at an average rate of 5 percent between 1963 and 1966. Real per capita income grew from 48.1 naira (N) in 1960 to N53.8 in 1965, while overall GNP rose from N2,244.6 million in 1960 to N3,140.8 million in 1968. These kinds of data led many to believe that Nigeria was on track to achieve economic independence. The military coup of January 1966 and subsequent political developments brought an unfortunately abrupt end to development planning efforts.

It must be noted that the successes of the FNDP and other development schemes were accompanied by many failures and negative trends. First, although the economy was becoming more diversified, the decline in the agricultural sector was not a good sign. As formal education opened up opportunities for increasing numbers of rural Nigerians, agricultural families were diverting revenues from investment in agriculture towards sending their children to schools. Once educated, these children were less likely to return home to work on the farms. This meant that, at the same time that private investments in agriculture were declining, so too was the agricultural labor force. Bad weather conditions in the 1960s further hurt production and affected transportation. The growth rate of agriculture was −0.5 percent in the 1960s, with the result that increasing amounts of food had to be imported. Food imports reached N46.1 million in 1965 and continued to grow thereafter. The decline in agriculture boded ill for Nigeria's long-term economic independence.

Further complicating Nigeria's push for economic independence was the anticipated reliance on foreign investment to fund development projects. In order to encourage this investment, the government instituted tax breaks, protective tariffs, and other incentives for investors. Foreign capital investments were made in private enterprise, such as manufacturing and industry; these investments, while increasing the overall productivity and diversity of Nigeria's economy, actually perpetuated the dependence of the Nigerian economy on foreign sources, however. As of 1965, foreign private investments accounted for 61 percent of all paid-up capital, compared to figures of 27 percent for the Nigerian government and 12 percent for Nigerian private investment. One hundred and ten firms in Nigeria were fully owned by foreigners, with a paid-up capital value of N28 million, compared to fifty-two Nigerian-owned companies, with a combined value of N4 million. Further illustrating the continued economic dependence of Nigeria on outside forces, the machinery and technology necessary for manufacturing and industrial upgrades had to be bought entirely from overseas producers. Foreign public investment, however, was harder to come by. The FNDP called for 50 percent of the budgeted N2,366 million to be raised through foreign investment. By the outbreak of civil war in 1967, however, foreign investment in the FNDP stood at only 14 percent.[13]

POLITICS OF THE FIRST REPUBLIC

No doubt the main factor inhibiting foreign public investment was the widespread political instability that characterized Nigeria's First Republic.

The federal system that had solidified regional divisions in the 1950s devolved into utter dysfunction in the period from 1960 to 1966, as the main political parties in each region fought bitterly and without scruples to gain or maintain control of both the federal and regional assemblies, which controlled the bulk of Nigerian resources, with the result that control at the regional and federal level was the key to power over how Nigeria's resources would be distributed. Those parties that had control over the assemblies were able to distribute government resources among themselves and their supporters and, equally, were able to deny these resources to their opponents. For instance, regional governments collected import and export taxes, and controlled the produce marketing boards, which consistently underpaid producers for their goods and, by doing so, were able to maintain huge annual surpluses. Revenues from these sources were then used to fund development projects. The parties that controlled the regional and federal assemblies were therefore able to determine where these projects would be undertaken, which ones would be prioritized, who would get the contracts to complete the projects, and so on. Control of the branches of government therefore had strong implications for the future development of Nigeria.

The fear that emerged in the 1960s was that of "domination." Southerners feared that an NPC-controlled government representing the interests of the Northern Region would divert resources to the north, cut southerners out of their positions in the administration and the military, and gradually Islamize the country. Northerners feared that southern "domination" by Awolowo's Action Group and Azikiwe's newly renamed National Convention of Nigerian Citizens would allocate resources to the more developed Western and Eastern Regions, which would prevent the north from ever developing in a competitive way. They also feared that southern "domination" would mean that southerners would come to control the civil service and educational institutions of the north, since northerners would continually be denied the resources to develop an educated class to compete on merit with southerners. These fears of "domination" clouded any sense of national unity in Nigeria in the 1960s, as residents in each region increasingly came to fear that other regions intended to use the political system to enrich themselves at the expense of their Nigerian "brothers" in other regions. Under such conditions, it became imperative for parties once in power to stay in power and for those out of power either to ally with the majority party or to wrest control of the government away from that party in the next election, as opposition parties faced the prospect of perennial marginalization.[14]

These fears, while certainly exaggerated for political purposes, were not unfounded. The NPC–NCNC coalition that governed at the federal level from 1959 quickly became dominated by the NPC, which under the leadership of federal Prime Minister Balewa and northern Premier Ahmadu Bello, the *Sardauna* of Sokoto, undertook many measures specifically to improve the condition of the Northern Region and northerners within the federation. The NPC-led government regularly handed out appointments and promotions to underqualified northerners at the expense of more qualified southerners in an effort to bring about greater parity between the regions in the public service sector. For example, from 1958 a quota system had determined admissions to the military: 50 percent of military recruits were to come from the Northern Region and 25 percent each from the Eastern and Western Regions. Historically, a majority of the armed service enlistments had come from the north (although 60 percent of northern recruits came from the non-Muslim middle belt areas). Colonial policy had been to appoint officers almost solely from among the more formally educated southern recruits, however. The result at independence was an armed forces staffed predominantly by northerners but led predominantly by southerners, particularly by Igbos from the Eastern Region.[15] In 1961 the NPC reversed this trend by extending the quota system to officer recruitment. Thereafter, 50 percent of all officers came from the Northern Region, regardless of their relative qualifications vis-à-vis those of their southern compatriots.[16] Policies such as these infuriated southerners, who saw their hard-won skills disregarded by a federal system that increasingly seemed to value ethnicity over merit.

Further illustration of the NPC-led federal government's intention to use the federal apparatus to boost a northern agenda was to be seen in the particulars of the FNDP. Although the FNDP claimed to be a national development plan, in actuality the bulk of the allocations went to projects in the north. Nearly all the funds earmarked for defense and a majority of the funds for health, education, and roads went to projects in the north, while the Niger dam project, estimated at £68.1 million but ultimately costing over £88 million, accounted for over 10 percent of all federal spending.[17] The NPC could legitimately argue that in the spirit of national unity the Northern Region should have the chance to catch up with the south after suffering the deliberate underdevelopment that had characterized the region during the colonial era. Southerners, however, saw such policies as a slippery slope that they felt signified a long-term plan for northern domination of the politics and economy of Nigeria.

Furthermore, the emphasis on improving conditions for the north and northerners strained relations with the NCNC, which increasingly felt that it was not receiving benefits at the federal level commensurate with its position as a coalition partner. From 1962 the NCNC leadership began actively to court new allies against the NPC in the south and among minority parties in the north.

In the Western Region, the AG-dominated government faced a crisis in 1962 over its position as opposition party to the NPC–NCNC coalition. Some members of the AG believed that the party and the region were becoming irrelevant at the national level and would be better served by abandoning their position as opposition party and allying more closely with the NPC. By doing so, they felt, they would have greater access to federal power and to the resources that the NPC doled out as the ruling party. Among the adherents of this line of thought was Chief S. L. Akintola, who had succeeded Chief Awolowo as Premier of the Western Region in 1959. Awolowo was not in concert with this plan, however. Awolowo had increasingly been arguing for what he called "democratic socialism," declaring the need for the Western Region to nationalize industries and seek every means of becoming self-sufficient as a region in order to reduce its dependence on the federal government, thereby making the NPC irrelevant in the west. In May 1962 a parliamentary crisis ensued when Awolowo broke with Akintola and tried to have him removed as premier and replaced by Awolowo's ally, Chief Adegbenro. At this point Prime Minister Balewa, who hoped to align with Akintola and gain a foothold in the Western Region, declared a state of emergency, and suspended the AG government for six months. At the end of the six months, Akintola was placed back in the premiership under the auspices of a new party, the United People's Party, which formed a coalition government with the NCNC in the Western Region. The AG was now a minority party in its own stronghold.

Things only became worse for the AG. The interim government during the state of emergency brought Awolowo up on charges of corruption, and found him guilty of diverting regional funds in the amount of over N5 million, which he was accused of using for political purposes to strengthen the AG in the Western Region. Several other AG leaders, including Chief Anthony Enahoro and Alhaji Lateef Jakande, were tried for treasonable felonies and imprisoned along with Awolowo in 1962. The AG was further weakened in 1963 when the Mid-Western Region was carved out of the Western Region, creating a new political unit in Nigerian politics and fracturing the AG base.

By 1963 it had become clear to most minority parties in Nigeria that there was little to be gained by joining with the NPC government. The best way to gain power in the existing federal system was to attack the northern basis of power by whatever means necessary. One opportunity for the southern parties to erode northern political power was through the census that was commissioned in 1962. The number of seats allocated to each region in the federal House of Representatives and revenue-sharing provisions at the federal level were based on regional population figures from the 1953 census. Southern governments realized that, if they could manipulate the census numbers in 1962, they could reverse the northern population majority and gain more seats for the southern regions in the federal assembly. When the census figures were released in May, they indicated an incredible 70 percent increase in the population of the Eastern and Western Regions since 1953, compared to a 30 percent increase in the Northern Region. These figures were no doubt grossly inaccurate, and the NPC-led government refused to ratify them, instead ordering another census to be held the next year.

When the results of the second census were released in November 1963, the new figures indicated that the Northern Region had grown at a pace commensurate with the East and West: some 8 million new northerners had been discovered. Again, the results were widely regarded as fraudulent. There were even reports that in some areas livestock had been counted as people.[18] The NCNC bitterly opposed the ratification of the new census figures, but failed to prevent them becoming official. Akintola, who was in the pocket of the NPC, accepted the figures on behalf of the Western Region, while the newly formed Mid-Western Region's premier, Dennis Osadebey, accepted the figures "for the sake of national unity."[19] The new Nigerian population officially stood at 55,620,268, of whom 29,758,875 resided in the Northern Region.[20] These figures meant that the proportional allocation of federal representation and revenues continued to favor the Northern Region. The census crisis indicated to many Nigerians, however, the extent to which governments in all regions were willing to lie and cheat in pursuance of political power.

What the census crisis revealed about the corruption of the First Republic, the federal elections of 1964 only reinforced.[21] Having lost the fight to gain control through a realignment of the seat allocations in the federal assembly, the southern-based political parties now turned all their energies towards winning the upcoming elections. The NCNC and AG united with minority parties in the Northern Region, such as Aminu Kano's NEPU and Joseph Tarka's United Middle Belt Congress, to form the United Progressive Grand Alliance (UPGA). The main goals of the UPGA were the ousting of the NPC from control of the federal government and the reinstatement of AG supremacy in the Western Region, and deposing the highly unpopular regime of Premier Akintola and his newly formed Nigerian National Democratic Party. The stakes were also high for the NPC, which faced political marginalization and the possible reversal of its policies if the UPGA were to win. Therefore, the NPC joined with the NNDP and a few fringe parties in the south to form the Nigerian National Alliance (NNA), the main goal of which was the prolongation of the status quo.

The campaign season that led up to the December 30, 1964, elections was abominable, particularly in the Northern and Western Regions, where the NPC and NNDP respectively did everything in their power to stymie the opposition. UPGA officials protested consistently that their candidates were physically prevented from campaigning in the north. Sometimes UPGA candidates were denied entry into towns where rallies were planned. Often UPGA candidates and supporters were arbitrarily detained or arrested, as in Kano in October 1964, when local police arrested a reported 297 UPGA supporters. Refused recourse to lawyers when brought before the local *alkalai* court, sixty-eight were released and ordered to return to their home districts, while 134 were held for over six months and ninety-five were imprisoned for terms ranging from six months to a year.[22] On October 17, Joseph Tarka, leader of the UMBC and one of the highest-ranking UPGA members, was arrested on charges of incitement, further hampering the UPGA campaign in the north.

It was in the Western Region that the campaign was most competitive, however. The AG had strong hopes of regaining control of regional politics from Akintola, whose NNDP party was largely seen as a puppet of the NPC and therefore a symbol of northern "domination." Indeed, Akintola's party was quite unpopular, but it enjoyed one major advantage: it controlled the regional government, the civil service, and the electoral machinery. To an even greater extent than in the north, the campaign in the west was characterized by violence and corruption as the NNDP tried to quash the UPGA and its supporters. Thugs regularly beat up UPGA supporters, destroyed UPGA property, and promoted a general atmosphere of fear.

The most common form of obstruction used against the UPGA in the north and the west was the use of the state apparatus to prevent UPGA candidates from competing as candidates. A main goal of the NNA was to prevent UPGA candidates from being legally nominated to stand for election. In this way, the NNA hoped to present as many of their own candidates as possible unopposed. Since NNA supporters controlled the election machinery in both the north and the west, they could easily hamper the nomination process for UPGA candidates. When the time came to turn in paperwork, election officials were often difficult to locate. Once forms had been turned in, there was no way to guarantee that they would be processed. In the end, eighty-eight out of 174 seats in the Northern Region went unopposed to NNA candidates, while the NNDP claimed nearly 30 percent of the seats in the Western Region uncontested. The NCNC, which controlled the Eastern Region government, employed similar tactics, returning 30 percent of its candidates unopposed as well.[23]

Outraged by the intimidation and obstruction faced by UPGA candidates and supporters, NCNC officials called for an UPGA boycott of the election. At the last minute, on December 29, the AG fell into line with the NCNC and agreed to boycott, but it was too late to stop the election from going forward. The boycott was a success only in the Eastern Region. In the west, the NNDP made sure that voting went forward, although election day was marred by allegations of voter intimidation and violence at the polls. In the Mid-Western Region, Premier Osadebay, who was an NCNC man, inexplicably ordered the election to go ahead against the wishes of his party. The result was a botched boycott that allowed the NNA to declare a sweeping victory, far larger than it could have achieved had the UPGA contested whole-heartedly.

After the election, Prime Minister Balewa called upon President Azikiwe to invite the creation of an NNA government, but Azikiwe, loyal to the NCNC that he had helped to found, refused to do so. A constitutional stalemate ensued, which was ended by negotiations between Azikiwe and Balewa. The "Zik-Balewa Pact" that came out of these negotiations gave the election to the NNA with a few conditions. First, Balewa was required to form a "broad-based government" that incorporated UPGA members wherever possible. Second, the seats that had been successfully boycotted in the election were to be recontested in March 1965. Finally, elections for the Western Region assembly were to go ahead in October 1965. The UPGA won most of the seats in the "little election" that took place in March, the vast majority going to NCNC candidates in the Eastern Region, but this was not enough to threaten the majority claimed by the NNA. In the end, the NPC and NNDP combined won 198 of the 312 seats in the federal assembly. Although this was a clear victory, the conduct of the election had been disastrous, causing resentment among UPGA supporters and causing many Nigerians to question the fairness of the country's democratic system.

Nigerians' faith in their system of government, already weakened by the 1964 elections, was further strained by the Western Region elections of October 1965. In style and substance, the Western Region elections were little more than a repeat of the 1964 federal debacle. Fearing that it would lose a fair election against the more popular AG candidates of the UPGA, the NNDP again used force to intimidate UPGA supporters and again prevented the UPGA from making nominations for many seats. Other problems also plagued the alliance. An original agreement to split the ninety-four seats between NCNC and AG candidates fell apart when the AG decided to make a push for more seats. Therefore, in twenty constituencies both an NCNC and an AG candidate ran, splitting the UPGA vote. Fighting at some polling places also caused some polls to close early. On top of these issues, however, was the general rigging of the election by the NNDP. Reports on election day, October 11, 1965, indicated cases of multiple voting and stuffing of ballot boxes in the NNDP's favor. Also, in a highly irregular move, Akintola decided that the results of the elections were to be disseminated only from the central headquarters in Ibadan and were not to be announced at local polling places, as was normal practice, giving NNDP electoral officials the time and secrecy to alter results as necessary. Without access to NNDP archives, the extent to which the NNDP rigged the election may never be known, but in such a zero-sum climate the NNDP preferred a concrete victory over the illusion of a fair election.

When the preliminary results were announced on October 13, both sides declared victory. Officially, Akintola and the NNDP had claimed fifty-one seats to the UPGA's eleven, with thirty still to be decided. Chief Adegbenro, the acting leader of the AG, immediately declared sixty-eight victories for the UPGA, however, and announced that he was forming an interim government. Adegbenro and other UPGA leaders were taken into detention for disregarding the official results. Across the Western Region, people took to the streets to protest the election results. Throughout November and December the Western Region was a battle zone, as UPGA supporters rioted, clashing with police, looting and burning the homes of NNDP supporters, and even killing them in some cases. Further fueling violence against the NNDP government was the government's ill-timed reduction in the price of cocoa. As the ruling party, the NNDP controlled the marketing boards, which set the price for cocoa. Usually, cocoa prices were set each year in late September or early

October; fearing the political repercussions of a price decrease in the days before the election, however, NNDP officials had left the price artificially high until after the election. Shortly after the election the price was dropped from £120 per ton to just £65, a nearly 50 percent drop. Cocoa farmers erupted in anger, creating a peasant revolt that joined with the UPGA rioting to make the Western Region virtually ungovernable.[24]

Rather than call a state of emergency in the Western Region, Prime Minister Balewa instead decided to send forces for the sole purpose of supporting his ally Akintola, but to little avail. The Western Region was out of control, bitter over yet another failure of the First Republic to provide democratic governance. Nowhere was this bitterness more heartfelt than among Igbo military officers, who, tired of the inability of the federal system to keep the peace and work in the best interests of all Nigerians, now began plotting to overthrow the government.

MILITARY INTERVENTION

In the early hours of January 15, 1966, Nigeria's first military coup began. The coup was led by the "five majors," as Kaduna Nzeogwu, E. Ifeajuna, D. Okafor, C. I. Anuforo, and A. Ademoyega were later dubbed, and operated out of each of the three regions of Nigeria and Lagos. The leaders of the coup claimed that their goal was to bring an end to the tribalism and corruption that had characterized the First Republic. In the process, the majors arrested all the regional premiers, and killed federal Prime Minister Tafawa Balewa, Premier S. L. Akintola of the Western Region, and Premier Ahmadu Bello of the Northern Region, who, the young military officers believed, were responsible for the chaos of 1964 and 1965. Many northern military officers were also killed in the coup. Despite the many high-profile murders carried out by the five majors, the coup was not a complete success.[25] In fact, it remains unclear what, if any, plan the coup leaders had to govern the country once the civilian leadership had been removed. Nevertheless, with so many of the most powerful political figures in Nigeria dead or imprisoned, the country was thrown into yet another major political crisis.

Power quickly devolved to the commanding officer of the Nigerian army, Major General John Aguiyi-Ironsi, who immediately went about restoring order. The main goals of the Ironsi regime, however, dovetailed with those of the coup leaders: re-establishing law and order, maintaining essential services, eradicating regionalism and tribalism, and ending corruption. Ironsi said his government would last only "until such a time when a constitution is brought out according to the wishes of the people."[26] Ironsi outlawed political parties and placed military governors in each of the regions. Included among these new military governors was the new governor of the Eastern Region, Lieutenant Colonel Chukwuemeka ("Emeka") Odumegwu Ojukwu.

Initially the military coup and the ascendancy of Ironsi were viewed very positively, particularly in the south. To many southerners, the removal of the civilian government marked the end of an agenda of northern "domination." In the Western Region, the collapse of the unpopular NNDP regime was greeted with jubilation, and the rioting and unrest that had plagued the region since the October elections came to an almost immediate end. Ironsi's subsequent policies as head of state alarmed many northerners, however, who came to view the coup and Ironsi as part of a plan by southern – specifically Igbo – officers to use the military as a means of imposing a new era of Igbo domination. In many ways, circumstantial evidence corroborated such a view. In the first place, four of the five majors who led the January coup were Igbo. Of all the officers and politicians killed in the coup, only one had been Igbo, while the majority had been northerners. While the two most prominent figures in northern politics – Balewa and Bello – had been murdered along with their ally Akintola, the Igbo premiers of the Mid-Western and Eastern Regions had been arrested but later released. To many, this pattern indicated that the coup was primarily an Igbo strike against the north.

Making matters worse, Ironsi made several moves in the first half of 1966 that led many northerners to believe that he was part of an Igbo conspiracy. Ironsi was himself an Igbo, and, in an unwise political move, he tended to surround himself with Igbo advisers throughout his time in power. He allowed the coup plotters to remain in detention, rather than bringing them to trial for the crimes that northerners believed they had committed. He has also been accused of accelerating the promotion of Igbo officers in the military, counter to the dictates of the quota system. The most damning evidence against Ironsi in the eyes of northerners, however, came in the form of Decree no. 34 of May 24, 1966, in which he officially abolished the federal system and replaced it with a unitary system. The regional structure of Nigeria ceased to exist, and was replaced by "groups of provinces." Both the military and the civil service, which had previously been administered regionally, were to be integrated and administered from the center.

To northerners this was Igbo domination in practice. The north now faced the prospect of being occupied by southern military officers, of being administered by southern civil servants. Furthermore, northerners now lacked the safeguards placed in the federal system that made sure that northerners were involved in governance to an extent commensurate with their population. Not willing to let their position slip any further, on July 29, 1966, a group of northern NCOs and officers carried out a countercoup, capturing and killing Ironsi in Ibadan. For three days the country teetered without a head of state, until the leading northern officers selected thirty-one-year-old Lieutenant Colonel. Yakubu ("Jack") Gowon as supreme commander of the armed forces and the new head of state.

Gowon immediately announced the repeal of Decree no. 34, indicating that Nigeria was committed to unity within a federal structure with respect for regional differences. Gowon was to find reconciliation difficult, however, particularly with Lieutenant Colonel Ojukwu, the Igbo military governor of the Eastern Region, who had many grave reservations about the legitimacy of the countercoup. In the first place, Ojukwu did not believe that Gowon had the authority to become supreme commander of the armed forces. Several still living officers had higher rank and more experience than Gowon, and Ojukwu argued that any of these officers had a greater claim to the title of supreme commander than the usurper Gowon. A far more pressing issue, however, was the safety of Igbos in Nigeria and the ability or willingness of the military government to protect them. Between May, when Ironsi had abolished the federal structure, and September 1966 continuous violence had been directed at Igbos and other easterners living in the north. A spate of massacres, many conducted by northern soldiers, took the lives of between 80,000 and 100,000 easterners during this period, the worst occurring in September. These massacres sparked revenge killings of northerners resident in the Eastern Region. Such events led Ojukwu to question whether Igbos could ever live in harmony within a federal Nigeria. He urged all easterners outside the region to return home and suggested that all northerners in the east do likewise. This led to large population movements in the latter half of 1966 and the early part of 1967.

While Ojukwu was already pondering the possibility of secession on the grounds that easterners were no longer safe within Nigeria, Gowon was determined to keep the east within the federation. A series of meetings between Gowon and Ojukwu took place in Aburi, Ghana, on January 4–5, 1967. These negotiations produced only a vague and loosely worded resolution. Gowon believed that the federation had been preserved at

Aburi, while Ojukwu claimed the Aburi agreement gave him wide-ranging powers to control the government of the Eastern Region and even to secede from the federation if he so chose. In March Ojukwu announced that as of April 1 the government of the Eastern Region would take over all federal departments, taxes, and other revenues, essentially making the region independently administered. Gowon responded by blockading the coast and instituting economic sanctions against the east. Last-ditch efforts at a peaceful settlement broke down, and, on May 30, Ojukwu declared the independence of the Eastern Region, which he renamed the Independent Republic of Biafra.

CIVIL WAR

From the perspective of Gowon and the Federal Military Government, Biafra could not simply be allowed to secede, for three main reasons. First, many in the FMG, including Gowon, sincerely believed in the practicability of Nigerian unity and were willing to fight to preserve it. Second, to allow the secession of Biafra would be to invite the secession of any minority group within the federation at any time. The prospect of Nigeria fragmenting into many small, hostile states was not appetizing to the FMG. Finally, the lands claimed by Biafra contained 67 percent of the known petroleum reserves in Nigeria. The secession of Biafra thus threatened what had the potential to be a very lucrative revenue base for the FMG.

Civil war ensued. Sometimes called the Biafran war, but most commonly referred to as the Nigerian Civil War, the fighting that took place between the FMG and the forces of Biafra lasted for two and a half years, ending in Biafra's collapse and surrender on January 12, 1970.[27] The FMG initially considered the war a "police action" that would not take long to settle; the Biafrans considered it a war for their very survival, however. Biafrans claimed throughout the war that the ultimate goal of the federal government was the "genocide" of the Igbo people. By presenting the war as first and foremost a self-defense effort, Ojukwu and his cohort of advisers were able to galvanize public opinion within Biafra around a growing sense of Igbo nationalism, while also engendering a great deal of sympathy in the international arena.

In some ways, the actions of the FMG to preserve the Nigerian federation seemed to support Biafra's interpretation that the main goal of the FMG was the eradication of the Igbo. Gowon's war strategy focused on the isolation of Igbo territory and the impoverishment of Biafra.

Immediately after Ojukwu declared the independence of Biafra, Gowon declared a state of emergency in Nigeria and announced the creation of new states. The three regions and the Federal Capital Territory of Lagos were carved up into twelve new states, three of which were created in the former Eastern Region. In this way, Gowon appeased minority groups across the country that had been clamoring for new states since before independence. Only one of the three states created out of the Eastern Region, the East Central State, was predominantly Igbo. Moreover, the East Central State was landlocked while the other two states in the Eastern Region, Rivers and South-eastern, accounted for the entire coastline of Biafra and contained most of the oil wealth of the country. The creation of these states within Biafra was largely symbolic – Biafra controlled the entire territory of the former Eastern Region at the time – but it did weaken support for the Biafran government among non-Igbo citizens, who viewed the creation of the states as an indication of the FMG's ability to act in their interests.

While the creation of new states was designed to isolate the Igbo and make political matters more difficult for the Biafran government, Gowon undertook measures to dampen the Biafran economy as well. The blockade of the coast continued, and a military cordon surrounding the country made it difficult for Biafra to ship food and other items into or out of the country. Although the FMG did allow regular shipments of relief goods carried by humanitarian organizations, the overall effect of the embargo was detrimental. In January 1968 Gowon announced that the Nigerian currency would be changed. This meant that any Nigerian currency that the Biafrans had amassed to fund the war and their government quickly became worthless. Over time, these economic factors took their toll on Biafra. Food became increasingly scarce and high inflation made even existing goods prohibitively expensive within Biafra. For example, the price of beef rose from 3 shillings a pound to 60, dried fish from 5 shillings a pound to 60, and a chicken, which went for roughly 15 shillings before the war, cost as much as £30 by its end.[28]

After some initial military successes achieved by the Biafran army, which actually occupied the Mid-Western Region in the first months of the war and threatened an invasion of the Western Region, FMG forces began to make advances, slowly pushing the Biafrans back deep into their own territory. Federal troops quickly pushed the Biafran army out of the Mid-Western region, occupied Enugu, Biafra's first capital, on October 4, 1967, and had taken Calabar by October 18. It seemed as if the war would end with a swift federal victory. The Biafran Igbos refused to surrender so

Figure 7.1 A motor park in Umuahia (collection of Roy Doron)

easily, however. The capital was moved south to Umuahia, and the fighting slackened for some time. Part of the reason for this was Gowon's hope that his policies of economic strangulation and the political propitiation of minority groups would cause those within Biafra to rise up against the Biafran government on their own.[29]

This proved to be a mistake. Malnourishment and starvation increased rapidly within Biafra, allowing Ojukwu and other Biafran leaders to exploit Gowon's policies as proof of a genocidal conspiracy against the Igbo. Biafra produced massive amounts of propaganda within the country and even hired the European advertising firm H. Wm. Bernhardt Inc., which published under the imprint Markpress, to promote the Biafran cause – particularly the allegations of "genocide" – to the international community. Deprivation was indeed a tool of the FMG's strategy; Gowon decried accusations of genocide, however, repeatedly noting the millions of Igbo currently living safely in territories occupied by federal forces. Nevertheless, the propaganda produced by Biafra helped to galvanize feeling against the FMG among Biafran Igbos and earned sympathy for Biafra from many international sources.

International involvement in the Nigerian Civil War undoubtedly helped to prolong the conflict. Initially, Biafra had difficulty finding sympathetic ears. The Organization of African Unity (OAU) refused to recognize Biafra and treated the war as an internal Nigerian conflict. The United Kingdom and the United States chose to sit on the fence, preferring to withhold support for either side until it was evident who was going to win. The unwillingness of the United States and the United Kingdom to support the federal cause wholeheartedly angered the FMG, which turned to the USSR for support. The Soviets were more than willing to oblige, and became the chief supplier of aircraft and advisers to the FMG over the course of the war. Things began to change in Biafra's favor in 1968, however. Several member states of the OAU – Tanzania, Gabon, the Ivory Coast, and Zambia – broke ranks and formally recognized Biafra. Influenced by the international reports of "genocide," several European and Asian countries also expressed solidarity with Biafra, although never officially recognizing it as an independent country. France and Portugal in particular provided Biafra with supplies and logistical support, while Israel saw Biafra, like Israel itself, as a state surrounded by enemies intent on its destruction. China, seeing a chance to challenge the USSR for leadership of the communist world, also expressed its sympathy for Biafra, although very little tangible support followed.[30]

International non-governmental actors also played a role in the war. The Catholic Church, to which many Biafrans belonged, worked hand in hand with the International Red Cross to provide humanitarian aid to Biafrans, flying nightly shipments of food, medicine, and other non-military supplies into Biafra's famous airstrip at Uli. Both Biafra and the FMG also employed mercenaries, particularly as fighter pilots, during the war. The ability of international actors to move supplies into Biafra across the blockade allowed the embattled state to survive for much longer than it would otherwise have done.

With the aid of international organizations and governments, and buoyed by an ideology of self-preservation, Biafran Igbos held out as long as possible against the stronger FMG. Eventually, however, the Biafran state collapsed, overrun by federal troops in December 1969 and January 1970. Seeing the writing on the wall, Ojukwu fled to the Ivory Coast, claiming that as long as he lived the revolution was not dead. On January 12, 1970, Major General Phillip Effiong, to whom Ojukwu had ceded power before his flight, officially surrendered to Gowon in Lagos.

Figure 7.2 A neighborhood in present-day Kano (collection of Jonathan T. Reynolds)

LEGACIES OF THE WAR

The war had taken the lives of between 1 and 3 million Nigerians, mostly in the Eastern Region and many through starvation, leaving perhaps another 3 million displaced, but the "genocide" that Igbos so feared did not materialize after the war. Gowon stressed that there was to be no vengeance and no reparations, and that there had been no winners or losers in the "war of brothers." The process of reintegration and reconciliation began immediately, buoyed by a rapid and enormous growth in petroleum production in the 1970s.

The civil war did leave a significant legacy to Nigeria, despite the rapid reintegration of the country and concerted efforts on the part of Nigerians to put the past behind them. The national question would continue to plague Nigerian political rhetoric. On the political level, however, these tensions were overshadowed by the fact that the military remained in power after the war. Committed to unity and order, the military government was by no means democratic. In fact, the military learned that it could ignore the public almost completely in the years after the civil war, becoming every bit the corrupt, bloated bureaucracy that the First Republic had been. The military government was not as fragile as the First Republic, however, despite its increasing corruption and ineffectiveness. If anything, the military emerged from the civil war more powerful and dominant than it had been previously. At the time of the January 1966 coup the Nigerian military was made up of roughly 10,000 soldiers. By the end of the war it had ballooned to over 270,000 soldiers. Cognizant of the need to keep people employed and also aware that its own power lay in its ability to exert force where necessary, the military regime retained large armed forces in the years after the war. As a percentage of the total budget, military spending jumped from 0.2 percent in 1961 to 6 percent in 1970. By the end of the war the military had become the driving force of Nigerian government and politics.

CHAPTER 8

Oil, state, and society, 1970 – 1983

As Nigeria emerged from the civil war, it was clear that severe ethnic and regional fissures continued to exist, preventing the establishment of a strong national identity and therefore inhibiting the development of a stable, democratically elected federal government. These issues were temporarily marginalized, however, as the Nigerian economy grew drastically due to the rapid expansion of the petroleum sector in the early 1970s. Located mostly in the Niger delta region, petroleum became Nigeria's chief export and single-handedly made Nigeria the wealthiest country in Africa during the 1970s. Rather than contributing to the overall development of Nigeria and to improved living conditions for Nigerian citizens, however, this wealth was distributed unequally, bene-fiting primarily those people who had access to state power and, therefore, to the licenses, contracts, and revenues that accrued to the government from the petroleum sector. The result was a government apparatus that became increasingly divorced from its subjects, creating a stark discon-nection between the will of the people and the actions of government officials – a disconnection that continues to afflict Nigeria. Three dif-ferent regimes, two military and one civilian, oversaw the growth of the oil economy in the period between 1970 and 1983, but all three mis-managed government funds and contributed to the development of a kleptocracy that continues to plague Nigeria today.[1] While a small class of politicians and entrepreneurs has become exceedingly wealthy via the oil economy, the majority of Nigerians remain mired in perpetual poverty.

Commercial quantities of petroleum had first been discovered in Nigeria at Olobiri in the eastern Niger delta, where the Shell-BP Development Company (a joint venture of Royal Dutch Shell and British Petroleum) first struck oil in 1956. Commercial drilling began two years later in 1958. Petroleum became an ever more important commodity in the Nigerian export economy during the 1960s, but the civil war of 1967–70 hampered the expansion of the industry. Two-thirds of the known petroleum reserves had been in areas controlled by Biafra, and, while the FMG did increase production in the fields it controlled, its main pre-occupation was with winning the war and reincorporating Biafra into the federation.

As soon as the war ended, the FMG led by Yakubu Gowon undertook the rapid expansion of the petroleum sector in the Niger delta, ushering in the oil boom of the early 1970s. Crude oil production had grown from 5,100 bpd in 1958 to over 417,000 bpd in 1966 on the eve of the war.[2] The most rapid expansion of the petroleum sector occurred in the first half of the 1970s, however. In 1970 total production rose to 396 million barrels, rising further to 643 million in 1972 and 823 million in 1974.[3] The Shell Petroleum Development Corporation, the Nigerian subsidiary of Royal Dutch Shell, accounted for the majority of petroleum production in the 1970s: roughly 1.3 million bpd of the 2.3 million bpd average during this period.

As petroleum production grew in the 1970s, so too did the revenue that the Nigerian government generated from petroleum. Government rev-enues from petroleum were a mere N200,000 in 1958, the first year of commercial production. Revenues in 1970 were N166 million, but they rose exponentially from that time. In 1974 revenues from petroleum were N3.7 billion and in 1976 they were over N5.3 billion.[4] The massive growth in the productivity and profitability of the petroleum industry in Nigeria in the early 1970s was fueled by a global scarcity at the time. In 1971 Nigeria joined OPEC, which in late 1973 set up an embargo on Western countries over their support of Israel in the Yom Kippur War in October that year. Prices of petroleum skyrocketed, rising from $3.80 a barrel in October 1973 to $14.70 by January 1974, and remained high for most of the remainder of the 1970s. Nigeria reaped the benefits. As revenues from petroleum rose, so too did Nigerian reliance on those revenues. Petrol-eum revenues allowed the government to reduce or eliminate other forms of revenue allocation, such as customs duties and income taxes. By 1974 82 percent of Nigerian government revenues came from petroleum,[5] making the Nigerian economy extremely dependent upon this single source.

This dependence on petroleum for the vast bulk of government rev-enue has caused many problems from the Gowon era onwards.[6] The Nigerian economy became extremely vulnerable to fluctuations in the world price of petroleum. Development planning and revenue allocation for the future were based on the going rate for petroleum in the early 1970s, when crude prices were high. The influx of wealth led to enormous rises in state expenditure. Gowon increased the size of the public service, granted huge wage and salary increases to government employees (known as the "Udoji Award"), and went about investing in large infrastructural projects such as restoring farms, roads, and airports that had been damaged during the war. Gowon undertook the building of new schools and military barracks, and spent massively on preparations for the Festival of Black Arts and Culture (FESTAC). He also increased military spending, maintaining a standing army of over 200,000 soldiers – much larger than needed during peacetime. Total military expenditure rose from N314.5 million in 1970 to N1,116.7 million in 1975. Much of this state spending was undertaken to buy loyalty for the military regime at the expense of future growth. When petroleum prices dropped between 1976 and 1979, and again during the oil glut years of the early 1980s, the Nigerian economy suffered greatly.

The focus on petroleum as the basis for the Nigerian economy led to the neglect of other sectors that are necessary for a stable and balanced economy. The agriculture sector continued its decline during the oil boom years, and Nigeria became more dependent on food imports, even beginning to import items such as palm oil and groundnuts, which had been staples of the agricultural economy. Manufacturing decreased as a percentage of gross domestic product (GDP) from 9.4 percent in 1970 to 7.0 percent in 1973/4.[7] The oil boom, rather than providing an impetus to grow the productive sector of the Nigerian economy, instead encouraged a rise in imports. As more money entered the domestic economy, it led to greater consumption, particularly in the urban areas. Greater consumption led to inflation, as more money was being used to buy the same amount of goods. For example, food prices ballooned by 273 percent between 1973 and 1981.[8] To offset inflation, the government sharply reduced tariff rates in order to encourage import growth, thereby flooding the market with imported goods. Nevertheless, this policy failed to end inflation within Nigeria, and at the same time it discouraged growth in agriculture and manufacturing by providing competition in the form of cheap imports.

The oil boom also resulted in widespread corruption on the part of the government officials responsible for the collection and allocation of revenues. The oil boom led to the development of a "rentier state" in Nigeria. Unlike most countries, where government revenue is generated within the country through taxes on citizens, service provision, or internal borrowing, in a "rentier state" the bulk of government revenue comes from outside the country. In the case of Nigeria, the vast bulk of

Figure 8.1 An oil tanker delivering fuel (collection of Matthew M. Heaton)

government revenue since the 1970s has come from "rents" paid to it through licenses and royalties from the multinational petroleum corporations such as Shell, BP, Fina, Agip, and so on. Under such a system, corruption can – and has – run rampant, since there is no accountability other than that owed to the multinational corporations that pay the rents. Citizens' opinion of the government becomes irrelevant, since the government does not maintain its power through popularity but through coercion and the control of resources. Under military regimes, government is inherently undemocratic. The military maintains power through the threat or act of violence. Under civilian administrations, rent moneys can be used to bribe election officials, buy votes, or hire thugs to harass political opponents. Rent seeking therefore creates a marked division between those who have access to rents and those who do not, and it creates a governing apparatus that can maintain power while disregarding the needs of the majority of its subjects. It creates a comprador class of politicians and bureaucrats, who work in conjunction with foreign companies to siphon off surplus wealth for personal benefit.

During the Gowon era there was minimal oversight of how petroleum revenues were spent. Millions of naira went missing as government officials at the federal and state levels lined their own pockets with revenues earmarked for other purposes. Several different methods developed for stealing government money. Sometimes money could simply be taken by distorting the books. Often government officials would award government contracts or licenses to friends or business partners and would accept a percentage of the contract as a kickback, a reward for securing the contract for a particular person or firm. Efforts were also made to indigenize businesses, taking control of economic activity out of the hands of foreigners and placing it in the hands of Nigerian investors. Indigenization programs rapidly increased the overall percentage of businesses owned by Nigerians; indigenization did little to improve the lot of the average Nigerian, however. Only those who already had money could afford to invest in business. Indigenization therefore created a small class of wealthy businessmen whose interests were aligned with those of foreign investors and rent-seeking politicians, who were content to use a booming economy to enrich themselves at the expense of the majority of the population.

The oil boom also created a crisis over revenue allocation. Federal and state governments alike wanted access to as much of the new wealth as possible. The federal government quickly went about making sure that it would be the body to control the bulk of oil revenues. In 1971 it established the Nigerian National Oil Company (NNOC) to supervise oil extraction and provide guidelines to the multinational corporations that carried out the production. In 1976 the NNOC was merged with the Ministry of Mines and Power to form the Nigerian National Petroleum Corporation (NNPC), which still exists today. The main argument over revenue allocation was over how to distribute revenues across the country. Those in the oil-rich states of the Niger delta preferred an allocation process known as "derivation," whereby oil revenues would be allocated to states based on the portion of petroleum derived from each state. Those in regions that did not produce petroleum objected to this concept, and instead proposed that revenues be allocated based on the populations of states.

In 1970 the federal government adopted a compromise position. Oil-producing states were to split 45 percent of the total revenues based on the concept of derivation; the remaining 55 percent went to the federal government. Of that 55 percent, half went directly to federal government coffers and half went to a fund known as the Distributable Pool Account (DPA). The DPA was to be distributed among all the states based on two criteria. Half of the DPA was to be divided equally among the states, while the other half was distributed to all the states in proportion to their populations. The 45 percent allocated by derivation was later reduced to 20 percent, before finally being eliminated in 1979 in favor of a federally controlled account for mineral-producing regions. The federal government also declared at this time that all rents and royalties from offshore drilling would accrue to the federal government.

The downfall of Gowon's regime was precipitated by the evident rise in corruption in his government during the oil boom years. Emboldened by the Federal Military Government's victory over Biafra, Gowon announced shortly after the war a nine-point plan to return the country to civilian rule. He proposed to reorganize the civil service and the military, root out official corruption, invest in development ventures, draw up a new constitution, create new states, conduct a new census, establish new, national political parties, and return the government to democratic rule. By doing all these things he intended to set the country on a path of reconciliation, rehabilitation, and reconstruction. Originally he declared that all of this would be accomplished and power returned to civilians by 1974, but later he moved the date back to 1976.

Despite the windfall of the oil boom years, Gowon was not able to achieve many of these goals. Rather than reorganizing the civil service and military, he expanded them. On the political front, little was accomplished to create a new constitution, establish new states, or encourage the formation of political parties. When Gowon tried to hold a census in 1973 the results were clearly fraudulent, as each state inflated its population figures to garner a greater percentage of the Distributable Pool Account. The 1973 census declared that the population of Nigeria had risen to 79.9 million, 43 percent higher than the grossly inflated figures of the 1963 census just a decade earlier. The results were so outlandish that Gowon rejected them. To many, however, Gowon's refusal to accept the census was an indication that he was dragging his heels on the democratic transition.

The Gowon regime was losing credibility, not only because of its failure to take the necessary steps to transition to democratic rule but also because of the corruption being exhibited by many of its high-ranking officers, particularly the military governors of the states, who were developing reputations for abuses of power and the plundering of government coffers. In 1974 two officers close to Gowon, both in Benue-Plateau State, were implicated in corruption scandals: Joseph Gomwalk, the governor, and Joseph Tarka, the commissioner of elections. Tarka resigned his post over these allegations, but Gowon refused to discipline Gomwalk and allowed him to retain his office. This action illustrated Gowon's tendency to remain loyal to his subordinate officers through thick and thin, even in cases of corruption and abuse of power. The growing belief in the extreme corruption of the Gowon administration was proven to be well founded after Gowon's removal from power, when inquiries into the personal assets of Gowon's military governors indicated that only two were innocent of illegally enriching themselves under his tenure.

Corruption in the Gowon regime was accompanied by gross mis-management of government revenues. For example, in early 1975 Gowon announced the purchase of 16 million metric tons of cement to build a new army barracks, among other projects. This amount alone nearly quadrupled the total Nigerian imports over the previous year, which had stood at 4.49 million metric tons.[9] As ships bearing cement poured into Lagos harbor, congestion became a major problem. Some ships were forced to wait for as long as a year to unload their cargo, all the while collecting demurrage fees in compensation. It was later revealed that many ships arrived at Lagos with inferior goods simply in order to wait in line and collect the demurrage fees. The amount ordered was later determined to have been a huge overestimation of the necessary tonnage, as contractors had inflated their bids in order to squeeze as much money out of the federal government as possible. The "cement armada" episode came to epitomize the wasteful mismanagement of government resources that took place under the Gowon regime.

Despite the glaring corruption and mismanagement that was coming to characterize his rule, Gowon was in no hurry to hand power back to a civilian government. Frustrated by the failure of the 1973 census and what he called the "sectional politicking" and "intemperate utterances and writings" of prospective politicians, in October 1974 he announced that he was further delaying the transition to democratic rule beyond his self-imposed 1976 deadline. He refused to lift the ban on the formation of political parties, but promised to move forward on drafting a constitution and on the creation of more states in an effort to bring the country closer to a peaceful democratic transition in the future. He also promised to reform his own government by clamping down on corruption, even hinting that there would be a shake-up in the personnel and distribution of the country's military governors.

Gowon's announcement of these reforms marked the beginning of the end of his regime. To many Nigerians, Gowon's speech was an indication of his own megalomania, corruption, and abuse of power. By 1975, he had lost respect in nearly every segment of Nigerian society. Average Nigerians resented the failure of the Gowon regime to manage the windfall of oil wealth, which had so much potential to improve living conditions. Non-military politicians resented Gowon's postponement of the democratic transition that promised to put them into power. Finally, many within the military felt that Gowon had damaged the reputation of the armed forces by favoring friends and allies for top jobs while refusing to discipline them when their corruption became apparent.

On July 30, 1975, a group of young officers led by Gowon's own chief of security, Colonel Joseph Garba, and Lieutenant Colonel Musa Yar'adua led a bloodless coup that removed Gowon from power while he was attending a meeting of the OAU in Uganda. The coup leaders agreed on a northerner, General Murtala Mohammed, as the new head of state. Mohammed was a battlefield hero of the civil war and had been Gowon's main adversary in the post-war regime. The coup was widely supported in Nigeria, and was heralded as the beginning of a new era of honest government and the transition to civilian rule. Mohammed immediately went about instituting reforms in order to live up to these expectations. He announced that his would be a "corrective" regime that would restore dignity to the military, which had been so maligned as a result of Gowon's misrule. He also committed himself to returning Nigeria to democratic rule.

Mohammed initiated many efforts to achieve these goals, but, unfortunately, his rule lasted only six months. On February 13, 1976, Mohammed was assassinated in an abortive coup, bringing to power his second in command, Lieutenant General Olusegun Obasanjo, a southern Yoruba who had also distinguished himself as a field commander during the civil war. Mohammed's short but vigorous tenure and his untimely demise have made him a populist hero in Nigeria. Today the international airport in Ikeja (Lagos) is named for him, and he appears on the N20 note, one of the most commonly used bills in the country today.

Obasanjo's regime continued in the footsteps of Mohammed. In fact, the transition between them in terms of goals and methods was so smooth that their tenures are usually considered together as the Mohammed/ Obasanjo regime. The goals of the Mohammed/Obasanjo regime can be broken down roughly into three: rooting out corruption in the government, promoting "national unity," and transitioning to civilian rule. In some ways, the Mohammed/Obasanjo regime built upon efforts already begun by Gowon, but in other ways it charted its own course. Measures to achieve all three of these goals had been instigated before Mohammed's assassination and were continued afterwards by Obasanjo.

In an effort to remove the corruption that had developed under the Gowon regime, Mohammed went about purging the military government. Gowon and most of the high-ranking military officials associated with his regime were compulsorily retired, and a new set of military governors was established throughout the country within days of the coup. Next, Mohammed turned his attention to the civil service, which had ballooned under Gowon and which was regularly accused of corruption, poor performance, and low productivity. In the course of eight weeks over 11,000 civil servants were dismissed or retired, most for purported malfeasance or ineptitude. Purges also spread to the police and judiciary, and four vice chancellors of Nigerian universities were retired as well.

Overall, however, these efforts to reduce corruption were unsuccessful, because they simply replaced individuals within the rent-seeking system without reforming the system itself. In many cases, people in positions of power used the purges to get rid of rivals or critical underlings. In cases where high-ranking military or civil employees were purged for corrupt practices, they were immediately replaced by people who could easily take advantage of the same corrupt system that had illegally enriched their predecessors. Without serious reforms to the "rentier" state system that encouraged corruption, little progress could be made in rooting out corruption. In effect, the purges of 1975–6, combined with the growing incapacity of the federal government to pay civil servants their wages regularly, had the effect of dampening morale and efficiency in the civil service and government administration, turning what were once considered secure and respectable careers into veritable symbols of the corruption and misgovernance of the Nigerian state.

The Mohammed/Obasanjo regime also undertook many efforts to improve the sense of "national unity" in Nigeria. Just like the attempt to root out corruption, however, the moves to promote national unity were unsuccessful, and often illustrated powerfully the negative attributes of the relationship between Nigerian state and society. Mohommed and Obasanjo were not the first heads of state to promote national unity. In 1973 Gowon had instituted the National Youth Service Corps (NYSC), which required all university and polytechnic graduates to perform one year of government service after graduation. This was designed to promote national unity in two ways. First, it made young Nigerians active participants in the activities of government, the desired result of which was supposed to be an increased sense of patriotism. Second, it brought together young Nigerians from across the country to work together towards common goals. NYSC service was also intended to guarantee that young Nigerians would develop relationships with Nigerians of religious and ethnic backgrounds that were different from their own, by requiring that their service take place in a part of the country other than their own.

The results of the NYSC program have been mixed at best. Since only university and polytechnic graduates are required to serve in the Corps, only a small percentage of Nigeria's youths are exposed to the multi-cultural environment that the NYSC promotes. Even within the NYSC itself, the program does not seem to be having the intended effect of promoting national unity and patriotism. While some participants have claimed to have gained greater respect for different cultures, many others have inidicated that they have less faith in the prospect of national integration after their year of service. Efforts to recruit NYSC participants to stay and work permanently in the states to which they were assigned have largely failed. Rather than developing a sense of patriotism, many participants have declared their resentment of the Nigerian government, which they believe is forcinig them to make sacrifices that the military and political elite members are themselves unwilling to make.[10]

When Mohammed took power one of the first acts of his administration was to begin the process of moving the federal capital from Lagos to a new site in Abuja, in the center of the country. Government officials argued that Lagos had become too crowded, and appeasing them was certainly one of the reasons for relocating the capital, a move that was not finally accomplished until 1991. Another compelling reason for moving the capital to Abuja, however, was to bring the seat of power closer to other regions of the country, and to carve out a Federal Capital Territory from the states surrounding Abuja that would be fully controlled by the federal government and not in any way administered by any state government, as had been the case in Lagos. Abuja and the FCT would therefore, in theory, be owned by all Nigerians and representative of all Nigerians, although this assumption has been widely criticized subsequently, as Abuja has become a place from which many Nigerians have been deliberately excluded rather than welcomed.[11]

The Mohammed/Obasanjo regime also promoted national unity through the creation of new states. Since each state was guaranteed a share of the oil revenues from the DPA, minority groups within existing states saw it as in their best interests to create new states, so as to have direct access to oil revenues that otherwise might not be spent in their areas or for the good of their communities. To minority groups, the creation of states promised greater political and economic autonomy for their communities, which tended to be neglected by the majority groups that controlled state governments in the twelve-state structure. Demands for new states had been prevalent throughout the Gowon administration, but Gowon had refused to create more states, fearing the inevitable fragmentation of the country into an ungovernable collection of interest groups. Mohammed went ahead with the formation of new states, however, and in February 1976 he announced the creation of seven new states out of the existing twelve, bringing the total to nineteen.

In theory, state creation would promote national unity by distributing the resources of the federal government more equitably, thereby engendering respect for the federal government and allaying fears that government was a tool used by the majority to oppress the minority. The creation of new states in 1976 also led to some criticism, however. Three of the new states were created out of existing states in the Yoruba-dominated southwestern part of the country. Some critics complained that this was an example of the rich getting richer, as these states were already within a part of the country that was relatively wealthy and developed compared to other parts. The creation of new states also established new majority populations with access to DPA revenues, but also created new minorities who argued for yet more states so that they could have their appropriate proportion of federal revenues. The Mohammed/Obasanjo regime announced that there would be no further state creation during its tenure, but the demands for new states did not go away, and they have continued to affect Nigerian politics ever since.

While the Mohammed/Obasanjo regime was trying to promote national unity through material benefits, it was also trying to promote national unity through symbolic acts. In 1977 Nigeria hosted FESTAC '77, an international festival of black and African arts and culture designed to showcase the "traditional" cultures of Nigeria and facilitate interaction and discussion amongst the greatest leaders and minds of Africa and its diaspora. Preparations for FESTAC had begun under the Gowon regime, which had allocated massive federal funds to build the major venues for the festival. When Mohammed came to power he postponed the festival and scaled down the public works projects associated with it, but the event was nevertheless impressive when Obasanjo convened it in 1977. FESTAC festivities centered on the National Theatre, a round structure encompassing 23,000 square meters and standing 31 meters tall, built in Lagos at an estimated cost of N144 million. The theater had been equipped on the inside with the most up-to-date technological

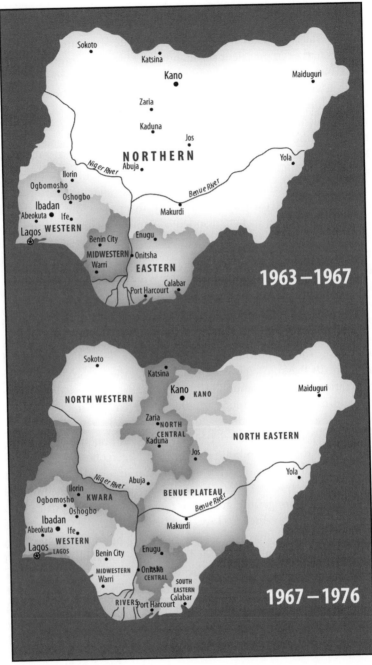

Map 8.1 Creation of new states, 1963–1976 (courtesy Saverance Publishing Services)

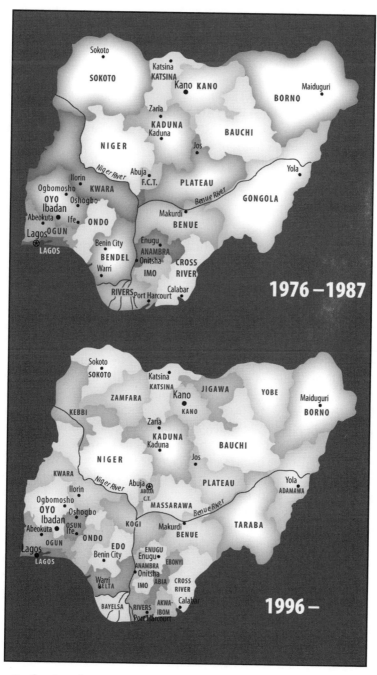

Map 8.2 Creation of new states, 1976–present (courtesy Saverance Publishing Services)

innovations that the burgeoning oil economy could buy: a 33- by 44-meter rotating stage with an extravagant lighting system, all of which could be operated by remote control; a closed circuit television system; and a 5,000-seat gallery with "a set of earphones at every seat which were hooked up to interpreters' booths equipped for simultaneous translation into eight major languages."[12] The theater was surrounded by a 5,000-unit housing complex known as FESTAC Village, built in modernist European-style architecture to accommodate FESTAC's international participants, including eight African heads of state.

FESTAC's facilities were apparently meant to inculcate national pride in Nigerians and to show the rest of the world Nigeria's great wealth and power, as well as its ability to modernize along the lines of Western countries. At the same time, the events that took place in the National Theatre were meant to bring Nigerians together by promoting collective pride in Nigeria's diverse and varied traditions and histories. On stage, "traditional" theatrical and dance performances were presented by troupes from around Nigeria that had won local and state competitions for the honor of performing at FESTAC. The arena also served as the site for conferences of black scholars from around the world, making Nigeria the locus for knowledge production on issues relevant to the black and African world. Two large exhibition halls housed artifacts from Nigeria's past, as well as works of art by contemporary Nigerian artists.

FESTAC '77 achieved some of its goals. It clearly illustrated the wealth of Nigeria and buttressed Nigerian aspirations to be recognized as a leading representative of black and African affairs in the international sphere. Within Nigeria, however, opinions on FESTAC's relevance were mixed. The event had brought together Nigeria's diverse cultures to be represented under one banner and for a united cause, but at what cost? In many ways, FESTAC was as much an illustration of the extravagance and corruption of the "rentier" state as it was a symbol of national pride and unity. In July 1975 Mohammed had instituted a tribunal of inquiry to look into the massive spending on FESTAC undertaken during the Gowon era. The tribunal presented a scathing report in May 1976 that revealed widespread mismanagement of funds. Many contracts for construction and supplies had been grossly inflated, with many companies being paid millions of naira for work that was never done. For example, the Bulgarian firm Technoexportsroy received a large contract for work related to the construction of the National Theatre. The tribunal found that the company had received over N12.6 million in excess profits over and above those stipulated in the contract, including N403,000 for redundant surveying. The figure did not even take into account losses to the federal government due to the shoddy access roads the company had built, roads that sank because the land on which they were built had not been properly drained.[13]

While contracts for FESTAC were grossly inflated and poorly supervised, FESTAC officials themselves were receiving kickbacks from these contracts and living lavishly on federal money. The tribunal accused Alhaji Umaru Dikko, who supervised FESTAC activities in Kaduna, of awarding contracts in cases where the contractors never even visited the sites after collecting their fees. Dikko was also accused of awarding unauthorized consultancy fees and of using FESTAC monies to fund projects on his own private property. FESTAC officials lived in expensive hotels, and traveled first-class to visit FESTAC liaison offices in London, Paris, and Washington, DC. A further illustration of the wasting of resources was the allocation to FESTAC officials of automobiles that were eventually simply given to them as gifts. The revelation that FESTAC funds had been allocated in such a way as to increase the wealth and improve the lifestyle of government officials and their contractor cronies undermined the goals of FESTAC itself. Rather than illustrating the magnanimity of the Nigerian state and the unity of Nigerian peoples, FESTAC became a symbol of the extravagance of the rentier state and the growing socio-economic rift between those with access to state resources and those whom the state ignored.

Although most of the mismanagement of funds associated with FESTAC had taken place under the Gowon regime, the Obasanjo regime also contributed to the alienation of large sections of the Nigerian population. In 1978 oil prices fell significantly for the first time in the decade, precipitating a decline in production from 2.1 million bpd to 1.5 million, with a resultant huge rise in Nigeria's balance of payments deficit. To offset the loss in revenue Obasanjo instituted some small-scale austerity measures, which included import restrictions, new taxes, and cuts to social service expenditure.[14] One such cut resulted in an increase in tuition fees at Nigerian universities. This action brought protests from students and lecturers, who called for the unseating of the education commissioner, Lieutenant Colonel Ambrose Ali.

Other alienated Nigerians included those who had lost their positions in the purge of the civil service and other branches of government. Many of those who had been retrenched moved to the private sector, taking high-paying jobs in the very companies that lobbied for contracts and licenses and paid rents to the federal government. Many of these people, resentful of the government and now benefiting from private enterprise, began to argue for less government control of the economy, although such calls were largely ignored. In 1979, on the eve of transferring power to the new civilian regime, Obasanjo nationalized the operations of British Petroleum (BP) in Nigeria, alleging that BP had been illegally trading Nigerian oil to South Africa in violation of existing embargoes.

Still other people accused the Obasanjo government of covertly pushing a northern agenda through its association with a group of young businessmen and technocrats in the north, known collectively as the "Kaduna mafia." The Kaduna mafia is not a criminal organization in the way that the name implies. It is, rather, a loose term used to describe a group of powerful northerners with a shared agenda, but a group that maintains informal ties and chooses to wield influence behind the scenes rather than as an open political organization. Because of its underground nature, the inner workings of the Kaduna mafia are not well known, but during the Obasanjo administration it was widely believed that Musa Yar'adua, Obasanjo's second in command, was an associate if not a member of the Kaduna mafia and therefore represented a strong voice for northern lobbyists within the military government.

Despite such incidents and suspicions, criticism of the Mohammed/ Obasanjo regime was largely stifled by threats and co-optation. In 1976 Mohammed announced a decree making it illegal for anyone to bring false accusations of corruption or mismanagement against government officials. In 1977 the federal government bought 60 percent of the equity of two of Nigeria's largest newspapers, *The Daily Times* and *The New Nigerian*. Television and radio were already mostly state-owned. Public figures criticized military regimes at their own peril.

One of the most famous critics of the Nigerian government during the 1970s and 1980s was Fela "Anikulapo" Kuti, the son of famed political activist Olufunmilayo Ransome-Kuti. Fela had emerged in the early 1970s as the leading performer of a new style of popular music known as Afrobeat, which was a fusion of Yoruba musical styles with American jazz and funk music. Through his music Fela became an international attraction, and through his opposition to the military government he became a national hero to many Nigerians. Eccentric by nature, Fela practiced polygamy, taking twenty-seven wives, and was politically influenced by the Black Power movement in the United States. In Nigeria he founded the Kalakuta Republic, a commune that he declared independent from the government of Nigeria and from where he composed many songs criticizing the corruption and violence of Nigeria's military regimes. For his actions he earned the ire of the Obasanjo government, which raided the Kalakuta commune with as many as 1,000 soldiers in 1978. During the raid the entire compound was burned to the ground, and Fela's mother was thrown from a window, receiving injuries from which she later died.

Fela later wrote the famous song "Coffin for Head of State" as a eulogy to his mother. Written in pidgin English, the song stands as a profoundly personal indictment of the Obasanjo regime, while at the same time resonating with the experiences of the many Nigerians who felt forgotten and betrayed by their government. The following is just one part of the song:

> I go many places
> I go government places
> I see, see, see
> All the bad, bad, bad things
> Den dey do, do, do
> Dem steal all the money
> Dem kill many students
> Dem burn many houses
> Dem burn my house too
> And killed my mama
> So I carry the coffin
> I Waka waka waka
> Movement of the People
> Dey Waka waka waka
> Young African Pioneers
> Waka waka waka
> We go Obalende,
> We go Dodan barracks
> Reach dem gatee-o
> And put the coffin down
> Obasanjo dey there,
> With him big fat stomach
> Yar'adua dey there,
> With him neck like ostrich
> We put the coffin down.

Fela actually did present his mother's coffin at the military barracks before having her buried. Afterwards, he twice ran for president of Nigeria, in 1979 and 1983, and was prevented from registering and campaigning both times. He died in 1997 of heart failure, which, it was later revealed, had been triggered by AIDS.[15]

Criticisms such as Fela's were well founded. The Mohammed/ Obasanjo regime failed to end the corruption that was becoming

Figure 8.2 The minibus, a common form of public transit (collection of Roy Doron)

increasingly endemic to the Nigerian government, and it used its military might to quell criticism. At the same time, it did accomplish one thing that the Gowon regime had failed to do: it transferred power to a new, democratically elected civilian administration, in 1979. The elections of 1979 were the culmination of a four-year transition process. In 1975 Mohammed initiated a Constitution Drafting Committee (CDC), which produced a draft constitution that was voted on by a Constituent Assembly in 1978, ultimately leading to federal and state elections in 1979.

The new constitution that was approved by the Constituent Assembly in 1978 was designed to prohibit the kind of regional polarization that had characterized the First Republic. Unlike the constitution that had governed the First Republic, which had been based on the Westminster model, the new constitution drew much of its influence from the constitution of the United States, which itself exhibited a three-tiered federal structure like Nigeria's. Under the new constitution, the offices of president and vice-president were created. Unlike the ceremonial presidency of the First Republic, however, the new president and vice-president were to have wide-ranging and well-defined powers. The federal legislature, called the National Assembly, was made up of a House of Representatives and a Senate, and checked the powers of the executive on many issues, such as fiscal appropriations and appointments to high-ranking government positions. The judiciary made up the third branch of government. Power was shared similarly at the state level, with the governor and deputy governor as the executive leaders. The powers of local governments were also enshrined in the constitution, and included, among other things, registration of births and deaths, regulation of markets, motor parks, public conveniences, cemeteries, refuse disposal, and "concurrent" powers with state governments over primary education, agriculture, and natural resources (other than minerals).[16]

New rules for the organization of political parties were also established, in order to prevent the deterioration of campaigns into the activities of regional cabals that had characterized the First Republic. In order to register with the Federal Electoral Commission (FEDECO) to contest the 1979 elections, political parties had to demonstrate their "national" character by opening membership to all Nigerians, locating their headquarters in the federal capital, featuring national symbols – not ethnic or religious ones – in their party emblems and mottoes, and maintaining party branches in at least two-thirds of the states. Students, academics, civil servants, and members of labor unions were prohibited from taking part in the elections and campaigns unless they first resigned their positions. When the official ban on politics was lifted on September 21, 1978, parties rushed to register with FEDECO. Over fifty parties attempted to register, but, in the end, only five were cleared by FEDECO to campaign. These were the Unity Party of Nigeria (UPN), led by Obafemi Awolowo; the Nigerian People's Party (NPP), which later split into two, with the NPP under the leadership of Nnamdi Azikiwe and the newly formed Great Nigeria People's Party (GNPP) under the Bornoan politician Waziri Ibrahim; the National Party of Nigeria, which ultimately won the allegiance of most of the politicians left over from the First Republic and the Gowon years and became the largest party; and, finally, the People's Redemption Party, led by Aminu Kano, previously of NEPU fame.

Despite the regulations that supposedly ensured the "national" character of the parties, only the NPN had any semblance of a "national" following. The leadership of the NPN came from all three of the former regions. Its presidential candidate, Alhaji Shehu Shagari, was a northerner; the vice-presidential candidate, Alex Ekwueme, was an Igbo; while its party secretary was A. M. A. Akinloye, a Yoruba. The NPN also gained members from minorities in the south, who preferred the more "national" party to the other parties, which were coming to resemble the ethnic and regional organizations of the First Republic. The UPN became essentially a rebirth of Awolowo's AG. When the NPP split into two over the issue of its presidential candidate, the GNPP, under northerner Waziri Ibrahim, became a much more northern-dominated party, while the NPP under Azikiwe tried to reconstitute itself as the second coming of the NCNC. The PRP of Aminu Kano gained most of its support in the area around Kano and Kaduna, just as NEPU had done previously.

Because of its ability to garner votes from across the country to a greater extent than the other parties, the NPN fared the best in the state and federal elections, which took place in five separate rounds between July 7 and August 11, 1979. When the votes were tallied, the NPN controlled the governorships and state assemblies in seven states (Sokoto, Bauchi, Benue, Cross River, Kwara, Niger, and Rivers), and controlled 168 out of 449 seats in the federal House of Representatives and thirty-six out of ninety-five Senate seats. While it did not gain an overall majority, the NPN won more seats than any other party. Although the NPN had its highest level of support in states carved out of the former Northern Region, it is important to note that the NPN was more "national" and less "northern" than the NPC of the First Republic had been. First, three of the states won by the NPN – Rivers, Cross River, and Benue – were in the southeast, where the NPN had significant support from non-Igbos. Second, the NPN failed to win several states in the north, including two of the most populous, Kano and Kaduna. The PRP won the governorship and a majority in the legislative assembly in Kano, while, in Kaduna, a PRP governor shared power with an NPN-led legislative assembly. The PRP also took seven Senate seats and forty-nine House seats at the federal level. The GNPP won control in two northern states, Borno and Gongola, and earned eight Senate seats and forty-three House seats.

Although the NPN proved itself to be not strictly a "northern" party, support for all the other parties largely followed regional lines. The PRP and GNPP gained almost all their support in the north, while Awolowo's UPN took control in five states (Lagos, Oyo, Ogun, Ondo, and Bendel) within which was contained the Yoruba heartland of western Nigeria. The NPP won in three states (Anambra, Imo, and Plateau), gaining most of its support in the Igbo heartland of southeastern Nigeria. At the federal level, the UPN won the second highest number of seats, with twenty-eight and 111 seats in the Senate and House respectively, while the NPP took sixteen Senate seats and seventy-eight House seats.

Although the elections to state offices and the National Assembly went relatively smoothly, the first tensions over the new constitution emerged in the controversial results of the presidential election. In keeping with the concept that politics should be "national" in the new civilian government, the 1979 constitution declared that, in order to avoid a run-off election involving the top two candidates, the leading candidate after the first round of voting had to have the most total votes cast as well as 25 percent of all votes cast in at least two-thirds of the states. After the presidential election of August 11, 1979, the NPN candidate, Alhaji Shehu Shagari, had 5,688,857 total votes; his nearest rival, the UPN's Obafemi Awolowo, won 4,916,651 votes. Shagari gained the requisite 25 percent of the vote in only twelve of the federation's nineteen states, however, less than the two-thirds needed to win the presidency outright. In a thirteenth state, Kano, Shagari claimed only 19.4 percent of the total vote. Awolowo declared that the situation required a run-off election between himself and Shagari, but NPN advocates disagreed. They argued that two-thirds of nineteen was not thirteen but twelve and two-thirds. This meant that, in order to win the election, Shagari should have to win only 25 percent of two-thirds of the total vote in Kano state. The issue led to a protracted legal battle, but ultimately the Supreme Court found in favor of Shagari. On October 1, 1979, Obasanjo transferred power to Shagari, marking the end of thirteen years of military rule with the establishment of the Second Republic.

The Second Republic quickly proved itself to be unequal to the challenges of securing the hoped-for truly "national" governance outlined in the constitution. Despite the efforts to prevent regionalism and sectional interests from prevailing at the federal level, the refusal to allow students, academics, civil servants, and members of labor unions to influence the political process meant that leadership in the new parties fell to prominent businessmen and old-guard career politicians from the First Republic such as Awolowo, Azikiwe, and also Shagari, who had held various ministerial positions in the Balewa Cabinet and was federal minister of finance under Gowon. Although the NPN was the largest party in the new civilian administration, its position was initially fragile. Incensed at the outcome of the presidential election, the UPN-controlled state governments did not recognize the results, and even refused to hang pictures of the new president in public buildings in their states. At the federal level, the NPN required a coalition partner in order to form a government. It found a ready partner in the NPP, the Igbo leaders of which saw an opportunity to reintegrate themselves into national politics. Once in office, however, NPN officials quickly went about using federal resources and revenues to establish a patronage system similar to that which had prevailed in the First Republic, drawing allies from elements of other parties that wanted access to federal power and wealth. This situation made the coalition with the NPP irrelevant, and in 1981 it was dissolved.

The patronage network of the NPN government during the Second Republic was every bit as corrupt as that of the First Republic had been. The added element of rent seeking, however, which had developed during the military regimes of the 1970s, made for a volatile mix that resulted in severely irresponsible governance and rapid economic decline between 1979 and 1983. For all the corruption that had characterized the First Republic, it could at least be said that the NPC-led federal government followed an agenda that represented the interests of a segment of the population, insofar as it pushed a "northernization" agenda. In the Second Republic, however, the make-up of the ruling party was far less regional, and supposedly represented the interests of diverse groups throughout the country. This made it difficult for the NPN to establish a clear agenda that would satisfy its broad base of constituents.

Ultimately, the NPN-led administration of the Second Republic became concerned only with representing its own interests as a political class, building up a huge patronage network that distributed resources solely for the enrichment of politicians and their cohorts and seeking to entrench NPN incumbency in the 1983 elections. By distributing federal revenues to political and business allies and by diverting revenues towards projects in their home districts, federal office-holders were able to use money and access to money to build up support from the people and places whose support they most needed. Second Republic politicians embarked on huge federal housing projects, attempted to build federal universities, colleges of education, and polytechnic institutions in every state, and attempted to establish federal radio and television stations in every state. Construction of the new Federal Capital Territory also continued. All these projects required heavy state expenditure and the awarding of contracts for the execution of the projects, which quickly became the means by which politicians enriched themselves and extended their power.

Corruption and rent seeking therefore continued, as politicians scrambled to buy the loyalty of clients and constituents. Millions upon millions of naira disappeared into contracts and kickbacks for work that was not accomplished or was done shoddily, while other officials blatantly raided government coffers. For example, an audit of Nigerian External Telecommunications revealed that N53 million had gone missing, while N43 million disappeared from a federal housing scheme. NYSC officials were discovered to have stolen over N16 million, while contracts for the

Figure 8.3 A view of Aso Rock in Abuja (collection of Dr. Okpeh Okpeh)

construction and development of the FCT and Abuja were grossly inflated and lacked effective oversight. A single manager of the Nigerian National Supply company in London stole £1.9 million between April 1979 and December 1980.[17] These are representative examples of the widespread corruption of the Second Republic, but they are by no means a complete list.

As in previous administrations, the massive corruption of the Second Republic was initially fueled by high oil yields, which rebounded in 1979 after a brief dip in 1978. When the "oil glut" hit in 1981, however, oil prices dropped significantly, throwing Nigeria into a recession that lasted until 1992. Total oil revenues declined from N12.3 billion in 1980 to N7.3 billion in 1983.[18] The response of Second Republic politicians, however, was not to curb their corrupt ways or to embark on a fundamental restructuring of the economy, but to seek outside aid. In 1982 the federal government took N1.5 billion in foreign aid from the International Monetary Fund (IMF), and secured a N400 million loan from Saudi Arabia. Over the course of the Second Republic, Nigeria's foreign reserves declined from N5.462 billion to just N798.5 million, not even enough to cover one month's imports in 1983, while external debt doubled, growing from roughly $9 billion in 1980 to $18 billion by 1983.[19]

The massive borrowing that the Second Republic undertook did little to halt the economic slide. Oil production dropped from over 2 million bpd in 1980 to 1.3 million bpd in 1983, and GDP dropped by 8.5 percent in real terms between 1981 and 1983, while inflation rose between 30 and 50 percent, illustrating the fact that the Nigerian economy had become entirely dependent on oil revenues. The purchasing power of the average Nigerian dropped significantly. Adding to the difficulties of the Nigerian worker, by mid-1981 the federal government and many state governments had failed to pay public servants for several months – a problem that has continued to plague the country since that time. Schools and universities regularly went on strike as teachers and administrators demanded pay for work already done. The poor state of the economy also meant that many unskilled laborers lost their jobs as companies could no longer afford to keep them on.

High inflation and rising joblessness gave rise to growing rates of urban crime, most noticeably in southern cities, and an increasingly lucrative black market in smuggled goods, particularly across the border with Benin. The most prominent smuggled goods were petroleum products, automobiles, and construction materials, but the smuggling of consumer items such as cigarettes, alcoholic beverages, and foodstuffs also took place. Smuggling increased dramatically as people sought to circumvent government import and export controls and increase profit margins by selling directly to foreign markets and domestic consumers. Searching for a scapegoat for the country's economic difficulties, the federal government expelled many alien workers, most of whom came from Ghana, in January and February 1983, suggesting that these workers were responsible for the hardships of the Nigerian working class because they took jobs away from Nigerian nationals and drove down the wages of the rest. As many as 2 million workers may have been affected by this forced removal. The move was popular within Nigeria, but it led to widespread criticism from abroad, most notably from neighboring west African governments, which saw the expulsions as undermining the Economic Community of West African States (ECOWAS) protocol of 1979, which guaranteed the free movement of goods and persons between ECOWAS member states.

The growing resentment of Nigerians at the corruption and mis-management of the Second Republic led to an outpouring of dissent that took various forms. The press, which experienced a resurgence under the civilian regime, as each party developed print media outlets to promote its own agenda and attack its political opponents, regularly pointed out the corrupt dealings of politicians.[20] The labor movement, which had been denied the ability to contest the 1979 elections, made its opinion of the economic policies of the Second Republic known in a number of ways. Smuggling, absenteeism, drunkenness, and poor and inefficient work habits increased during this time, as did petty corruption on the part of employees, who increasingly resorted to taking bribes from customers and clients to offset the loss of wages they were experiencing. Labor unions also organized multiple strikes and demonstrations for workers' rights. In 1980 alone the Nigerian workforce lost over 2.5 million worker days, involving over 220,000 workers, in 416 registered strikes.[21] In May 1981 a general strike shut down nearly all essential services and businesses in Nigeria. Even oil workers took part in the strike, despite the fact that a military decree of 1975 allowed oil workers to be executed or imprisoned for up to twenty-one years for such behavior.[22]

Other disaffected elements turned to religion. Most religious movements that developed in this time were peaceful, self-help organizations that saw community solidarity as a form of social organization providing an alternative to citizenship. Other religious movements, however, organized with the goal of bringing about reforms in what they saw as a decadent secular government. Both Islamic and Christian groups criticized the government for discriminating against them in such areas as job allocations and the takeover of schools, among other things.

By far the biggest religious issue of the times was the debate over the implementation of Islamic *shari'a* law at the federal level. As early as 1978, when Nigeria's new constitution was being drafted, northern Muslim activists lobbied for the inclusion of a *shari'a* court of appeals so that Muslims could be judged by Islamic law at the federal level. Christians and practitioners of indigenous religions opposed this move, however, arguing that it was a violation of the dedication to a secular state and marked the beginning of an "Islamization" of Nigeria. The proposed *shari'a* appellate court provoked a walkout from the Constitutional Assembly on the part of Christian elements from the middle belt states. In the end, a compromise was reached, allowing judges versed in *shari'a* law to sit on cases in the regular appellate court that had originated in local *shari'a* courts. The politicization of religious identity represented in the *shari'a* dispute marked a growing tension between Christian and Muslim world views, however – a tension that has expressed itself ever more violently since the 1970s, with the development of radical religious movements that are more interested in fighting their religious adversaries than in lobbying for government reform.

One such radical sect emerged in Kano in 1980. Led by Mohammed Marwa, an immigrant from northern Cameroon, the Maitatsine movement, as it came to be called, was explicitly opposed to the corrupt and decadent Nigerian government, which Marwa's followers believed consisted of "infidels" who had to be resisted. The Maitatsine were accused of smuggling large numbers of weapons into Kano, and the state government attempted to force them out of the area, prompting large-scale rioting on the part of Marwa's followers, many of whom had joined the movement because of their disaffection with the current state of affairs, although many others had reportedly been forced to join. The riots had to be put down by the military. More than 5,000 people died in the riots, including Marwa himself, and substantial property damage was incurred. The Maitatsine movement was officially banned by the federal government in 1982, but it lived on and was not fully crushed until the mid-1980s. The Maitatsine riots were followed in 1982 by religious riots in Kano, in which Muslims burned churches in the Christian areas of the town. The riots quickly spread to Zaria and Kaduna, illustrating the extent to which religious polarization was beginning to affect Nigeria.[23]

The resentment of Nigerian citizens against the Second Republic government did not concern the NPN, however. As frustrated voters flocked to opposition parties in anticipation of the 1983 elections, the NPN used its patronage system and power of incumbency to secure its position as the predominant political party. At the same time that the government was failing to pay its employees, the NPN was also increasing the size of the police force exponentially, raising the total number of policemen in Nigeria from 10,000 in 1979 to over 100,000 by 1983. The government also increased expenditure on the police force, arming police departments with weapons and equipment previously reserved for the military. This larger and more lethally equipped police force was then let loose on critics of the Second Republic and other malcontents. Police forces violently put down protests, harassed critical press outlets, and disrupted the meetings and campaigns of rival political parties, all for the sake of maintaining the power of the NPN government and keeping criticism of it to a minimum.

By the time of the 1983 elections the NPN had extended its patronage network and grip on power so far and wide that its leaders haughtily declared there were only two parties in Nigeria: the NPN and the military. As the elections grew closer, opposition forces tried to combine against the NPN, but found it impossible to forge a strong, broad-based alliance. The UPN and NPP came together with elements of the PRP and GNPP to form the Progressive Parties Alliance (PPA) to oppose the NPN. The alliance was less than complete, however, as many politicians in the PRP and GNPP in particular chose to maintain their positions as members of the patronage system established by the NPN, and therefore did not join the opposition alliance. The PPA was wracked by internal dissension. The GNPP eventually pulled out of the alliance, fearing that the UPN and NPP were using the alliance as a way to make inroads into GNPP territory for the benefit of their own parties. Tensions between the UPN and NPP emerged when the two parties were unable to decide on a common list of candidates or a common presidential candidate.

The fragmentation of the opposition gave the NPN the advantage in the upcoming elections, but the NPN did not take victory for granted. Throughout the campaign, opposition candidates accused the NPN of using its control of the police and the election commissions to prevent opposition parties from meeting and campaigning. The NPN also recorded astronomical increases in the voter registries of territories they controlled, an early indication that vote rigging lay ahead. The elections were spread out between August 6 and September 3, 1983. The results indicated a big win for the NPN, far greater than could have been expected in a free and fair election. Shagari won re-election as president, defeating Awolowo, while the NPN expanded its control in the National Assembly, winning two-thirds of all the seats and taking the governorship in thirteen of the nineteen states. The numbers were astounding and indicated widespread fraud, especially since many of the gains made by the NPN came in UPN and NPP strongholds, making their validity highly suspect. In fact, the election of the NPN gubernatorial candidate, Akin Omobiriowo, in Ondo State, the heart of UPN territory, provoked riots that took the lives of hundreds and resulted in the destruction of federal property. The electoral fraud in this case was undeniable, and an electoral tribunal eventually overturned the result.

Despite the obvious rigging of the elections in favor of the NPN, opposition forces were unable to prevent the inauguration of the new government on October 1, 1983. Public opinion was so strongly against the NPN regime, however, that calls for military intervention were already on people's lips. It was widely believed that Shagari's second term was starting out on "borrowed time." In just four years the Second

Republic had descended into the same kind of chaos that had characterized the First Republic. Corruption, mismanagement, and blatant disregard for the democratic process, fueled by the rent-seeking opportunities of the oil economy, led members of the military to believe that their services were once again needed to right the sinking ship of state. On December 31, 1983, the military struck again, removing Shagari in yet another coup, and installing Major General Muhammadu Buhari as head of state. The military would rule Nigeria for the next fifteen years, presiding over the further decline of the country's economy and civil society.

CHAPTER 9

Civil society and democratic transition, 1984 – 2007

INTRODUCTION

The military coup that ended the Second Republic and brought General Muhammadu Buhari to power on December 31, 1983, ushered in a new period of military rule in Nigeria that lasted fifteen years. Three military regimes ruled during this period – those of Buhari, General Ibrahim Badamasi Babangida (IBB for short), and General Sani Abacha – before power was finally transferred back, in 1999, to a civilian administration under the leadership of President Olusegun Obasanjo, the former military ruler now turned politician. The three military regimes oversaw the further decline of the Nigerian economy, particularly after the imposition of the Structural Adjustment Program in 1985.

Far from revitalizing the shattered government apparatus left behind by the Second Republic, these regimes presided over the further entrenchment of official and everyday corruption in Nigeria, and sought to maintain power through oppression, coercion, and the manipulation of the democratic transition process. Government officials and their patrons continued to plunder government coffers at the expense of the population, causing many Nigerians to turn to corrupt and illegal activities such as bribe taking, smuggling, armed robbery, and fraudulent schemes in order to make enough money simply to survive. While a few Nigerians became exceedingly wealthy through their corrupt practices, most remained mired in extreme poverty. Since the transfer to democratic rule in 1999, a few of the ills of the Nigerian political, economic, and social situation have seen minimal amelioration, while others continue to plague the country, with no resolution in sight.

The policies and actions of the military regimes did not go unchallenged, however. The period since 1984 in Nigeria can be characterized as one in which civil society organizations have increasingly become galvanized around a variety of issues and institutions, in an effort to have their needs addressed and their voices heard.

CIVIL SOCIETY AND DEMOCRACY

"Civil society" is a term that has been defined in many different ways. For the purposes of this chapter, we use Michael Bratton's definition of civil society as "an arena where manifold social movement organizations from all classes attempt to constitute themselves in an ensemble of arrangements, so that they can express themselves and advance their interests."[1] This definition implies that civil society can exist in direct opposition to the state, which is often the main target at which civil society organizations aim in order to try to advance their interests. This definition does not imply that civil society exists *only* in opposition to the state, however. In fact, in Nigeria, it will be seen that civil society organizations have often been constituted to meet the needs of their members in a way that is completely separate from the state. Sometimes civil society organizations serve both functions: making their needs known to the state while simultaneously meeting the needs of their constituencies in ways that are completely separate from state involvement. The fundamentalist Christian charismatic movement, for example, serves both these purposes for its congregations.

This definition of civil society is very broad, and it clearly indicates that civil society existed in Nigeria well before the 1980s. Secret societies, progress unions, labor movements, student protests, press activities, and religious organizations have all made up strong elements in Nigerian civil society for as long as the country has existed, and even longer in many cases, and have frequently engaged the state in debates about citizens' rights and privileges. The stirring of civil society organizations was not a new phenomenon in the 1980s, but what this chapter focuses on is the groundswell of civil society organizations that have developed since the 1980s and the ever-increasing role that these organizations have played in the lives of everyday Nigerians, both in terms of their mobilization of forces to confront what they saw as a decrepit, authoritarian military government and in terms of their ability to provide for Nigerians goods, services, and peace of mind that the state could not or would not provide.

The military regimes of Buhari, Babangida, and Abacha were often characterized by their high levels of oppression and coercion, because of their willingness to suppress criticism in the name of promoting stability. It must be recognized, however, that the heavy-handedness of these regimes was a response to the growth of grassroots political activism among Nigerians who were not willing to let the misrule of the governing class go uncontested. Civil society organizations during this period took a number of forms and pushed many different agendas. Labor unions continued to oppose the economic model that has relied exclusively on oil revenues at the expense of diversified, sustainable development planning and has led to high unemployment rates and low wages for Nigerian workers. Religious organizations, both Muslim and Christian, have grown rapidly as Nigerians turned towards God for salvation from a decrepit state. Pro-democracy organizations have also developed, to pressure the government into greater transparency and to push for the solidification of stable, free and fair democratic processes in the country. In the Niger delta, groups have organized both politically and militantly to demand greater control over oil revenues and the environment, which has become seriously polluted as a result of poor regulation of the oil companies.

The growth of active civil society organizations and institutions has had a two-pronged effect. On the one hand, the willingness to oppose the military regimes resulted in unprecedented levels of oppression and coercion, but at the same time it forced the military regimes to address some of the needs of Nigerian citizens. In order to maintain power and stability in the face of opposition groups that were more than willing to foment instability when displeased, the military regimes were more or less forced to consult public opinion on some key policies, most notably structural adjustment of the economy and the transition to democratic rule. Although the military regimes attempted to manipulate these policies, ultimately they were unable to escape the ire of the Nigerian people, who were increasingly organized to oppose unpopular government positions. The ability of pro-democracy civil society organizations to thrive despite the coercive and oppressive tactics of the military regimes led first to an abortive attempt to transfer power to a Third Republic in 1993, and finally to a successful transfer of power to a Fourth Republic under Olusegun Obasanjo in 1999.

On the other hand, the growth of civil society organizations with differing agendas has exacerbated social tensions, which have frequently erupted into violence. Christian and Muslim populations have clashed regularly since the 1980s, particularly in northern Nigeria, while armed rebels in the Niger delta have taken their battle for the control of territory and oil revenues directly to the oil companies, destroying property and kidnapping expatriate employees. Since the return to democratic rule in 1999 there has been a more open dialogue between government and civil society, as politicians have to acknowledge the power of civil society organizations to maintain legitimacy and secure re-election, and as leaders of civil society organizations have been co-opted into government in many cases.[2]

This convergence of state and civil society can have both good effects and bad effects. On the one hand, greater communication and coopera-tion between state and civil society can lead to the objectives of civil society organizations being addressed and sometimes achieved. On the other hand, the fraternization of state and civil society organizations could lead to complacence on the part of one or both, and the ultimate corruption of civil society organizations, which might over time come to identify more with their partners in government than with their con-stituent members. The outcome of this dynamic is yet to be analyzed in Nigeria's Fourth Republic; nevertheless, civil society organizations find themselves in a more auspicious position than in the 1980s and 1990s.

THE BUHARI REGIME (1984–5)

The rousing of civil society organizations to protest government policies has occurred frequently in Nigeria since colonial times. Since the Buhari years, however, such organizations have become impossible to ignore. Buhari came to power after the overthrow of the NPN-dominated Sec-ond Republic, citing the corruption of the Shagari administration and its failure to monitor the country's economy as justification for the coup. Therefore, it is no surprise that the main preoccupation of the Buhari administration was to clean up government and institute reforms to get the Nigerian economy back on track. Buhari and his supporters believed that the most expedient way to tackle both of these issues was by pro-moting an ideology of "discipline" within Nigeria. Buhari believed that the problems that had plagued Nigeria in recent years did not originate with bad policies but, rather, with poor implementation and a lack of will on the part of Nigeria's ruling elite to govern ethically.

Buhari's main goal as head of state was, therefore, to instill in Nigerians the importance of following the law and of behaving in a manner that benefited society as a whole. As a result, Buhari did little to change the economic system that had governed the Second Republic. In fact, he followed very closely the short- and medium-term austerity measures imposed by the Shagari administration in 1982. Buhari's main emphasis was to root out corrupt persons and practices so as to ensure that austerity measures were followed appropriately. The idea was that, if Nigerian government and businesses made a concerted and conspicuous effort to live by ethical and legitimate business practices and to pay off loans in a timely manner, foreign investors would be more willing to see Nigeria as a safe and potentially lucrative place to do business. Once the credibility of the Nigerian government and economy had been restored, foreign investment, foreign exchange levels, and foreign trade would all increase, leading to an economic turnaround.

As part of his austerity measures, Buhari curbed government spending, reducing public expenditure by 50 percent in his first year. To do this, his administration shrank the size of the government by making 53,000 public sector employees redundant between January and September 1984 and reducing capital expenditures and educational subsidies. He also reduced the number of local government areas from over 1,000 to 301. To control inflation, particularly of food prices, Buhari set up a system of government rations of "essential commodities" such as rice, sugar, salt, and toiletries, which were sold directly to the public at controlled prices. Buhari also expelled over 700,000 illegal immigrants, claiming that they were a burden on the Nigerian economy. At the same time that Buhari was reducing government expenditure and attempting to control aspects of the economy, he also forced state governments to pay arrears of wages and salaries to government employees who had not been paid for the last several months of Second Republic rule.

In order to realize his goal of manufacturing a corruption-free, "disciplined" Nigerian society, Buhari introduced a broad collection of authoritarian measures. He aggressively prosecuted corrupt Second Republic politicians. Most Second Republic governors and many National Assembly politicians were tried, convicted, and sentenced to long terms of imprisonment, most commonly on charges of corrupt dealings. President Shagari and Vice-president Alex Ekwueme were notable exceptions. In a particularly notorious affair, Buhari operatives attempted to kidnap the former minister of transport and Shagari loyalist Umaru Dikko, who had fled to London during the coup that brought down the Second Republic. Dikko was widely known to have used his political positions to enrich himself, and, after his flight, he became among the most wanted fugitives sought by the Buhari administration. When Buhari operatives found him in London, they drugged him, stuffed him in a crate labeled "Property of Nigeria," and attempted to have the crate flown from London to Nigeria. British authorities uncovered the plot and refused to extradite Dikko. The affair put a severe strain on relations between the United Kingdom and Nigeria, but it illustrated the extremes to which Buhari would go to bring corrupt officials to justice.

Beyond prosecuting former politicians, Buhari also went to great lengths to root out corruption and criminality in Nigerian society at large. In so doing, he set up what has often been called a "police state," taking public surveillance to levels never before seen in Nigeria and imposing harsh penalties on corruption and criminal activities. Buhari used the National Security Organization (NSO) to spy on military officers within the administration. He instituted the death penalty for drug smuggling, tampering with electric cables or oil pipelines, and counterfeiting currency, while long prison terms were provided for such offenses as postal tampering, cheating on examinations, and illegally exporting produce. Cases were tried in military tribunals, not by a jury of one's peers.

Buhari also used his authoritarian powers to silence criticism of his regime. He instituted a decree that allowed persons considered to be a national security risk or to have contributed to the country's economic troubles to be detained by police for up to three months, renewable without trial. Another decree allowed for the detention of journalists and the closing of any media outlet that disseminated false statements, false information, or rumors likely to bring embarrassment or ridicule on public officials. Buhari also outlawed strikes and lockouts, in an attempt to cripple the ability of unions to express their grievances. He used these measures to remove his critics and opponents from the public space, thereby promoting to the outside world the image of Nigeria as a stable and happy place under his leadership.

Buhari is perhaps most remembered for his broad-based social reform program known as the War Against Indiscipline. The WAI consisted of five phases, each of which sought to instill a desired character trait in Nigerian citizens. In the end, Nigerians were supposed to have developed a sense of work ethics, patriotism, nationalism, anti-corruption, patience (waiting in lines for goods and services was a major component of one phase of the WAI), timeliness, and the importance of urban and environmental sanitation. The WAI was greeted with considerable enthusiasm, as many people believed that Nigeria's problems stemmed precisely from a lack of discipline and the preponderance of unethical and unpatriotic behavior by citizens that had developed in the 1960s and 1970s as a result of the political instability and corruption of the ruling class during those decades.

The many facets of the WAI proved practicable only under the watchful eye of the police state, however, which promised heavy penalties for failure to comply. Many of the changes to Nigerian society under the WAI were little more than cosmetic, and they tended to conceal the deeper social ills of the country, such as widespread poverty and a lack of basic services, beneath a veneer of orderliness. For example, cities were charged to undertake a weekly exercise of environmental sanitation to remove garbage and other unsightly evidence of the urban decay that had occurred since the late 1960s. In doing so, however, many state governments used the opportunity to tear down "illegal" structures – shacks and lean-tos built by petty traders and market people – and forced the poor and homeless out of city centers. Of course, such actions did nothing to alleviate poverty and deprivation; they simply made these problems less visible to the naked eye. The WAI, while initially popular and well intentioned, ultimately failed to address any of the root causes of Nigeria's social malaise.

The motives for Buhari's authoritarian response to Nigeria's political, economic, and social crises are largely considered to have been pure. Unfortunately, Buhari's actions, however well meant, gave little short-term help to the majority of Nigerians, who were already suffering greatly from the mismanagement of previous administrations. The police state surveillance and erosion of civil liberties that characterized Buhari's regime also stimulated ill will towards the regime on the part of many Nigerians. Although hampered by Buhari's repressive measures against free speech, many civil society organizations openly challenged his policies. The Nigerian Bar Association (NBA) unsuccessfully attempted to boycott participation in the military tribunal system of law enforcement. The National Association of Nigerian Students (NANS) protested consistently over Buhari's decision to reduce student subsidies. Eventually, Buhari proscribed the NANS altogether. The Nigerian Labour Congress (NLC), Nigeria's largest umbrella group of labor unions, staged many strikes over the massive retrenchment of public servants and the high unemployment and low wages that resulted from Buhari's austerity measures, despite the fact that the regime had made strikes illegal. Buhari's response to such opposition was violent and oppressive. Many critics and leaders of civil society organizations were detained, while student protests were greeted with violence. Dozens of students were killed in clashes with armed military and police personnel during Buhari's tenure of power.

Buhari's measures were therefore unsuccessful in arresting Nigeria's economic decline or alleviating the social malaise of the country in the short term. Further complicating Buhari's management of the sinking economy was his inability to strike a deal with the IMF to secure a rescheduling of Nigeria's external debt. By 1985 the federal government was spending 38.7 percent of its total revenue just to service its debts.[3]

Debt rescheduling would have lengthened the repayment period and reduced the annual amount that Nigeria would have had to pay to avoid defaulting on its loans. The idea was that lower repayments would allow Nigeria to invest more of its revenue in development projects, which would improve the domestic economy and eventually allow Nigeria to make larger repayments. In order to secure such a rescheduling of the external debt, however, the IMF demanded that Nigeria undertake a series of economic reforms. Known as the Structural Adjustment Program, these reforms, which most debtor African nations instituted in the 1980s, were designed to stabilize ailing economies by rationalizing tariffs, reducing government expenditure, privatizing government-owned or government-operated businesses, particularly public utilities, deregulating the economy by ending government subsidies and price controls, and devaluing currencies. Believing his own austerity measures were enough to set the Nigerian economy back on track, and not wishing to sacrifice Nigerian national pride by turning over its economic policy-making to Western creditors, Buhari refused to institute a Structural Adjustment Program, and was therefore unable to conclude a deal to reschedule Nigeria's debt.

THE BABANGIDA REGIME (1985–93)

On August 27, 1985, Buhari was overthrown in a palace coup staged by Major General Ibrahim Badamasi Babangida. The new military regime cited several factors as justification for the coup, including Buhari's inability to bring the economy under control or to secure a rescheduling of the debt; his authoritarian tendencies, which had resulted in a poor human rights record; his self-righteous refusal to consult with or seek advice from other military officers; and his failure to set forth a clear plan to transfer power back to a civilian administration. Babangida had served in the Supreme Military Council under the Mohammed/Obasanjo and Buhari regimes, and during the Second Republic he had been the head of Operations and Military Planning. He had also been personally involved in both the 1975 and 1983 coups. As head of state, he proved himself to be politically adept, mixing authoritarian repression with a feigned interest in public opinion. He also embarked on a complicated and malleable democratic transition process that always appeared to be moving forward yet at the same time seemed infinitely far from completion.

In order to generate credibility for the new regime, Babangida initially took a more conciliatory approach to governance than had Buhari.

Babangida brought some of Buhari's harshest critics into his government, including Olikoye Ransome-Kuti (brother of Fela Kuti), a medical doctor who had led a strike by public health employees protesting the decline of public health services under Buhari. Babangida also opened an investigation into human rights abuses perpetrated by the Buhari regime, and reduced or overturned the jail sentences of many of those prosecuted for corruption and other offenses under Buhari. He repealed the decree that had strangled the press during Buhari's administration, and released several journalists from detention. To address the image perpetrated by Buhari that the military did not care about the opinions of the general public, Babangida encouraged public debate on issues pertaining to the governance of Nigeria. The press was encouraged to report on all sides of these issues and to print public responses and opinions. Such actions painted a picture of a government that no longer wished to suppress contrasting opinions but, instead, sought to learn from them. Babangida also took the title "president" rather than "head of state," as an indication that he served as chief executive in the new regime, not just as a military overlord, and also to imbue his tenure with legitimacy by using more democratic rhetoric.

The most important issue over which Babangida encouraged such public debate was that of the SAP. Babangida was intent on securing an agreement to reschedule Nigeria's debts, but realized that allowing the IMF to dictate the terms and control the process by which SAP measures would be enforced was unpopular in Nigeria. Babangida threw the issue open to the public, asking for an open debate over whether Nigeria should accept the IMF package outright, instituting a full-scale SAP and taking the IMF loan that came with it, or whether Nigeria should decline the loan and institute SAP reforms on its own. Public opinion overwhelmingly supported the latter option, as it allowed Nigeria to avoid the image of a beggar nation willing to compromise its sovereignty for Western aid. The public debate legitimized Babangida's desire to institute SAP measures, therefore making possible a debt rescheduling, although it took the strange form of declining an IMF loan to help with the transition process. Since there was no IMF involvement, most of the monitoring of the SAP occurred through the World Bank. In June 1986 Nigeria officially instituted a Structural Adjustment Program, opening the doors to debt rescheduling and new lines of credit. The debt rescheduling allowed the bulk of the repayment of existing loans to be pushed back to 1991 and later.

There is evidence that the SAP had some positive impact on the country, but, by and large, its tangible effects were devastating to the

Figure 9.1 A landscape of underdevelopment (collection of Roy Doron)

average Nigerian.[4] On the positive side, the annual debt service declined from 38.7 percent of federal revenues in 1985 to around 30 percent in 1988. Tariff rationalization and devaluation of the naira led to a decrease in imports, which had slightly positive effects on the production of agricultural and other raw materials. Agricultural output, which grew at an annual average rate of 1.0 percent from 1980 to 1985, increased at an average of 5.3 percent per year in the period from 1986 to 1991.[5] The increased cost of imports meant that Nigerian industry had to boost its consumption of locally produced raw materials. Local sourcing of raw materials for industry grew from 38.5 percent of the total in 1985 to 50 percent by 1988.[6] The growth in the agricultural market also brought about a shift in wealth from the cities to rural areas, bringing a greater, although far from perfect, balance to wealth accumulation, which had heavily favored urban areas in recent decades.

Despite such positive steps in restructuring the economy, the SAP also caused serious hardships for Nigerian citizens and failed to achieve many of its anticipated results. Unemployment levels increased markedly under the SAP, for a variety of reasons. While the rising cost of imports encouraged local sourcing by industry, it also caused much Nigerian industry to operate at below-capacity production levels. External sources of raw materials became more expensive, which meant that companies purchased less and, consequently, produced fewer finished goods. As a result, profits often decreased, leading to a reduction in wages and/or staff. Government and public service departments cut staff and reduced salaries as part of the austerity measures designed to reduce government expenditure. Devaluation of the currency brought with it rapid inflation and a decrease in the purchasing power of the average Nigerian. The naira, which had stood at N1 = $1 in 1985, fell to N4.21 to the dollar in 1988, N7.48 in 1989, and N22 by 1994.[7] The inflation rate stood at between 40 and 70 percent from about 1988 to 1995, and per capita income declined from an estimated $778 in 1985 to just $105 in 1989,[8] making it difficult for people to afford basic necessities such as food, clothing, electricity, health care, education, and anything else that cost money.

The harsh economic climate was exacerbated by SAP demands for a deregulation of the economy and, in particular, the removal of government subsidies for basic necessities, particularly fuel. Subsidies from the federal government had for a long time meant that fuel prices within Nigeria were artificially low. In 1988 the government raised the price of a liter of gasoline from 39.5 kobo (k) to 42k (100 kobo = 1 naira), then to 60k in 1989 and 70k in 1990. By 1993 the price of a liter of gasoline had risen to N3.25, and it has continued to rise steadily.[9] The increase in fuel prices put a heavy burden on Nigerians, whose budgets for cooking, transportation, and electricity (for those fortunate enough to own generators) were strained even further.

The reduction in government expenditure required by the SAP meant that social services and utilities in Nigeria continued their downward trend. Electricity provision became incredibly erratic, with frequent and sustained blackouts becoming increasingly common. The acronym NEPA, standing for the Nigerian Electric Power Authority, took on a new meaning, as people frustrated by the poor quality of service farcically renamed the public utility "Never Expect Power Always." The state of Nigerian health services and education facilities declined, as these institutions were unable to afford regular maintenance or basic supplies. More and more people, unimpressed by the quality of these social services and unable to afford them in any case, increasingly took their children out of government schools and stopped attending government clinics, preferring instead to have traditional medical practitioners treat their physical and spiritual ailments. At the same time that the quality of social services deteriorated, the prices for them rose, making people even less likely to seek these services.

The SAP also required the Nigerian government to divest itself of its ownership in many companies, including many of those that offered public services, in favor of a privatization of business and industry. Privatization also required the relaxation of the indigenization regulations, which had limited the shares that foreign interests could hold in certain kinds of companies and industries. Babangida moved slowly on this provision of the SAP, because allowing more foreign ownership of Nigerian businesses carried the political liability of enhancing the appearance of selling out Nigeria's economic independence to the highest bidder, increasing the perception of dependence on Western creditors and financiers. Eventually, however, Babangida announced a widespread privatization plan in 1988, in which the Nigerian government attempted to privatize completely or partially 135 enterprises. These included government holdings in such wide-ranging ventures as hotels, textile producers, breweries, banks, dairies, insurance companies, Nigeria Airways, and the national shipping line. Many companies were also to be partially or completely commercialized. These included, among others, the Nigerian National Petroleum Corporation, Nigerian Telecommunications (NITEL), and NEPA. As of 1990, however, only fifty of these 135 companies had been sold, indicating the main problem with the SAP: it failed to attract the foreign investment that was supposed to boost the Nigerian economy and encourage the creation of sustainable development programs. Foreign direct investment (FDI) remained low; in fact, many foreign firms divested themselves of their Nigerian holdings during the late 1980s and early 1990s.[10] Despite the modest growth in the agricultural sector, petroleum has continued to account for the vast majority of all Nigeria's export earnings since the introduction of the adjustment program.

The Babangida administration created many organizations to help the country ease into the SAP and to give the austerity measures something of a human face. For example, the Directorate of Food, Roads, and Rural Infrastructure (DFRRI) was created to coordinate rural development plans, while the Better Life Programme was designed to help improve living conditions for rural women. The National Directorate of Employment (NDE) was created to help place people in non-public-sector jobs, and "people's banks" were created to help poor Nigerians gain access to credit and loans. These organizations were well intentioned and helped many people early on, but over time they became avenues for corruption and patronage building through which the regime could buy support.

Nigerians reacted to the economic turmoil of structural adjustment in a number of ways. Many turned to religion as the answer to the problems of their society. The redemptive power of fundamental Islam and charismatic and evangelical Christianity, notably the Pentecostal sects, had been increasingly attractive to many Nigerians since the 1970s. This attraction carried on growing through the 1980s and 1990s, and has continued up to the present day, as religious organizations have offered a message of individual salvation through prayer and faith in God. Churches of the charismatic movement have grown exponentially, particularly in southern Nigeria. By 1991 there were an estimated 6 million evangelical Christians in Nigeria, with the largest single charismatic organization, called Deeper Life, claiming between 330,000 and 400,000 members by 1994. Charismatic churches tend to be based in urban areas, which give them the greatest access to resources and infrastructure, while also making their congregations very multi-ethnic. Their members are also known as "born-again" Christians, and charismatic churches tend to be evangelical in nature, seeing the active spread of Christianity through Bible-based preaching as the supreme duty of Christians.

The charismatic movement offers an alternative path to social and spiritual well-being, and attracts members by addressing people's needs for community development, physical, mental, and spiritual healing, and the hope of prosperity in this life and the next, all of which the Nigerian state has been unable to provide. Charismatic churches preach that only God can provide the answers to Nigerians' many problems, through the power of prayer. Charismatic church communities pool their resources to provide their congregants with social services that the state has not been able to provide, developing church-based schools and health dispensaries, while also arguing that God will provide for the prosperity of the devoted through miraculous transformations in this life and eternal salvation in the hereafter. Charismatic churches argue that not only can individual Nigerians be healed by the power of prayer, but so too could the Nigerian state. Charismatic church congregants are urged to pray for the salvation of Nigeria as well as themselves, and they believe that, by bringing about the effective "rebirth" of the Nigerian state as a compassionate, Christian state, they might save Nigeria itself from suffering and deprivation.[11]

While the charismatic movement remained largely apolitical throughout the 1970s, by the 1980s charismatic churches were beginning to take an active part in Nigerian civil society, lobbying the Nigerian government to be more responsive to the needs of the Christian community. In entering the political arena, Christian organizations came into direct conflict with Islamic organizations that had been engaged in politics since the 1970s. Islamic organizations such as the Supreme Council for Islamic Affairs (SCIA) and the Jama'atu Nasril Islam (JNI) had long been pushing for the Nigerian government to adhere more to Islamic norms of governance. These included, among other things, changing the weekly day of rest from Sunday to Friday, removing symbols of Judeo-Christian traditions from public space, and, above all, allowing the spread of *shari'a* law and courts. Islamic organizations were opposed at the political level from the late 1970s by Christian organizations, most notably the Christian Association of Nigeria (CAN), which pushed to prevent the "Islamization" of Nigeria while also lobbying the government for greater employment opportunities for Christians and a state-sponsored pilgrimage for Christians to complement the state sponsorship of the Islamic *hajj*, which had benefited many Muslims since 1975.

The politicization of religion that occurred as Muslim and Christian civil society organizations clashed over government policies intensified tensions between the religions. These tensions were further heightened in 1986, when Babangida announced that he had made Nigeria an official member of the Organization of the Islamic Conference (OIC). The OIC is an international body with the stated goal of promoting Islamic issues and the spread of Islamic norms of governance and social organization. The announcement that Babangida had made Nigeria a member of the OIC without consulting the population, or even Christian members of his own administration, provoked widespread outrage on the part of Nigeria's Christian community. Ultimately, Babangida was forced to announce that the issue of Nigeria's membership in the OIC had been shelved, thereby putting the crisis to rest for the time being. But the damage had been done. To many Christians it now appeared that Babangida intended slowly and secretly to "Islamize" Nigeria, and their opposition to his regime mounted.

This politicization of Christian and Muslim identity over such issues resulted in increased violence between Christians and Muslims, particularly in northern Nigeria, where riots involving clashes between Muslims and Christian minorities have become very common since the 1980s. During the Babangida years, riots occurred in Ilorin in 1986; Kafanchan, Kaduna, Katsina, Funtua, Kano, and Zaria in 1987; Bauchi in 1991; and Zaria in 1992. Most of these riots were characterized by the burning of churches and violent clashes between Christians and Muslims, in which many adherents to both faiths were killed or injured. In the Bauchi riots alone at least 1,000 were killed, with many more wounded, although the official numbers were much smaller. A similar number of deaths resulted from the 1992 Zaria riots.[12] It is important to note, however, that tensions between Muslims and Christians in Nigeria do not always degenerate into riots and widespread violence. In the southwestern part of the country, where the majority Yoruba population is more or less evenly split between Muslims and Christians, competition between Muslims and Christians has rarely escalated to violent levels.

Religious activism was not the only response to the rapidly deteriorating economy. Those with means or marketable skills began to leave Nigeria in increasing numbers. Professionals such as doctors, lawyers, engineers, and businessmen found that they could find more stable employment and higher salaries working as expatriates in the United States and Europe. Likewise, their children could receive a better education outside Nigeria. This outflow of skilled professionals from the country, dubbed the "brain drain," has in itself contributed to the decline of the Nigerian economy, as the lack of highly trained doctors has negatively affected health service provision throughout Nigeria, while the lack of engineers, scientists, architects, and the like has made it difficult for Nigeria to improve its infrastructure and technology sectors. By 1993 there were an estimated 21,000 Nigerian doctors practicing in the United States alone. It has been estimated that, by 2000, between 25 and 50 percent of all Nigerians with university educations lived outside the country.[13]

Those who lacked the ability to leave the country made their displeasure with the economic consequences of the SAP known through protest. In December 1986 students at Ahmadu Bello University staged protests in remembrance of the students killed during the 1978 riots over student subsidy reductions. Labor unions and university and polytechnic students joined together to stage anti-SAP riots in 1988, protesting the increase in petroleum costs that resulted from the reduction of government subsidies. Strikes were commonplace, and the press used its relative freedom to criticize government policies. As public discontent with Babangida grew, so too did Babangida's willingness to use repression and violence to suppress his critics. All protest activities were met with violence, with demonstrators killed and injured as troops sought to restore order. Unions were dissolved again, the NANS in 1986 and the NLC in 1988. The press came under government scrutiny again as well. By the end of 1987 several of Nigeria's largest newspapers, including *Newswatch, The*

Guardian, *Punch*, and *Lagos News*, had experienced periods of closure and/or had had journalists detained for leaks or "libelous" comments. The editor of *Newswatch*, Dele Giwa, was killed by a letter bomb in 1987. The timing of his death, just days after an interrogation by government operatives, led many to believe the Babangida regime may have been responsible.

DEMOCRATIC TRANSITION AND THE 1993 ELECTIONS

Babangida's program for the transition to civilian rule also provoked widespread frustration and, ultimately, a civil society response the like of which had not been seen since the days of the civil war. Although Babangida declared the transition to democratic rule to be one of his main goals, the transition process proved long and at times baffling. Babangida consistently manipulated the transition process by moving timelines, amending procedures, and frequently banning and unbanning politicians and government officials from taking part in the political process. Babangida justified his interference in his own transition process in the name of preventing corruption and building a more stable democratic system than had previously existed in Nigeria, but, over time, it became clear to many that Babangida was willing to use any pretext to derail the transition process and maintain his own position at the top of the political ladder. Although the transition process was begun in January 1986, presidential elections to determine Babangida's replacement did not take place until June 12, 1993, and ultimately did not result in a transfer of power, although they did mark the beginning of the end of Babangida's rule.

Babangida began the transition process within months of taking power. In January 1986 he set up a political bureau charged with developing an acceptable procedure for transferring power back to a civilian administration. The report of the political bureau, released the next year, led to the Transition to Civilian Rule Decree no. 19 of 1987, which laid out the procedure for the formation of political parties and the holding of elections. In practical terms, Babangida's transition program resembled very closely the transition program of the Second Republic. In fact, very few changes were made to the 1979 constitution of the Second Republic in the drafting of the new constitution for the Third Republic, which was released in 1989.

The fact that procedures for transition were set in place as early as 1987 did not make the transition process transparent or smooth. The

Transition to Civilian Rule Decree was amended many times at Babangida's whim. Babangida postponed elections on several occasions. The original transfer date had been set for October 1, 1990, but it was later pushed back to October 1, 1992, then to January 2, 1993, and, finally, to August 27, 1993. The date changes were always accompanied by some crisis that resulted in a change in the transition procedure, often involving the banning of politicians or political parties. In June 1986 Babangida declared that all past politicians were banned from taking part in transition politics and from holding office for ten years after the ban on politics was lifted. In 1987 he announced a lifetime ban on all former office-holders who had ever been convicted of corruption, and claimed the right to ban from engaging in transition politics anyone who might pose a threat to the stability or integrity of the process, regardless of whether they had ever been convicted of a crime. In 1989 the political ban was extended to chairmen and members of governmental institutions engaged in effecting the transition process, institutions such as the newly formed National Electoral Commission (NEC) or the Directorate for Social Mobilization. Those banned from running for political office were also banned from forming, joining, or funding any political party or organization. Interestingly, however, some of these bans were later lifted. In 1991 the ban on former politicians was lifted (as long as they had not been convicted of corruption), and in 1992 former chairmen and members of transition institutions were also unbanned.

In May 1989 Babangida lifted the ban on forming political organizations, allowing groups to apply to the NEC for recognition as full-fledged and legal political parties. Thirteen organizations applied. The NEC later shortlisted six organizations, but submitted a report to the Armed Forces Ruling Council (AFRC) in which it raised concerns about the "national" character of many of these organizations, as well as their links to banned politicians, and did not recommend any of them for formal recognition. The government subsequently proscribed all thirteen associations and replaced them with two artificially created parties: the Social Democratic Party, which the government described as a right-leaning party, and the National Republican Convention (NRC), a left-of-center party. The fabrication of two parties with strong links to the federal government ensured on the one hand that "corrupt" – or, at the very least, banned – politicians could not manipulate the parties, but on the other hand it meant that the military regime could exert a strong influence on the actions of the parties. As a result, the tenor of political campaigns was muted, as neither of the government-created parties could dare to distance itself from government policies or to criticize the existing regime, for fear of proscription or expulsion. The creation of the SDP and the NRC, accompanied by the prohibition of all other political parties, made for a very undemocratic transition from this point onwards and ensured that political debate would not revolve around any of the major political, economic, or social ills affecting Nigerians.

Nevertheless, the desire for elections was strong among Nigerians, and political consciousness was fostered by the government. The Babangida administration created the Mass Mobilization for Economic Recovery, Self-reliance, and Social Justice (MAMSER). MAMSER was designed to build support for the transition program, educate citizens about the political process, and encourage them to vote in the upcoming elections, among other things. In 1991 Babangida submitted to popular demands for the creation of more states, creating nine new states and bringing the total number of states to thirty. These new states participated in the elections to state assemblies, governorships, and the National Assembly that took place in 1992. In these elections, the SDP won control of sixteen state assemblies and won fourteen governorships at the state level, compared to the NRC's twelve state assemblies (the parties took an equal number of seats in Enugu and Taraba States) and sixteen governorships. At the federal level, the SDP took control of the National Assembly, winning 312 House of Representative seats and fifty-two Senate seats to the NRC's 275 and thirty-eight.

All that remained to complete the transition to democratic rule was a presidential election. Cracks in the democratic process appeared, however, when the two parties held conventions to nominate presidential candidates. Twenty-three candidates competed for the two nominations, with former deputy head of state Shehu Yar'Adua emerging as the victor for the SDP and Adamu Ciroma, the former general secretary of the NPN during the Second Republic, taking the NRC nomination. The losing candidates from both parties disputed the results, arguing that the nomination process had been rigged. In October 1992 the government chose to cancel the primaries and disqualified all twenty-three candidates from seeking their party's nomination in the future. The failure to certify presidential nominees meant that the date for the presidential election had to be postponed from December 5, 1992, to June 12, 1993, while presidential candidates were vetted to determine their acceptability.

In the end, the government cleared only two candidates to run for the presidency. Chief M. K. O. Abiola, an extraordinarily wealthy Yoruba businessman who rose to political significance as owner of the Concord group of newspapers and as an official in the Second Republic's ruling NPN, became the nominee of the SDP.[14] The NRC nominated Bashir Tofa, a Kanuri businessman from Kano State. Both candidates were Muslim; Abiola was a Yoruba from the southwest, however, while Tofa was a northerner. The presidential election in which these two candidates took part, on June 12, 1993, is widely considered to have been the freest, fairest, and most peaceful election in Nigerian history to date. Some analysts believe that Babangida cleared two Muslims to run in the hope that they would split the vote across the country and this would result in an election with no clear winner. Had this happened, Babangida could have used the ensuing chaos to maintain his own power. This did not occur, however. In the end, Abiola and the SDP mounted the more effective campaign. Abiola won 58 percent of the vote, even taking a majority of the vote in his opponent's home base of Kano.

Faced with the prospect of finally having to relinquish power, Babangida annulled the election result on June 23, citing several preposterous justifications. He declared that Abiola had won on a platform that sowed ethnic discord, that both parties had illegally used funds to buy votes, and that the national election machinery had not been secure enough to prevent electoral malpractices. All these reasons provided an ample pretext for invalidating the election in Babangida's eyes. Unfortunately for Babangida, most politicians and a formidable proportion of the Nigerian populace disagreed. The explosion of protests, riots, and demonstrations that followed the annulment of the presidential election was so widespread and passionate that it could not be contained by military suppression alone.

Indeed, Nigeria teetered on the brink of anarchy throughout the summer of 1993. Civil society groups tried to organize demonstrations, but these were only partially successful and often degenerated into chaos and rioting. In many ways, the atmosphere of protest reflected regional alliances, as southern protestors pushed for a restoration of the June 12 decision, while the north became the breeding ground for government-organized pro-Babangida rallies. In the south, the Campaign for Democracy (CD), which was a coalition of many pre-existing civil society organizations including the NLC and the NANS, was formed to push for the restoration of the election results. The NLC itself tried to institute a general strike, but this was only partially successful, as many northern members refused to comply. On the government side, the Association for a Better Nigeria (ABN), a pro-Babangida group funded by the government, which had taken many steps even before the elections to obstruct the process and keep Babangida in power, continued to rouse support for the annulment. Fringe groups, such as the Movement for the Advancement of Democracy (MAD), organized terrorist activities against the state. MAD hijacked a Nigerian Airways plane in Niger in protest against the annulment, while several bombings directed at military installations also occurred.

The unrest brought about by the annulment caused Babangida to declare a state of emergency in many places. Even his machinery of state suppression was insufficient to curtail the violence and disturbances caused by the activities of pro-democracy groups, however. Some Yoruba activists began to talk openly about the possibility of the southwest seceding from the federation if the election results were not restored. Rumblings of the possible resurgence of Biafra in the east could be heard, as Nigerians again contemplated the possibility that the federal system was simply unworkable. Fears of an impending civil war provoked large-scale migrations, as people uprooted their families from the places where they had lived and worked in order to return to their places of origin.

Under such widespread conditions of crisis, Babangida could no longer retain legitimacy, and a compromise was reached with the civilian politicians. The issue of the June 12 election remained on hold, but to quell the violence and unrest for the time being Babangida agreed to hand over power to an Interim Governing Council, led by his friend and ally Ernest Shonekan, on August 27, 1993 – the day that Abiola would have been inaugurated. The ousting of Babangida allayed fears that he intended to remain in power at any cost, but the IGC still faced questions of credibility and legitimacy. Pro-democracy factions believed that the purpose of the IGC should have been to hand over power to Abiola as quickly as possible, thus affirming the democratic process and ushering in the long-awaited Third Republic. The IGC did not do this, however. Further undermining the credibility of the IGC was its decision to raise gasoline prices exponentially, from 70k to N5 per liter. The response to this policy was so negative that eventually the price was lowered to N3.25, although this still placed a significant economic burden on most Nigerians.

The final nail in the IGC's coffin, however, came on November 10, 1993, when the Lagos High Court declared the IGC itself illegal and unconstitutional, since, at the time that the decree bringing it into existence was promulgated, Babangida no longer technically held legislative authority. According to the court, only the winner of the presidential election, M. K. O. Abiola, had the legal authority under the 1989 constitution to govern Nigeria after August 27. The IGC, of course,

Figure 9.2 The okada, another form of public transport (collection of Roy Doron)

disputed these claims and filed an appeal. The weakness of the IGC, coupled with the questions about its legitimacy, made it easy prey for another military coup, however.

THE ABACHA REGIME (1993–8)

On November 17, 1993, General Sani Abacha, a very ambitious senior military officer in the IGC and long considered a "president in waiting," pushed Shonekan aside, dissolved the IGC, and declared himself head of state and commander-in-chief of the armed forces. Abacha has been the most vilified of all Nigeria's post-independence rulers for his severe oppression in the name of personal power, the further decline of the Nigerian economy, and the relegation of Nigeria to the status of a pariah state in international affairs. Abacha's initial coup resulted in mixed feelings among Nigerians, however. Many saw the coup as a step backwards, a move away from democracy, and a threat to the democratically elected state and national assemblies. Those who feared the implications of the Abacha coup included sixty-seven federal senators, who wrote a letter urging Nigerians to resist the retrogression into autocratic rule.

Others, however, were willing to give Abacha the benefit of the doubt, in the hope that he could exert enough strength and discipline to bring the political situation under control. Many supporters of Abiola and members of the pro-democracy groups hoped that Abacha would accept the June 12 election result, something that the IGC, with all its links to Babangida, was unlikely to do. Even Abiola himself praised Abacha as a man of reason and offered the services of several of his closest allies and advisers, including his vice-president elect, Babagan Kinigbe, to the new government. Abacha initially took a couple of steps that encouraged feelings that he might be a real reformer intent on righting the wrongs of the Babangida regime. He immediately sent into forcible retirement many of Babangida's closest military advisers and announced a suspension of the SAP measures that had been so devastating to so many average Nigerians.

Those who expected Abacha to hand power over to Abiola were to be severely disappointed, however, as Abacha quickly showed that he had no intention of ceding power any time soon. Shortly after taking over Abacha abolished all the existing political institutions of the Third Republic, including the state and national assemblies, the governorships, and the electoral bodies. He banned all political parties and embarked on a campaign to eliminate all opposition to his rule. He incarcerated and detained any military officer or civilian he considered a threat, sometimes going so far as to invent coups against himself in order to accuse opponents of orchestrating them. Many political activists, journalists, and former high-ranking military officers found themselves behind bars as perceived national security threats. Abacha claimed that there were no "sacred cows" in his regime. No one was too powerful or influential to face his wrath. For example, former head of state Olusegun Obasanjo and his deputy, Shehu Yar'Adua, were both imprisoned by Abacha in 1995 for alleged involvement in a coup intended to unseat him.

Civil society organizations were not willing to accept his termination of democratic institutions, however, and mounted vigorous opposition to the regime throughout Abacha's tenure. As the first anniversary of the June 12 election approached in 1994, pro-democracy organizations once again rallied support, taking to the streets in a reinvigorated series of protests and riots. The CD joined with a newly formed organization called the National Democratic Coalition (NADECO), led by many well-established politicians, to support the acceptance of the election result. Chief Abiola declared himself president of Nigeria and held a public inauguration in Lagos, while many labor unions staged strikes, which brought much of southern Nigeria, including parts of the petroleum sector, to a standstill in June and July.

Abacha's response was swift and brutal. He ordered the executive committees of Nigeria's labor unions dissolved, and he appointed sole administrators for them. NADECO was outlawed, and the leaders of the pro-democracy organizations were arrested. Abiola was arrested and held without bail pending trial. The trial became a long-drawn-out legal process, and Abiola remained in indefinite detention until his untimely death in prison in 1998, which brought to an ignominious end the prospects for the realization of the Third Republic. Protesters were dispersed by violence, with the military and the police killing many people in the effort to restore order. By the end of August the pro-democracy movement had effectively been removed from the public space in Nigeria. Many pro-democracy activists fled Nigeria, however, and carried on their campaign against the Abacha regime from new bases in the United States, the United Kingdom, Europe, and other African countries.

The event that solidified Abacha's reputation as a tyrant for Nigerians and the international community was the execution of Ken Saro-Wiwa and the rest of the Ogoni Nine on November 10, 1995. For many years ethnic groups in the oil-rich Niger delta had argued that, while the wealth extracted from their lands was being used to fund the state and federal governments, the peoples of the delta saw very little of this wealth and continued to live in poverty. At the same time, the oil companies that operated in the delta showed little concern for the environmental degradation that accompanied their drilling. Oil spills threatened the land and waterways, while the flaring of natural gas polluted the air to dangerous levels. The facilities and infrastructure themselves posed serious dangers to the communities that surrounded oil installations. Pipeline explosions were common, and often killed many innocent bystanders (and sometimes not so innocent parties who were attempting to tap pipelines to siphon off some of the precious oil).

The Ogoni, a group of about 500,000 people resident mostly in Rivers State, were one such ethnic community negatively affected by oil production. Their livelihood revolved around fishing, making it extremely important that their environment remain unpolluted. Despite their small population, the territory on which the Ogoni lived yielded roughly a half of all the oil extracted annually in Nigeria. The position of the Ogoni as a small minority in a larger state meant that no federal revenue and very little state revenue from oil production went to improving their living conditions. The Ogoni were, therefore, intent on gaining greater control over their environment and greater access to the revenues that originated in their territory.

In 1990 a well-known Ogoni author and political activist named Ken Saro-Wiwa founded the Movement for the Survival of the Ogoni People to push for greater autonomy for the Ogoni people. Although this was never specified, autonomy most probably would have meant the creation of a separate Ogoni state, which would then have had a right to an equitable share of oil revenues. In 1993 MOSOP presented an "Ogoni Bill of Rights" to Babangida and to the governor of Rivers State, demanding, among other things, the right of the Ogoni to adequate representation in all Nigerian political institutions, a larger share of oil revenues, and the right to protect their environment from degradation at the hands of oil producers. Saro-Wiwa and other Ogoni activists equated the existing government policies with regard to the oil companies as tantamount to the "genocide" of the Ogoni people.

The Ogoni demands fell on deaf ears within the government. Among the Ogoni themselves, however, MOSOP became a powerful voice, able to mobilize protests in January 1993 that turned into riots. Unrest grew in Ogoniland, as young activists in particular began to promote the use of tactical violence against oil company personnel and facilities. The Ogoni uprising soon affected stability in the oil-producing areas, jeopardizing federal revenues and, by extension, rent-seeking opportunities for Abacha and his associates. The government used the killing of four conservative local chiefs in May 1994 as the pretext to arrest Saro-Wiwa and eight other leaders of MOSOP, who were then charged with the murders. The resulting trial was a farce, roundly condemned by international human rights groups. The tribunal in which the defendants were tried went ahead with the trial despite the fact that a case regarding the impartiality of the judges was pending in a higher court. The tribunal also suppressed important evidence that pointed to the innocence of the defendants. Despite these complaints, eight of the nine defendants were found guilty and sentenced to death by hanging. Saro-Wiwa's final words, "Lord take my soul, but the struggle continues," became a rallying cry for civil society organizations inside and outside Nigeria in their fight to end the tyranny of the Abacha regime.[15]

The hanging of Ken Saro-Wiwa and the other seven Ogoni activists cemented Nigeria's position as a pariah state in the international community. Pro-democracy elements that had fled Nigeria successfully raised international awareness of the case, which illustrated Abacha's blatant disregard for justice and human rights. After the hanging of Saro-Wiwa, the Commonwealth of Nations, consisting of the United Kingdom and its former colonies, went so far as to suspend Nigeria's membership in the organization. Other factors also negatively affected Nigeria's foreign relations under Abacha. Abacha's refusal to accept the June 12 election result annoyed democratic countries, particularly the United Kingdom and the United States. The abrogation of the SAP in 1994 indicated to Western creditors that Abacha was not a trustworthy leader (although he did reintroduce the program a year later, albeit under duress).

Unsurprisingly, the poor standing of Nigeria in the international community had negative consequences for the Nigerian economy. Rather than encouraging investment, Abacha oversaw the further divestment of foreign holdings in Nigeria. Even the oil sector declined under Abacha. By 1994 only fourteen drilling rigs were active in Nigeria, compared to thirty-six in 1991.[16] This divestment was offset somewhat by rising oil prices, which increased total federal export revenues from oil from $7,898 million in 1995 to $11,994 million in 1997.[17] Massive corruption and rent-seeking activities on the part of government officials, however, meant that this increased revenue had little effect on living conditions for most Nigerians. The value of the naira spiraled downwards to over N90 to the dollar by 1998. Abacha also took to the disastrous policy of printing excessive amounts of money. The total amount of money in circulation rose from just over N4 billion in 1985 to N144 billion in 1997, leading to inflation rates of over 150 percent per annum. Petroleum shortages within Nigeria became common and, coupled with the reduction of state subsidies on petroleum products, forced prices for gasoline and kerosene still higher. The price of gasoline rose from N3.25 to N11 per liter under Abacha.

The weak economy and the poor record on human rights and social justice made Abacha a very unpopular leader both at home and abroad. Politically, Abacha wanted to cement his legitimacy as ruler and consolidate his power, but without resorting to a fair, competitive election process. He therefore moved forward with a transition to civilian rule, but in a way that ensured he would transfer power to himself. In 1996, in an effort to build some support for his regime, he announced the creation of six new states, bringing the total to thirty-six. He also created 138 new local government areas and allowed the registration of five new political parties. These parties, however, were not able to develop into true representations of the public will. Through patronage and intimidation, Abacha managed to get all five parties to nominate him as their presidential candidate, thereby eliminating the possibility of a democratic election process while at the same time legitimizing himself as the next "civilian" leader of Nigeria.

Before this sham of a transition could be completed, Abacha was found dead from an apparent heart attack on the morning of June 8, 1998. Top military officials handed power over to General Abdulsalami Abubakar, who quickly dissolved the five existing political parties, released many of those detained and imprisoned by Abacha, and set the country on a hasty course to a democratic transition. Investigations into the financial dealings of Abacha and his cohort revealed an astonishing level of corruption, even by Nigerian standards. Abacha and his family had embezzled an estimated $3 billion, which was traced to bank accounts around the world. Abacha's governors were equally corrupt. The governor of the central bank, for example, was found to have owned thirty-seven homes, which, when searched, turned up millions of dollars in various foreign currencies. Since 1999 the Nigerian government has negotiated with many European banks for the return of funds stolen by Abacha, and has used much of the returned money to pay off its staggering foreign debt.

TRANSITION TO THE FOURTH REPUBLIC

The transitional government of Abubakar opened the doors to the registration of political parties shortly after it took power. Twenty-six organizations applied for recognition, but, after many of them had combined with each other, three major parties emerged. The Alliance for Democracy (AD) became the dominant party in southwestern Nigeria, while the All People's Party (APP) contained many of the supporters and allies of the Abacha regime. The People's Democratic Party became the most "national" of the parties, containing powerful eastern politicians such as Alex Ekwueme and links to northern interests through Shehu Yar'Adua and his protégé Atiku Abubakar. Olusegun Obasanjo, recently released from prison, was nominated as the presidential candidate of the PDP. Despite the fact that he is himself Yoruba, Obasanjo was unpopular among Yorubas, who saw him as indebted to northern interests. As a result, the AD and APP agreed to field a common presidential candidate in the hope of preventing Obasanjo from attaining the presidency. Olu Falae, who had been minister of finance under Babangida and one of the architects of the SAP in Nigeria, became the AD/APP candidate.

Elections for state assemblies, governorships, the National Assembly, and the presidency were staggered. In the elections for state assemblies and governorships, held on January 9, 1999, the PDP emerged as the dominant party, taking control of twenty-one of the thirty-six states compared to the APP's nine states and the AD's six, all of which were in the southwest. Across Nigeria, PDP candidates won 528 state assembly seats compared to the APP's 251 and the AD's 166. In the National Assembly elections, held on February 20, the PDP won an outright majority, taking fifty-nine of the 109 Senate seats and 206 of the 360 House of Representatives seats, compared to the APP's twenty-four and seventy-four and the AD's twenty and sixty-eight respectively. In the presidential election, which followed on February 27, Obasanjo took over 62 percent of the vote, easily defeating Falae. All the elections were relatively peaceful, but all were marred by accusations of electoral mal-practices, by all parties. Since all parties were involved in the vote rigging that took place, it is difficult to say what the actual will of the Nigerian people might have been in this election, but the desire to put an end to the long period of abusive military rule far outweighed concerns over the legitimacy of the elections, and Obasanjo was sworn in as the first civilian president of the Fourth Republic on May 29, 1999, with Atiku Abubakar as his vice president.[18] Obasanjo won re-election in 2003 under equally controversial circumstances, this time defeating former military dictator Muhammadu Buhari, who stood as the main opposition candidate under the banner of the All Nigerian Peoples Party.[19]

THE OBASANJO ADMINISTRATION (1999–2007)

Obasanjo's eight-year term as president has yielded mixed opinions. While, on the one hand, it has been the longest period of civilian rule in the country's history, on the other hand many believe that Obasanjo achieved this milestone through manipulation of the political system, and, as a result, that he has not helped to create a stable or sustainable democratic system. While he had some success in at least slowing the economic decline of the country, he did not do so in a way that has improved standards of living for the majority of Nigerians. Little effort was made under Obasanjo to address the many social ills that continue to plague Nigeria, including ethnic and regional tensions, and the political situation in the Niger delta has degenerated into chaos as people continue to fight against the degradation of their lands and for greater access to oil revenues, in ways that have become destructive and violent.[20]

Obasanjo's economic policies in many ways served as a continuation of the SAP measures. His priorities were courting foreign investment, reducing Nigeria's external debt, and continuing the privatization of Nigerian business and industry. In these efforts, he was at least partially successful. Under Obasanjo, the annual amount of FDI grew from

$1.1 billion in 2000 to $1.9 billion in 2004.[21] Real GDP growth, which stood at 2.9 percent in 2000, rose to 4.9 percent in 2004 and remained over 5 percent between 2004 and 2006.[22] The naira continued to decline in value, but at a slower rate than in the 1980s and 1990s, and in recent years it has stabilized at about N140 to the dollar. Inflation rates have also improved, dropping from official rates of 40 to 50 percent under Abacha to 8.9 percent in 2006.[23] Although oil continues to account for the vast bulk of Nigerian revenue, the non-oil sector has grown substantially since 2004. In 2006 the non-oil sector grew at a rate of 8.9 percent, while the oil sector shrank by 4.7 percent, largely due to violence and unrest in the Niger delta region.[24]

The rapid expansion of the telecommunications industry since 2001 has proven the viability of Nigerian markets and has provided much-needed infrastructure. In the 1990s NITEL, the state-owned telecommunications company, supplied roughly 450,000 telephone lines for the whole country. With the coming of mobile phone companies such as MTN and Econet, Nigerians have had access to reliable telephone services at a reasonable rate for the first time in decades. In 2002 there were an estimated 350,000 mobile phone users in Nigeria; by 2006 this number had risen to over 28 million, and the industry continues to grow at an annual rate of over 30 percent.[25] Those who do not personally own a mobile phone line can access mobile phones at small booths that have been set up in most neighborhoods in urban areas, and make phone calls for rates of N15 or N20 a minute. The growth of internet cafés in urban areas of Nigeria has also been remarkable. For about N100, anyone can purchase an hour of internet access, while "night browsing" options allow people to pay a slightly higher price to use internet facilities for as long as they want during off-peak hours. Phone booths and internet cafés have provided entrepreneurial opportunities for young Nigerians that did not exist even five years earlier.

The growth of the Nigerian economy has allowed the government to pay off a substantial portion of its foreign debt. In 2006 Obasanjo struck a deal with the Paris Club, a group of nineteen countries that, combined, accounted for over $30 billion of Nigeria's foreign debt, by agreeing to pay off $12.4 billion of its loans in exchange for the cancellation of its remaining debts. After this payment, Nigeria had reduced its total foreign debt from $35 billion to $5 billion, which it still owed to the World Bank and private sector creditors.[26]

Although Obasanjo's economic policies improved Nigeria's reputation with international investors and donors, domestically Nigeria remains a

Figure 9.3 Girl at a mobile phone booth (collection of Roy Doron)

poverty-stricken country. The development of new industries and the rise in GDP have benefited only a small number of Nigerians living in urban areas. Although the annual per capita income in Nigeria rose from $280 in 2000 to $560 in 2005,[27] most of this increase has padded the pockets of those who were already financially secure. The poor and rural communities saw little improvement in their everyday lives while Obasanjo was in power. In fact, the development of a few wealthy districts in Nigeria's urban areas has become a symbol of the corruption of the elite class of comprador businessmen and government officials, who continue to enrich and empower themselves at the expense of Nigeria's poor majority. For example, Abuja, which became the seat of the federal government in 1991, is not accessible to the average Nigerian. Government policies have made housing prohibitively expensive in the city and have made it illegal for people to build their own homes or to hawk wares on the street, all in an effort to keep the city pristine in the eyes of Nigerian bigwigs and foreign dignitaries. Civil servants, who work in modern, electrified, air-conditioned offices in the city, are forced to commute from their homes in the shanty villages that have grown up on the outskirts of the city.[28]

Despite the growth in GDP and government revenues, civil servants, teachers, and university employees continue to go for months on end without pay, which prompted many strikes and school closures during

Obasanjo's term in office. Public services remain in poor shape. Electricity supply is erratic, pipe-borne water is nearly non-existent unless privately supplied, and roads remain poorly maintained. Health services have not recovered from the cuts the sector took in the 1980s and 1990s. The "brain drain" continues to attract Nigerian health personnel to better-paying jobs in Europe or the United States. Conditions have become so poor in Nigerian hospitals that those with resources, including the politicians responsible for improving these services, often travel out of Nigeria to meet their own health needs. Two of the main front-runners in Nigeria's presidential election in 2007, Umaru Yar'Adua and Vice-president Atiku Abubakar, flew out of Nigeria to attend hospitals in Germany and the United Kingdom respectively in March 2007, less than a month before the scheduled presidential election was to take place![29] The poor state of health services in Nigeria has contributed to Nigeria's low life expectancy of forty-five to forty-six years and high child mortality rates of nearly 200 per 1,000 live births.[30] Malaria remains prevalent, and outbreaks of cholera, meningococcal meningitis, and yellow fever are not uncommon. Although Nigeria is not as heavily affected as other sub-Saharan African countries, the HIV prevalence rate is on the rise, and, as of 2003, was estimated at somewhere between 3.6 and 8.0 percent of the population.[31]

Religious tensions remained high throughout Obasanjo's term. When the country returned to democratic rule in 1999 most of the northern states instituted new, stricter forms of *shari'a* law, which have resulted in both national and international controversy. For example, in many states thieves can now be punished with the amputation of a hand, and those convicted of adultery can be put to death by stoning. In 2002 a woman named Safiyatu Husaini of Sotoko State was sentenced to death by stoning for the crime of adultery. Although she claimed to have been raped, the sentence was upheld, because rape convictions under the new *shari'a* laws require four male witnesses. The judgment brought outrage from human rights groups inside and outside Nigeria. Although Safiyatu Husaini's sentence and others like it were later commuted, such cases have led to increased tensions in northern Nigeria, as Christians have criticized the harshness of *shari'a* law while Muslims argue that the new legal codes have brought significant reductions in crime rates.[32]

Violent conflicts between Christians and Muslims have remained common, and have increasingly been linked to international events. In 2002 the Miss World beauty pageant was relocated from Abuja to London after violent protests in Kaduna in which over 200 people were killed. Sparked by a newspaper article in Nigeria suggesting that the Prophet Mohammed would probably have approved of the protests, the riots illustrated the frustrations that Nigerian Muslims have felt over the perceived alliance between their government and Western, secular powers.[33] In 2006 demonstrations were held throughout the Islamic world in response to cartoons printed in a Danish newspaper lampooning the Prophet Mohammed. In Nigeria these demonstrations turned violent, with dozens killed in riots in Maiduguri, Katsina, Bauchi, and Onitsha, illustrating the extent to which religious tensions in Nigeria are now directly linked to events elsewhere in the world.[34] The stakes remain high, as Muslims and Christians both want greater control and representation for themselves in the state and federal governments. Obasanjo was unable to defuse these tensions in his eight years as president.[35]

Ethnic tensions also run high throughout the country. The wounds of 1993 have not yet healed, particularly between Yoruba and Hausa. In the southeast, the Movement for the Actualization of the Sovereign State of Biafra (MASSOB) was founded in 1999 by Ralph Uwazuruike. The movement calls for the reassertion of the failed Biafran state of the 1960s. MASSOB has made little headway, as federal forces have cracked down on the group decisively, arresting many of its leaders, including Uwazuruike, who was charged with treason in 2001. In the Niger delta, the fight of the Ogonis and other ethnic minorities for control over oil resources and an end to the pollution of their territories has continued and has taken a violent and destructive turn. Since the late 1990s armed bands of anti-government and anti-oil-company activists have been attacking oil installations and kidnapping expatriates in the delta region, particularly in and around the oil-rich city of Port Harcourt. The most publicized of these groups is the Movement for the Emancipation of the Niger Delta (MEND). While little is known about the actual dealings and negotiations of these armed groups, it is widely speculated that they collect ransom payments for their hostages from the oil companies and use the funds from these transactions to secure more weapons, which they then use to mount more and bigger attacks against oil infrastructure and personnel.[36] The Obasanjo administration was unable to curb the activities of these groups. The result has been a decline in the oil sector in recent years. It has been estimated that total oil exports declined as much as 20 percent in 2006 as a result of the violence and instability fomented by such groups in the delta region.[37]

Corruption also continued to run rampant in Nigeria under Obasanjo. Many state governors and other high-ranking politicians have been accused of graft since 1999; under the 1989 constitution, however, sitting governors and federal executives are immune from prosecution during their terms of office. This has resulted in the impeachment of three state governors in Nigeria, as opposition political parties have sought to remove from office governors accused of corruption in order to prosecute them and gain political control of the state for themselves. The most famous case to occur during Obasanjo's term was that of Bayelsa State Governor Diepreye Alamieyeseigha, who was arrested in London in 2005 after being caught with £1.8 million in stolen funds. He later fled the United Kingdom in disguise, returning to Nigeria, where he was promptly removed from office by the Bayelsa State legislature and put under arrest.

At the level of everyday society, corruption has become a normal aspect of life. From paying policemen at highway checkpoints to bribing public officials for legitimate or falsified documents, Nigerians deal with corruption on a daily basis. Elaborate fraud schemes, known colloquially as "419" after the legal code number under which they are prosecuted, have cheated Nigerians, and foreigners as well, out of millions of dollars. Some fraudsters attempt to sell homes that they do not own to unsuspecting buyers; others impersonate doctors, selling fictitious remedies for common or invented ailments.

The most famous form of 419 that has emerged since 1999, however, is the use of the internet to perpetrate advance fee scams on greedy foreigners. For a few naira, enterprising fraudsters can get a list of foreign e-mail addresses. They then craft fictitious messages promising foreigners a large return for a minimal initial investment. Sometimes these messages claim that the author is the son, daughter, or widow of a famous African leader such as Abacha, Charles Taylor of Liberia, or Mobutu Sese Seko of Zaire (now the Democratic Republic of Congo). Sometimes the author claims to be an employee of the NNPC or of a multinational oil company. In all cases, however, the scam is the same. The author claims to know how to get his or her hands on a large sum of money – tens of millions of dollars – but also claims that he or she needs the recipient's help to access this money. If the recipient is willing to pay thousands of dollars in fees and bribes, or to provide a bank account into which the money can be deposited, the author promises to repay this investment by handing over a large percentage of the take after it is released. Of course, those foolish enough to fall for these scams soon realize the folly of their trust. They never receive their millions, and the fraudsters laugh all the way to the bank.[38] Through such high-profile cases of official and unofficial corruption, Nigeria has consistently earned a ranking as one of the most corrupt countries in the world from the international watchdog group Transparency International.[39]

Obasanjo himself declared the ending of corruption to be one of the main goals of his administration. On taking office in 1999 he immediately had the Corrupt Practices and Other Related Offences Act passed, and set up the Economic and Financial Crimes Commission (EFCC) to investigate alleged instances of corruption among public officials. As of 2006 the EFCC had recovered more than $5 billion in stolen funds and had successfully prosecuted over eighty people. To some this indicated Obasanjo's dedication to an anti-corruption agenda. To others, however, Obasanjo's use of the EFCC was itself an example of official corruption run amok. Critics of Obasanjo argued that he used the EFCC to investigate and prosecute his political opponents to weaken them in election years and to cripple opposition parties. In the most notable instance, the EFCC charged Vice-president Abubakar with graft after he and Obasanjo came into conflict over the issue of whether or not Obasanjo should be allowed to stand for a third term in 2007. Abubakar opposed the measure, as did the Nigerian Senate, paving the way for a "competitive" presidential election in 2007. Shortly thereafter, Abubakar was charged with the misappropriation of $125 million in government funds and suspended from the PDP. Abubakar then defected from the PDP and began a campaign for president on an opposition ticket, the Action Congress (AC). Many believe the graft indictment was politically motivated, timed as it was to prevent Abubakar from running for president on the PDP ticket. The subsequent fallout and the conduct of the 2007 elections is discussed in the concluding chapter of this volume.

CONCLUSION

Over the course of the 1980s and 1990s civil society organizations in Nigeria grew expansively, both to demand changes from a non-democratic, authoritarian military regime and to provide goods, services, and peace of mind to average Nigerians who had been ignored by their government. Over this period the Nigerian economy continued to suffer, as SAP measures brought massive inflation, substantial devaluation of the naira, and a scarcity of basic goods and public services. The economic situation continued its decline in the 1990s, particularly as the annulment of the 1993 presidential election and the human rights abuses of the Abacha regime turned Nigeria into a pariah state that overseas governments and corporations sought to divest from rather than invest in. Official corruption continued to plague the country as well, resulting in the loss of billions of naira that could have been spent to improve living conditions for Nigerian citizens. Under such conditions, the Nigerian people increasingly fought to have their voices heard during the long period of military rule under Buhari, Babangida, and Abacha, which lasted from 1984 to 1998. The actions of pro-democracy groups helped to bring about an attempted transition to democracy in 1993, which ultimately failed, and a successful transition in 1999.

From 1999 to 2007 President Olusegun Obasanjo went about restoring the image of Nigeria in international circles, pushing a pro-democracy agenda and courting increased foreign investment. In some ways these efforts have been successful; in others they have not. Despite Obasanjo's stated aims of bringing democracy and development to Africa, Nigerians continued to suffer. Obasanjo's administration oversaw the longest period of civilian rule in the country's history, but it was accused by local and international observers of achieving this through undemocratic practices in Nigerian elections. Although Obasanjo's plans for economic development resulted in some improvements in small pockets of the country and for a small class of elites, in most of the country Nigerians remained poor, lacking basic necessities and social services such as health care, public transportation, and adequate educational facilities. Obasanjo's two terms as president have therefore led to very mixed reviews, and his final legacy is yet to be determined.

CHAPTER 10

Nigeria and Nigerians in world history

INTRODUCTION

The previous chapters have focused on historical processes within the geographic region of Nigeria and the ways in which internal and external factors have helped to shape that history. This chapter diverges from the pattern to discuss the ways in which Nigeria and Nigerians have influenced and affected historical processes in the rest of the world. For many centuries people from social groupings within modern-day Nigeria have traveled beyond their homelands, spreading throughout the African continent and beyond, to the Middle East, south and east Asia, Europe, and the Americas. In so doing, many migrants have established permanent homes in new lands, representing an important sector of the African diaspora that has so impacted world history. Others, particularly in the twentieth century, have established semi-permanent, transnational communities throughout the world.

Both the diasporic and transnational types of migrants have maintained social and cultural connections to their homelands in Nigeria, while simultaneously influencing social and cultural patterns in the lands through which they have traveled and in which they have settled. These diasporic and transnational communities of Nigerians abroad have served as important connections between Nigeria and the rest of the world, while also illustrating Nigeria's impact on human development across the globe. The first half of this chapter discusses the spread of people from the Nigerian geographical zone through time and space and the circumstances that influence their movement, with a focus on how these migrants have had an impact on the places to which they have traveled and in which they have settled.

Just as Nigerian people have influenced world history, so too has the country of Nigeria itself. The second half of this chapter focuses on the ways in which Nigeria has influenced foreign affairs since its independence from British colonial rule in 1960. Nigeria's position as the most populous country in Africa and its massive oil wealth have made it a strategically important country in world affairs in general and in African affairs in particular. Although in the 1960s Nigerian governments found it difficult to assert a strong, independent foreign policy because of political instability and civil war in Nigeria itself, during the oil boom years of the 1970s Nigeria inserted itself distinctively into international relations. Taking the stance of non-alignment in the Cold War, Nigeria promoted an Africa-centered foreign policy in which Nigeria sought to become the leading spokescountry on African issues in international affairs.

Backing its policy rhetoric with its huge oil revenues, Nigeria pushed heavily for decolonization and African majority rule throughout the continent. Nigeria strongly supported liberation movements in Angola, Rhodesia, and South Africa, among others, and took an anti-Israeli position in the Middle East conflict. Nigeria also argued for greater continental unity in Africa and greater regional integration in west Africa, becoming a leading force in international organizations such as the Organization of African Unity and the Economic Community of West African States. As Nigeria's economy faltered from the 1980s onwards, however, the country's influence in international affairs began to wane. Nigeria's decline in foreign policy effectiveness continued during the 1990s, reflecting its poor records on democracy, human rights, and internal stability, but since the return to democratic rule in 1999 Nigeria has become poised to take on a leadership position in African and world affairs in the twenty-first century.

DIASPORIC AND TRANSNATIONAL COMMUNITIES

The Hausa diaspora

The borders of modern-day Nigeria were drawn arbitrarily in the late nineteenth century by Europeans, during the Berlin Conference of 1884–5 and in line with other mutual agreements between the United Kingdom, France, and Germany, as part of the colonization of west Africa. They do not correspond to any pre-existing social, geographical, or ecological boundaries. It is therefore not surprising that, until recent times, people and goods moved freely across these borders, establishing commercial connections and historical linkages with other societies across Africa. In the pre-colonial period, in what is now northern Nigeria, the Hausa established social and commercial connections as far west as the Senegal valley and as far east as the Arabian Peninsula. The kingdoms of Kanem-Borno and Borno established relationships with the Hausa states to the west and with their neighbors to the east. Both the Hausa states and Borno had long-standing commercial ties with the Maghrib states of north Africa through their engagement in the trans-Saharan trade, in which goods and people moved back and forth, creating relationships of mutual commercial interactions.[1]

Over the course of time, many northern Nigerians, particularly Hausa, came to settle in the various societies with which they regularly traded, establishing communities that were integrated into their host settings but retained kinship connections with their places of origin. Through inter-marriage or long-term residence in host communities outside Hausaland, Hausa merchants developed close relationships with suppliers while at the same time being able to maintain relationships with itinerant Hausa traders, with whom they shared kinship and language ties. This Hausa diaspora spread from east to west across the savannah, creating a wide-spread commercial network that proved beneficial for all involved. In this way the Hausa people and their language spread across Africa, to the point at which the Hausa were recognized throughout the savanna as a trading people, and in many places the Hausa language became the language of commerce.

The Hausa and Borno kingdoms also engaged prominently in the trans-Saharan trade, through which goods and people traversed the desert on north–south routes, connecting north Africa and Europe with sub-Saharan African societies. The "golden age" of the trans-Saharan trade occurred between the fourteenth and sixteenth centuries, during which time the most important items of trade were gold and slaves. Other goods were also important over the centuries, however, including salt, leather goods, textiles, and ostrich feathers. Slaves came from different back-grounds. Some were Hausa or Bornoan, captured during wars or raids in the savanna or Sahelian states of west Africa. Most slaves, however, came from the forest zone to the south, passed along trade routes that connected communities all the way from the Atlantic coast to the lucrative interregional trading centers of the savanna. Although Hausa and Borno traders tended not to conduct caravans across the Sahara themselves, preferring to act as middlemen between the trans-Saharan travelers and the goods they sought, the thousands of slaves who passed along these routes to new homes abroad contributed to the spread of peoples out of the geographical area of modern-day Nigeria, throughout the period from the thirteenth to the twentieth centuries.

The trans-Saharan trade had declined to negligible levels by the early twentieth century. As trade with Europeans grew on the Atlantic coast from the sixteenth century, the significance of the trans-Saharan routes declined. With the coming of British colonial rule and the establishment of official boundaries for Nigeria, the trans-Saharan trade became even more difficult to sustain.[2]

The trans-Saharan and cross-savanna trading routes that transferred goods and people to and from Nigerian territories also carried ideas. It was along these routes that Islam first came to the Hausa and Bornoan states of northern Nigeria during the eleventh to fourteenth centuries. With Islam came yet another opportunity for the interregional movement of peoples from Nigerian territories, as a small number of devout Muslims began to make the pilgrimage to Mecca. It is not known exactly when the first pilgrimages out of the savanna and Sahelian states of northern Nigeria began. The Bornoan King Humai is said to have adopted Islam in his realm in the late eleventh century, and Yaji of Kano, the first Hausa king to become a Muslim, converted in 1370. Mai Idris Aloma of Borno is reported to have made the pilgrimage in the late sixteenth century.[3]

Until the twentieth century most pilgrimages were made by royals or other wealthy elite members. This was the case for a couple of reasons. First, Islam remained largely a religion of the ruling class, and little effort was made to extend it to the masses until the jihad of Usman dan Fodio in the early nineteenth century. Even after the jihad, however, pilgrimage remained an elite occupation for most of the nineteenth century. The journey to Mecca was long and difficult. Prior to the eighteenth century the most common way to travel was overland along the trans-Saharan trade routes to the Mediterranean and then eastwards along the Maghrib to Arabia. In the eighteenth century alternative routes developed, leading across the savannas to the Red Sea through what are today the countries of Chad and Sudan. One had to have ample resources to be able to organize and carry out such a project. As a result, only the wealthy would have had the resources to make such a long and treacherous journey. Those commoners who undertook the journey to Mecca faced the possibility of starvation, disease, and deprivation, as well as the possibility of being forced into slavery along the way.

In the twentieth century pilgrimage to Mecca became a much more common undertaking for poorer Nigerian Muslims. With the collapse of the Sokoto Caliphate and the British conquest of northern Nigeria in 1903, many Muslims refused to live under alien rule and left northern

Nigeria, moving eastwards on pilgrimage to Mecca. During the colonial period the British implemented several measures to control the pilgrimage, in an effort to arrest the spread of disease, prevent the accumulation of large numbers of penurious Nigerian pilgrims stranded in Sudan and Saudi Arabia, and combat the surreptitious trade in slaves that reportedly occurred along pilgrimage routes. During the 1930s the British instituted a Nigerian Pilgrims' Scheme, whereby the colonial authorities negotiated with traditional rulers in Nigeria, as well as with the colonial governments of Sudan and Chad, to standardize the pilgrimage route and to ensure that pilgrims had proper pilgrim passports and enough money to complete the journey and return to Nigeria. The scheme was only partially successful. The borders between Nigeria, French West Africa, and Sudan were porous, and it was difficult to prevent anyone who so wished from embarking upon a pilgrimage or using whatever route he or she chose.

The overland pilgrimage route across the savannas remained treacherous and filled with hardships. Many Nigerians who began overland pilgrimages were unable to complete them, and ended up living in Chad and Sudan as "permanent pilgrims," always claiming their intent to continue their journey to Mecca but never financially able to do so. In Sudan, many pilgrims found employment in agriculture, particularly in the famous Gezira Scheme, one of the largest cotton-producing organizations in the world. Many continue to live and work in Sudan to this day. Some Nigerian pilgrims work in the Sudan for a short time, just long enough to make enough money to continue their journey. Others have taken up semi-permanent or even permanent residence in the country. Many also migrate to Sudan's urban areas, where they live from hand to mouth in conditions of extreme poverty. These permanent residents often become social organizers, able to recruit and help settle new itinerant Nigerian laborers. Many of these residents are now third-, fourth-, or fifth-generation settlers. Current estimates of the total number of west Africans resident in Sudan range from 900,000 to 3 million, and the majority of them are Hausa from northern Nigeria or Niger. The trail of "permanent pilgrims" between Nigeria and Saudi Arabia has become another component of the Hausa diaspora.[4]

Since the 1950s air travel has become the most common means of transportation for Nigerians embarking on pilgrimage to Mecca. This has significantly reduced the flow of pilgrims overland through Sudan, although a few, the very poor or very devout traditionalists, still attempt this route. Air travel has led to large increases in the overall number of pilgrims traveling from Nigeria to Mecca, however. The numbers of

Nigerian pilgrims arriving in Mecca are difficult to calculate, because, prior to the 1960s, immigration officials recorded west African pilgrims together as a single demographic with no differentiation for specific territory of origin. In 1938, just a few years into the Nigerian Pilgrims' Scheme, 6,046 west African pilgrims crossed the Red Sea from Sudan to Saudi Arabia, and it is safe to assume that well over a half of these pilgrims were from northern Nigeria.[5] By 1961 over 9,000 pilgrims were completing the pilgrimage annually, and this number continued to rise. During the oil boom years of the 1970s Nigeria sometimes sent over 100,000 pilgrims to Mecca in a single year. During the military regimes of the 1980s and 1990s the annual pilgrim numbers dropped, as the Nigerian government set up strict screening processes to limit the number of pilgrims to only the most "respectable" and "trustworthy" candidates, in an effort to prevent pilgrims from disappearing into Saudi Arabia on arrival or in any other way embarrassing the Nigerian regime. During this period, the average annual number of pilgrims hovered around 20,000. Since the return to civilian rule in 1999 pilgrim numbers have begun to rise again, reaching over 50,000 in 2005.

Modern-day pilgrims to Mecca serve as unofficial cultural ambassadors. Through their pilgrimages they partake in the largest annual multicultural event in the world, mixing, mingling, and developing relationships with people from across the globe. At the same time, they represent Nigeria's strong links to the larger Islamic world.

Since the 1980s the government has also sponsored Christian pilgrimages to Jerusalem, in an effort to promote parity of government policies and expenditures between the Muslim and Christian communities. Between 1995 and 1998 an average of nearly 2,500 Christian pilgrims visited Jerusalem each year under this system.[6] Christian pilgrims from Nigeria have become a common sight in Jerusalem. There is a sizable Nigerian community resident in Jerusalem today. Christian pilgrims from Nigeria have also served as cultural ambassadors between Nigeria and greater Christendom, promoting interactions between disparate peoples through a shared religious experience.

The transatlantic diaspora

Large numbers of people from the territory of modern-day Nigeria have also spread throughout Europe and the western hemisphere in the period since the 1500s. In the period before the mid-nineteenth century most intercontinental migration of Nigerians was involuntary and permanent, as millions of people from Nigerian territory were taken into slavery and shipped across the Atlantic Ocean to new homes in the Americas. Enslaved people resisted their conditions of servitude in the western hemisphere while also adapting to their new surroundings, retaining many key elements of their indigenous cultures and blending others with European and American cultural forms. In this way, enslaved people in the western hemisphere coming from Nigerian territories both maintained connections to their homelands despite their diasporic existences and simultaneously contributed to the development of new and unique cultures throughout the Americas.

The exact number of slaves taken from territories inside what is today Nigeria is impossible to calculate. In fact, even to speak of the area as "Nigeria" prior to the British colonial takeover in the late nineteenth century is anachronistic. The possibility of calculating with any accuracy the number of slaves taken from each specific ethnicity in the region is equally small, as by no means all slaves were categorized methodically or correctly by the European slave traders, whose records provide the largest source of information on the demographics of the transatlantic slave trade. What it is possible to estimate is the total number of slaves shipped from the Bights of Benin and Biafra, the two main slave-trading regions that overlap with the current boundaries of Nigeria. Paul Lovejoy has estimated that the Bight of Benin shipped approximately 2,019,300 slaves between 1600 and 1867,[7] while David Eltis and David Richardson have estimated that some 1,491,000 were shipped from the Bight of Biafra between 1650 and 1850.[8] It is no stretch to assume that a sizable majority of these 3.5 million unfortunate souls came from within the boundaries of modern-day Nigeria, although exactly how many will never be known.

The slaves taken from these areas consisted of individuals from every ethnicity within Nigeria. Yorubas and Igbos were certainly taken in large numbers, in accordance with their relatively large population sizes compared to other ethnic groups in southern Nigeria, with an increasing influx of Hausa slaves in the nineteenth century as a result of the jihad of Usman dan Fodio in the north and the unrelated decline of the trans-Saharan trade routes. Slaves from the Bights of Benin and Biafra were dispersed throughout the western hemisphere, where they became mostly agricultural laborers in the plantation economies of the Caribbean, the southern United States, and Brazil.

Enslaved Nigerians did not submit quietly to their new conditions of servitude. Like enslaved peoples from across the African continent, they found ways to resist their oppressors. Sometimes this resistance was

aggressive. On the journey across the ocean, known as the Middle
Passage, slaves occasionally mounted violent rebellions against their
enslavers, although the harsh conditions of the journey made opportunities
for such revolts scarce. More commonly, enslaved persons resisted their
conditions passive-aggressively, by refusing to eat or, in many instances,
committing suicide, throwing themselves overboard, preferring a watery
death to a life of servitude in the Americas. Igbo slaves, rightly or wrongly,
developed a particular reputation for taking their own lives.[9] Slaves also
resisted on the plantations of the New World, through such means as
working slowly, breaking tools, and running away.[10]

Full-scale slave rebellions also occurred on occasion in the Americas,
and slaves of Nigerian origin were often involved in these. In particular,
several slave rebellions in the Brazilian province of Bahia during the first
four decades of the nineteenth century were mostly led by Hausa and
Yoruba Muslim slaves. The largest such rebellion occurred in the city of
Salvador in 1835, as Muslim slaves rose up and took control of the city
streets for over three hours before being brought down by local police.
Seventy people were killed in the rebellion, mostly slaves, but the
rebellion led to panic among the slave-owning class in Brazil. Over 500
Africans were sentenced to death, whipping, prison, or deportation for
their involvement in the rebellion. Afterwards, local police attempted to
wipe out African cultural practices, believing the rebellions to have been
instigated by slaves' thoughts of returning to their homelands.[11] Such
efforts were futile, however. Yoruba and Hausa cultural elements continue to resonate in Brazilian society to this day.

One Nigerian in particular became famous for his negotiation of the
American slave system and his fight for the abolition of the slave trade.
Olaudah Equiano was born in Igbo territory around 1745.[12] Kidnapped as
a child and sold into slavery, he lived as a slave in Barbados and Virginia
before being purchased by a British naval officer, who renamed him
Gustavus Vassa, the name he went by for the rest of his life. Equiano
served in the British navy during the Seven Years War, after which he was
sold to a plantation owner in the West Indies. He worked as an overseer
while trading on his own account on the side and was able to save enough
to buy his freedom in 1766. For the next ten years he worked as a shipper,
before relocating to London in 1776. While in London Equiano became
heavily involved in the abolitionist movement, fighting for an end to the
transatlantic slave trade. He was involved in the scheme to resettle former
and "recaptive" slaves in Sierra Leone and became a renowned public
speaker and editorialist on the subject of slavery and the slave trade. In

1789 he published his autobiography, *The Interesting Narrative of the Life of Olaudah Equiano, or Gustavus Vassa, the African. Written by Himself.*[13] Detailing the horrors and injustices of slavery and the slave trade through a recounting of his own experiences, *The Interesting Narrative* was a huge success and went through nine editions in the span of five years. The personal experiences of hardship and injustice illustrated in the *Narrative* helped to put a human face on the slave trade for many Britons and helped fuel the drive for the abolition of the slave trade. After 1794 Equiano retired from public life, and spent his time raising two daughters with his English wife, until his death in 1797, ten years before the official British abolition of the slave trade.

Although the British abolished the slave trade in 1807, the trafficking in slaves from the Bights of Benin and Biafra (among other slaving zones) continued for several decades afterwards. Many slaves taken during the first half of the nineteenth century were intercepted by the British anti-slaving squadron along the coast of west Africa and were deposited in the newly founded British west African colony of Sierra Leone. Many slaves resettled permanently in Sierra Leone, but others, such as Bishop Samuel Ajayi Crowther,[14] who were educated in mission schools and converted to Christianity, became proselytizers for Christianity and the anti-slavery movement, moving throughout west Africa to fight against the abominable institution that had uprooted their lives and nearly led to their enslavement overseas. These nineteenth-century transplants in Sierra Leone represent yet another part of the diaspora of peoples from the territories of modern Nigeria.

Most African slaves were not lucky enough, unlike Equiano and the recaptives of Sierra Leone, to have their freedom restored. Most were settled in the Americas, where they retained major aspects of their traditional cultures despite the efforts of the slave-owning classes to eradicate those cultures in many places. An emerging literature on the Yoruba diaspora in the Americas is beginning to bring to light many of the elements of Yoruba culture that have been retained and adapted in the western hemisphere. Perhaps the most recognizable and distinctly Yoruba cultural retentions have been in the sphere of religious belief and practice. Over the course of time, Yoruba religion mixed with other African religions and with Christianity in the Americas to form new religions unique to the western hemisphere. Elements of Yoruba religion can be found in a number of religious movements throughout the Americas, including Haitian Voodoo, Cuban Santeria, and Brazilian Candomblé. In each of these religions, Yoruba religious beliefs and practices can still be discerned, most notably the worship of Yoruba *orisas*, or gods, such as Orunmila, Olodumare, and Sango (sometimes written Xango). Rituals from Yoruba religion, such as animal sacrifice, continue to hold significance in these diasporic religions, as does the use of the Yoruba language for ritual purposes in many cases.[15]

Religious belief and practice are not the only forms of Yoruba culture that have been adapted and retained in the Americas. Versions of Yoruba (and other west African) prepared foods also exist throughout the Americas. Bean cakes made and sold by people of African descent in Brazil resemble those made by the Yoruba and other west African peoples. Gumbo, a favorite food in the southern United States, particularly in the Louisiana area, is a variation of popular west African (including Yoruba) stews in which similar ingredients, such as okra and spicy peppers, are served over a starchy substance. In west African stews the starch is usually yam or cassava; in gumbo it is usually rice. West African language patterns have also merged with the English language over time. For example, the Yoruba language does not conjugate verbs. Therefore, the English "I *am*," "you *are*," "he/she/it *is*," translates into Yoruba simply as "emi *ni*," "iwo *ni*," and "oun *ni*" respectively. Scholars equate this lack of conjugation with colloquial African-American speech patterns that would conjugate the same phrase in English as "I *be*," "you *be*," "he/she/it *be*," representing the retention of African language patterns over time and space. This is just one example among many of west African, including Yoruba, speech patterns that have influenced spoken English.[16]

Although the examples given have been primarily Yoruba, similar examples of cultural retentions originating from other ethnic groups from territories in modern-day Nigeria certainly exist as well. For example, it has been argued that the English word "okra" comes from the Igbo *okro*, and that certain cultural phenomena in the Americas, particularly forms of masquerades, have Igbo, as well as Yoruba, origins.[17] Regardless of the community of origin, slaves in the diaspora retained links with their motherlands in Nigeria and elsewhere, while simultaneously contributing to the cultural development of the Americas in ways that have linked the two regions both culturally and historically over time.

Transnational communities in the twentieth century

The transatlantic slave trade came to an end in the mid-nineteenth century, but the intercontinental migration of Nigerians did not end with it. With the coming of British colonial rule over the territories of modern-day Nigeria between 1861 and 1903, the peoples of these territories became British subjects, free to move anywhere within the British Empire, including the United Kingdom as means permitted. Since independence in 1960 many Nigerians have continued to travel abroad for employment and education opportunities. Unlike the forced migrations of the transatlantic slave trade, however, Nigerian migration since the twentieth century has been mostly elective, and in many cases these migrants see their relocations as temporary. Nigerians who have relocated to Europe and the United States since the early twentieth century have established what can be called transnational communities, in which migrants become partially assimilated to their new environments but remain socially and culturally committed to their homelands.

During the colonial period travel outside Nigeria was voluntary and most often temporary or semi-permanent, as Nigerians went to the United Kingdom and the United States in search of Western education and possible employment, mostly with the ultimate goal of returning to Nigeria to utilize their new skills for the benefit of their families and communities. A few Nigerians settled permanently in the United Kingdom or the United States during the first half of the twentieth century, but prevailing sentiments of race prejudice in these places made permanent relocation unattractive to many Nigerians.

While studying in the United Kingdom, Nigerians interacted with students from other British west African colonies. Due to a shared experience of racial prejudice encountered in the United Kingdom and a growing desire to see their homelands free of British colonial rule, many Nigerians joined with other west Africans to form political organizations aimed at securing greater rights for blacks in the United Kingdom and throughout the diaspora. One of the largest such organizations formed in the early twentieth century was the West African Students' Union, which was founded in 1925 by a group of west African students led by a Nigerian named Ladipo Solanke. WASU's goals were the establishment of a hostel in London for west African students and the promotion of issues relevant to west Africans, primarily through a newsletter, *Wasu*. While it was founded in Britain, WASU developed branches in west Africa and as far away as Harlem in the United States. Many prominent Nigerian intellectuals and nationalists were associated with WASU, including H. O. Davies, Julius Ojo-Cole, and Louis Mbanefo.

The United States also offered opportunities for enterprising Nigerian students to interact with Africans, Afro-Caribbeans, and African-Americans while obtaining higher education. In fact, in many ways the prospect of an

American education was more stimulating than a British education for many young Nigerians. Whereas most students who earned degrees from British universities took only a first degree, African students in the United States had greater opportunities to attain master's and doctorate degrees. Also, in the United States there was a sizable black minority, and even black universities such as Lincoln and Howard, which attracted African students by offering a greater sense of community and incorporation than could be claimed in British universities. Finally, the United States was seen by many young Nigerians as the "land of democracy," the place where the rudiments of majority rule and the democratic selection of leaders could be learned and brought back to Nigeria. It is not surprising, then, that Nigerians who studied in the United States, most notably Nnamdi Azikiwe himself, developed strong nationalist sentiments and established ties with other black nationalists with origins throughout the diaspora. During his time in the United States Azikiwe developed friendships with such noted black intellectuals, nationalists, and cultural promoters as George Padmore, Langston Hughes, and Alain Locke.[18]

Political thought among Africans in the United Kingdom and the United States in the first half of the twentieth century was grounded in the ideology of Pan-Africanism, the idea that people of African descent both in Africa and in the diaspora must come together to combat a world dominated by white, European racism and imperialism. Pan-Africanism promoted the need to preserve African cultures in the face of European ideas of modernity, while also arguing for the independence of African colonies from European rule and for greater equality for blacks in the diaspora. Nigerians participated in all the Pan-African congresses that took place in the first half of the twentieth century. Azikiwe sent a delegate to represent his nationalist movement, the National Council of Nigeria and the Cameroons, at the famous Manchester Conference of 1945.

Over time Pan-Africanism took on a nationalist component, as Africans in particular began to promote the agenda of independence for African colonies. In west Africa, Pan-African organizations such as WASU originally promoted a west African nationalism – that is, independence for all of British west Africa collectively. Over time, however, these organizations fragmented into colony-specific nationalist movements, and Nigerian nationalism became very pronounced. Many of the nationalist leaders of Nigeria from the 1930s to the 1950s had studied abroad and had influenced and been influenced by these Pan-African organizations. Through their experiences abroad, Nigerians made political and social connections with people throughout the African diaspora as well as with liberal-minded white Europeans and Americans. In so doing, Nigerians contributed to the growth of Pan-African and west African political activism in the United Kingdom and the United States in the first half of the twentieth century, while at the same time developing their own political ideologies under the influence of Pan-African organizations in ways that ultimately led to independence for Nigeria from British colonial rule.[19]

In the years since Nigeria achieved independence in 1960 Nigerians have continued to travel abroad, mainly to neighboring African countries, but also increasingly to Europe and the United States for education and employment opportunities. Particularly since the 1980s, large numbers of trained Nigerian professionals in such fields as medicine, engineering, and law have left the crumbling Nigerian economy for more stable and remunerative employment overseas.

The Nigerian population in the United States as of 2000 was over 164,000, of whom over 104,000 were Nigerian-born. Over 91,000 of the Nigerians in the United States were over the age of twenty-five, with a median age of thirty, and, of those 91,000, over 54,000 had a college degree or higher.[20] As of 2001 over 88,000 Nigerian-born persons resided in the United Kingdom, and were overwhelmingly concentrated in and around London.[21] As of 1993 an estimated 21,000 Nigerian doctors were practicing in the United States alone.[22]

This "brain drain" of Nigerian talent has benefited the health care, engineering, and academic sectors of European and American economies at the expense of Nigerian social service and economic institutions. Nigerians have contributed to the fields of scientific research, medicine, business, and all manner of academic disciplines in European and American universities. Many have won awards in various fields and are listed in *Who Is Who in the World*.[23] Nigerians have also made international contributions to business entrepreneurship. Kase Lukman Lawal, originally from Ibadan, has become one of the leading businessmen in the Houston, Texas, area, serving as the CEO of the CAMAC International Corporation and the Allied Energy Corporation. He is also a large shareholder in the Unity National Bank, the only federally insured African-American-owned bank in Texas.

The migration of Nigerians abroad for employment purposes must be seen as, by and large, only a semi-permanent relocation, however. Many Nigerians who have moved overseas as part of the "brain drain" have been able to bring their immediate families with them and settle permanently in Europe or the United States, but many have not. A large number of professionals are forced to leave their families behind in Nigeria. Even those who do bring their immediate families continue to have connections with extended families and kinship networks within Nigeria. Therefore, at the same time that Nigerian talent is being drained from the country, that same talent is sending a constant influx of foreign exchange in the form of remittances to support family and friends back in Nigeria. Statistics on the total value of remittances sent to Nigeria vary, ranging from as low as $1.3 billion[24] to as high as $4 billion annually.[25] Regardless of which figures are used, remittances have become the second leading source of foreign exchange earnings for Nigeria, after oil. Remittances are an example of the social and cultural connections that Nigerians in the diaspora have retained, but they cannot be seen as an adequate replacement for the lack of professionals in the Nigerian economy.

The social and cultural connections between Nigeria and its exported professionals continue to hold resonance. Most Nigerian expatriates overseas claim the desire to return to Nigeria one day, once they have earned enough money to support themselves and send their children to school. These expatriates recognize that it may take many years abroad to accomplish their goals, but the intention to retire, die, and be buried in their homeland remains strong. Many Nigerians abroad send money to their families in Nigeria for the erection of a retirement home in their hometown, ready and waiting for them when they finally return from overseas. Many Nigerians have used the skills they acquired abroad for the benefit of their homeland.

Not all Nigerians migrating abroad are highly trained professionals. Nigerians also immigrate to and travel between European and African countries illegally as smugglers and criminals. For example, in recent years large numbers of girls and young women have migrated out of Nigeria to work as prostitutes in Europe, Saudi Arabia, and various African countries. Traffickers agree with the families of the young women that they will pay the cost of smuggling them out of Nigeria, and, once settled in a new country, the young women will work to pay off their debt to the traffickers. Some of the young women are aware that they will have to repay this debt through prostitution, but are willing to make this sacrifice in order to travel abroad and earn good money. Many, however, are unaware of the fate that awaits them, thinking that they will work off their debts through some unspecified form of unskilled labor, such as domestic service. The illicit trafficking of young people is very much an underground phenomenon. As a result, no reliable statistics on the number of those trafficked exist. The problem has become so obvious, however, that Nigeria passed a law in 2003 banning human trafficking, and is currently making efforts to curb the practice.[26] In South Africa, among other places, resident Nigerians are commonly believed to be "419ers," in the country only for the purpose of running scam operations. This is obviously an exaggeration, as most Nigerians travel abroad for legitimate business or social purposes, but it is an example of the extent to which the Nigerian image has been damaged by the illegal and extra-legal activities of some of its emigrants.

Several Nigerians have become extremely well known as international sports superstars. For example, Hakeem Olajuwon became a famous basketball player for the Houston Rockets, leading the team in the National Basketball Association (NBA) championships in 1994 and 1995. Born and raised in Lagos, Olajuwon attended the University of Houston before being drafted into the NBA in 1984. Nicknamed "the Nigerian Nightmare" for his prowess on the court, Olajuwon was named one of the fifty greatest players in NBA history in 1996. The most popular sport in the world is not basketball, however, but football (soccer), and in international football Nigerians have also made a significant contribution. Such players as Jay Jay Ochoa, who played for Bolton in the English Premier League before moving to the Qatar league in 2006, Nwankwo Kanu, who plays for Portsmouth, and Taribo West, who has played for many European clubs, such as A.C. Milan and F.C. Kaiserslautem, have brought international recognition to Nigeria as cultural ambassadors. Nigeria's national football team has also done quite well in international competitions, reaching the second round of the World Cup in 1994 and 1998 and winning Olympic gold in 1996.

FOREIGN POLICY

Although Nigeria has developed global connections through the dispersion of its peoples throughout the world, its diplomatic presence has often been important as well. Because Nigeria is such a diverse, populous, and resource-rich country with political, economic, and cultural connections throughout Africa and the world, it is not surprising that it has been a vocal and active participant in international affairs. The agenda of Nigerian foreign policy has shifted somewhat as new regimes have taken power, and it has adapted to geopolitical circumstances over time, but for the most part Nigerian foreign policy can be summarized under two related goals: (1) opposition to colonialism and imperialism, in both its political and economic forms, throughout the world but with special emphasis on Africa; and (2) the promotion and coordination of continental unity and regional integration within Africa so as to improve political stability and economic growth, as well as enhancing the negotiating power of African countries vis-à-vis Western powers.

Nigerian governments have advanced these foreign policy agendas through bilateral and multilateral negotiations with other countries, as well as through active participation in many international organizations, such as the United Nations and many of its constituent bodies, the Commonwealth group consisting of the United Kingdom and its former colonies, OPEC, the Non-Aligned Movement, the OAU (reconstituted in 2000 as the African Union, or AU), ECOWAS, and the African Development Bank.

Prior to the 1970s Nigerian foreign policy was very conservative, dictated for the most part by the need to maintain strong relationships with Western countries, most importantly the United Kingdom, upon which Nigeria's economy largely depended as a market for its exports and as the source of imports. Throughout the period of British colonial rule Nigerian foreign policy was directed by the British, and therefore it conformed entirely to British foreign policy interests. During the First World War, for example, Nigerian troops were instrumental in the occupation of the German colonies of Togo and the Cameroons, which bordered Nigeria. A Nigerian contingent also traveled to east Africa to aid in the British occupation of German East Africa. After helping to drive the Germans from their African colonies, Nigerian troops were in line to be sent to the Middle East to help with the fight against the Ottomans, but the war came to an end before the final preparations were completed.[27] During the Second World War, Nigerian troops served in transport and support roles in the north African campaign, and the Nigerian economy was geared towards increasing production in necessary war materials such as palm oil and tin in order to aid Britain's war effort.

The strong link between Nigerian foreign policy and British foreign policy continued after Nigerian independence in 1960. The Balewa government of the First Republic sought to maintain strong ties with the former colonial power, as well as with western Europe, and took a pro-West position in global affairs on most matters. Upon independence, Nigeria took up membership in the Commonwealth, in recognition of the historical ties between Nigeria and the United Kingdom. The Balewa government kept its distance from the Soviet Union, allowing the establishment of a Soviet consulate in Nigeria but without establishing a Nigerian consulate in the USSR, and refused to recognize the People's Republic of China. Nigeria also rejected Soviet aid and scholarships for Nigerian students during the First Republic. On the Arab–Israeli conflict, Nigeria took a neutral stance during the First Republic, often condemning both Israelis and Arabs for violent acts against each other.

In African affairs, Nigeria called for the decolonization of the continent; the approach of the Balewa government was conservative in tone, however, pushing for diplomatic negotiation in ways that often angered allies in other African countries. Nigeria pushed for peaceful negotiations with the apartheid regime of South Africa, while simultaneously calling for the ousting of South Africa from the Commonwealth because of its racist policies. Nigeria backed the West in its opposition to Patrice Lumumba in the Congo, and sent a large force to aid with the UN peacekeeping mission there. Overall, the First Republic walked a very fine line in foreign affairs, trying to promote independence and sovereignty for African countries while at the same time trying not to alienate the Western powers against which African nationalist movements fought.

The Nigerian Civil War of 1967–70 marked a shift in Nigerian foreign policy formulation and implementation. During the civil war the main foreign affairs goal of the Gowon regime was to gain allies for the Federal Military Government and to prevent international intervention on the side of the Biafran secessionists. In some ways, the FMG was successful. Gowon convinced the OAU to treat the Nigerian Civil War as an internal conflict and to respect the sovereignty of the FMG by not getting involved. In other ways, however, the FMG was unsuccessful. Most Western powers adopted a "wait and see" approach to the civil war and refused to offer full-scale support to the FMG in the conflict. The United States and the United Kingdom even refused to sell heavy artillery, other highly destructive weapons,[28] and fighter jets to the FMG for fear of alienating the Biafrans, who controlled the territories of the Niger delta, where the majority of Nigeria's petroleum reserves lay. With its traditional allies deliberately non-committal, the FMG found a ready ally in the USSR. For the first time the Nigerian government embraced Soviet aid, purchasing several aircraft from Eastern bloc countries and accepting Soviet technicians and advisers.

The FMG was unsuccessful in its efforts to forestall international support for Biafra. Several African countries, including Tanzania, Gabon, the Ivory Coast, and Zambia, all members of the OAU, officially recognized Biafra in 1968. France and Portugal provided significant aid and logistical support for the Biafran cause; supplies were flown regularly to Biafra from Portuguese bases in west Africa. Both Portugal and France believed that permanently destabilizing Nigeria was in the best interests of their own foreign policy. Portugal was fighting to retain its own colonies in Africa, and as long as Nigeria was preoccupied with its own civil war it could not aid the liberation movements in Portuguese colonies. France, for its part, feared the establishment of Nigeria as a hegemonic influence in west Africa, believing that any increase in Nigerian influence in the region would lead to a decrease in French influence in its own former west African colonies. Israel also expressed solidarity with the Biafran position, although the exact extent of tangible Israeli aid to the Biafrans is unclear.[29]

With the ending of the civil war and the reincorporation of Biafra into Nigeria, Nigerian foreign policy took a radical turn. From the FMG's standpoint, its inability to gain the full support of Western powers coupled with the extent of external support for Biafra had prolonged the conflict and represented a deliberate attempt by Western powers to weaken Nigeria. Furthermore, the ability of Western powers such as France and Portugal to use African countries as launching points for support of the secessionists revealed a regional security risk to Nigeria.[30] The USSR's support for Nigeria during the war also led to a loosening of Western ties and a more pronounced policy of non-alignment in Cold War politics. From 1970 the Gowon regime pursued an aggressive, Africa-centered foreign policy that promoted the complete decolonization of Africa, the end to white minority rule in South Africa and Rhodesia, and the achievement of greater regional interdependence in west Africa in particular. The Mohammed/Obasanjo regime retained these foreign policy goals after taking over in 1975, and even intensified them in many respects. Over the course of the 1970s Nigerian foreign policy became more radicalized, often resulting in direct confrontations with Western powers, most notably the United States and the United Kingdom.

The radicalization of foreign policy in the 1970s coincided with the height of Nigerian influence in foreign affairs, thanks in no small part to the oil boom that occurred in the years after the conclusion of the civil war. The wealth that accrued to Nigeria from oil revenues allowed the country to become an important source of philanthropy throughout Africa. At the same time, Nigeria was able to use its oil as a bargaining chip with the Western powers that purchased it and used it to meet their energy needs. By 1974 Nigeria had become the sixth largest oil producer in the world, and was the second largest supplier to the United States, after Saudi Arabia. As long as oil prices remained high, as they did for most of the 1970s, Nigeria was a force to be reckoned with in international affairs. The "oil weapon" therefore became an important instrument in Nigerian foreign policy; it could be used both to reward allies and to punish opponents.

Nigeria took a strong stance against the white minority regimes that governed South Africa and Rhodesia. A central tenet of Nigerian foreign policy became the strangulation of these regimes by boycotting them and threatening to impose harsh sanctions on countries that did business with them. Nigeria frequently addressed the UN on the apartheid issue, and took the chairmanship of the UN's anti-apartheid committee. Nigeria lobbied for the exclusion of South Africa and Rhodesia from international bodies such as the Commonwealth and the OAU, and organized boycotts of international sporting events, including the 1972 and 1976 Olympic Games and the 1978 Commonwealth Games, refusing to take part unless South Africa, Rhodesia, and all their allies were excluded. Nigeria also used economic disincentives to try to force Western powers to break their ties with the South African and Rhodesian regimes. In 1979 Obasanjo nationalized all British Petroleum's holdings in Nigeria in retaliation for BP's continued commercial relations with Ian Smith's white minority regime in Rhodesia.

The fight against white minority rule in southern Africa was part and parcel of a broader foreign policy devoted to anti-imperialism throughout Africa. Nigeria was more than willing to use its newfound oil wealth to give financial support to liberation movements across the continent. By 1979 it is estimated that Nigeria was donating approximately $5 million annually to aid the various liberation movements in southern Africa, including the Zimbabwean African National Union (ZANU) and the Patriotic Front (PF) in Rhodesia, the South West Africa People's Organization (SWAPO), which fought for the independence of what is now the country of Namibia from South African control, and the African National Congress (ANC) and Pan-African Congress (PAC) in South Africa. Nigeria also came out on the side of the socialist Popular Movement for the Liberation of Angola (MPLA) in its fight for control of Angola against the US-backed National Front for the Liberation of Angola (FNLA) and the South-African-backed Union for the Total Independence of Angola (UNITA). Nigeria is estimated to have given $20 million in cash to the MPLA, as well as $80 million in military supplies and economic aid. This infuriated the Western powers, particularly the United States and the United Kingdom, which opposed the establishment of a socialist government in Angola. In addition to providing financial support to liberation movements, Nigeria also provided training to Angolan students and soldiers in Nigerian institutions.[31]

Nigeria extended its hard-line anti-imperialist agenda to the Middle East crisis in the 1970s. Whereas previously Nigeria had maintained a relatively neutral position on the Arab–Israeli conflict, even accepting aid packages from Israel in the early 1960s and embarking on several joint commercial ventures with Israeli firms, in the 1970s Nigeria became increasingly anti-Israeli and pro-Palestinian. Anti-Israeli sentiment had grown in much of Nigeria during the civil war, when Israel announced its support of the Biafran secession. After the war the Gowon regime became increasingly anti-Israel, seeing the country as itself an occupying force in the Middle East, backed up by Western imperialist powers, in particular the United States. With the outbreak of the Yom Kippur War in 1973 Nigeria broke off diplomatic relations with Israel and participated in the OPEC oil embargo against the United States, illustrating its solidarity with its oil-producing Arab allies while simultaneously using the "oil weapon" against a formidable Western foe. Since the 1970s Nigeria has been a vociferous advocate of Palestinian rights in the UN and the OAU.

Nigeria also gave substantial amounts of economic and technical assistance to independent African countries. For example, in 1972 the Gowon administration donated $150,000 to Kenya, $75,000 to Guinea, $150,000 to Sudan, and 10 million CFA francs to Senegal.[32] The Obasanjo administration continued the policy of distributing largesse to other African countries, giving drought relief funds to Ethiopia, Chad, and Mali, and various other kinds of economic assistance to Cameroon, Sudan, Zambia, and The Gambia. Meanwhile, Nigeria offered technical assistance to Algeria, Botswana, The Gambia, and Swaziland, among others. Nigeria also offered scholarships to students across the continent to study in Nigeria. In addition, Nigeria financed projects in other African countries, including the building of a presidential palace and petroleum refinery in Togo, among other investments. Many of these investments involved bilateral agreements with other countries, but Nigeria also contributed $80 million to the establishment of the African Development Bank, to which African countries could apply for loans at generous rates.[33]

Such generosity was paid for with oil revenues, which by 1974 accounted for over 90 percent of Nigeria's export earnings and over 80 percent of its total revenue.[34] In 1975 Nigeria started to use oil itself as economic assistance and began selling petroleum directly to African countries at concessionary rates. African countries were allowed to purchase Nigerian crude oil at three-quarters of the market price on two conditions: (1) that the purchasing country had its own refineries; and (2) that the purchasing country agreed not to resell the oil to third parties.[35] By such measures, Nigeria hoped to strengthen relations with African countries and help struggling African economies get on their feet.

In west Africa, Nigeria went about fostering regional integration. In addition to providing economic aid to west African countries, Nigeria also became the leading proponent of the establishment of the Economic Community of West African States. The push to build a strong economic community in west Africa developed in the early 1970s out of Nigeria's desire to strengthen its own ties with neighboring countries and, simultaneously, weaken ties between neighboring countries and the member states of the European Economic Community (EEC), particularly France, which had a historic connection with its former colonies in west Africa. Originally many of the francophone west African countries were reluctant to join a west African economic community with Nigeria, preferring instead to forge their own regional pacts, most notably the Communauté Economique de l'Afrique de l'Ouest, but eventually, in 1975, fifteen west African states, including the francophone states, agreed to the formation of ECOWAS.

The objectives of ECOWAS were to foster regional economic integration through standardizing tariffs in the region, and to facilitate the movement of people, goods, and capital across borders. In doing so, member states would become more unified economically and would therefore be able to negotiate from a more powerful position with the EEC for more favorable terms of trade. ECOWAS also established a fund to finance development projects in member states. Since its inception, Nigeria, as the largest and wealthiest of the member states, has contributed roughly a third of all the funds for the maintenance and implementation of ECOWAS objectives.[36] The establishment of ECOWAS has largely been seen as a foreign policy triumph for Nigeria, establishing Nigeria as a bulwark in west Africa, in direct competition with the former colonial powers.

Nigeria's efforts to promote liberation movements, its Africa-centered approach to foreign policy goals in the 1970s, and its use of oil and oil revenues as leverage in its foreign policy objectives masked Nigeria's ultimate goal: that of becoming the most powerful and respected country in African affairs. Indeed, scholars and analysts have viewed Nigeria as an extremely important actor in international affairs, particularly in relation to Africa, during this period. There can be little doubt that Nigeria went to great lengths to promote its policy agenda and did become one of the most vocal and active African countries in international affairs during the 1970s. Nigeria's efforts therefore deserve to be lauded. Some analysts of Nigerian foreign policy in the 1970s argue, however, that it is difficult to determine how instrumental or effective the Gowon and Mohammed/Obasanjo administrations were in achieving their foreign policy goals. For example, in the liberation struggle against white minority regimes in southern Africa, Nigeria's actions were valiant, but cannot be said to have been decisive in the struggle.

At the time when Obasanjo nationalized BP's holdings in Nigeria in 1979 to protest against British relations with the Rhodesian regime, the United Kingdom was purchasing only 3.66 percent of Nigeria's annual oil production and had recently expanded crude production in the North Sea. Total British revenues from trade with Nigeria reached over £1 billion in 1977, of which BP accounted for only about £30 million. The nationalization of BP was, therefore, more symbolic than substantive, in that it caused no major hardship in the United Kingdom and did not represent a watershed change in the trajectory of British–Nigerian trade relations.[37] Nigeria's participation in the OPEC oil embargo of 1973 was effective largely because it was in conjunction with other OPEC countries. Indeed, the United States was the largest purchaser of Nigerian oil, and it could be argued that Nigeria was, and is, far more dependent on the United States to buy its oil, from which the government derives most of its revenue, than the United States is dependent on Nigeria to sell it.

Nigeria's direct aid to liberation movements in southern Africa and Angola, among others, must be seen as quite helpful to those movements, but most analysts give the credit for victory in those movements to the forces on the ground that fought so tenaciously for independence. Nigerian sanctions on South Africa had minimal impact, as trade between the two countries had been negligible prior to the sanctions.

In terms of west African regional integration, ECOWAS was unable to break the ties between member countries and their European trade partners. Member states by and large remained heavily indebted to Western business interests and creditors, a situation Nigeria itself was soon to encounter. By the early 1980s ECOWAS was becoming increasingly irrelevant, as some member states could not afford their obligations to the organization while others came to resent it, seeing it as a veiled attempt by Nigeria to achieve its own hegemony over the west African region.

After the transition to civilian rule in 1979 Nigerian influence in foreign affairs began a decline that lasted through the 1990s. The Second Republic presided over the end of the oil boom, and the fiscal irresponsibility of the Shagari administration led to a rising debt crisis in Nigeria. As Nigeria's foreign debt rose, its ability to position itself in opposition to Western powers in the international arena faded. The oil glut that replaced the oil boom ushered in an era of cheap oil, which made it difficult for Nigeria to use the "oil weapon" effectively. At the same time, the liberation movements that Nigeria had supported throughout the 1970s had been largely successful by the early 1980s. The Portuguese colonies had gained independence in the second half of the 1970s, and Rhodesia ushered in African majority rule in 1980, changing its name to Zimbabwe. As a result of these victories, Nigeria lost one of the major planks of its foreign policy agenda. South Africa continued under apartheid throughout the 1980s, however, and Nigeria continued to be among the strongest opponents of the white minority regime there. The introduction of the SAP under Babangida in 1985 further weakened the Nigerian economy, and the austerity measures associated with the program made it increasingly difficult for Nigeria to distribute economic aid to other countries in the way that it had done in the 1970s, mired as it was in an economic crisis of its own.

Two major foreign policy initiatives were undertaken by the Babangida administration after the implementation of SAP measures in Nigeria. The first was Babangida's attempt in 1986 to develop Nigerian relations with the Islamic world by making the country a member of the Organization of the Islamic Conference, an international body in which member states worked together to promote the implementation of Islamic norms of governance and social justice. Within Nigeria, the decision came as a blow to the Christian community, which fought to have Nigeria's membership cancelled. Tensions became so high over the issue that Babangida shelved the issue of Nigeria's membership in the OIC, and the country has yet to become a full member. For perhaps the first time, a military leader of Nigeria was unable to progress with a personal foreign policy agenda for fear of destablilizing the country, illustrating the capacity of domestic crises to affect Nigeria's foreign policy implementation from the 1980s.

The second major foreign policy initiative of the Babangida years was Nigeria's involvement in the peacekeeping efforts in Liberia and Sierra Leone. Between 1989 and 1991 both Liberia and Sierra Leone began long, bloody civil wars, in which fighting not only took place within the borders of these countries but also spilled over into neighboring countries in ways that threatened to destabilize large parts of west Africa. At the time of the outbreak of the Liberian Civil War, in 1989, Babangida was a close ally of the Liberian military dictator, Samuel Doe, who was under attack from various militant groups, most notably the National Patriotic Front of Liberia (NPFL), led by Charles Taylor. Nigeria spearheaded a mission by ECOWAS to serve as a peacekeeper in the region, establishing the ECOWAS Monitoring Group (ECOMOG). The goals of ECOMOG were to enforce a negotiated ceasefire, help with the transition to an interim government and the eventual election of a permanent government in Liberia, and aid in stemming the growing refugee crisis in the region, which involved over 500,000 refugees by the early 1990s. Nigeria provided 70 percent of the troops and 80 percent of the funding for the ECOMOG mission in Liberia.[38] By 1991 ECOMOG operations had spread into Sierra Leone as well.

The ECOMOG mission received support and encouragement from the United States, the UN, and the OAU, but the process of negotiating peace became protracted. In 1993 the Cotonou Agreement was signed between the interim government of Liberia and the main rebel groups, marking the beginning of an effective ceasefire; final settlement of the conflict did not occur until 1997, however, when elections were finally held in Liberia – elections that Charles Taylor won with 75 percent of the vote. In Sierra Leone, elections put Ahmad Tejan Kabbah in the presidency in 1996. Kabbah was overthrown in a coup within a year, however, and only through the efforts of ECOMOG forces was he restored, in 1998. Ceasefire negotiations continued until 2000, with Kabbah winning re-election in 2002, ending the decade-long civil war in Sierra Leone.

The capacity and willingness of ECOMOG to work towards peace in Liberia and Sierra Leone, and to cooperate with larger organizations such as the UN and OAU in the process, have been seen by many as a major success of Nigerian foreign policy. Indeed, without Nigerian personnel and resources the ECOMOG mission would never have been implemented. Others have seen ECOMOG's protracted deployment in the region as less than triumphant, however. Within Nigeria, many criticized the willingness of Babangida to divert huge amounts of money to ECOMOG operations during a time of economic crisis at home. Babangida's motives were seen as suspect: it was widely recognized that Doe was a friend of Babangida's, and many believed that Babangida pushed for the establishment of ECOMOG so that Nigerian forces could be used to protect Doe in the guise of a regional peacekeeping effort.

Doe's death in 1990, at the hands of rebel forces who successfully abducted him from ECOMOG headquarters in Monrovia, was also seen as a failure of ECOMOG forces to keep the peace. There were also concerns that ECOMOG violated UN and OAU declarations against interference in the internal affairs of sovereign states. By the end of the conflict, however, both the UN and the OAU had become staunch supporters of ECOMOG's peacekeeping effort.[39]

Any political capital that Nigeria had gained in international affairs through its involvement in the ECOMOG peacekeeping mission was squandered during the 1990s, however, as Nigeria itself became wracked with political instability and violence. Babangida's annulment of the presidential election of June 12, 1993, which was considered by the international community to have been free and fair, led to harsh criticisms from Western powers, most notably the United States and the United Kingdom. In the late 1990s Nigeria became a pariah state in international affairs due to the poor record of the Abacha administration. Abacha's abrogation of the Third Republic and his moves to install himself as president brought strong criticisms, as did flagrant human rights abuses, most notably the execution of Ken Saro-Wiwa and other Ogoni activists on trumped-up charges in 1995. Under these circumstances, Nigerian foreign policy effectiveness suffered greatly as Abacha's regime came under widespread condemnation.

Since Abacha's death in 1998 and the return to civilian rule in 1999 under President Olusegun Obasanjo, Nigeria has begun to improve its international reputation again. Obasanjo has long been considered a mastermind of international affairs; at one point he was even a serious candidate for the position of Secretary General of the United Nations. The main thrust of Obasanjo's foreign policy agenda was to make Nigeria a leader in the promotion of democracy and economic investment in Africa. First, Obasanjo leveraged ECOWAS to use its economic power to pursue pro-democracy objectives in west Africa. Nigeria claimed responsibility for negotiating Charles Taylor's abdication from the presidency of Liberia in 2003 after rebel forces threatened to ignite the flames of civil war again, and was instrumental in persuading ECOWAS to reject flawed elections in Togo in 2005, threatening economic sanctions unless new elections were held. Obasanjo also attempted to get ECOWAS involved in negotiations for an end to the civil war in the Ivory Coast.

Obasanjo is also credited, along with South Africa's Thabo Mbeki and Senegal's Abdoulaye Wade, as being instrumental in formulating the

New Partnership for Africa's Development (NEPAD), in 2001. NEPAD is founded on the belief that strong democratic and human rights records are prerequisites for attracting foreign investment and developing African economies. NEPAD offers oversight of human rights and democracy records in African countries through an independent African Peer Review Mechanism. The goal is for African countries to take a proactive role in promoting democracy and human rights and in ostracizing those governments that do not comply with NEPAD's standards. In this way, it is hoped that African countries will be able to allay the fears of foreign investors and bring about more stable and beneficent governance in African countries. For his own part, Obasanjo attempted to appease Nigeria's creditors by paying off the vast bulk of Nigeria's external debt during his term.

For all his efforts at promoting democracy, human rights, and economic development, Obasanjo came under criticism for not living up to his own rhetoric. In both 1999 and 2003 Obasanjo was elected president in polls widely believed to have been "flawed." Although foreign investment increased in Nigeria during his term of office, this has not yet resulted in the kinds of economic development that benefit the majority of the population, which still lives in abject poverty.[40] Indeed, some Nigerians believed that Obasanjo was more concerned with pushing his foreign policy agenda than with governing his own country. One of Obasanjo's critics noted that, in his first term, the president took a total of ninety-three international trips, totaling 340 days abroad.[41] Despite Obasanjo's pronounced respect for international law and oversight, he balked on this issue as well when it came to Nigeria. In 2002 Obasanjo defied an International Court ruling declaring that Nigeria had to surrender the Bakassi Peninsula to Cameroon, meant to be the final resolution of a long-standing border dispute between the two countries. It was not until 2006 that Nigeria finally handed over Bakassi to Cameroon, after negotiations with a UN-chaired joint commission.[42] Despite these criticisms, however, Nigeria improved its international reputation under Obasanjo in comparison to the 1990s.

Nigerians have also had a growing influence in international affairs through their involvement in non-governmental institutions in recent years. Particularly in branches of the Christian Church, Nigerians have risen to levels of great prominence. In 2005 the Nigerian Cardinal Francis Arinze was considered one of the leading candidates for the papacy after the death of Pope John Paul II.[43] Nigerian Bishop Peter Akinola has achieved great international success as the spiritual leader of Anglican and

Episcopal congregations in Nigeria, in other African countries, and even in the United States, where, as of 2006, twenty-one congregations had broken with the Episcopal Church over its tolerance of homosexuality and joined Akinola's ultra-conservative Nigerian Anglican Church.[44] Nigeria's influence in world religious affairs appears to be on the rise.

The rise of the Nigerian film industry is also quickly becoming an important factor influencing Nigeria's international image. Known as "Nollywood," the Nigerian film industry produces over 2,000 low-budget films each year, two-thirds of which are in English. In terms of numbers of movies released, Nollywood is more productive than both the United States' Hollywood and India's "Bollywood."[45] Nollywood movies are wildly popular not only in Nigeria but, since the early years of the twenty-first century, also throughout Africa and beyond. The success of Nollywood movies has resulted in stronger links between Nigerian film-makers and actors and those of other countries, most notably the United States. The spread of Nollywood films has also been an avenue through which Nigerian cultural traits are expressed to the outside world. Despite the fact that Nollywood films are consumed worldwide, the target audience for most films is Nigerians themselves. As such, the focus of most Nollywood films is on issues central to Nigerians; crime, corruption, witchcraft, family values, and the emerging youth culture are just a few of the themes tackled in Nollywood films. Many Nollywood movies also provide film versions of historical events, as well as legends and stories familiar to Nigerians. The distribution of Nollywood films throughout Africa and the world is therefore contributing to the spread of Nigerian culture across the globe.

CONCLUSION

Through the movement of its people throughout the world, Nigeria has played important roles in the social and cultural histories of many parts of the world over the course of many centuries. The migrants have come from many different backgrounds and from historical eras long before the establishment of the political boundaries of Nigeria in the early twentieth century. At all times, however, migrants from the Nigerian geographical region have taken their cultures with them. Both diasporic and trans-national communities have retained connections to their homelands through the retention of cultural traits. These cultural traits have mingled with other cultures to create new, unique cultures, illustrating the extent to which peoples from Nigeria have influenced social development in other parts of the world. Transnational communities have also retained bonds with their home areas in Nigeria, connecting Nigeria to other parts of the world through networks of Nigerians abroad. The connection of Nigeria with the rest of the world through its emigrant population will no doubt continue into the future.

The Nigerian state has also influenced world affairs through its foreign policy since its independence in 1960. Although Nigeria's period of greatest influence in international affairs thus far occurred in the 1970s with its dedication to an Africa-centered agenda of anti-colonialism, African majority rule, continental unity, and regional integration, Nigeria seems poised again to take a leading role in African and world affairs after more than two decades of decline. Nigeria's large oil reserves at the very least will ensure that the country continues to play a role in global affairs, as countries throughout the world become ever more dependent on this precious natural resource to meet their growing energy needs.

Concluding remarks: corruption, anti-corruption, and the 2007 elections

INTRODUCTION

On May 29, 2007, Olusegun Obasanjo stepped down as president of Nigeria, having served the maximum two terms allowed under the constitution. Alhaji Umaru Yar'Adua, the brother of Obasanjo's deputy head of state in the 1970s, was inaugurated as the new president of Nigeria, marking the first time in Nigeria's history that power was transferred from one civilian ruler to another. The PDP extended its domination of political offices throughout the country, controlling both federal houses as well as the governorships and state legislatures in twenty-eight of the thirty-six states of the federation.

The 2007 elections highlighted several of the internal contradictions of Nigerian politics as they relate to the issue of political corruption. On the surface, the transfer of power to Yar'Adua served as an indication of the potential for stability and longevity of democratic, civilian rule in the Fourth Republic. The lead-up to the elections saw an unprecedented crackdown on corruption in the country. The federal anti-corruption body, the Economic and Financial Crimes Commission, along with various state legislatures, brought charges against many powerful politicians. The elections, which took place for local and state offices on April 14 and for federal offices on April 21, were conducted with a minimum of violence. All these factors are encouraging, and they illustrate the extent to which the Fourth Republic has been able to accomplish things that other civilian regimes have not.

These positive steps are relatively superficial, however. Just beneath the surface, the 2007 elections also demonstrated dangerous levels of political corruption. The transfer of power to Yar'Adua was a foregone conclusion. He came from the same party as Obasanjo, the PDP, which dominated the government and therefore was able to control the electoral process and outcome. The allegations of corruption leveled at many politicians were selective; they were used by Obasanjo and several state legislatures primarily to discredit opponents and try to prevent them from contesting the elections at all. Finally, although the elections were held with relatively little violence, polling itself was marred by irregularities and vote rigging, which led local and international electoral observers to declare the elections severely flawed. This brief conclusion discusses the role of corruption in the 2007 elections, and the implications of the PDP's sweeping victory for the future of Nigeria.

ANTI-CORRUPTION AND POLITICS

The Obasanjo administration had claimed its anti-corruption campaign to be an important priority throughout Obasanjo's two terms in office. The establishment of the EFCC had resulted in the return of over $5 billion in stolen funds and the prosecution of over eighty individuals for corruption charges by 2006. In that year Obasanjo and the EFCC intensified investigations of politicians at all levels in anticipation of the 2007 polls. The EFCC declared that it was investigating two-thirds of all state governors over allegations of corruption. Over the course of 2006 four state governors – Rashidi Adewolu Ladoja of Oyo State, Ayo Fayose of Ekiti State, Joshua Dariye of Plateau State, and Peter Obi of Anambra State – were impeached by their state legislatures over allegations of corruption and/or gross misconduct. Eventually even Vice-president Atiku Abubakar became the focus of the EFCC, and was indicted for graft in September 2006. In February 2007, just two months before the elections, the EFCC released a list of 135 candidates it deemed "unfit to hold public office because of corruption."[1]

The crackdown on corruption was justified by the administration on the grounds that it was the federal government's job to provide oversight and root out corrupt politicians at all costs. Impeachments in state legislatures were necessary because the Nigerian constitution guaranteed immunity from prosecution for politicians as long as they held office. Therefore, it was impossible to try and convict a sitting politician on corruption charges until that politician had been forced from office. Many people criticized the timing of the indictments, however, and argued that it was Obasanjo who was, in fact, the corrupt one, in that he was using the state agency of the EFCC, which he controlled, to target political opponents in an effort to influence and manipulate the upcoming elections. The Obasanjo administration fired back at these critics, arguing that such accusations were simply an attempt by corrupt politicians to divert attention from their own corrupt dealings by pretending that the charges were politically motivated.

The most publicized case of politically motivated corruption charges occurred in the race for the presidency. The leading contender to succeed Obasanjo as the presidential candidate of the PDP, and therefore to become the front-runner for the presidency, was the sitting vice-president, Atiku Abubakar. During 2006, however, a movement gathered steam to have the Nigerian constitution changed to allow President Obasanjo to run for a third term. Obasanjo never officially stated whether he was in favor of amending the constitution to allow him to stay on; nevertheless, a bill was introduced in the federal legislature for this purpose. Vice-president Abubakar, seeing his prospects for the presidency threatened by such a move, led the opposition to the bill. In May the Senate threw out the bill, thus ending the possibility that the constitution would be amended and guaranteeing that the PDP would have a new presidential candidate in 2007.[2] The row over the possibility of a third term strained relations between Obasanjo and Abubakar. Abubakar, for his part, saw Obasanjo as reneging on a promise to hand over the PDP nomination to him in 2007, while Obasanjo saw Abubakar's maneuvering against him as disloyal and embarrassing. The ensuing quarrel between the president and the vice-president became intensely vitriolic and public.

In many ways, Abubakar was caught in a catch-22 situation. If he had supported Obasanjo's bid for a third term, he would have been signing away his own ambitions for the presidency. His open opposition to Obasanjo, however, cost him the PDP nomination in the 2007 elections. In September the EFCC charged Abubakar with graft, claiming that he had diverted $125 million in public funds into personal business ventures.[3] Abubakar denied the charges and, in turn, accused Obasanjo of graft and of using the EFCC as a political tool to discredit him. Abubakar's spokesman, Garba Shehu, warned that Nigeria under the Obasanjo administration was becoming a "police state."[4] Realizing that his ambitions within the PDP were dead, Abubakar defected from the party and joined the Action Congress, an opposition party based in Lagos.

The Obasanjo administration argued that the Nigerian constitution stipulates that any politician indicted for corruption cannot run for public office, and the Independent National Election Commission (INEC), under the leadership of Maurice Iwu, attempted to bar Abubakar from running. The administration also argued that once Abubakar had defected from the PDP he had also effectively vacated the office of vice-president, since the constitution stipulated that the president and the vice-president must be from the same party. Believing the motivation of the Obasanjo administration to be purely political, Abubakar took the EFCC and INEC to court over their efforts to remove him from office and block him running for the presidency in 2007.

The Nigerian court system became the arbiter of the disputes over corruption charges in 2006, and, in most cases, the courts ruled against the Obasanjo administration, the EFCC, and the state legislatures that removed unpopular governors from office. The impeachments of the governors of Oyo, Ekiti, and Anambra States were overturned by Nigerian courts – in two cases by the Supreme Court. The Supreme Court also ruled in Abubakar's favor in both cases involving his falling-out with the PDP, declaring that he could not be removed from office as vice-president because of his defection from the ruling party, and that INEC did not have the power to bar him from contesting the elections. The three governors were reinstated and Abubakar retained the vice-presidency; INEC chose to defy the court's ruling on Abubakar's eligibility to run in the 2007 presidential election, however, claiming that the constitution clearly prohibited INEC from allowing candidates indicted for corruption to stand. When the list of INEC-approved presidential candidates was released in March 2007, Abubakar's name was not on it.[5] Abubakar again took INEC to court, winning a Supreme Court decision, on April 17, just four days before the election, declaring that INEC did not have the power to disqualify candidates and ordering that Abubakar's name be added to the ballot at the eleventh hour.[6]

THE ELECTIONS

The rulings of Nigeria's courts nullifying the indictments and impeachments of corrupt officials certainly contributed to the interpretation that the allegations had been politically motivated and were themselves indications of the corruption of the Obasanjo administration and the ruling parties in the states in which the impeachments took place. Even if the politicians indicted for corruption were, in fact, guilty, the courts had clearly decided that the actions of their accusers were equally illegal. Accusations of corruption had therefore become a political tool that politicians could use for their own corrupt purposes. In the end, twenty-four candidates were cleared to run for the presidency. The PDP chose Umaru Yar'Adua, the little-known governor of Katsina State, as its candidate. Although Yar'Adua was not a particularly high-profile or powerful politician, he did have a reputation as an upright, fair-dealing person with a strong anti-corruption record. His anonymity mattered little, since his candidature in the ruling PDP guaranteed him rapid publicity and the backing of a strong political machine with the benefit of incumbency. Yar'Adua immediately became the front-runner in the election as the hand-picked successor to Obasanjo. Two powerful opposition candidates also contested the elections: Atiku Abubakar, who became the candidate of the Lagos-based AC, and former military ruler Muhammadu Buhari, now a civilian and the leader of the All Nigeria People's Party, based mainly in the north.

The conduct of the elections themselves further illustrated the corruption that remains inherent in the political process. The elections were marred by irregularities. Where PDP efforts to derail opponents through legal means had failed, good old-fashioned vote rigging succeeded. Although only about fifty voting-related deaths were recorded in the elections of April 14 and 21, a relatively low number by Nigerian standards, reports of voter intimidation were widespread. PDP thugs appeared at many polling stations, where, after scaring voters away from the polls, they simply filled out ballot after ballot paper for PDP candidates. In some places, thugs forced voters to cast ballots for PDP candidates. In many places, polling stations opened late or not at all. Ballot papers were delivered to some polling stations in insufficient numbers or not at all, and reports of ballot box theft were common.[7] The irregularities in the voting process were so widespread that independent election observers from the Nigeria-based Transition Monitoring Group and National Democratic Institute, the European Union, the Commonwealth monitoring group, and the US-based International Republican Institute all declared them seriously flawed. The UK High Commission condemned the elections as "not credible," and the United States State Department called them "seriously flawed." Only the monitoring group from ECOWAS declared the elections "fairly acceptable."[8]

The flawed results of the election almost universally favored the PDP. In the state and local elections held on April 21, the PDP took twenty-eight of the thirty-six state legislatures and governorships. Three opposition parties managed to win state offices: the All Nigeria People's Party, led by former military ruler Muhammadu Buhari, took five states, all in the north, while the People's Progressive Alliance won in the heavily Igbo states of Imo and Abia. The Action Congress took Lagos State. The PDP also won hefty majorities in the Federal House of Representatives and

Senate in the elections held on April 21. In the presidential race, Yar'Adua declared victory with 70 percent of the total votes cast.[9] Opposition candidates rejected the results of the elections, citing the findings of the independent observers. Since the PDP was already the ruling party and had won such a large majority of the seats in the 2007 elections, however, there was little that the weakened and fragmented opposition could do to prevent the PDP from handing power over to itself.

REACTIONS AND IMPLICATIONS

The reaction of Nigerians to the 2007 elections has been one of frustration accompanied by resignation. Although voter turnout was estimated to have been high in most places, there is nevertheless a widespread belief that the elections were rigged and that the majority of politicians are corrupt power seekers more concerned with self-interest than public service. This frustration with politicians is not directed solely at the PDP, however. Support for opposition candidates is equally tepid, as many Nigerians have little faith that the opposition would govern any differently. Nigerians have seen too many politicians make grandiose promises only to disappoint them once in power. The fact that Abubakar could defect from the ruling party and immediately become the presidential candidate of an opposition party is indication enough that politics in Nigeria is not based on ideology, policies, or platforms but on proximity to the locus of power, access to money, and ability to mobilize resources. It is not surprising, therefore, that protests against the elections within Nigeria have been minimal. The Nigerian Bar Association organized a boycott in May, but rallies organized by the opposition candidates themselves have failed to materialize, as most Nigerians do not feel sufficiently involved with the messages of the politicians to mobilize behind them to any significant degree.

There is every indication that the Yar'Adua administration will be a continuation of the Obasanjo administration in most respects. Yar'Adua was the hand-picked successor of Obasanjo and a member of a family historically allied with Obasanjo. Meanwhile, although Obsanjo has stepped down as president, he retains his post as chairman of the PDP's board of trustees, a strong indication that he will continue to be influential in government.[10] The PDP's proven ability to manipulate and control the results of elections has dire implications for the future governance of the country as well. With such strong PDP control, Nigeria seems to be moving towards the establishment of what amounts to a one-party state, in which the avenue to power comes not through contesting elections but through appeasing officials within the dominant party. Under such circumstances, there is little accountability in government and little incentive for the PDP to rule in the best interests of the citizens. The "rentier state" mentality seems likely to continue, as government officials can continue to use oil revenues derived from foreign sources to maintain their power by any means necessary.

Despite these negative prospects, there are some positive signs associated with the transfer of power. Although religious and ethnic tensions remain strong in Nigeria, there are signs that the Yar'Adua administration might be able to reduce some of these tensions. All three of the main candidates in the 2007 presidential election were northern Muslims, as opposed to Obasanjo, who is a born-again Christian. This transfer from a southern Christian to a northern Muslim could serve to lessen tensions, in the sense that the power-sharing arrangement whereby the presidency rotates between the main ethno-religious regions of the country seems to be on track. Also, the new vice-president, Goodluck Johnson, hails from the troubled Niger delta state of Bayelsa. The choice of a "south-south" vice-presidential candidate has been seen by some as an indication that the Yar'Adua administration will play a more active and involved role in reconciling tensions in the Niger delta, where militants continue to attack oil installations in an effort to force oil companies and the Nigerian government to meet their demands for greater access to oil revenues and for stricter environmental regulations.

There is also some positive spin that can be put on the conduct of the 2007 elections themselves. Despite the fact that the elections were rigged, this did not provoke violence or instability in the country. While ethnic and religious tensions continue to be prevalent throughout the country, for the time being these tensions are not linked to the elections, as has been the case in the past. Because the elections were carried out relatively smoothly, however flawed they may have been, the military has not seen it necessary to step in and reclaim control of the government. This bodes well for the Fourth Republic, which is already the longest-tenured civilian regime in the history of Nigeria. The longer that a stable civilian regime can stay in power the better the chances are of developing more solid democratic institutions in the future, as little along these lines can be accomplished under military dictatorship.

The fact that corruption has entered the political debate is also a good thing. It is important that government in Nigeria becomes more transparent, and the prospect of corruption charges surfacing and threatening

Figure C.1 The future of Nigeria (collection of Roy Doron)

the careers of politicians may possibly reduce the instances of corruption among politicians. For those who argue that watchdog groups such as the EFCC have been used for political purposes, it is also important to note that the courts were able to overrule government agencies when they were proven to be overzealous. In such cases, the separation of powers in the Nigerian constitution seems to be functioning adequately, as the judiciary has successfully checked the powers of both the executive and the legislature in recent years. The legislature itself effectively checked the power of the executive by denying Obasanjo the constitutional amendment needed to gain a third term as president. The existence of a vigilant judiciary bodes well for the establishment of more responsible and democratic governance in the long term.

The possibilities for the future seem endless and impossible to predict. Nigeria continues to combat serious political, economic, and social problems that are deeply embedded in the country's unique and complex history. Despite all that Nigeria has gone through, the potential remains for the country to be strong, powerful, wealthy, and internationally esteemed. The conditions are currently more favorable for long-term stability than they have been for many years. There is still a long way to go, however. Most Nigerians continue to live in extreme poverty; political consciousness is waning as people search for leaders they can trust to govern responsibly and ethically; and the majority of Nigerians lack access to proper medical and educational facilities. The elections of 2007 did little to address these basic concerns; nevertheless, the prospects for long-term stability represented in the transfer of power and the functioning of effective checks and balances in the political system leave room to hope that the future might hold brighter days.

Notes

INTRODUCTION

1 Tom Forrest, *Politics and Economic Development in Nigeria* (Boulder, CO: Westview Press, 1995), 134.
2 BBC News, "Population in Nigeria Tops 140m," December 29, 2006, available online at http://news.bbc.co.uk/2/hi/africa/6217719.stm.
3 Central Intelligence Agency (CIA), *World Factbook: Nigeria*, updated May 15, 2007, available online at www.cia.gov/library/publications/the-world-factbook/geos/ni.html.
4 Ibid.
5 *World Gazetteer*, "Nigeria: Largest Cities and Towns and Statistics of Their Population," updated January 1, 2006, available online at www.world-gazetteer.com/wg.php?x=&men=gcis&lng=en&des=gamelan&dat=32&geo=-158&srt=npan&col=aohdq.
6 Population Division of the Department of Economic and Social Affairs of the United Nations Secretariat, *World Population Prospects: The 2006 Revision and World Urbanization Prospects: The 2005 Revision*, available online at http://esa.un.org/unpp.
7 CIA, *World Factbook: Nigeria*.

I EARLY STATES AND SOCIETIES, 9000 BCE – 1500 CE

1 Archeologists have often used the dating system years before present (YBP); since the Gregorian calendar is used as the dating system throughout the remaining chapters of this book, however, it seems appropriate to extend the Gregorian system to the archeological discussion for consistency. Accordingly, the BCE (before the Common Era) system is employed to indicate dates before the Christian era and CE is used for dates during the Christian era.
2 More detailed discussion of these sites can be found in Raphael A. Alabi, "Late Stone Age technologies and agricultural beginnings," in *Precolonial Nigeria: Essays in Honor of Toyin Falola*, ed. Akinwumi Ogundiran (Trenton, NJ: Africa World Press, 2005), 87–104.
3 Ibid.

4 See P. Breunig, K. Neumann, and W. V. Neer, "New research on the Holocene settlement and environment of the Chad Basin in Nigeria," *African Archaeological Review* 13, no. 2 (1996): 111–45.

5 David A. Aremu, "Change and continuity in metallurgical traditions: origins, technology and social implications," in *Precolonial Nigeria*, 136–7.

6 P. A. Oyelaran, "Early settlement and archaeological sequence of northeast Yorubaland," *African Archaeological Review* 15, no. 1 (1998): 65–79.

7 E. E. Okafor, "New evidence on early iron smelting from southeastern Nigeria," in *The Archaeology of Africa: Food, Metals and Towns*, ed. T. Shaw, P. Sinclair, B. Andah, and A. Okpoko (London: Routledge, 1993), 432–48; and E. E. Okafor, "Opi: the earliest iron smelting site in Africa?," *Nigerian Heritage* 9 (2000): 146.

8 D. D. Hartle, "Archaeology in eastern Nigeria," *Nigeria Magazine* 93 (1969): 134–43.

9 G. Connah, "Radiocarbon dates for Benin City and further dates for Daima, northeast Nigeria," *Journal of the Historical Society of Nigeria* 4, no. 2 (1968): 313–20.

10 Aremu, "Change and continuity," 141–3.

11 Ibid., 148.

12 A fuller description of this decentralized political structure can be found in A. E. Afigbo, "The indigenous political systems of the Igbo," in *Igbo History and Society: The Essays of Adiele Afigbo*, ed. Toyin Falola (Trenton, NJ: Africa World Press, 2005), 155–66.

13 Aremu, "Change and continuity," 141.

14 See chapter 2, this volume.

15 For more on the importance of Ife to Yoruba identity, see Samuel Johnson, *The History of the Yorubas from the Earliest Times to the Beginning of the British Protectorate* (reprint, Lagos: CSS, 2001).

16 On Benin social formation, see R. E. Bradbury, *The Benin Kingdom and the Edo-speaking Peoples of South-western Nigeria* (London: International African Institute, 1957, 1970).

17 For more on Kanem and Bornu, see, for example, John O. Hunwick, "Songhay, Bornu and Hausaland in the sixteenth century," in *History of West Africa*, vol. I, ed. J. F. A. Ajayi and Michael Crowder (New York: Columbia University Press, 1972), 202–39; and Mervyn Hiskett, *The Development of Islam in West Africa* (London and New York: Longman, 1984), passim.

18 For more on the early Hausa states, see Hiskett, *The Development of Islam*.

19 As noted in J. Spencer Trimingham, *A History of Islam in West Africa* (Oxford: Oxford University Press, 1962), 107–8.

20 Hiskett, *The Development of Islam*, 55–8.

21 Trimingham, *A History of Islam*, 107–8.

22 This information does come from a sixteenth-century source, however, far removed from the time of the supposed pilgrimages. See Hiskett, *The Development of Islam*, 14, 60.

23 Nehemia Levtzion, "Islam in the Bilal-al Sudan to 1800," in *The History of Islam in Africa*, ed. Nehemia Levtzion and Randall L. Pouwels (Athens, OH: Ohio University Press, 2000), 65.

24 Ibid., 81.
25 For more on the trans-Saharan trade, see, for example, Edward William Bovill, *The Golden Trade of the Moors* (Oxford: Oxford University Press, 1958).
26 Robin Horton, "Stateless societies in the history of west Africa," in *History of West Africa*, vol. I, 109–19, provides an excellent discussion of these issues.

2 SLAVERY, STATE, AND SOCIETY, *c.* 1500 – *c.* 1800

1 Toyin Falola and Paul E. Lovejoy, eds., *Pawnship in Africa: Debt Bondage in Historical Perspective* (Boulder, CO: Westview Press, 1994).
2 Paul E. Lovejoy and David Richardson, "Competing markets for male and female slaves: prices in the interior of west Africa, 1780–1850," *International Journal of African Historical Studies* 28, no. 2 (1995): 261–93.
3 A more detailed discussion of traditional slavery in African societies can be found in Paul E. Lovejoy, *Transformations in Slavery: A History of Slavery in Africa*, 2nd edn. (Cambridge: Cambridge University Press, 2000), 1–23.
4 For instance, H. R. Palmer, *The Bornu Sahara and Sudan* (London: J. Murray, 1936), 218, reports that Mai Uthman ibn Idris complained in 1391–2 to the Egyptian government that "the Arab tribes of Jodham and others have taken our free subjects, women and children and old men of our own family and other Muslims," and requested that the Egyptian government send messengers to enquire after Bariba Muslim slaves who might be living in Egypt. Cited in Lovejoy, *Transformations in Slavery*, 30.
5 A good source on the institution of slavery in Islamic Africa is Allan G. B. Fisher and Humphrey J. Fisher, *Slavery and Muslim Society in Africa: The Institution in Saharan and Sudanic Africa and the Trans-Saharan Trade* (Garden City, NY: Doubleday, 1971).
6 See especially the discussion of the slave trade in the Bight of Biafra, below.
7 Lovejoy, *Transformations in Slavery*, 24.
8 This is because data for the trans-Saharan trade in slaves is mostly confined to the markets of north Africa, the terminal points of the trade, where slaves were categorized spottily if at all. Little data on the make-up of the trans-Saharan slave trade exists in the kingdoms of origin in the western or central Sudan, making it difficult to estimate the percentage of slaves that originated in each sub-Saharan kingdom. See the data tables in Ralph A. Austen, "The trans-Saharan slave trade: a tentative census," in *The Uncommon Market: Essays in the Economic History of the Atlantic Slave Trade*, ed. H. A. Gemery and J. S. Hogendorn (New York: Academic Press, 1979), 23–76, in which the data is compiled almost exclusively from sources in the trading centers of north Africa.
9 Hunwick, "Songhay, Borno and Hausaland," 207–8.
10 R. A. Adeleye, "Hausaland and Borno, 1600–1800," in *History of West Africa*, vol. I, 503.
11 Ibid., 505–6.
12 Hunwick, "Songhay, Borno and Hausaland," 215–17.

13 Adeleye, "Hausaland and Borno."

14 Hunwick, "Songhay, Borno and Hausaland," 216.

15 Rasheed Olaniyi, "Kano: the development of a trading city in central Sudan," in *Precolonial Nigeria*, 311.

16 B. Agbaje-Williams, "New dates for Old Oyo," *African Notes* 10, no. 1 (1986): 1–3.

17 As described in Johnson, *The History of the Yorubas*, 11–16.

18 Robin Law, *The Oyo Empire c. 1600–c. 1836: A West African Imperialism in the Era of the Atlantic Slave Trade* (Oxford: Clarendon Press, 1977), 85–90.

19 Ibid., 80–1.

20 Ibid., 67–9, 110–18, for a discussion of the role of slaves in the *alafin*'s palace administration.

21 On the slave trade in Oyo, see Peter Morton-Williams, "The Oyo Yoruba and the Atlantic trade, 1670–1830," *Journal of the Historical Society of Nigeria* 3, no. 1 (1964): 25–45. See also Law, *The Oyo Empire*, chap. 10.

22 Paul E. Lovejoy and J. S. Hogendorn, "Slave marketing in west Africa," in *The Uncommon Market*, 222–3.

23 Benin maintained restrictions on the slave trade for roughly 150 years, re-entering the slave market only in the last decades of the seventeenth century. Even from this point, however, Benin's contribution to the transatlantic slave trade remained minimal relative to the great slaving ports on the Bights of Benin and Biafra. For a discussion of Benin's relationship with European traders, see A. F. C. Ryder, *Benin and the Europeans 1485–1897* (London: Longman, 1969).

24 Calculation from Lovejoy, *Transformations in Slavery*, 51, 56.

25 Ibid., 55.

26 Ibid., 59–60.

27 Ibid., 51.

28 Law, *The Oyo Empire*, 220–2. Discussions of the geopolitics of the slave trade in the Bight of Benin can be found in ibid., chap. 10. See also Lovejoy, *Transformations in Slavery*, 55–7, 80–3; and I. A. Akinjogbin, "The expansion of Oyo and the rise of Dahomey, 1600–1800," in *History of West Africa*, vol. I, 373–412.

29 Law, *The Oyo Empire*, 221–2.

30 For a discussion of this eastward shift over time, culminating in the rise of Lagos, see Robin Law, "Trade and politics behind the Slave Coast: the lagoon traffic and the rise of Lagos, 1500–1800," *Journal of African History* 24, no. 3 (1983): 321–48. Morton-Williams, "The Oyo Yoruba and the Atlantic trade," also discusses this subject.

31 E. J. Alagoa, "The Niger Delta states and their neighbours, 1600–1800," in *History of West Africa*, vol. I, 280–1. Houses are also discussed at length in G. I. Jones, *The Trading States of the Oil Rivers* (London: Oxford University Press, 1963).

32 A. J. H. Latham, *Old Calabar, 1600–1891: The Impact of the International Economy upon a Traditional Society* (Oxford: Clarendon Press, 1973), 37–8.

33 As discussed in Lovejoy, *Transformations in Slavery*, 84–6, and in Pat Uche Okpoko and Paul Obi-Ani, "The making of an oligarchy in the Bight of Biafra: perspectives on the Aro ascendancy," in *Precolonial Nigeria*, 435–6.

34 Okpoko and Obi-Ani, "The making of an oligarchy," 437–8.

3 POLITICAL AND ECONOMIC TRANSFORMATIONS IN THE NINETEENTH CENTURY

1 More on these jihads and their relationship (or lack thereof) to the jihad of Usman dan Fodio can be found in Hiskett, *The Development of Islam*, 142–7.

2 An engaging biography of Usman dan Fodio is Mervyn Hiskett, *The Sword of Truth: The Life and Times of the Shehu Usman dan Fodio* (New York: Oxford University Press, 1973).

3 H. A. S. Johnston, *The Fulani Empire of Sokoto* (London: Oxford University Press, 1967), 28–9.

4 Murray Last, *The Sokoto Caliphate* (London: Longman, 1967), lxviii, 7–8.

5 Johnston, *The Fulani Empire*, 38.

6 Ibid.

7 Brief histories of all the emirates that made up the Sokoto Caliphate can be found in S. J. Hogben, *An Introduction to the History of the Islamic States of Northern Nigeria* (Ibadan: Oxford University Press, 1967).

8 Last, *The Sokoto Caliphate*, 69.

9 See chapter 2, this volume.

10 Johnston, *The Fulani Empire*, 128.

11 On the function and ideology of *ribats*, see Hiskett, *The Development of Islam*, 174–6, 188–9; and Last, *The Sokoto Caliphate*, 74–80, 229–31.

12 Sa'ad Abubakar, "The established caliphate: Sokoto, the emirates, and their neighbours," in *Groundwork of Nigerian History*, ed. Obaro Ikime (Ibadan: Heinemann Educational Books [Nigeria], 1980), 304; and Last, *The Sokoto Caliphate*, 160–1.

13 R. A. Adeleye, *Power and Diplomacy in Northern Nigeria, 1804–1906: The Sokoto Caliphate and Its Enemies* (New York: Humanities Press, 1971), 95. Adeleye actually presents the Buhari revolt as an indication of the strength of the Sokoto Caliphate at this time, in the sense that all the emirs supported the caliph in this dispute, against Buhari. See also Johnston, *The Fulani Empire*, 181–3; and Last, *The Sokoto Caliphate*, 88–9, 159–61.

14 A good, concise description of the Kano civil war can be found in Abubukar, "The established caliphate," 309–11. See also Adeleye, *Power and Diplomacy in Northern Nigeria*, 97–103; Johnston, *The Fulani Empire*, 181–3; and Last, *The Sokoto Caliphate*, 88–9, 159–61.

15 For instance, Trimingham, *A History of Islam*, presents a decidedly negative interpretation of the achievements of the Sokoto Caliphate.

16 Johnston, *The Fulani Empire*, 172. It does appear, however, that, for the most part, taxation was reformed to meet classical Islamic standards in the Sokoto Caliphate. See Hiskett, *The Development of Islam*, 183–4.

17 Slavery and enslavement are a major aspect of the analysis provided in Trimingham, *A History of Islam*. See also Abdullahi Mahadi, "The aftermath of the *jihad* in the central Sudan as a major factor in the volume of the trans-Saharan slave trade in the nineteenth century," in *The Human Commodity: Perspectives on the Trans-Saharan Slave Trade*, ed. Elizabeth Savage (London: Frank Cass, 1992), 111–28; and Beverley B. Mack, "Women and slavery in nineteenth century Hausaland," in *The Human Commodity*, 19–110.

18 A more complete description of this debate can be found in Johnston, *The Fulani Empire*, 105–10.

19 This is the interpretation taken in Johnston, *The Fulani Empire*, for example.

20 Debunking this interpretation is the primary goal of the essays in Y. B. Usman, ed., *Studies in the History of the Sokoto Caliphate: The Sokoto Seminar Papers* (Zaria: Ahmadu Bello University, Department of History, 1979).

21 Although Adeleye, *Power and Diplomacy*, 20, reminds us that "[t]o what extent the Fulani reaction was ethnocentric rather than religious cannot be definitely decided since the distinction between loyalty to kin and to religion cannot be demarcated beyond doubt."

22 This is the argument put forward in Last, *The Sokoto Caliphate*.

23 This is the analysis of Adeleye, *Power and Diplomacy*, 19–22.

24 Ibid., 20.

25 Although dan Fodio opposed praise of himself and of music in general unless it served a religious purpose. See Veit Ehrlemann, *Music and the Islamic Reform in the Early Sokoto Empire* (Stuttgart: Deutsche Morgenländische Gesellschaft, 1986).

26 Ibid., 233–5.

27 Mary Wren Bivins, *Telling Stories, Making Histories: Women, Words, and Islam in Nineteenth-century Hausaland and the Sokoto Caliphate* (Portsmouth, NH, and London: Heinemann, 2007), 126.

28 See Trimingham, *A History of Islam*, on this interpretation. See also Dean S. Gilliland, *African Religion Meets Islam: Religious Change in Northern Nigeria* (Latham, MD, and London: University Press of America, 1986); and Roman Loimeier, *Islamic Reform and Political Change in Northern Nigeria* (Evanston, IL: Northwestern University Press, 1997).

29 For more on Nupe activities in the eighteenth and nineteenth centuries, see Michael Mason, *Foundations of the Bida Kingdom* (Zaria: Ahmadu Bello University Press, 1981).

30 Law, *The Oyo Empire*, 263–4.

31 All these revolts against Oyo's authority are discussed in greater detail in Law, *The Oyo Empire*, chap. 13.

32 These wars and their tactics have been the subject of much detailed historical work, including J. F. A. Ajayi and Robert Smith, *Yoruba Warfare in the Nineteenth Century*, 2nd edn. (Cambridge: Cambridge University Press, 1971); J. F. A. Ajayi, "The aftermath of the fall of Old Oyo," in *History of West Africa*, vol. II, eds. J. F. A. Ajayi and Michael Crowder (New York: Columbia University Press, 1973), 129–66; Toyin Falola and G. O. Oguntomisin, *The*

Military in Nineteenth Century Yoruba Politics (Ile-Ife: University of Ife Press, 1984); and Toyin Falola and G. O. Oguntomisin, *Yoruba Warlords of the Nineteenth Century* (Trenton, NJ: Africa World Press, 2001).

33 Ajayi, "The aftermath of the fall of Old Oyo," 146–7.

34 For reasons that will be discussed in chapter 4, this volume.

35 David Northrup, *Trade without Rulers: Pre-colonial Economic Development in South-eastern Nigeria* (Oxford: Clarendon Press, 1978), 182–3.

36 Ibid.

37 Lovejoy, *Transformations in Slavery*, 146.

38 A. G. Hopkins, *An Economic History of West Africa* (New York: Columbia University Press, 1973), 113.

39 This argument is laid out concisely in David Northrup, "The compatibility of the slave and palm oil trades in the Bight of Biafra," *Journal of African History* 17, no. 3 (1976): 353–64.

40 This estimate comes from A. F. B. Bridges, "Report on oil palm survey in Ibo, Ibibio and Cross River area," 1938, appendix VII, p. 1, Rhodes House Library, Oxford, MSS. Afr. s. 679, cited in Northrup, *Trade without Rulers*, 186.

41 The degree and meaning of these changes have been the subject of rather intense historical debate, particularly over the relative importance of large-scale versus small-scale production of palm oil. For a detailed discussion of the various viewpoints, see Robin Law, "The historiography of the commercial transition in nineteenth-century west Africa," in *West African Historiography: Essays in Honour of Jacob Ade Ajayi*, ed. Toyin Falola (Harlow: Longman, 1993), 91–115.

42 Julian Clarke, "Households and the political economy of small-scale cash crop production in south-western Nigeria," *Africa* 51 (1981): 807–23; and Robin Law, "'Legitimate' trade and gender relations in Yorubaland and Dahomey," in *From Slave Trade to "Legitimate" Commerce: The Commercial Transition in Nineteenth-century West Africa*, ed. Robin Law (Cambridge: Cambridge University Press, 1995), 195–214.

43 As discussed in Lovejoy, *Transformations in Slavery*, 179–80.

44 Ibid., 187.

45 For a discussion of gender roles in palm oil production, see Law, "'Legitimate' trade and gender relations." Similar gender roles existed in the southeast. See Susan Martin, "Slaves, Igbo women and palm oil in the nineteenth century," in *From Slave Trade to "Legitimate" Commerce*, 172–94.

46 J. N. Oriji, "A re-assessment of the organisation and benefits of the slave and palm produce trade amongst the Ngwa-Igbo," *Canadian Journal of African Studies* 16, no. 3 (1982): 542.

47 For a detailed discussion of slave mobility in the Lagos area, see Kristin Mann, "Owners, slaves and the struggle for labour in the commercial transition at Lagos," in *From Slave Trade to "Legitimate" Commerce*, 144–71.

48 Ja Ja's remarkable story can be found in most general histories of Nigeria or west Africa. Perhaps one of the best and most detailed descriptions is contained in the classic work by K. O. Dike, *Trade and Politics in the Niger*

Delta, 1830–1885 (Oxford: Clarendon Press, 1956), 182–202. A similar discussion of slave opportunities related to the palm oil trade in Calabar can be found in Latham, *Old Calabar*, 91–102.

49 A broad discussion of this process across west Africa can be found in Martin Lynn, "The west African palm oil trade in the nineteenth century and the 'crisis of adaptation,'" in *From Slave Trade to "Legitimate" Commerce*, 57–77.

50 Martin, "Slaves, Igbo women and palm oil," 181–9.

51 Latham, *Old Calabar*, 96–102, 111–12.

4 TRANSITION TO BRITISH COLONIAL RULE, 1850 – 1903

1 The spread of Christian missions in the second half of the nineteenth century has been a highly researched topic. For the spread of Christianity in Nigeria generally, see J. F. A. Ajayi, *The Christian Missions in Nigeria, 1841–1891: The Making of a New Elite* (Evanston, IL: Northwestern University Press, 1965); E. A. Ayandele, *The Missionary Impact on Modern Nigeria, 1842–1914: A Political and Social Analysis* (New York: Humanities Press, 1967); and Michael Crowder, *The Story of Nigeria*, 3rd edn. (London: Faber and Faber, 1973), 134–49. For the spread of Christianity in Yorubaland, see James Bertin Webster, *The African Churches among the Yoruba, 1888–1922* (Oxford: Clarendon Press, 1964); J. D. Y. Peel, *Religious Encounter and the Making of the Yoruba* (Bloomington: Indiana University Press, 2000); and Jean Hersokvits Kopytoff, *A Preface to Modern Nigeria: The "Sierra Leonians" in Yoruba, 1830–1890* (Madison: University of Wisconsin Press, 1965). For the Niger delta region and the southeast, see G. O. M. Tasie, *Christian Missionary Enterprise in the Niger Delta, 1864–1918* (Leiden: E. J. Brill, 1978); and F. K. Ekechi, *Missionary Enterprise and Rivalry in Igboland, 1857–1914* (London: Frank Cass, 1971); as well as E. A. Ayandele's critique of Ekechi in E. A. Ayandele, "The collapse of 'pagandom' in Igboland," in *Nigerian Historical Studies*, ed. E. A. Ayandele (London: Frank Cass, 1979), 167–91. On the arrest of Christianity in the north, see E. A. Ayandele, "The missionary factor in northern Nigeria, 1870–1918," in *Nigerian Historical Studies*, 138–66.

2 Johnson's *The History of the Yorubas* has, in fact, been the foundational source for Yoruba history since its publication in 1921. Johnson was himself the son of recaptive slaves who moved back to Nigeria from Sierra Leone. He became an Anglican pastor in 1876 and spent the better part of his career compiling the manuscript of his *History*, which was completed in 1897 but not published until decades later. On the importance of Johnson's work to Yoruba historiography, see Toyin Falola, ed., *Pioneer, Patriot and Patriarch: Samuel Johnson and the Yoruba People* (Madison: University of Wisconsin – Madison, African Studies Program, 1991). For the contribution of missionaries such as James Frederick Schön and Samuel Ajayi Crowther to the study of language in the Niger delta area and among the Igbo, see Ajayi, *The Christian Missions*, 127–30; and Ekechi, *Missionary Enterprise*, 228. For more sources on the early writings of missionaries on Nigerian languages, see P. E. H. Hair, *The Early*

Study of Nigerian Languages: Essays and Bibliographies (Cambridge: Cambridge University Press, 1967).

3 The role of recaptive slaves in the spread of Christianity in west Africa is the focus of Kopytoff, *A Preface to Modern Nigeria*, as well as Lamin Sanneh, *Abolitionists Abroad: American Blacks and the Making of Modern West Africa* (Cambridge, MA: Harvard University Press, 2001).

4 Few missionaries, however, especially Nigerian ones, promoted the full-scale colonization that eventually occurred. Samuel Ajayi Crowther went to London to ask for British intermediation over the Kosoko affair, asking that the British support Akitoye's claim to the throne but not suggesting that the British take over the administration of Lagos completely. Crowther protested when a British gunship shelled Onitsha over trade disputes in 1879, claiming that force could not be used to promote free trade. The role of Christian missionaries in local politics can be found throughout Crowder's elaboration on the transition to British colonial rule in *The Story of Nigeria*, 134–84.

5 See chapter 3, this volume.

6 The perils of the trust system are discussed at length in Dike, *Trade and Politics in the Niger Delta*, 108–27; Latham, *Old Calabar*, 79–90; and Obaro Ikime, *The Fall of Nigeria: The British Conquest* (London: Heinemann, 1977), 15–35.

7 The process of river Niger exploration is also neatly summed up in Crowder, *The Story of Nigeria*, 134–49.

8 Mungo Park's book detailing the experience of his early expeditions became a best-seller in the United Kingdom. Mungo Park, *Travels in the Interior Districts of Africa, in 1795, 1796, and 1797, etc.* (London, 1799).

9 In actuality, the Conference of Berlin established rules for territorial acquisition only on the coasts, leaving the interior open for future dispute. As the scramble continued and interior territories became more and more important, however, it became clear to all that the validity of treaties could be contested but "effective occupation" could not be so easily undermined. Therefore, by 1885 the true signifier of control of an area in the interior was not the possession of a treaty but the ability to defend the territory against military aggression, as in the case of Goldie's conflict with French forces at Bussa, discussed below. For more on the "Scramble for Africa," see Thomas Pakenham, *The Scramble for Africa: White Man's Conquest of the Dark Continent from 1876–1912* (New York: Avon Books, 1991); and H. L. Wesseling, *Divide and Rule: The Partition of Africa, 1880–1914*, trans. Arnold J. Pomerans (Westport, CT: Praeger, 1996).

10 See Ikime, *The Fall of Nigeria*, 112–18.

11 This was done even though Old Town had not even been a signatory to the 1850 treaty. Ibid., 107–8.

12 The story of Ja Ja's resistance can be found in greater detail in Sylvanus Cookey, *King Jaja of the Niger Delta: His Life and Times, 1821–1891* (New York: NOK Publishers, 1974), 103–60; and see Ikime, *The Fall of Nigeria*, 40–3.

13 For detailed discussion of Nana's resistance, see Obaro Ikime, *Merchant Prince of the Niger Delta: The Rise and Fall of Nana Olomu, Last Governor of the Benin River* (London: Heinemann, 1968).

14 For a detailed discussion of the fall of Benin, see Ryder, *Benin and the Europeans*.

15 The most authoritative work on Goldie and the Royal Niger Company is John E. Flint, *Sir George Goldie and the Making of Modern Nigeria* (London: Oxford University Press, 1960), which, while perhaps overly flattering with regard to the personal characteristics of Goldie, is nevertheless relatively critical of the ideology and practices of the Royal Niger Company itself.

16 Detailed discussions of the Brass revolt can be found in Flint, *Sir George Goldie*, 187–215; and Ikime, *The Fall of Nigeria*, 130–44.

17 This crisis that led ultimately to the revocation of the company's charter is discussed in detail in Flint, *Sir George Goldie*, 264–94.

18 The company continued to trade on the river, however, without any administrative power.

19 An explication of the fall of the Sokoto Caliphate can be found in a number of sources. Among the most explicit are Ikime, *The Fall of Nigeria*, 62–90, 185–209; Adeleye, *Power and Diplomacy*, 213–313; Richard R. Dusgate, *The Conquest of Northern Nigeria* (London: Frank Cass, 1985); and Risto Marjomaa, *War on the Savannah: The Military Collapse of the Sokoto Caliphate under the Invasion of the British Empire, 1897–1903* (Helsinki: Academia Scientiarum Fennica, 1998).

20 On the fall of Borno, see Ikime, *The Fall of Nigeria*, 178–84.

21 The campaign against the Aro is the main focus of A. E. Afigbo, "The Aro Expedition of 1901–1902: an episode in the British occupation of Iboland," *Odu: A Journal of West African Studies*, New Series, no. 7 (1972), reprinted in Falola, ed., *Igbo History and Society*, 321–40.

22 Don C. Ohadike, *The Ekumeku Movement: Western Igbo Resistance to the British Conquest of Nigeria, 1883–1914* (Athens, OH: Ohio University Press, 1991), is a full-length account of Ekumeku activity over the period of the organization's existence.

23 This point is raised repeatedly in Ikime, *The Fall of Nigeria*. Treaties with the emirs and caliphs of Sokoto are treated in Ayandele, *Power and Diplomacy*, 117–64.

5 COLONIAL SOCIETY TO 1929

1 Lord Lugard, *The Dual Mandate in British Tropical Africa*, 5th edn. (London: Archon Books, 1965).

2 A. E. Afigbo, *The Warrant Chiefs: Indirect Rule in Southeastern Nigeria, 1891–1929* (London: Longman, 1972), 55. Other important works on indirect rule in eastern Nigeria include Harry A. Gailey, *The Road to Aba: A Study of British Administrative Policy in Eastern Nigeria* (New York: New York University Press, 1970); Elizabeth Isichei, *A History of the Igbo People* (London: Macmillan,

1976), 140–60; and I. F. Nicholson, *The Administration of Nigeria 1900–1960: Men, Methods and Myths* (Oxford: Clarendon Press, 1969), 82–124.

3 See, for example, Afigbo, "The indigenous political systems of the Igbo," 155–66.

4 Afigbo, *The Warrant Chiefs*, 56–77, discusses the various processes by which warrant chiefs were chosen and empowered.

5 On colonial administration in Lagos, see, for example, Nicholson, *The Administration of Nigeria*, 46–81; T. N. Tamuno, *The Evolution of the Nigerian State: The Southern Phase, 1898–1914* (London: Longman, 1972); and Robert S. Smith, *The Lagos Consulate, 1851–1861* (London: Macmillan, 1978).

6 Tanumo, *The Evolution of the Nigerian State*, 82. On colonial administration in southwestern Nigeria, see Nicholson, *The Administration of Nigeria*, 46–81.

7 Lord Lugard, *Report on the Amalgamation of Northern and Southern Nigeria* (London: HM Stationery Office, 1920), 14–15, quoted in Crowder, *The Story of Nigeria*, 245.

8 For glowing reports on colonial administration in northern Nigeria and Lugard's form of indirect rule, see Margery Perham, *Native Administration in Nigeria* (London: Oxford University Press, 1937); and Robert Heussler, *The British in Northern Nigeria* (London: Oxford University Press, 1968). For a more critical perspective, see Nicholson, *The Administration of Nigeria*, 124–79.

9 Nicholson, *The Administration of Nigeria*, 54–5.

10 A. E. Afigbo, "Sir Ralph Moor and the economic development of southern Nigeria: 1896–1903," in *Nigerian History, Politics and Affairs: The Collected Essays of Adiele Afigbo*, ed. Toyin Falola (Trenton, NJ: Africa World Press, 2005), 185–212.

11 Crowder, *The Story of Nigeria*, 240.

12 In fact, "Protectorate of Southern Nigeria" had been the official name of the Niger Coast Protectorate since 1900.

13 For instance, Lugard believed that to allow native courts to fill their treasuries with court fines and fees tempted warrant chiefs to abuse their power, imposing outrageous fines in order to fill their coffers. See Afigbo, *The Warrant Chiefs*, 145–6.

14 On economic policy in colonial Nigeria, see R. Olufemi Ekundare, *An Economic History of Nigeria 1860–1960* (London: Methuen, 1973); Hopkins, *An Economic History of West Africa*, 167–292; W. I. Ofonagoro, *Trade and Imperialism in Southern Nigeria, 1881–1929* (New York: Nok, 1979); and Toyin Falola, ed., *Britain and Nigeria: Exploitation or Development?* (London: Zed Books, 1987).

15 Ekundare, *An Economic History of Nigeria*, 166–72, contains several tables indicating the growth in these export commodities between 1900 and 1944.

16 For instance, gold exports in 1914 stood at 350 ounces. In 1916–17 exports were over 2,000 ounces. By 1929, however, exports of gold had dropped to a mere 192 ounces. See Ekundare, *An Economic History of Nigeria*, 181; see also Toyin Falola, "'An ounce is good enough': the gold industry in colonial southwestern Nigeria," *African Economic History* no. 20 (1992): 27–50.

17 Ekundare, *An Economic History of Nigeria*, 182–4; and A. G. Adebayo and Toyin Falola, "Production for the metropolis: the extractive industries," in Falola, *Britain and Nigeria*, 96–7.

18 Ekundare, *An Economic History of Nigeria*, 179.

19 Railway construction is discussed more extensively in Ekundare, *An Economic History of Nigeria*, 134–42.

20 Crowder, *The Story of Nigeria*, 233–4.

21 Ekundare, *An Economic History of Nigeria*, 172.

22 Akinjide Osuntokun, *Nigeria in the First World War* (London: Longman, 1979), 25–6.

23 O. N. Njoku, "Trading with the metropolis: an unequal exchange," in Falola, *Britain and Nigeria*, 127.

24 Adebayo and Falola, "Production for the metropolis," 95.

25 Ekundare, *An Economic History of Nigeria*, 175–6.

26 Sara S. Berry, *Cocoa, Custom, and Socio-economic Change in Rural Western Nigeria* (Oxford: Clarendon Press, 1975), 168–9. Berry goes on to note that in Ilorin many people chose not to roof their houses with iron sheets lest the British authorities should think people were getting too wealthy and raise their taxes.

27 This was not always the case, however. Don C. Ohadike, "Exploitation of labour: waged and forced," in Falola, *Britain and Nigeria*, 151–2, points out that, in the Agbor district of western Igboland, forced laborers were often sent to work on the railway lines for five days at a time. At the end of their tour, they were sent away without pay.

28 The authoritative text on labor conditions among tin miners in colonial Nigeria is W. M. Freund, *Capital and Labour in the Nigerian Tin Mines* (London: Routledge and Kegan Paul, 1981).

29 Sara S. Berry, "Christianity and the rise of cocoa-growing in Ibadan and Ondo," *Journal of the Historical Society of Nigeria* 4, no. 3 (1969): 439–51.

30 Ekundare, *An Economic History of Nigeria*, 187.

31 S. A. Olanrewaju, "The infrastructure of exploitation: transport, monetary changes, banking, etc.," in Falola, *Britain and Nigeria*, 71–2.

32 For the effects of colonial rule on one urban center, see Toyin Falola, *Politics and Economy in Ibadan 1893–1945* (Lagos: Modelor, 1989).

33 W. M. Freund, "Labor migration to the northern Nigerian tin mines, 1903–1945," *Journal of African History* 22 (1981): 76.

34 S. A. Aluko, "How many Nigerians: an analysis of Nigeria's census problems, 1901–1963," *Journal of Modern African Studies* 3, no. 3 (1965): 372. By 1951 the population of Lagos had risen to 272,000, and by 1963 it had risen to 675,000. For a more current account, see Hakeem Ibikunle Tijani, "Census: a factor in Nigeria's instability – lessons for the 1991 head counts," in *Readings in Selected Nigerian Problems*, ed. S. Johnson (Lagos: Okanlawon, 1990), 30–8.

35 On Nigerian troops in the First World War, see Osuntokun, *Nigeria in the First World War*, 169–290. On the influenza pandemic of 1918–19 in Nigeria, see Don C. Ohadike, "The influenza pandemic of 1918–19 and the spread of

cassava cultivation on the lower Niger: a case study in historical linkages," *Journal of African History* 22 (1981): 379–91. It is estimated that the influenza pandemic killed as much as 3 percent of Nigeria's entire population, exacerbating labor shortages at a time when labor was already scarce.

36 Although Susan Martin, "Gender and innovation: farming, cooking and palm processing in the Ngwa region, south-eastern Nigeria, 1900–30," *Journal of African History* 25, no. 4 (1984): 424, argues that, over time, young men began to engage in cassava production.

37 Two recent works on the role of women in the colonial economy of southeastern Nigeria are Nwando Achebe, *Farmers, Traders, Warriors, and Kings: Female Power and Authority in Northern Igboland, 1900–1960* (Portsmouth, NH: Heinemann, 2005); and Gloria Chuku, *Igbo Women and Economic Transformation in Southeastern Nigeria, 1900–1960* (New York: Routledge, 2005).

38 Jane I. Guyer, "Food, cocoa and the division of labor by sex in two west African societies," *Comparative Studies in Society and History* 22, no. 3 (1980): 368–9. It should be noted, however, that Berry, *Cocoa, Custom, and Socio-economic change*, 171, argues that it is difficult to determine the extent to which this amounted to a transformation in women's roles during the colonial period, since the extent to which women were involved in the import economy in pre-colonial times remains undetermined.

39 For more on Bishop Crowther, see chapter 4, this volume.

40 Philip S. Zachernuk, *Colonial Subjects: An African Intelligentsia and Atlantic Ideas* (Charlottesville: University of Virginia Press, 2000), 50–1.

41 Ibid.

42 Ibid., 48–9.

43 A. Babs Fafunwa, *History of Education in Nigeria* (London: George Allen and Unwin, 1974), 110–12. Lugard's Education Ordinance, passed in 1916, did allow for schools to receive grants-in-aid from the government, but, in order to receive this money, schools had to agree to government inspections and to restrict their religious teachings. Most mission schools declined the offer.

44 Zachernuk, *Colonial Subjects*, 50; Fafunwa, *History of Education*, 112, says that primary school enrollment in southern Nigeria in 1913 was 35,716, compared to a mere 1,131 in northern Nigeria.

45 At least to a greater extent than other social groups. On the marriage practices of the European-educated middle class in colonial Nigeria, see Kristin Mann, *Marrying Well: Marriage, Status and Social Change among the Educated Elite in Colonial Lagos* (Cambridge: Cambridge University Press, 1985).

46 On elite consumption patterns, see H. H. Smythe and M. M. Smythe, *The New Nigerian Elite* (Stanford, CA: Stanford University Press, 1971); Olufunke Adeboye, "Elite lifestyle and consumption in colonial Ibadan," in *The Foundations of Nigeria: Essays in Honor of Toyin Falola*, ed. Adebayo Oyebade (Trenton, NJ: Africa World Press, 2003), 281–303; and H. I. Tijani, "The career of Seriki Abass (Faremi Williams) in Badagry, 1870–1919," in *Badagry: A Study in History, Culture and Traditions of an Ancient City*, ed.

G. O. Ogunremi, M. O. Opeloye, and S. Oyeweso (Ibadan: Rex Charles, 1994), 354–64.

47 Margery Perham, *Lugard: The Years of Authority, 1898–1945* (London: Collins, 1960), 586.

48 See chapter 4, note 2, this volume, for a discussion of the historical writings of European-educated Nigerians.

49 For a more specific discussion of African churches in Nigeria, see Webster, *The African Churches among the Yoruba*; and Ayandele, *The Missionary Impact on Modern Nigeria.*

50 Fred I. A. Omu, *Press and Politics in Nigeria, 1880–1937* (London: Longman, 1978), 26.

51 Although the colonial government went ahead with the scheme, it continued to be a thorny political issue for the government for several years. See Tamuno, *The Evolution of the Nigerian State*, 113–21; and Omu, *Press and Politics*, 222–7.

52 Crowder, *The Story of Nigeria*, 247–8.

53 Nina Emma Mba, *Nigerian Women Mobilized: Women's Political Activity in Southern Nigeria, 1900–1965* (Berkeley: Institute of International Studies, University of California, Berkeley, 1982), 135–9.

54 Crowder, *The Story of Nigeria*, 259–61.

55 With certain restrictions. To vote, one had to have been a resident of Lagos for twelve months and to have an annual income of at least £100. Herbert Macaulay's National Democratic Party won all three seats in 1923, 1928, and 1933. Crowder, *The Story of Nigeria*, 256–7.

56 Michael Mason, "The history of Mr. Johnson: progress and protest in northern Nigeria, 1900–1921," *Canadian Journal of African Studies* 27, no. 2 (1993): 196–217.

6 NATIONALIST MOVEMENTS AND INDEPENDENCE, 1929 – 1960

1 On the concept of race consciousness and west African nationalism, see Toyin Falola, *Nationalism and African Intellectuals* (Rochester, NY: University of Rochester Press, 2001), 97–180; P. Olisanwuche Esedebe, *Pan-Africanism: The Idea and the Movement, 1776–1991*, 2nd edn. (Washington, DC: Howard University Press, 1994), 3–94; and Hakeem Adi, *West Africans in Britain, 1900–1960: Nationalism, Pan-Africanism and Communism* (London: Lawrence and Wishart, 1998). On the concept in Nigeria specifically, see James S. Coleman, *Nigeria: Background to Nationalism* (Berkeley: University of California Press, 1963), 141–229; and Zachernuk, *Colonial Subjects*, 19–79.

2 See chapter 5, this volume.

3 Zachernuk, *Colonial Subjects*, 85–6.

4 Compiled from table 14, "Differential development of Western education in southern and northern Nigeria," in Coleman, *Nigeria*, 134.

5 Ibid., 214.

6 Ekundare, *An Economic History of Nigeria*, 367–74. For a more in-depth analysis of trade unions in colonial Nigeria, see Wogu Ananaba, *The Trade Union Movement in Nigeria* (New York: Africana, 1970).

7 Ekundare, *An Economic History of Nigeria*, 377.

8 For more on the role of women as anti-colonial and nationalist activists, see Mba, *Nigerian Women Mobilized*. For a fascinating biography of Ms. Ransome-Kuti, see Cheryl Johnson-Odim and Nina Emma Mba, *For Women and the Nation: Funmilayo Ransome-Kuti of Nigeria* (Urbana and Chicago: University of Illinois Press, 1997).

9 Zachernuk, *Colonial Subjects*, 224–9.

10 Michael Crowder, *The Story of Nigeria*, 4th edn. (London: Faber and Faber, 1978), 263.

11 Michael Crowder, *West Africa under Colonial Rule* (London: Hutchinsons, 1968), 301.

12 On the effect of the Second World War on political activism in Nigeria, see G. O. Olusanya, *The Second World War and Politics in Nigeria 1939–1953* (Lagos: University of Lagos and Evans Brothers, 1973).

13 These are the numbers given in Coleman, *Nigeria*, 259.

14 Later the National Council of Nigerian Citizens.

15 Azikiwe's autobiography provides a personal look at the development of Nigeria's most influential nationalist. See Nnamdi Azikiwe, *My Odyssey: An Autobiography* (London: C. Hurst, 1970).

16 On Zikism and other left-wing movements in Nigeria, see Hakeem Ibikunle Tijani, *Britain, Leftist Nationalists and the Transfer of Power in Nigeria, 1945–1965* (New York and London: Routledge, 2006).

17 Ekundare, *An Economic History of Nigeria*, 357.

18 On the growth of university education in Nigeria, see Nduka Okafor, *The Development of Universities in Nigeria* (London: Longman, 1971).

19 On development planning in Nigeria, see Toyin Falola, *Development Planning and Decolonization in Nigeria* (Gainesville: University Press of Florida, 1996); and Toyin Falola, *Economic Reforms and Modernization in Nigeria, 1945–1965* (Kent, OH, and London: Kent State University Press, 2004).

20 Ekundare, *An Economic History of Nigeria*, 225.

21 Coleman, *Nigeria*, 313.

22 On the issue of the *shari'a*, see Jonathan T. Reynolds, *The Time of Politics (Zamanin Siyasa): Islam and the Politics of Legitimacy in Northern Nigeria, 1950–1966* (San Francisco: International Scholars Publications, 1999), 83–104. On the role of tradition in northern Nigerian political development, see C. S. Whitaker, Jr., *The Politics of Tradition: Continuity and Change in Northern Nigeria, 1946–1966* (Princeton, NJ: Princeton University Press, 1970).

23 Awolowo's autobiography tells the story of his rise to political greatness. See Obafemi Awolowo, *Awo: The Autobiography of Chief Obafemi Awolowo* (Cambridge: Cambridge University Press, 1960).

24 On the rise of political consciousness in the north, see Reynolds, *The Time of Politics*; J. B. Dudley, *Parties and Politics in Northern Nigeria* (London: Frank

Cass, 1968); and Alhaji Mahmood Yakubu, *An Aristocracy in Political Crisis: The End of Indirect Rule and the Emergence of Party Politics in the Emirates of Northern Nigeria* (Brookfield, VT: Ashgate, 1996).

25 On the growth of political parties in Nigeria, see, for example, Richard Sklar, *Nigerian Political Parties: Power in an Emergent African Nation* (Princeton, NJ: Princeton University Press, 1963); and Coleman, *Nigeria*.

26 The NCNC continued to contend strongly in the Western Region, however. In 1954 the NCNC actually gained more seats than the AG in the central legislature, twenty-three to eighteen, as explained in Crowder, *The Story of Nigeria*, 289.

27 Mensah was actually from the Gold Coast (Ghana), but he built up a wide following in the cities of Nigeria in the 1950s, once again illustrating their cosmopolitan nature.

28 For more on the development of post-war musical styles in Nigeria, see E. J. Collins, "Post-war popular band music in west Africa," *African Arts* 10, no. 3 (1977): 53–60; and Afolabi Alaja-Browne, "The origin and development of juju music," *The Black Perspective in Music* 17, no. 1–2 (1989): 55–72.

29 See H. I. Tijani, ed., *Nigeria's Urban History: Past and Present* (Lanham, MD: University Press of America, 2006).

7 INSTABILITY AND CIVIL WAR, 1960 – 1970

1 Historians and political scientists have written much on this topic. Good concise overviews of the various ways in which the national question has affected Nigerian society and institutions can be found in Abubakar Momoh and Said Adejumobi, eds., *The National Question in Nigeria: Comparative Perspectives* (Aldershot, UK, and Burlington, VT: Ashgate, 2002).

2 Technically, Nigeria did not become a republic until 1963, when the Nigerian constitution was amended to make Governor General Azikiwe the first president of Nigeria, replacing Queen Elizabeth II and becoming the first Nigerian head of state. Nevertheless, the entire period from 1960 to 1966 is customarily referred to as the First Republic.

3 Chinua Achebe, *Things Fall Apart* (London: Heinemann, 1958).

4 Amos Tutuola, *The Palm-wine Drinkard and His Dead Palm-wine Tapster in the Deads' Town* (London: Faber and Faber, 1952).

5 Wole Soyinka, *A Dance of the Forests* (London: Oxford University Press, 1963).

6 Wole Soyinka, *The Swamp Dwellers* (London: Oxford University Press, 1963).

7 Much of the above analysis comes from Dapo Adelugba, "The development of drama and theatre in Nigeria," in *Nigeria since Independence: The First Twenty-five Years*, vol. VII, *Culture*, eds. Peter P. Ekeh and Garba Ashinwaju (Ibadan: Heinemann Educational Books, 1989), 66.

8 On English language as a cultural medium in Nigeria, see Umaru Ahmed, "The cultural content in Nigerian education: the language curriculum," in *Nigeria since Independence*, vol. VII, *Culture*, 32–59.

9 On the growth and value of the use of oral history in Nigerian scholarship, see, for instance, any of the chapters in Toyin Falola, ed., *Myth, History and Society: The Collected Works of Adiele Afigbo* (Trenton, NJ: Africa World Press, 2006).

10 For more on the visual arts, see Gani Odutokun, "Art in Nigeria since independence," in *Nigeria since Independence*, vol. VII, *Culture*, 139–51.

11 On the growth of university education in independent Nigeria, see Fafunwa, *History of Education in Nigeria*, 202–6.

12 For more on development planning in the 1960s, see Falola, *Economic Reforms and Modernization in Nigeria*.

13 Eghosa E. Osaghae, *Crippled Giant: Nigeria since Independence* (London: C. Hurst, 1998), 50.

14 For a more detailed analysis of the federal structure of the First Republic, see Uma O. Eleazu, *Federalism and Nation-building: The Nigerian Experience, 1954–64* (Ilfracombe, UK: Arthur H. Stockwell, 1977); Eme O. Awa, *Federal Government in Nigeria* (Berkeley and Los Angeles: University of California Press, 1964); John P. Mackintosh, *Nigerian Government and Politics* (London: George Allen and Unwin, 1966); and William D. Graf, *The Nigerian State: Political Economy, State Class and Political System in the Post-colonial Era* (London: James Currey, 1988), 1–40.

15 N. Miners, *The Nigerian Military: 1956–1966* (London: Methuen, 1971), 52, claims that, at independence, two-thirds of all commissioned officers in the military came from the Eastern Region, and half of those were Igbo.

16 On the history of the military in Nigeria, see Said Adejumobi, "The military and the national question," in *The National Question in Nigeria*, 155–82; and Siyan Oyeweso, *Perspectives on the Nigerian Civil War* (Lagos: Campus Press, 1992).

17 J. B. Dudley, *An Introduction to Nigerian Government and Politics* (London: Macmillan, 1982), 63.

18 Osaghae, *Crippled Giant*, 41.

19 Quoted in ibid., 42.

20 The populations of the southern regions in the 1963 census were as follows: East – 12,394,462; West – 10,265,846; Mid-west – 2,535,839; Lagos – 665,246.

21 A particularly in-depth analysis of the elections of 1964 and 1965 can be found in Kenneth Post and Michael Vickers, *Structure and Conflict in Nigeria, 1960–1966* (London: Heinemann, 1973).

22 Ibid., 168–9.

23 Osaghae, *Crippled Giant*, 44–5.

24 Post and Vickers, *Structure and Conflict*, 221–2.

25 A detailed description of the January coup and the Ironsi regime can be found in John de St. Jorre, *The Brothers' War: Biafra and Nigeria* (Boston: Houghton Mifflin, 1972), 27–64. On the significance of the military coups of 1966, see, for example, Toyin Falola, A. Ajayi, A. Alao, and B. Babawale, *The Military Factor in Nigeria, 1966–1985* (Lewiston, NY: Edwin Mellen Press, 1994).

26 Quoted in Osaghae, *Crippled Giant*, 57.
27 Many works have been written on the Nigerian Civil War. Among the most descriptive are de St. Jorre, *The Brothers' War*; John de St. Jorre, *The Nigerian Civil War* (London: Hodder and Stoughton, 1972); Joseph Okpaku, ed., *Nigeria: Dilemma of Nationhood, an African Analysis of the Biafran Conflict* (New York: Third Press, 1972); Sir Rex Niven, *The War of Nigerian Unity* (Ibadan and London: Evans Brothers, 1970); Tekena N. Tamuno and Samson C. Ukpabi, eds., *Nigeria since Independence: The First Twenty-Five Years*, vol. VI, *The War Years* (Ibadan: Heinemann Educational Books Ltd., 1989); and Oyeweso, *Perspectives*.
28 De St. Jorre, *The Brothers' War*, 225.
29 For a view of life inside Biafra during the war, see Bernard Odugwu, *No Place to Hide (Crises and Conflicts inside Biafra)* (Enugu: Fourth Dimension, 1985).
30 For more on the international dimensions of the war, see de St. Jorre, *The Brothers' War*, 233–366; John J. Stremlau, *The International Politics of the Nigerian Civil War, 1967–70* (Princeton, NJ: Princeton University Press, 1977); Suzanne Cronje, *The World and Nigeria: The Diplomatic History of the Biafran War 1967–1970* (London: Sidgwick and Jackson, 1972); and Oyeweso, *Perspectives*.

8 OIL, STATE, AND SOCIETY, 1970 – 1983

1 Several comprehensive works on the military regimes of the 1970s exist. See, for instance, O. Oyediran, ed., *Nigerian Government and Politics under Military Rule, 1966–1979* (London: Macmillan, 1979); K. Panter-Brick, ed., *Soldiers and Oil: The Political Transformation of Nigeria* (London: Frank Cass, 1978); T. O. Odetola, *Military Politics in Nigeria: Economic Development and Political Stability* (New Brunswick, NJ: Transaction Books, 1978); and A. Kirk-Greene and D. Rimmer, *Nigeria since 1970* (London: Hodder and Stoughton, 1981). For a comprehensive look at the civilian administration of the Second Republic, see R. Joseph, *Democracy and Prebendal Politics in Nigeria: The Rise and Fall of the Second Republic* (Cambridge: Cambridge University Press, 1987); and Toyin Falola and Julius Ihonvbere, *The Rise and Fall of Nigeria's Second Republic, 1979–1984* (London: Zed Books, 1985).
2 Federal Office of Statistics, *National Accounts of Nigeria, 1960–61, 1975–76* (Lagos: Federal Office of Statistics, 1977).
3 Forrest, *Politics and Economic Development*, 134.
4 Ibid.
5 Ibid.
6 For a more detailed discussion of the characteristics of the Nigerian oil economy, see J. K. Onoh, *The Nigerian Oil Economy: From Prosperity to Glut* (New York: St. Martin's Press, 1983); Sarah Ahmad Khan, *Nigeria: The Political Economy of Oil* (New York: Oxford University Press, 1994); Goddy Ikeh, *Nigerian Oil Industry: The First Three Decades (1958–1988)* (Lagos: Starledger

Communications, 1991); and A. A. Ikein, *The Impact of Oil on a Developing Country* (New York: Praeger, 1990). To see how the Nigerian oil economy compares to those of other oil-producing countries, see Toyin Falola and Ann Genova, *The Politics of the Global Oil Industry* (Westport, CT: Praeger, 2005).

7 Osaghae, *Crippled Giant*, 78.

8 Forrest, *Politics and Economic Development*, 136.

9 Ibid., 57.

10 On the ambivalent reaction of NYSC participants to their year of service, see Otwini Marenin, "National service and national consciousness in Nigeria," *Journal of Modern African Studies* 17, no. 4 (1979): 629–54.

11 For more on the controversy surrounding Abuja. see chapter 9, this volume.

12 Andrew Apter, *The Pan-African Nation: Oil and the Spectacle of Culture in Nigeria* (Chicago: University of Chicago Press, 2005), 47.

13 Ibid., 202–3.

14 Osaghae, *Crippled Giant*, 98–9.

15 On the life and work of Fela Kuti, see Tejumola Olaniyan, *Arrest the Music! Fela and His Rebel Art and Politics* (Bloomington: Indiana University Press, 2004).

16 Osaghae, *Crippled Giant*, 92.

17 Forrest, *Politics and Economic Development*, 86.

18 Ibid., 134.

19 Osaghae, *Crippled Giant*, 155–6.

20 On the role of the press in the Second Republic, see Adigun A.B. Agbaje, *The Nigerian Press, Hegemony, and the Social Construction of Legitimacy, 1960–1983* (Lewiston, NY: Edwin Mellen Press, 1992), 176–99.

21 Falola and Ihonvbere, *The Rise and Fall*, 155.

22 Ibid. 160–1.

23 For a much more in-depth look at the Maitatsine riots and religious violence in Nigeria since the 1970s, see Toyin Falola, *Violence in Nigeria: The Crisis of Religious Politics and Secular Ideologies* (Rochester, NY: University of Rochester Press, 1998).

9 CIVIL SOCIETY AND DEMOCRATIC TRANSITION, 1984 – 2007

1 Michael Bratton, *Democratic Experiments in Africa: Regime Transitions in Comparative Perspective* (Cambridge: Cambridge University Press, 1997).

2 On the civil society resurgence in Nigeria since the 1980s, see, for example, Matthew Hassan Kukah, *Democracy and Civil Society in Nigeria* (Oxford: Africa Books Collective, 1999); and Rita Kiki Edozie, *People Power and Democracy: The Popular Movement against Military Despotism in Nigeria, 1989–1999* (Trenton, NJ: Africa World Press, 2002).

3 Forrest, *Politics and Economic Development*, 219.

4 Much has been written on the effects of the SAP on Nigeria. See, for example, Effiong Essien, *Nigeria under Structural Adjustment* (Ibadan: Fountain Publications, 1990).

5 Osaghae, *Crippled Giant*, 203.
6 Forrest, *Politics and Economic Development*, 219.
7 Osaghae, *Crippled Giant*, 205.
8 Ibid., 204.
9 Ibid., 206.
10 Forrest, *Politics and Economic Development*, 242–3.
11 For an in-depth discussion of the Charismatic movement in Nigeria, see Matthews A. Ojo, *End-time Army: Charismatic Movements in Modern Nigeria* (Trenton, NJ: Africa World Press, 2006).
12 Osaghae, *Crippled Giant*, 249–51.
13 Devesh Kapur and John McHale, *The Global Migration of Talent: What Does It Mean for Developing Countries?* (Washington, DC: Center for Global Development, 2005).
14 On the life and times of Chief Abiola, see Yemi Ogunbiyi and Chidi Amuta, *Legend of Our Time: The Thoughts of M. K. O. Abiola* (Lagos: Tanus Communications, 1993).
15 For more on Saro-Wiwa and the Ogoni uprising, see Abdul Rasheed Na'Allah, ed., *Ogoni's Agonies: Ken Saro-Wiwa and the Crisis in Nigeria* (Trenton, NJ: Africa World Press, 1998); and Onookome Okome, ed., *Before I Am Hanged: Ken Saro-Wiwa – Literature, Politics, and Dissent* (Trenton, NJ: Africa World Press, 2000).
16 Osaghae, *Crippled Giant*, 281.
17 Economist Intelligence Unit, *Quarterly Economic Review – Nigeria* (London: Economist Intelligence Unit, various years).
18 'Lai Olurode and Remi Anifowose, eds., *Issues in Nigeria's 1999 General Elections* (Ikeja: John West, 2004).
19 Remi Anifowoso and Tunde Babawale, eds., *2003 General Elections and Democratic Consolidation in Nigeria* (Lagos: Frankad, 2003).
20 For a balance sheet on Obasanjo's first term, see Aaron T. Gana and Yakubu B. C. Omelle, eds., *Democratic Rebirth in Nigeria,* vol. I, *1999–2003* (Plainsboro, NJ: African Centre for Democratic Governance, 2005). As of 2007, no synthesis on Obasanjo's full eight years as president has yet been published. On Obasanjo's legacy, however, see Sola Odunfa, "Obasanjo's legacy to Nigeria," *BBC's Focus on Africa Magazine*, March 16, 2007, available online at http://news.bbc.co.uk/2/hi/africa/6412971.stm.
21 World Bank, "World development indicators database," April 2006, available online at http://devdata.worldbank.org/external/CPProfile.asp?CCODE=NGA&PTYPE=CP.
22 World Bank, "ICT at a glance," available online at http://devdata.worldbank.org/ict/nga_ict.pdf. The *Economist* projects that Nigerian GDP growth rates will remain above 5 percent per annum through 2011: see *Economist*, "Country briefings, Nigeria, economic data," March 26, 2007, available online at www.economist.com/countries/Nigeria/profile.cfm?folder=Profile%2DEconomic%20Data.
23 *Economist*, "Country briefings, Nigeria."

24 Anas A. Galadima, "Nigeria: country retains Fitch's rating on economy," *AllAfrica.com*, March 16, 2007, available online at http://allafrica.com/stories/200703160457.html.

25 Abimbola Akosile, "Africa: foreign investment for poverty reduction," *ThisDay* (Lagos), February 20, 2007, available online at http://allafrica.com/stories/200702210482.html.

26 BBC News, "Nigeria settles Paris Club debt," April 21, 2006, available online at http://news.bbc.co.uk/2/hi/business/4926966.stm.

27 World Bank Group, "Nigeria data profile," available online at http://devdata.worldbank.org/external/CPProfile.asp?CCODE=NGA&PTYPE=CP.

28 See, for example, Senan Murray, "Life of poverty in Abuja's wealth," BBC News, February 13, 2007, available online at http://news.bbc.co.uk/2/hi/africa/6355269.stm.

29 Yar'Adua flew to Germany for treatment of a chronic kidney ailment: see BBC News, "Nigerian contender seeks check-up," March 7, 2007, available online at http://news.bbc.co.uk/2/hi/africa/6425875.stm. Atiku flew to London for treatment after damaging his knee in a fall from his treadmill: see BBC News, "Nigerian VP falls off treadmill," March 12, 2007, available online at http://news.bbc.co.uk/2/hi/africa/6442855.stm.

30 Based on 2004 statistics. World Health Organization, "Country profile: Nigeria," available online at www.who.int/countries/nga/nga/en/.

31 Ibid.

32 For an in-depth discussion of the *shari'a* debate, see Hakeem B. Harunah, *Shari'ah under Western Democracy in Contemporary Nigeria: Contradictions, Crises and the Way Forward* (Ikeja: Perfect Printers, 2002).

33 See, for example, BBC News, "Nigeria riots toll passes 200," November 24, 2002, available online at http://news.bbc.co.uk/2/hi/africa/2508131.stm.

34 See, for example, BBC News, "Riots in Nigeria leave many dead," February 22, 2006, available online at http://news.bbc.co.uk/2/hi/africa/4738726.stm.

35 On religious tensions since the 1990s, see Chima J. Korieh and G. Ugo Nwokeji, *Religion, History, and Politics in Nigeria: Essays in Honor of Ogbu U. Kalu* (Lanham, MD: University Press of America, 2005).

36 For more on MEND, see BBC News, "Nigeria's shadowy oil rebels," April 20, 2006, available online at http://news.bbc.co.uk/2/hi/africa/4732210.stm.

37 This statistic is widely used in pieces dealing with hostage taking in the delta. See, for example, BBC News, "Italians released in Niger delta," March 15, 2007, available online at http://news.bbc.co.uk/2/hi/africa/6452673.stm.

38 For more on everyday corruption in Nigeria, see Daniel Jordan Smith, *A Culture of Corruption: Everyday Deception and Popular Discontent in Nigeria* (Princeton, NJ: Princeton University Press, 2007).

39 For the most up-to-date version of Transparency International's Corruption Perceptions Index, as well as previous years' rankings, visit Transparency International's homepage: www.transparency.org.

10 NIGERIA AND NIGERIANS IN WORLD HISTORY

1 On the Hausa diaspora, see Mahdi Adamu, *The Hausa Factor in West African History* (Zaria: Oxford University Press, 1978). For a detailed history of one commodity in which the Hausa traded in the west African region, see Paul E. Lovejoy, *Caravans of Kola: The Hausa Kola Trade, 1700–1900* (Oxford: Oxford University Press, 1980). On the lives of Hausa migrants in one African country, see John A. Works, Jr., *Pilgrims in a Strange Land: Hausa Communities in Chad* (New York: Columbia University Press, 1976).

2 On the trans-Saharan trade, see Bovill, *The Golden Trade of the Moors.*

3 On the overland pilgrimage in west African history, see J. S. Birks, *Across the Savannas to Mecca: The Overland Pilgrimage Route from West Africa* (London: C. Hurst, 1978).

4 See C. Bawa Yamba, *Permanent Pilgrims: The Role of Pilgrimage in the Lives of West African Muslims in Sudan* (Washington, DC: Smithsonian Institution Press, 1995).

5 Birks, *Across the Savannas*, 25. Most of the other colonies in west Africa with large Muslim populations were governed by the French, who discouraged their colonial subjects from participating in the pilgrimage.

6 On the pilgrimage in contemporary Nigeria, see Robert R. Bianchi, *Guests of God: Pilgrimage and Politics in the Islamic World* (Oxford: Oxford University Press, 2004), 211–52.

7 Compiled from tables in Lovejoy, *Transformations in Slavery*, 42, 146.

8 David Eltis, David Richardson, and Stephen Behrendt, *The Trans-Atlantic Slave Trade: A New Census* (Cambridge: Cambridge University Press, forthcoming), cited in Mohammed Bashir Salau, "The Atlantic slave trade and the impact on the Nigerian hinterland, 1500–1900," in *Precolonial Nigeria*, 466. Both Lovejoy's work and that of Eltis, Richardson, and Behrendt are derived from and in collaboration with ongoing research associated with the W. E. B. DuBois Institute for African and African-American Research's Trans-Atlantic Slave Trade Database, the most comprehensive and up-to-date compilation of statistical data related to the transatlantic slave trade.

9 See, for example, Michael A. Gomez, "A quality of anguish: the Igbo response to enslavement in the Americas," in *Trans-Atlantic Dimension of Ethnicity in the African Diaspora*, ed. Paul E. Lovejoy and David V. Trotman (New York: Continuum, 2003), 82–95.

10 Such responses were by no means limited to slaves taken from the territories of modern-day Nigeria, but certainly applied to them.

11 For more on the slave rebellions in Bahia, see João José Reis, *Slave Rebellion in Brazil: The Muslim Uprising of 1835 in Bahia*, trans. Arthur Brakel (Baltimore: Johns Hopkins University Press, 1993).

12 Some scholars now believe that Equiano was, in fact, born in South Carolina, although the issue remains quite controversial. Nevertheless, Equiano's autobiography claims that he was born in Igboland. On the controversy surrounding Equiano's birthplace, see Vincent Carretta, *Equiano, the African: Biography of a*

Self Made Man (Atlanta: University of Georgia Press, 2005), who argues that Equiano was born in the Carolinas. For a defense of Equiano's African origin, see Paul E. Lovejoy, "Construction of identity: Olaudah Equiano or Gustavus Vassa?," *Historically Speaking: The Bulletin of the Historical Society* 7, no. 3 (2006), available online at www.bu.edu/historic/hs/janfeb06. html#lovejoy.

13 *The Interesting Narrative* is now in widespread circulation. See Olaudah Equiano, *The Interesting Narrative and Other Writings*, ed. Vincent Carretta (New York: Penguin Books, 2003).

14 See chapter 4, this volume, for more on Crowther.

15 For more on *orisa* worship in diasporic religions, see Toyin Falola and Ann Genova, eds., *Orisa: Yoruba Gods and Spiritual Identity in Africa and the Diaspora* (Trenton, NJ: Africa World Press, 2005).

16 Augustine H. Agwuele, "'Yorubaisms' in African American 'Speech' patterns," in *The Yoruba Diaspora in the Atlantic World*, ed. Toyin Falola and Matt D. Childs (Bloomington: Indiana University Press, 2006), 325–48.

17 Douglas B. Chambers, "'My own nation': Igbo exiles in the diaspora," *Slavery and Abolition* 18, no. 1 (1997): 72–97.

18 On the appeal of American education, see Mazi Okoro Ojiaku and Gene Ulansky, "Early Nigerian response to American education," *Phylon* 33, no. 4 (1972): 380–8.

19 For more on Nigerians and the Pan-African movement, see Hakim Adi, "Pan-Africanism and west African nationalism in Britain," *African Studies Review* 43, no. 1 (2000): 69–82; and Esedebe, *Pan-Africanism*.

20 From United States Census Bureau, *2000 Census*. Information on the Nigerian population in the United States can be found at http://factfinder. census.gov/.

21 BBC News, "Born abroad – an immigration map of Britain: Nigeria," available online at http://news.bbc.co.uk/1/shared/spl/hi/uk/05/born_abroad/ countries/html/nigeria.stm.

22 United Nations Development Project (UNDP), *Human Development Report, 1993*, available online at http://hdr.undp.org/reports/global/1993/en/.

23 For the activities of many of them, see www.toyinfalola.com.

24 Gumisai Mutume, "Workers' remittances: a boon to development," *Africa Renewal* 19, no. 3 (October 2005): 10.

25 Direct Expatriate Nationals Investment (DeniAfrica), "Nigeria: remittances hit $4 billion," July 26, 2006, available online at http://deniafrica.com/2006/ 07/26/nigeria-remittances-hit-4-billion/. The article, summarized from the newspaper *ThisDay*, reports that Nigerian minister of foreign affairs Dr. Ngozi Okonjo-Iweala declared Nigerian remittances to be nearly $3 billion, but notes that some economists believe that this number could be as much as 50 percent higher.

26 *Economist*, "Nigeria's other export: people trafficking from Nigeria," April 24, 2004.

27 See Osuntokun, *Nigeria in the First World War*, 237–69.

28 The United Kingdom did continue to supply light arms to the Federal Military Government throughout the war, however.

29 On foreign affairs during the civil war, see Stremlau, *The International Politics of the Nigerian Civil War*; and Cronje, *The World and Nigeria*.

30 On the effects of the civil war on Nigerian foreign policy, see, for example, Olajide Aluko, "The civil war and Nigerian foreign policy," in *Essays on Nigerian Foreign Policy* (London: George Allen and Unwin, 1981), 117–28.

31 Olayiwola Abegunrin, *Nigerian Foreign Policy under Military Rule, 1966–1999* (Westport, CT: Praeger, 2003), 64–6. See also Kelechi Amihe Kalu, *Economic Development and Nigerian Foreign Policy* (Lewiston, NY: Edwin Mellen Press, 2000); and Okon Akiba, *Nigerian Foreign Policy towards Africa: Continuity and Change* (New York: Peter Lang, 1998).

32 Abegunrin, *Nigerian Foreign Policy*, 63. The CFA (Communauté Financière d'Afrique) franc is the currency of France's ex-colonies in Africa.

33 Osaghae, *Crippled Giant*, 107–8.

34 Forrest, *Politics and Economic Development*, 134.

35 See Olajide Aluko, "Nigeria's oil at concessionary prices for Africa: a case study in decision-making," in *Essays in Nigerian Foreign Policy*, 193–211.

36 On the establishment and effectiveness of ECOWAS, see, for example, S. K. B. Asante, *The Political Economy of Regionalism in Africa: A Decade of the Economic Community of West African States (ECOWAS)* (New York: Praeger, 1986); Uka Ezenwe, *ECOWAS and the Economic Integration of West Africa* (New York: St. Martin's Press, 1983); and Timothy M. Shaw and Julius Emeka Okolo, eds., *The Political Economy of Foreign Policy in ECOWAS* (New York: St. Martin's Press, 1994).

37 Akanmu Gufaru Adebayo, "Oil and the Murtala/Obasanjo foreign policy, 1975–1979," in *Nigeria and the International Capitalist System*, ed. Toyin Falola and Julius O. Ihonvbere (Boulder, CO, and London: Lynne Rienner, 1988), 96–7.

38 'Funmi Oloni sakin, *Reinventing Peacekeeping in Africa: Conceptual and Legal Issues in ECOMOG Operations* (The Hague: Kluwer Law International, 2000), 109.

39 For more on ECOMOG's operations in Liberia and Sierra Leone, see Olonisakin, *Reinventing Peacekeeping*; and Adekeye Adebajo, *Liberia's Civil War: Nigeria, ECOMOG, and Regional Security in West Africa* (Boulder, CO: Lynne Rienner, 2002).

40 See chapter 9, this volume.

41 Adigun Agbaje and Wale Adebanwi, "The executive: four years of democratic rule in Nigeria," in *Democratic Rebirth in Nigeria*, vol. I, 50.

42 BBC News, "Nigeria hands Bakassi to Cameroon," August 14, 2006, available online at http://news.bbc.co.uk/2/hi/africa/4789647.stm. For more on Obasanjo's foreign policy, see R. A. Akindele, "Nigeria's foreign policy in the global diplomatic market place, 1999–2003," in *Democratic Rebirth in Nigeria*, vol. I, 187–218.

43 David Loyn, "Profile: Cardinal Francis Arinze," BBC News, April 18, 2005, available online at http://news.bbc.co.uk/2/hi/africa/4445821.stm.

44 Lydia Polgreen and Laurie Goodstein, "At axis of Episcopal split, an anti-gay Nigerian," *New York Times*, December 25, 2006, available online at www.nytimes.com/2006/12/25/world/africa/25episcopal.html?ex = 1324702800& en = 2d3ee7997f4872d7&ei = 5088.

45 *Economist*, "Nollywood dreams; Nigeria's film industry," July 29, 2006.

CONCLUDING REMARKS: CORRUPTION, ANTI-CORRUPTION, AND THE 2007 ELECTIONS

1 BBC News, "Nigeria's 'graft list' rejected," February 9, 2007, available online at http://news.bbc.co.uk/2/hi/africa/6346043.stm.

2 Alifa Daniel, "Senate dumps constitution review Bill," *The Guardian* (Lagos), May 17, 2006, available online at www.guardiannewsngr.com/news/article01/170506.

3 Alifa Daniel and Azimazi Momoh Jimoh, "Obasanjo presents panel, EFCC reports on Atiku to Senate," *The Guardian* (Lagos), September 6, 2006, available online at www.guardiannewsngr.com/news/article01/080906.

4 Martins Oloja and Saxone Akhaine, "SSS arrests Atiku's media side, Shehu," *The Guardian* (Lagos), September 20, 2006, available online at www.guardiannewsngr.com/news/article02/200906.

5 Mohammed Abubakar and Kodilinye Obiagwu, "Atiku not on INEC's list, goes to court," *The Guardian* (Lagos), March 16, 2007, available online at www.guardiannewsngr.com/news/article01/160307.

6 Gbolahan Gbadamosi, Lemmy Ughegbe, and Alifa Daniel, "INEC can't bar Atiku, others, Supreme Court rules," *The Guardian* (Lagos), April 17, 2007, available online at www.guardiannewsngr.com/news/article02/170407.

7 *New Nigerian* (Lagos), "Elections a 'failed process,'" April 24, 2007.

8 BBC News, "What Nigerian election observers say," April 23, 2007, available online at http://news.bbc.co.uk/2/hi/africa/6582979.stm.

9 Mohammed Abubakar, "AC, ANPP protest Yar'Adua's victory," *The Guardian* (Lagos), April 24, 2007, available online at www.guardiannewsngr.com/ArchiveIndex_html?pdate=240407.

10 BBC News, "Nigerian leader to retire to farm," May 21, 2007, available online at http://news.bbc.co.uk/2/hi/africa/6677039.stm.

Selected bibliography

GENERAL HISTORIES

Historical scholarship on Nigeria is both dense and broad, with works ranging from the very general to the very specific. Before discussing the specific works of note, it is important to note that there are many general histories of Nigeria that are quite useful for understanding the broad themes and major events that have affected Nigeria over the centuries. General works that cover the period up to the independence of Nigeria in 1960 include Michael Crowder, *The Story of Nigeria* (London: Faber and Faber, 1962, 1966, 1973, 1978, 1982); Sir Alan Burns, *History of Nigeria* (London: Allen and Unwin, 1972); Elizabeth Isichei, *History of Nigeria* (London and New York: Longman, 1983); and Toyin Falola, *The History of Nigeria* (Westport, CT: Greenwood, 1999).

More recent general histories have focused more heavily on the period since Nigeria's independence. These include Eghosa E. Osaghae, *Crippled Giant: Nigeria since Independence* (Bloomington: Indiana University Press, 1998); Tom Forrest, *Politics and Economic Development in Nigeria* (Boulder, CO: Westview Press, 1995); Stephen Wright, *Nigeria: Struggle for Stability and Status* (Boulder, CO: Westview Press, 1997); the series of volumes edited by Garba Ashiwaju and Olusegun Areola, *Nigeria since Independence: The First Twenty-five Years* (Ibadan: University of Ibadan Press, 1995); and the massive, 1,000-page collection edited by Toyin Falola, *Nigeria in the Twentieth Century* (Durham, NC: Carolina Academic Press, 2002). For general synopses of important people, places, and things, see Anthony Oyewole and John Lucas, eds., *Historical Dictionary of Nigeria*, 2nd edn (Lanham, MD, and London: Scarecrow Press, 2000).

In the bibliography that follows, works discussing specific aspects of Nigeria's history are listed under the chapter headings in which those aspects have been discussed in this volume.

CHAPTER 1

Archeological understanding of the prehistory of the Nigerian region has been under constant revision for the last thirty plus years. Some of the earlier but still important works include Thurstan Shaw, *Igbo-Ukwu: An Account of Archaeological*

Discoveries in Eastern Nigeria, two volumes (Evanston, IL: Northwestern University Press, 1970); his more general *Nigeria: Its Archaeology and Early History* (London: Thames and Hudson, 1978); and G. Connah, *Three Thousand Years in Africa: Man and His Environment in the Lake Chad Region of Nigeria* (Cambridge: Cambridge University Press, 1981). More recent works include the following edited volumes: Kit W. Wesler, ed., *Historical Archaeology in Nigeria* (Trenton, NJ: Africa World Press, 1998); Aliyu A. Idrees and Yakubu A. Ochefu, eds., *Studies in the History of Central Nigerian Area*, two volumes (Lagos: CSS, 2002); and Akinwumi Ogundiran, ed., *Precolonial Nigeria: Essays in Honor of Toyin Falola* (Trenton, NJ: Africa World Press, 2005). These latter volumes contain essays by many prominent and active archeologists in Nigeria, providing the most up-to-date analysis of topics as diverse as agricultural origins, iron smelting, and the beginnings of urbanism in Nigeria, and covering all regions of Nigeria from the Sahelian region around Lake Chad to the savanna and forest zones, as well as the Niger delta region.

Much has also been written concerning the origins of different societies in the Nigerian region. For the southwest, perhaps the most famous work on the origin of the Yoruba is Samuel Johnson, *The History of the Yorubas from the Earliest Times to the Beginning of the British Protectorate* (reprint, Lagos: CSS, 2001), originally published in 1921. Other works on Yoruba origins include Janet Stanley and Richard Olaniyan with Depo Adenle, *Ife: The Holy City of the Yoruba: An Annotated Bibliography* (Ile-Ife: University of Ife Press, 1982); S. O. Biobaku, *The Origin of the Yoruba* (Lagos: Government Printer, 1955); S. O. Biobaku, *Sources of Yoruba History* (Oxford: Oxford University Press, 1973); and P. A. Talbot, *The Peoples of South-western Nigeria* (London: Frank Cass, 1969). On the Benin kingdom and society, see R. E. Bradbury, *The Benin Kingdom and the Edo-speaking Peoples of South-western Nigeria* (London: International African Institute, 1957, 1970). Early social development in southeastern Nigeria is discussed at length in Elizabeth Isichei, *A History of the Igbo People* (London and New York: Macmillan, 1976); Simon Ottenberg, *Igbo Religion, Social Life and Other Essays*, ed. Toyin Falola (Trenton, NJ: Africa World Press, 2006); and Toyin Falola, ed., *Igbo History and Society: The Essays of Adiele Afigbo* (Trenton, NJ: Africa World Press, 2005).

On the foundations of societies in the savanna region, see Nehemia Levtzion, "The early states of the western Sudan to 1500," in *History of West Africa*, vol. I, eds. J. F. A. Ajayi and Michael Crowder (New York: Columbia University Press, 1972), 120–57; and Mahdi Adamu, *The Hausa Factor in West African History* (Zaria: Oxford University Press, 1978). For early histories of Kanem and Borno, see Abdullahi Smith, "The early states of the central Sudan," in *History of West Africa*, vol. I, 158–201; and John O. Hunwick, "Songhay, Bornu and Hausaland in the sixteenth century," in *History of West Africa*, vol. I, 202–39. Early histories of the Hausa and Kanem-Borno kingdoms are also contained in the works that discuss the coming of Islam to the region; for example, J. Spencer Trimingham, *A History of Islam in West Africa* (Oxford: Oxford University Press, 1962); and Mervyn Hiskett, *The Development of Islam in West Africa* (London and New York: Longman, 1984). On the development of the trans-Saharan trade, see Edward William Bovill, *The Golden Trade of the Moors* (Oxford: Oxford University Press, 1958).

CHAPTER 2

The literature on slavery and the slave trade and their effects on political and social developments in west Africa is enormous. Only a few examples can be given here. Paul E. Lovejoy, *Transformations in Slavery: A History of Slavery in Africa*, 2nd edn (Cambridge: Cambridge University Press, 2000), is a good starting point for discussions of slavery institutions and slave trading activities throughout Africa, including west Africa and the Bights of Benin and Biafra. Other studies of institutions of social bondage in west Africa include Allan G. B. Fisher and Humphrey J. Fisher, *Slavery and Muslim Society in Africa: The Institution in Saharan and Sudanic Africa and the Trans-Saharan Trade* (Garden City, NY: Doubleday, 1971); Toyin Falola and Paul E. Lovejoy, *Pawnship, Slavery and Colonialism in Africa* (Trenton, NJ: Africa World Press, 2003); Paul E. Lovejoy and David Richardson, "Competing markets for male and female slaves: prices in the interior of west Africa, 1780–1850," *International Journal of African Historical Studies* 28, no. 2 (1995): 261–93; H. A. Gemery and J. S. Hogendorn, eds., *The Uncommon Market: Essays in the Economic History of the Atlantic Slave Trade* (New York: Academic Press, 1979); and Elizabeth Savage, ed., *The Human Commodity: Perspectives on the Trans-Saharan Slave Trade* (London: Frank Cass, 1992).

For discussions of the growth, consolidation, and rivalries of the Hausa states and Borno, see R. A. Adeleye, "Hausaland and Borno, 1600–1800," in *History of West Africa*, vol. I, 485–530; M. U. Adamu, *Confluences and Influences: The Emergence of Kano as a City-state* (Kano: Munawwar Books Foundation, 1999); M. G. Smith, *Government in Kano, 1350–1950* (Boulder, CO: Westview Press, 1997); Yusuf Bala Usman, *The Transformation of Katsina, 1400–1883: The Emergence and Overthrow of the Sarauta System and the Establishment of the Emirate* (Zaria: Ahmadu Bello University, 1981); John Lavers, "Islam in the Bornu Caliphate," *Odu: A Journal of West African Studies* 5 (1971): 27–53. These issues are also discussed at length in Mervyn Hiskett, *The Development of Islam in West Africa* (London and New York: Longman, 1984); and J. Spencer Trimingham, *A History of Islam in West Africa* (Oxford: Oxford University Press, 1962).

The rise of the Oyo empire in the southwest is well chronicled in Robin Law, *The Oyo Empire c. 1600–c. 1836: A West African Imperialism in the Era of the Atlantic Slave Trade* (Oxford: Clarendon Press, 1977); and I. A. Akinjogbin, "The expansion of Oyo and the rise of Dahomey, 1600–1800," in *History of West Africa*, vol. I, 373–412. On Oyo's role in the slave trade in the Bight of Benin, see Peter Morton-Williams, "The Oyo Yoruba and the Atlantic trade, 1670–1830," *Journal of the Historical Society of Nigeria* 3, no. 1 (1964): 25–45; Robin Law, "Trade and politics behind the Slave Coast: the lagoon traffic and the rise of Lagos, 1500–1800," *Journal of African History* 24, no. 3 (1983): 321–48; and Robin Law, *Ouidah: The Social History of a West African Slaving "Port," 1727–1892*

(Athens, OH: Ohio University Press, 2004). On the relationship between the Benin kingdom and European traders, see A. F. C. Ryder, *Benin and the Europeans 1485–1897* (London: Longman, 1969).

Social and political developments in the Niger delta and southeastern Nigeria can be found in E. J. Alagoa, "The Niger delta states and their neighbours, 1600–1800," in *History of West Africa*, vol. I, 269–303; G. I. Jones, *The Trading States of the Oil Rivers* (London: Oxford University Press, 1963); K. O. Dike, *Trade and Politics in the Niger Delta, 1830–1885* (Oxford: Clarendon Press, 1956); A. J. Latham, *Old Calabar: The Impact of the International Economy upon a Traditional Society* (Oxford: Clarendon Press, 1973); and David Northrup, *Trade without Rulers: Pre-colonial Economic Development in South-eastern Nigeria* (Oxford: Clarendon Press, 1978). On the Aro and their control of the oracle of Arochukwu, see K. O. Dike and Felicia Ekejiubu, *The Aro of Southeastern Nigeria, 1650–1980* (Ibadan: University of Ibadan Press, 1990); and J. Okoro Ijoma, ed., *Arochukwu History and Culture* (Enugu: Fourth Dimension Publishers, 1980).

CHAPTER 3

The jihad of Usman dan Fodio and the emergence of the Sokoto Caliphate in the Hausa states of the savannas have been handled by many capable scholars, including Murray Last, *The Sokoto Caliphate* (London: Longman, 1967); R. A. Adeleye, *Power and Diplomacy in Northern Nigeria, 1804–1906: The Sokoto Caliphate and Its Enemies* (New York: Humanities Press, 1971); H. A. S. Johnston, *The Fulani Empire of Sokoto* (London: Oxford University Press, 1967); S. J. Hogben, *An Introduction to the History of the Islamic States of Northern Nigeria* (Ibadan: Oxford University Press, 1967); Sa'ad Abubakar, "The established caliphate: Sokoto, the emirates, and their neighbours," in *Groundwork of Nigerian History*, ed. Obaro Ikime (Ibadan: Heinemann Educational Books [Nigeria], 1980); Y. B. Usman, ed., *Studies in the History of the Sokoto Caliphate: The Sokoto Seminar Papers* (Zaria: Ahmadu Bello University, Department of History, 1979); Mervyn Hiskett, *The Sword of Truth: The Life and Times of the Shehu Usman dan Fodio* (New York: Oxford University Press, 1973); Sean Stilwell, *Paradoxes of Power: The Kano Mamluks and Male Royal Slavery in the Sokoto Caliphate, 1804–1903* (Portsmouth, NH, and London: Heinemann, 2004); and Mary Wren Bivins, *Telling Stories, Making Histories: Women, Words, and Islam in Nineteenth-century Hausaland and the Sokoto Caliphate* (Portsmouth, NH, and London: Heinemann, 2007).

The nineteenth-century transformations sparked by the collapse of Oyo in the southwest have also captivated scholars of Nigerian history. Notable works include J. F. A. Ajayi and Robert Smith, *Yoruba Warfare in the Nineteenth Century*, 2nd edn (Cambridge: Cambridge University Press, 1971); J. F. A. Ajayi, "The aftermath of the fall of Old Oyo," in *History of West Africa*, vol. II, eds. J. F. A. Ajayi and Michael Crowder (New York: Columbia University Press, 1973), 129–66; Toyin Falola, *The Political Economy of a Precolonial African City: Ibadan, 1830–1893* (Ile-Ife: University of Ife Press, 1984); Toyin Falola and

G. O. Oguntomisin, *The Military in Nineteenth Century Yoruba Politics* (Ile-Ife: University of Ife Press, 1984); and Toyin Falola and G. O. Oguntomisin, *Yoruba Warlords of the Nineteenth Century* (Trenton, NJ: Africa World Press, 2001).

The transition from slave trading to "legitimate" commerce in agricultural products has resulted in robust scholarly debate among historians of southern Nigeria. Some historians have argued that the end of the slave trade brought abrupt changes to the economies of southern Nigeria, while others characterize the period as one of remarkably stable adaptation. On the historiography of this transition period, see Robin Law, "The historiography of the commercial transition in nineteenth-century west Africa," in *West African Historiography: Essays in Honour of Jacob Ade Ajayi*, ed. Toyin Falola (Harlow: Longman, 1993), 91–115; A. G. Hopkins, *An Economic History of West Africa* (New York: Columbia University Press, 1973), 125–35; David Northrup, "The compatibility of the slave and palm oil trades in the Bight of Biafra," *Journal of African History* 17, no. 3 (1976): 353–64; Julian Clarke, "Households and the political economy of small-scale cash crop production in south-western Nigeria," *Africa* 51 (1981): 807–23; Robin Law, "'Legitimate' trade and gender relations in Yorubaland and Dahomey," in *From Slave Trade to "Legitimate" Commerce: The Commercial Transition in Nineteenth-century West Africa* (Cambridge: Cambridge University Press, 1995), 195–214; and J. N. Oriji, "A re-assessment of the organisation and benefits of the slave and palm produce trade amongst the Ngwa-Igbo," *Canadian Journal of African Studies* 16, no. 3 (1982): 542. Discussion of the transition to "legitimate" commerce also forms part of the narrative of K. O. Dike, *Trade and Politics in the Niger Delta, 1830–1885* (Oxford: Clarendon Press, 1956); A. J. Latham, *Old Calabar: The Impact of the International Economy upon a Traditional Society* (Oxford: Clarendon Press, 1973); and David Northrup, *Trade without Rulers: Pre-colonial Economic Development in South-eastern Nigeria* (Oxford: Clarendon Press, 1978).

CHAPTER 4

The growth of Christian missionary activity in southern Nigeria in the nineteenth century has been the subject of intense scrutiny by historians. On Christian missionary activities in southwestern Nigeria, see J. F. A. Ajayi, *The Christian Missions in Nigeria, 1841–1891: The Making of a New Elite* (Evanston, IL: Northwestern University Press, 1965); E. A. Ayandele, *The Missionary Impact on Modern Nigeria, 1842–1914: A Political and Social Analysis* (New York: Humanities Press, 1967); James Bertin Webster, *The African Churches among the Yoruba, 1888–1922* (Oxford: Clarendon Press, 1964); and J. D. Y. Peel, *Religious Encounter and the Making of the Yoruba* (Bloomington: Indiana University Press, 2000).

On the spread of Christian missions in the Niger delta and southeastern Nigeria, see G. O. M. Tasie, *Christian Missionary Enterprise in the Niger Delta, 1864–1918* (Leiden: E. J. Brill, 1978); F. K. Ekechi, *Missionary Enterprise and Rivalry in Igboland, 1857–1914* (London: Frank Cass, 1971); and the essay by E. A. Ayandele, "The collapse of 'pagandom' in Igboland," in E. A. Ayandele, ed.,

Nigerian Historical Studies (London: Frank Cass, 1979), 167–91. On the arrest of Christianity in the north, see E. A. Ayandele, "The missionary factor in northern Nigeria, 1870–1918," in *Nigerian Historical Studies*, 138–66.

The role of the repatriate Christians from Sierra Leone in the spread of Christianity, and ultimately British imperialism, in southern Nigeria is the subject of Jean Hersokvits Kopytoff, *A Preface to Modern Nigeria: The "Sierra Leonians" in Yoruba, 1830–1890* (Madison: University of Wisconsin Press, 1965); while Lamin Sanneh, *Abolitionists Abroad: American Blacks and the Making of Modern West Africa* (Cambridge, MA: Harvard University Press, 2001), discusses the broader goal of recaptive Christians in Sierra Leone and throughout west Africa to establish new African societies based on anti-slavery and their bottom-up approach to political and social institutions. For an understanding of Christianity and other aspects of religion and culture in Nigeria, see Toyin Falola, *Culture and Customs of Nigeria* (Westport, CT: Greenwood, 2001).

The European explorers who went to the Nigerian region in the late eighteenth and nineteenth centuries wrote best-selling travel narratives of their experiences. Mungo Park, *Travels in the Interior Districts of Africa, in 1795, 1796, and 1797, etc.* (London, 1799), detailed Park's journey down the Niger from Timbuktu to Nupe territory and was the first such account by a European. Subsequent travelogues were published by other explorers. These included Heinrich Barth, *Travels and Discoveries in Northern and Central Africa*, five volumes (London, 1857–8); Hugh Clapperton, *Journal of a Second Expedition into the Interior of Africa, from the Bight of Benin to Soccattoo* (London, 1829); Richard and John Lander, *Journals of an Expedition to Explore the Course and Termination of the Niger, etc.* (London, 1832); and Samuel Ajayi Crowther, *Journal of an Expedition up the Niger and the Tshadda Rivers, undertaken by Macgregor Laird, Esq. in Connection with the British Government, in 1854* (London, 1855). Crowther was a Nigerian who had returned from Sierra Leone, and he became one of the leading proponents of the spread of Christian missions into the interior of Nigeria.

The Europeans' explorations came in the context of increasing competition between European countries for access to and control of interior markets in Africa. This competition ultimately resulted in the "Scramble for Africa" in the last decades of the nineteenth century, in which Europeans carved up the continent into colonial holdings. On the larger "Scramble for Africa," see Thomas Pakenham, *The Scramble for Africa: White Man's Conquest of the Dark Continent from 1876–1912* (New York: Avon Books, 1991); and H. L. Wesseling, *Divide and Rule: The Partition of Africa, 1880–1914*, trans. Arnold J. Pomerans (Westport, CT: Praeger, 1996).

The British takeover of the territories in the Nigerian region was part of this larger "Scramble for Africa." See Obaro Ikime, *The Fall of Nigeria: The British Conquest* (London: Heinemann, 1977) for an in-depth description of how these territories came under British colonial rule in the late nineteenth century. On the Royal Niger Company's role in the colonial conquest of Nigeria, see John E. Flint, *Sir George Goldie and the Making of Modern Nigeria* (London: Oxford

University Press, 1960). The fall of the Sokoto Caliphate is discussed at length in R. A. Adeleye, *Power and Diplomacy in Northern Nigeria, 1804–1906* (New York: Humanities Press, 1971), 213–313; Richard R. Dusgate, *The Conquest of Northern Nigeria* (London: Frank Cass, 1985); and Risto Marjomaa, *War on the Savannah: The Military Collapse of the Sokoto Caliphate under the Invasion of the British Empire, 1897–1903* (Helsinki: Academia Scientiarum Fennica, 1998).

Local authorities, of course, resisted the takeover of their territories by the British. For in-depth case studies of anti-colonial resistance, see Sylvanus Cookey, *King Jaja of the Niger Delta: His Life and Times, 1821–1891* (New York: NOK Publishers, 1974); Obaro Ikime, *Merchant Prince of the Niger Delta: The Rise and Fall of Nana Olomu, Last Governor of the Benin River* (London: Heinemann, 1968); A. F. C. Ryder, *Benin and the Europeans 1485–1897* (London: Longman, 1969); A. E. Afigbo, "The Aro Expedition of 1901–1902: an episode in the British occupation of Iboland," *Odu: A Journal of West African Studies*, New Series, no. 7 (1972), reprinted in Toyin Falola, ed., *Igbo History and Society: The Essays of Adiele Afigbo* (Trenton, NJ: Africa World Press, 2005), 321–40; and Don C. Ohadike, *The Ekumeku Movement: Western Igbo Resistance to the British Conquest of Nigeria, 1883–1914* (Athens, OH: Ohio University Press, 1991).

CHAPTER 5

The goals, objectives, and effectiveness of colonial administration in Nigeria have been viewed differently by scholars over time. Favorable views of colonial administration tended to come earlier, with critiques becoming more and more prevalent and damning as anti-colonial and nationalist scholars increasingly revealed the flaws in both the ideology and the practice of colonial rule. Positive interpretations of the "Dual Mandate" can be found in Lord Lugard, *The Dual Mandate in British Tropical Africa*, 5th edn (London: Archon Books, 1965); Margery Perham, *Native Administration in Nigeria* (London: Oxford University Press, 1937); and Robert Heussler, *The British in Northern Nigeria* (London: Oxford University Press, 1968). More critical works include A. E. Afigbo, *The Warrant Chiefs: Indirect Rule in Southeastern Nigeria, 1891–1929* (London: Longman, 1972); Harry A. Gailey, *The Road to Aba: A Study of British Administrative Policy in Eastern Nigeria* (New York: New York University Press, 1970), 140–60; I. F. Nicholson, *The Administration of Nigeria 1900–1960: Men, Methods and Myths* (Oxford: Clarendon Press, 1969); T. N. Tamuno, *The Evolution of the Nigerian State: The Southern Phase, 1898–1914* (London: Longman, 1972); and Raphael Chijioke Njoku, *African Cultural Values: Igbo Political Leadership in Colonial Nigeria, 1900–1966* (New York: Routledge, 2006). On the nature of the colonial economy, see R. Olufemi Ekundare, *An Economic History of Nigeria 1860–1960* (London: Methuen, 1973); A. G. Hopkins, *An Economic History of West Africa* (New York: Columbia University Press, 1973), 167–292; W. I. Ofonagoro, *Trade and Imperialism in Southern Nigeria, 1881–1929* (New York: Nok, 1979); Toyin Falola, ed., *Britain and Nigeria: Exploitation or Development?* (London: Zed Books, 1987); and Ayodeji Olukoju, *The "Liverpool" of West Africa: The Dynamics and Impact of Maritime Trade in Lagos, 1900–1950* (Trenton, NJ: Africa World Press, 2004).

For case studies of the economic development of specific industries, the following are recommended: on cocoa production in southwestern Nigeria, see Sara S. Berry, *Cocoa, Custom, and Socio-economic Change in Rural Western Nigeria* (Oxford: Clarendon Press, 1975); Sara S. Berry, "Christianity and the rise of cocoa-growing in Ibadan and Ondo," *Journal of the Historical Society of Nigeria* 4, no. 3 (1969): 439–51; on palm oil and kernel production in the southeast, see Susan M. Martin, *Palm Oil and Protest: An Economic History of the Ngwa Region, South-eastern Nigeria, 1800–1980* (Cambridge: Cambridge University Press, 1988); F. K. Ekechi, "Aspects of palm oil trade at Oguta (eastern Nigeria), 1900–1950," *African Economic History* 10 (1981): 35–65; Simon Ottenberg, *Farmers and Townspeople in a Changing Nigeria: Abakaliki during Colonial Times (1905–1960)* (Ibadan: Spectrum Books, 2005); and Chima J. Korieh, "The invisible farmer? Women, gender, and colonial agricultural policy in the Igbo region of Nigeria, c. 1913–1954," *African Economic History* 29 (2001): 117–62; on groundnut production in the north, see Allister E. Hinds, "Colonial policy and the processing of groundnuts: the case of Georges Calil," *International Journal of African Historical Studies* 19, no. 2 (1986): 261–73; for tin mining in the Jos Plateau area, see W. M. Freund, *Capital and Labour in the Nigerian Tin Mines* (London: Routledge and Kegan Paul, 1981); and W. M. Freund, "Labor migration to the northern Nigerian tin mines, 1903–1945," *Journal of African History* 22 (1981): 73–84. For an encompassing study of political economy in one major urban center, see Toyin Falola, *Politics and Economy in Ibadan 1893–1945* (Lagos: Modelor, 1989). On urbanization in Nigeria more generally, see Hakeem Ibikunle Tijani, ed., *Nigeria's Urban History: Past and Present* (Lanham, MD: University Press of America, 2006); and Toyin Falola and Steve Salm, eds., *Nigerian Cities* (Trenton, NJ: Africa World Press, 2004).

The effects of colonial rule on the social structures and cultures of Nigeria have been tackled from a number of angles by historians. On transformations in gender roles, particularly in southeastern Nigeria, see Susan Martin, "Gender and innovation: farming, cooking and palm processing in the Ngwa region, south-eastern Nigeria, 1900–30," *Journal of African History* 25, no. 4 (1984): 411–27; Nwando Achebe, *Farmers, Traders, Warriors, and Kings: Female Power and Authority in Northern Igboland, 1900–1960* (Portsmouth, NH: Heinemann, 2005); Gloria Chuku, *Igbo Women and Economic Transformation in Southeastern Nigeria, 1900–1960* (New York: Routledge, 2005); and Judith A. Byfield, *The Bluest Hands: A Social and Economic History of Women Dyers in Abeokuta, 1890–1940* (Portsmouth, NH, and London: Heinemann, 2004). A comparison of gender roles between Yoruba and Igbo societies can be found in Jane I. Guyer, "Food, cocoa and the division of labor by sex in two west African societies," *Comparative Studies in Society and History* 22, no. 3 (1980).

The creation and establishment of a colonial elite of middle-class, European-educated Nigerians has been the subject of many scholarly endeavors. See, for example, Philip S. Zachernuk, *Colonial Subjects: An African Intelligentsia and*

Atlantic Ideas (Charlottesville: University of Virginia Press, 2000), 50–1; Kristin Mann, *Marrying Well: Marriage, Status and Social Change among the Educated Elite in Colonial Lagos* (Cambridge: Cambridge University Press, 1985); and H. H. Smythe and M. M. Smythe, *The New Nigerian Elite* (Stanford, CA: Stanford University Press, 1971). The missionary impact on the growth of this middle-class elite can be found in Webster, *The African Churches among the Yoruba*; and Ayandele, *The Missionary Impact on Modern Nigeria*. On the growth of European-style education facilities and curricula, see A. Babs Fafunwa, *History of Education in Nigeria* (London: George Allen and Unwin, 1974); and Nduka Okafor, *The Development of Universities in Nigeria* (London: Longman, 1971). The development of an indigenous press, owned and operated by members of the middle-class elite, helped to foment anti-colonial critiques and to build a sense of nationalism. On this phenomenon, see Fred I. A. Omu, *Press and Politics in Nigeria, 1880–1937* (London: Longman, 1978).

CHAPTER 6

On the growth of nationalism in colonial Africa, see Toyin Falola, *Nationalism and African Intellectuals* (Rochester, NY: University of Rochester Press, 2001). The relationship between pan-Africanism and African nationalisms is covered extensively in P. Olisanwuche Esedebe, *Pan-Africanism: The Idea and the Movement, 1776–1991* (Washington, DC: Howard University Press, 1994); and Hakeem Adi, *West Africans in Britain, 1900–1960: Nationalism, Pan-Africanism and Communism* (London: Lawrence and Wishart, 1998). For a Nigeria-wide narrative of the development of nationalist movements in Nigeria, see James S. Coleman, *Nigeria: Background to Nationalism* (Berkeley: University of California Press, 1963); and Richard Sklar, *Nigerian Political Parties: Power in an Emergent African Nation* (Princeton, NJ: Princeton University Press, 1963). On nationalism in the Lagos area of southern Nigeria, see Zachernuk, *Colonial Subjects*.

On the development of nationalist political parties in northern Nigeria, see Jonathan T. Reynolds, *The Time of Politics (Zamanin Siyasa): Islam and the Politics of Legitimacy in Northern Nigeria, 1950–1966* (San Francisco: International Scholars Publications, 1999); C. S. Whitaker, Jr., *The Politics of Tradition: Continuity and Change in Northern Nigeria, 1946–1966* (Princeton, NJ: Princeton University Press, 1970); J. B. Dudley, *Parties and Politics in Northern Nigeria* (London: Frank Cass, 1968); and Alhaji Mahmood Yakubu, *An Aristocracy in Political Crisis: The End of Indirect Rule and the Emergence of Party Politics in the Emirates of Northern Nigeria* (Brookfield, VT: Ashgate, 1996).

Many of the main figures in the nationalist movements wrote autobiographies detailing their experiences during this momentous period. For example, see Nnamdi Azikiwe, *My Odyssey: An Autobiography* (London: C. Hurst, 1970); Obafemi Awolowo, *Awo: The Autobiography of Chief Obafemi Awolowo* (Cambridge: Cambridge University Press, 1960); and Sir Ahmadu Bello, *My Life* (Cambridge: Cambridge University Press, 1962). For some of the speeches of Sir

Abubakar Tafawa Balewa, see Abubakar Tafawa Balewa, *Nigeria Speaks: Speeches Made between 1957 and 1964* (Ikeja: Longmans of Nigeria, 1964).

There are many other works of note on aspects of nationalism and independence in Nigeria. On the role of trade unions in anti-colonialism and nationalism, see Wogu Ananaba, *The Trade Union Movement in Nigeria* (New York: Africana, 1970). For the effects of the Second World War on nationalism and political developments in Nigeria, see G. O. Olusanya, *The Second World War and Politics in Nigeria 1939–1953* (Lagos: University of Lagos and Evans Brothers, 1973); and Ayodeji Olukoju, "'Buy British, sell foreign': external trade control policies in Nigeria during World War II and its aftermath, 1939–1950," *The International Journal of African Historical Studies* 35, no. 2/3 (2002): 363–84. For an analysis of the role of socialist thinking in nationalist movements, see Hakeem Ibikunle Tijani, *Britain, Leftist Nationalists and the Transfer of Power in Nigeria, 1945–1965* (New York and London: Routledge, 2006).

Women were important actors in trade unions and nationalist movements, particularly in southern Nigeria. For more on the role of women, see Nina Emma Mba, *Nigerian Women Mobilized: Women's Political Activity in Southern Nigeria, 1900–1965* (Berkeley, CA: Institute of International Studies, 1982); and Martin, *Palm Oil and Protest*. For a fascinating biography of Mrs. Ransome-Kuti, see Cheryl Johnson-Odim and Nina Emma Mba, *For Women and the Nation: Funmilayo Ransome-Kuti of Nigeria* (Urbana and Chicago: University of Illinois Press, 1997).

The process of decolonization was also accompanied by long-term development planning programs. For an in-depth analysis of the development planning and modernization schemes undertaken in the post-war years, see Toyin Falola, *Development Planning and Decolonization in Nigeria* (Gainesville: University Press of Florida, 1996); Toyin Falola, *Economic Reforms and Modernization in Nigeria, 1945–1965* (Kent, OH, and London: Kent State University Press, 2004); and Ekundare, *An Economic History of Nigeria.*

CHAPTER 7

For more on Nigerian literature, see Bernth Lindfors, *Early Nigerian Literature* (New York: Africana, 1982); Robert M. Wren, *Achebe's World: The Historical and Cultural Context of the Novels of Chinua Achebe* (Washington, DC: Three Continents Press, 1980); Ato Quayson, *Strategic Transformations in Nigerian Writing: Orality and History in the Work of Rev. Samuel Johnson, Amos Tutuola, Wole Soyinka and Ben Okri* (Bloomington: Indiana University Press, 1997); and Claudia Baldwin, *Nigerian Literature: A Bibliography of Criticism, 1952–1976* (Boston: G. K. Hall, 1980). Some of the important literary works of the 1950s and 1960s include Chinua Achebe, *Things Fall Apart* (London: Heinemann, 1958); Amos Tutuola, *The Palm-wine Drinkard and His Dead Palm-wine Tapster in the Deads' Town* (London: Faber and Faber, 1952); Wole Soyinka, *A Dance of the Forests* (London: Oxford University Press, 1963); and Wole Soyinka, *The Swamp Dwellers* (London: Oxford University Press, 1963).

On the visual arts, see Bernice M. Kelly, *Nigerian Artists: A Who's Who and Bibliography*, ed. Janet L. Stanley (London and New York: Hans Zell, 1993); Simon Ottenberg, *New Traditions from Nigeria: Seven Artists of the Nsukka Group* (Washington, DC: Smithsonian Institution Press, in association with the National Museum of African Art, 1997); and Gani Odutokun, "Art in Nigeria since independence," in *Nigeria since Independence: The First Twenty-five Years*, vol. VII, *Culture*, eds. Peter P. Ekeh and Garba Ashinwaju (Ibadan: Heinemann Educational Books, 1989), 139–51. On musical traditions in Nigeria, see Christopher Alan Waterman, *Juju: A Social History and Ethnography of an African Popular Music* (Chicago: University of Chicago Press, 1990); Beverly B. Mack, *Muslim Women Sing: Hausa Popular Song* (Bloomington: Indiana University Press, 2004); and Samuel Ekpe Akpabot, *Ibibio Music in Nigerian Culture* (East Lansing: Michigan State University Press, 1975). Although Fela Kuti is discussed in chapter 8 of this volume, his contribution to Nigerian music must be noted here. See Tejumola Olaniyan, *Arrest the Music! Fela and His Rebel Art and Politics* (Bloomington: Indiana University Press, 2004), for more on how Fela's music impacted Nigerian society.

Artists, like all Nigerians at the time, were contributing to a dialogue on what it meant to be "Nigerian" in the 1960s. For more on how this "national question" affected various, wide-ranging aspects of Nigerian politics, culture, and society, see Abubakar Momoh and Said Adejumobi, eds., *The National Question in Nigeria: Comparative Perspectives* (Aldershot, UK, and Burlington, VT: Ashgate, 2002). The problems of the federal system of government soon came to represent the largest impediment to solving the national question. On the breakdown of the federal system during the First Republic, see Uma O. Eleazu, *Federalism and Nation-building: The Nigerian Experience, 1954–64* (Ilfracombe, UK: Arthur H. Stockwell, 1977); Eme O. Awa, *Federal Government in Nigeria* (Berkeley and Los Angeles: University of California Press, 1964); John P. Mackintosh, *Nigerian Government and Politics* (London: George Allen and Unwin, 1966); William D. Graf, *The Nigerian State: Political Economy, State Class and Political System in the Post-colonial Era* (London: James Currey, 1988); and J. B. Dudley, *An Introduction to Nigerian Government and Politics* (London: Macmillan, 1982). For an in-depth look at the fateful elections of 1964 and 1965, see Kenneth Post and Michael Vickers, *Structure and Conflict in Nigeria, 1960–1966* (London: Heinemann, 1973).

The role of the military in Nigerian governance has been a topic of great interest to historians and political scientists. On the politicization of the armed forces prior to the 1966 coup, see N. Miners, *The Nigerian Military: 1956–1966* (London: Methuen, 1971). For more on the objectives and methods of military rule leading up to the civil war, see Toyin Falola, A. Ajayi, A. Alao, and B. Babawale, *The Military Factor in Nigeria, 1966–1985* (Lewiston, NY: Edwin Mellen Press, 1994); James J. Oluleye, *Military Leadership in Nigeria, 1966–1979* (Ibadan: University of Ibadan Press, 1985); and S. K. Panter-Brick, ed., *Nigerian Politics and Military Rule: Prelude to the Civil War* (London: Athlone Press, 1970).

For in-depth narratives and analysis of the Nigerian Civil War, see Siyan Oyeweso, *Perspectives on the Nigerian Civil War* (Lagos: Campus Press, 1992);

John de St. Jorre, *The Brothers' War: Biafra and Nigeria* (Boston: Houghton Mifflin, 1972); John de St. Jorre, *The Nigerian Civil War* (London: Hodder and Stoughton, 1972); Joseph Okpaku, ed., *Nigeria: Dilemma of Nationhood, an African Analysis of the Biafran Conflict* (New York: Third Press, 1972); Sir Rex Niven, *The War of Nigerian Unity* (Ibadan and London: Evans Brothers, 1970); and Bernard Odugwu, *No Place to Hide (Crises and Conflicts inside Biafra)* (Enugu: Fourth Dimension, 1985).

On the international dimensions of the Nigerian Civil War, see John J. Stremlau, *The International Politics of the Nigerian Civil War, 1967–70* (Princeton, NJ: Princeton University Press, 1977); and Suzanne Cronje, *The World and Nigeria: The Diplomatic History of the Biafran War 1967–1970* (London: Sidgwick and Jackson, 1972).

CHAPTER 8

The dynamics of military rule in Nigeria during the 1970s have been the subject of considerable analysis. See Theophilus Olatunde Odetola, *Military Politics in Nigeria: Economic Development and Political Stability* (New Brunswick, NJ: Transaction Books, 1978); Okey Onyejekwe, *The Role of the Military in Economic and Social Development: A Comparative Regime Performance in Nigeria* (Washington, DC: University Press of America, 1981); O. Oyediran, ed., *Nigerian Government and Politics under Military Rule, 1966–1979* (London: Macmillan, 1979); T. O. Odetola, *Military Politics in Nigeria: Economic Development and Political Stability* (New Brunswick, NJ: Transaction Books, 1978); A. Kirk-Greene and D. Rimmer, *Nigeria since 1970* (London: Hodder and Stoughton, 1981); Toyin Falola, A. Ajayi, A. Alao, and B. Babawale, *The Military Factor in Nigeria* (Lewiston, NY: Edwin Mellen Press, 1994); Augustine Ikelegbe, "Civil society, oil and conflict in the Niger delta region of Nigeria: ramifications of civil society for a regional resource struggle," *Journal of Modern African Studies* 39, no. 3 (2001): 437–69; and Adegboyega Isaac Ajayi, *The Military and the Nigerian State, 1966–1993: A Study of the Strategies of Political Power Control* (Trenton, NJ: Africa World Press, 2007).

Military rule in the 1970s has been extensively linked with the rise of the oil economy and, with it, the growth of official corruption. For more on the military's handling of the oil economy, see J. K. Onoh, *The Nigerian Oil Economy: From Prosperity to Glut* (New York: St. Martin's Press, 1983); S. K. Panter-Brick, ed., *Soldiers and Oil: The Political Transformation of Nigeria* (London: Frank Cass, 1978); Sarah Ahmad Khan, *Nigeria: The Political Economy of Oil* (New York: Oxford University Press, 1994); Goddy Ikeh, *Nigerian Oil Industry: The First Three Decades (1958–1988)* (Lagos: Starledger Communications, 1991); and A. A. Ikein, *The Impact of Oil on a Developing Country* (New York: Praeger, 1990). Andrew Apter, *The Pan-African Nation: Oil and the Spectacle of Culture in Nigeria* (Chicago: University of Chicago Press, 2005) provides a case study of FESTAC '77, which illustrates the ways in which the military regimes of Gowon and Mohammed/Obasanjo used oil prosperity for ostentatious purposes rather than for sustainable development projects. For a comparison of Nigeria's oil economy to other oil economies in the world, see Toyin Falola and Ann Genova, *The Politics of the Global Oil Industry* (Westport, CT: Praeger, 2005).

The authoritarian tendencies of the military regimes of the 1970s have been explored in several different contexts. On the consolidation of the power elite and its relationship to the military regimes, see Bala J. Takaya and Sonni Gwanle Tyoden, eds., *The Kaduna Mafia: A Study of the Rise, Development and Consolidation of a Nigerian Power Elite* (Jos: Jos University Press, 1987). For more on the clampdown on Fela Kuti and his criticism of the Obasanjo regime, see Olaniyan, *Arrest the Music!*. On the relationship between the military governments and the press, see Adigun A. B. Agbaje, *The Nigerian Press, Hegemony, and the Social Construction of Legitimacy, 1960–1983* (Lewiston, NY: Edwin Mellen Press, 1992); Bayo Oyolede, *The Press under Military Rule in Nigeria, 1966–1993: An Historical and Legal Narrative* (Lewiston, NY: Edwin Mellen Press, 2004); and Chris W. Ogbondah, *Military Regimes and the Press in Nigeria, 1966–1993: Human Rights and National Development* (Lanham, MD: University Press of America, 1994).

The ill-fated Second Republic brought a new hope for effective civilian rule in Nigeria, but quickly combined the corruption of the oil economy with the patronage system of political organization that alienated the public and the military. For more on the Second Republic, see R. Joseph, *Democracy and Prebendal Politics in Nigeria: The Rise and Fall of the Second Republic* (Cambridge: Cambridge University Press, 1987); and Toyin Falola and Julius Ihonvbere, *The Rise and Fall of Nigeria's Second Republic, 1979–1984* (London: Zed Books, 1985).

As government became ever more distanced from the people in the 1970s and 1980s, social tensions mounted, often spilling over into violent outbursts. These violent episodes were increasingly rooted in religious ideologies – focused either on the unsympathetic and corrupt government or on people of different religious persuasions. For more on the nature and causes of religious tensions in Nigeria, see Toyin Falola, *Violence in Nigeria: The Crisis of Religious Politics and Secular Ideologies* (Rochester, NY: University of Rochester Press, 1998); Simeon O. Ilesanmi, *Religious Pluralism and the Nigerian State* (Athens, OH: Ohio University Center for International Studies, 1997); Pat Williams and Toyin Falola, *Religious Impact on the Nation State: The Nigerian Predicament* (Brookfield, VT: Ashgate, 1995); Jacob K. Olupona and Toyin Falola, *Religion and Society in Nigeria: Historical and Sociological Perspectives* (Ibadan: Spectrum Books, 1991); and Ernest E. Uwazie, Isaac O. Albert, and Godfrey N. Uzoigwe, eds., *Inter-ethnic and Religious Conflict Resolution in Nigeria* (Lanham, MD: Lexington Books, 1999).

CHAPTER 9

On the definition of civil society and its relationship to contemporary Nigerian politics, see Michael Bratton, *Democratic Experiments in Africa: Regime Transitions in Comparative Perspective* (Cambridge: Cambridge University Press, 1997); Matthew Hassan Kukah, *Democracy and Civil Society in Nigeria* (Oxford: Africa

Books Collective, 1999); and Rita Kiki Edozie, *People Power and Democracy: The Popular Movement against Military Despotism in Nigeria, 1989–1999* (Trenton, NJ: Africa World Press, 2002).

The Babangida regime oversaw many important changes in Nigeria's political and economic structures. On the effects of the Structural Adjustment Program on Nigeria, see Effiong Essien, *Nigeria under Structural Adjustment* (Ibadan: Fountain Publications, 1990); Adebayo O. Olukoshi, *The Politics of Structural Adjustment in Nigeria* (London: J. Currey, 1993); Julius Omozuanvbo Ihonvbere, *Nigeria: The Politics of Adjustment and Democracy* (New Brunswick, NJ: Transaction, 1994); and Gary G. Moser, Scott Rogers, and Reinhold van Til, with Robin Kibuka and Inutu Lukonga, *Nigeria: Experience with Structural Adjustment* (Washington, DC: International Monetary Fund, 1997). On the effect of the SAP on identity politics, see Attahiru Jega, ed., *Identity Transformation and Identity Politics under Structural Adjustment in Nigeria* (Uppsala: Nordiska Afrikanstitutet, 2000).

Babangida's democratic transition process has also been scrutinized by many scholars. See, for example, Larry Diamond, Anthony Kirk-Greene, and Oyeleye Oyediran, eds., *Transition without End: Nigerian Politics and Civil Society under Babangida* (Boulder, CO: Lynne Rienner, 1997); Oyeleye Oyediran and Adigun A. B. Agbaje, eds., *Nigeria: Politics of Transition and Governance, 1986–1996* (Dakar: Council for the Development of Social Science Research in Africa, 1999); Uche O. Nnadozie, *The State, Civil Service and Underdevelopment in Nigeria: An Analysis of Policy-making Process in a Neo-colonial Society* (Enugu: Johnkens and Willy, 2004); and Ade Kunle Amuwo, "Between intellectual responsibility and political commodification of knowledge: Nigeria's academic political scientists under the Babangida military junta, 1985–1993," *African Studies Review* 45, no. 2 (2002): 93–121. For a biographical account of M. K. O. Abiola, the uninaugurated winner of the 1993 presidential election, see Yemi Ogunbiyi and Chidi Amuta, *Legend of Our Time: The Thoughts of M. K. O. Abiola* (Lagos: Tanus Communications, 1993).

The deterioration of Nigeria's domestic and international situation under the regime of Sani Abacha is discussed at length in Karl Maier, *This House Has Fallen: Midnight in Nigeria* (New York: PublicAffairs, 2000). The struggle of the Ogoni for the control of oil revenues and environmental policy in their Niger delta homeland became international news in the mid-1990s, when Ken Saro-Wiwa and seven other Ogoni activists were executed on trumped-up murder charges. Saro-Wiwa's activism and ultimate demise are discussed in depth in Abdul Rasheed Na'Allah, ed. *Ogoni's Agonies: Ken Saro-Wiwa and the Crisis in Nigeria* (Trenton, NJ: Africa World Press, 1998); and Onookome Okome, ed., *Before I Am Hanged: Ken Saro-Wiwa – Literature, Politics, and Dissent* (Trenton, NJ: Africa World Press, 2000).

In-depth analyses of the performance and legacy of the Fourth Republic under President Olusegun Obasanjo have yet to appear. For a thorough examination of the goals and policies of Obasanjo's administration in its first term, see Aaron T. Gana and Yakubu B. C. Omelle, eds., *Democratic Rebirth in Nigeria*, Vol. I, *1999–2003* (Plainsboro, NJ: African Centre for Democratic Governance, 2005). On the conduct of the 1999 and 2003 elections, both of which were widely viewed as having been significantly flawed, see 'Lai Olurode and Remi Anifowose, eds., *Issues in Nigeria's 1999 General Elections* (Ikeja: John West, 2004); and Remi Anifowoso and Tunde Babawale, eds., *2003 General Elections and Democratic Consolidation in Nigeria* (Lagos: Frankad, 2003), respectively.

Religious tensions have remained prevalent throughout the 1980s, 1990s, and 2000s. In the north, tensions have mounted over the introduction of new, more fundamentalist interpretations of *shari'a* law: see Hakeem B. Harunah, *Shari'ah under Western Democracy in Contemporary Nigeria: Contradictions, Crises and the Way Forward* (Ikeja: Perfect Printers, 2002). In the south, the rise of charismatic and evangelical Churches has been documented in Matthews A. Ojo, *End-time Army: Charismatic Movements in Modern Nigeria* (Trenton, NJ: Africa World Press, 2006). The continued politicization of religious identity in Nigeria is the subject of the essays in Chima J. Korieh and G. Ugo Nwokeji, eds., *Religion, History, and Politics in Nigeria: Essays in Honor of Ogbu U. Kalu* (Lanham, MD: University Press of America, 2005).

A fascinating account of the various ways in which corruption affects not just the political spectrum but also the daily lives of Nigerians can be found in Daniel Jordan Smith, *A Culture of Corruption: Everyday Deception and Popular Discontent in Nigeria* (Princeton, NJ: Princeton University Press, 2007).

CHAPTER 10

Studies of the commercial aspects of the Hausa diaspora can be found in Adamu, *The Hausa Factor in West African History*; and Paul Lovejoy, *Caravans of Kola: The Hausa Kola Trade, 1700–1900* (Oxford: Oxford University Press, 1980). The role of the pilgrimage in the Hausa diaspora is covered in depth in John A. Works, Jr., *Pilgrims in a Strange Land: Hausa Communities in Chad* (New York: Columbia University Press, 1976); J. S. Birks, *Across the Savannas to Mecca: The Overland Pilgrimage Route from West Africa* (London: C. Hurst, 1978); C. Bawa Yamba, *Permanent Pilgrims: The Role of Pilgrimage in the Lives of West African Muslims in Sudan* (Washington, DC: Smithsonian Institution Press, 1995); and Jonathan T. Reynolds, *Stealing the Road: Colonial Rule and the Hajj from Nigeria in the Early 20th Century* (Boston: African Studies Center, Boston University, 2003). Robert R. Bianchi, *Guests of God; Pilgrimage and Politics in the Islamic World* (Oxford: Oxford University Press, 2004), 211–52, provides an account of pilgrimage control in contemporary Nigeria.

The transatlantic diaspora has an immensely diverse historiography. On the contributions of Yoruba slaves to the cultural history of the Americas, see Toyin Falola and Ann Genova, eds., *Orisa: Yoruba Gods and Spiritual Identity in Africa and the Diaspora* (Trenton, NJ: Africa World Press, 2005); and Toyin Falola and Matt D. Childs, eds., *The Yoruba Diaspora in the Atlantic World* (Bloomington: Indiana University Press, 2006). Igbo migrants are discussed specifically in Michael A. Gomez, "A quality of anguish: the Igbo response to enslavement in the Americas," in *Trans-Atlantic Dimensions of Ethnicity in the African Diaspora,* ed. Paul E. Lovejoy and David V. Trotman (New York: Continuum, 2003), 82–95; and Douglas B. Chambers, "'My own nation': Igbo exiles in the diaspora," *Slavery and Abolition* 18, no. 1 (1997): 72–97. Olaudah Equiano, the famed freedman and abolitionist, was himself Igbo. Equiano's *Interesting Narrative* became an incredibly influential text on the terrors of slavery and the slave trade, and was used by abolitionists as evidence of why the slave trade should be ended: see Olaudah Equiano, *The Interesting Narrative and Other Writings*, ed. Vincent Carretta (New York: Penguin Books, 2003). Yoruba and Hausa slaves are also discussed as instrumental as organizers and participants in slave rebellions, particularly in Brazil: see João José Reis, *Slave Rebellion in Brazil: The Muslim Uprising of 1835 in Bahia*, trans. Arthur Brakel (Baltimore: Johns Hopkins University Press, 1993).

On west Africans and Nigerians in Europe and the United States during the first half of the twentieth century, see Adi, *West Africans in Britain*; Hakim Adi, "Pan-Africanism and west African nationalism in Britain," *African Studies Review* 43, no. 1 (2000): 69–82; Esedebe, *Pan-Africanism*; and Mazi Okoro Ojiaku and Gene Ulansky, "Early Nigerian response to American education," *Phylon* 33, no. 4 (1972): 380–8. While not specific to Nigeria, the extent and effects of the "brain drain" from African countries in recent decades are the subject of Devesh Kapur and John McHale, *The Global Migration of Talent: What Does It Mean for Developing Countries?* (Washington, DC: Center for Global Development, 2005).

Scholars of Nigeria's foreign policy have, by and large, been in agreement about what the major preoccupations of Nigeria's foreign policy have been, although they often disagree about the effectiveness and gravitas of Nigeria as an international power. During the civil war the focus of the Federal Military Government was on gaining support in its battle against Biafra, while simultaneously trying to stifle international aid to the Biafrans. On Nigerian foreign policy during the civil war, see Stremlau, *The International Politics of the Nigerian Civil War*; Cronje, *The World and Nigeria*; and Olajide Aluko, "The civil war and Nigerian foreign policy," in *Essays on Nigerian Foreign Policy* (London: George Allen and Unwin, 1981), 117–28.

During the 1970s the end of the war, coupled with the oil boom, allowed the military regimes of Gowon and Mohammed/Obasanjo to craft a more radical, anti-Western and Africa-centered foreign policy. See Olayiwola Abegunrin, *Nigerian Foreign Policy under Military Rule, 1966–1999* (Westport, CT: Praeger, 2003); Kelechi Amihe Kalu, *Economic Development and Nigerian Foreign Policy* (Lewiston, NY: Edwin Mellen Press, 2000); Okon Akiba, *Nigerian Foreign Policy towards Africa: Continuity and Change* (New York: Peter Lang, 1998); and Toyin Falola and Julius O. Ihonvbere, *Nigeria and the International Capitalist System* (Boulder, CO, and London: Lynne Rienner, 1988).

Nigeria's role in founding and funding ECOWAS and ECOMOG has been covered at length in such works as S. K. B. Asante, *The Political Economy of Regionalism in Africa: A Decade of the Economic Community of West African States (ECOWAS)* (New York: Praeger, 1986); Uka Ezenwe, *ECOWAS and the Economic*

Integration of West Africa (New York: St. Martin's Press, 1983); Timothy M. Shaw and Julius Emeka Okolo, eds., *The Political Economy of Foreign Policy in ECOWAS* (New York: St. Martin's Press, 1994); 'Funmi Olonisakin, *Reinventing Peacekeeping in Africa: Conceptual and Legal Issues in ECOMOG Operations* (The Hague: Kluwer Law International, 2000); and Adekeye Adebajo, *Liberia's Civil War: Nigeria, ECOMOG, and Regional Security in West Africa* (Boulder, CO: Lynne Rienner, 2002).

For a discussion of the foreign policy agenda of the Fourth Republic under Obasanjo, see Adigun Agbaje and Wale Adebanwi, "The executive: four years of democratic rule in Nigeria," in Aaron T. Gana and Yakubu B. C. Omelle, eds., *Democratic Rebirth in Nigeria,* Vol. I, *1999–2003* (Plainsboro, NJ: African Centre for Democratic Governance, 2005), 41–55; and R. A. Akindele, "Nigeria's foreign policy in the global diplomatic market place, 1999–2003," in *Democratic Rebirth in Nigeria,* 187–218.

Index

966.9 F196   INFCW
Falola, Toyin.
A history of Nigeria /

CENTRAL LIBRARY
04/10